⊙TOKYOPOP® SNEAKS™

Introduction

Welcome to the latest installment of TOKYOPOP Sneaks – your insider's guide to the wild and wonderful world of manga!

As you may already know, manga – the Japanese word for comics – has become a truly global phenomenon. Kids all over the world can't get enough of its irresistible visual storytelling and bleeding-edge graphic design. There's manga for every taste, too: science fiction, romance, comedy, fantasy, action...you name it and manga's got it covered!

Within the pages of this book you will find an extraordinary selection of TOKYOPOP's latest titles that are sure to fire your imagination like nothing you have ever read before. Once you pick out your favorites, remember that manga is available everywhere books are sold.

Check your local book or comic shop, go to your favorite e-commerce site, or visit TOKYOPOP's online store at www.TOKYOPOP.com/shop to buy the latest and greatest TOKYOPOP manga.

And, as always, for the freshest news and info, please visit us online at www.TOKYOPOP.com.

From all of us here at TOKYOPOP, thank you for your support – and welcome to the Manga Revolution!

left to right ▶ left to right ▶ left to r

TABLE OF CONTENTS

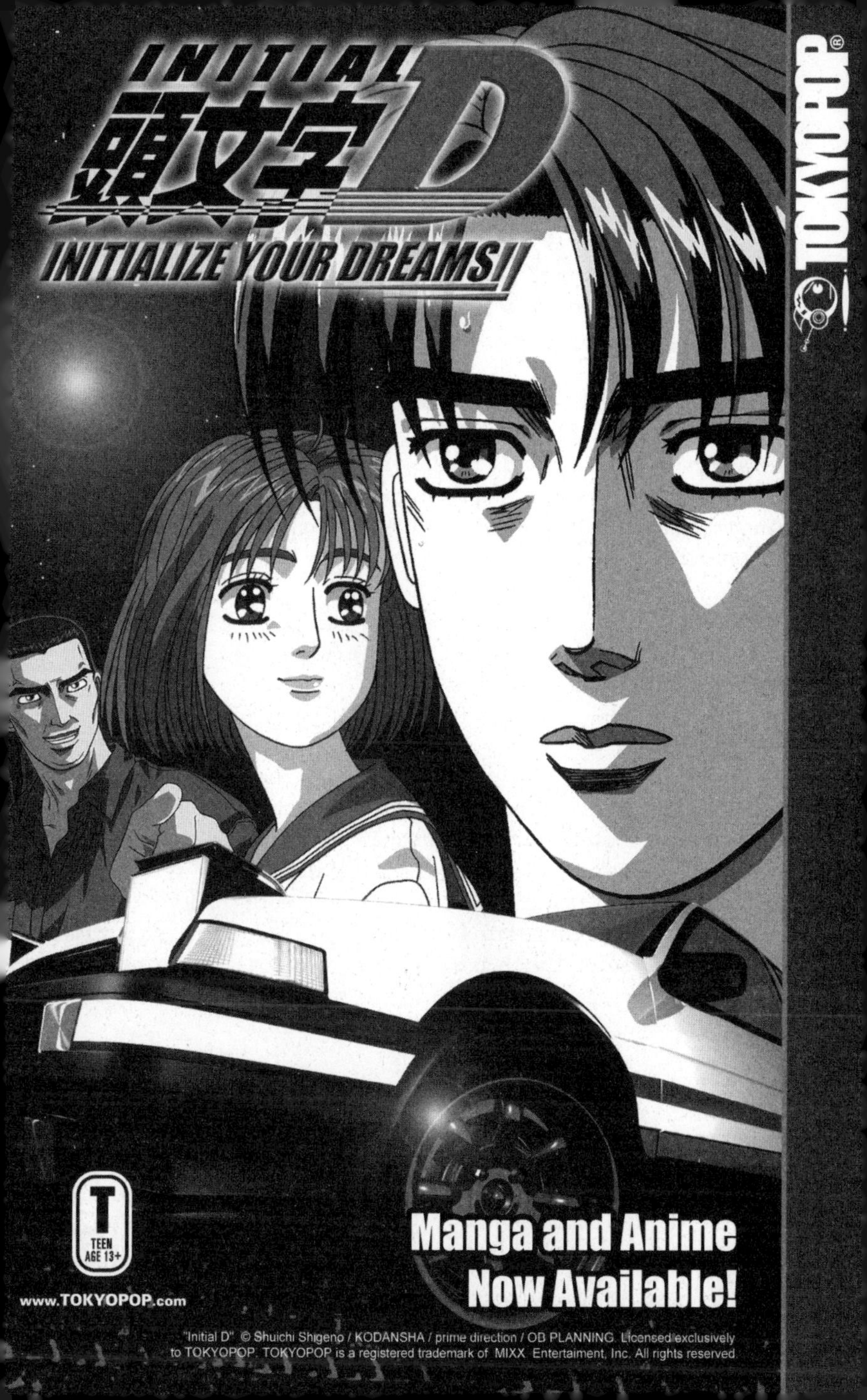
INITIAL
頭文字D
INITIALIZE YOUR DREAMS!
TOKYOPOP®
T
TEEN
AGE 13+
www.TOKYOPOP.com
Manga and Anime
Now Available!
"Initial D" © Shuichi Shigeno / KODANSHA / prime direction / OB PLANNING. Licensed exclusively
to TOKYOPOP. TOKYOPOP is a registered trademark of MIXX Entertaiment, Inc. All rights reserved.

The Story:

The forces of evil have come back to rip peace from the twice-peaceful Kingdom of Dikay! The land's only hope lies in the one man who many years ago vanquished the evil tyranny: Van Von Hunter, Hunter of Evil... Stuff! Together with his loyal, memory-challenged sidekick, he faces off against the deposed former ruler of Dikay, who has come back to reclaim his throne!

The Creators:

Mark Schwark and Ron Kaulfersch

Behind the Manga:

• Exclusive preview featured on www.TOKYOPOP.com.
Shrek meets the riotous humor of Monty Python and Mel Brooks.
• Created by Pseudomé Studios' Mike Schwark and Ron Kaulfersch—winners of TOKYOPOP's Rising Stars of Manga™ competition.
• The artists' online comic site (www.Pseudome.net) includes a forum in which fans come to chat with the creators and discuss upcoming releases.

Genre:

Comedy / Fantasy

SRP:

£ 6.99

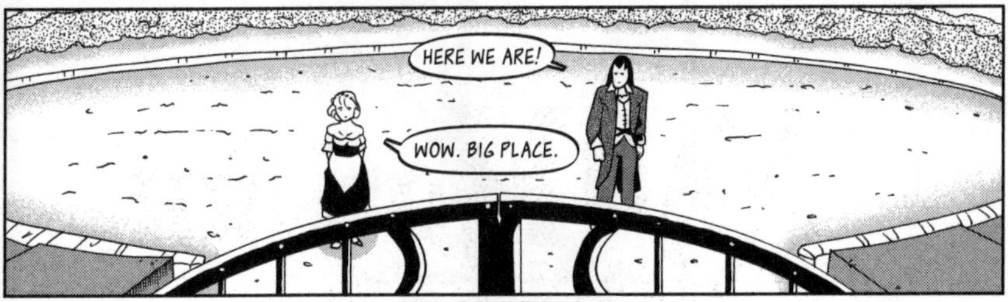
HERE WE ARE!
WOW. BIG PLACE.

CHAPTER 3
(WOW. THIS IS A REALLY SMALL SUBTITLE.)

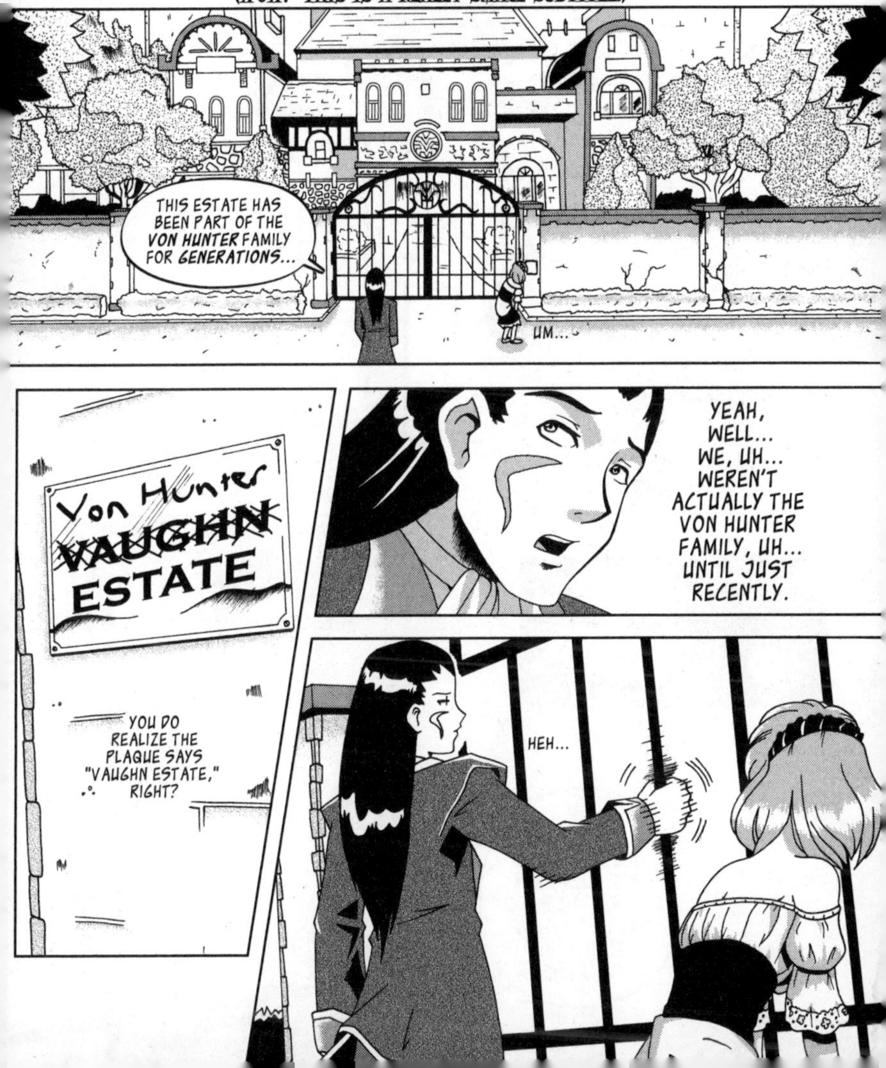
THIS ESTATE HAS BEEN PART OF THE *VON HUNTER* FAMILY FOR *GENERATIONS...*
UM...
Von Hunter
~~VAUGHN~~
ESTATE
YOU DO REALIZE THE PLAQUE SAYS "VAUGHN ESTATE," RIGHT?
YEAH, WELL... WE, UH... WEREN'T ACTUALLY THE VON HUNTER FAMILY, UH... UNTIL JUST RECENTLY.
HEH...

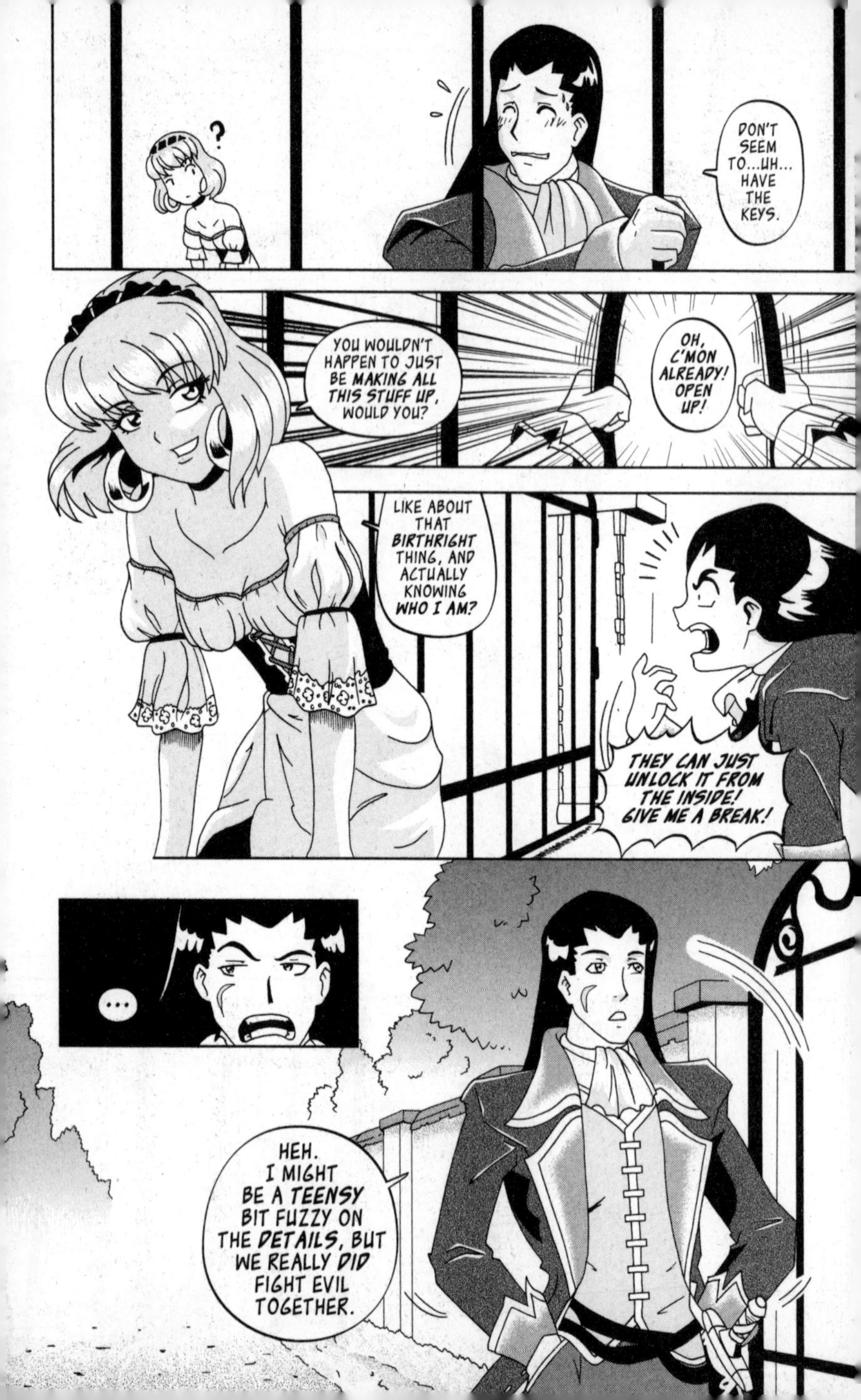
DON'T SEEM TO...UH... HAVE THE KEYS.
?
OH, C'MON ALREADY! OPEN UP!
THEY CAN JUST UNLOCK IT FROM THE INSIDE! GIVE ME A BREAK!
YOU WOULDN'T HAPPEN TO JUST BE MAKING ALL THIS STUFF UP, WOULD YOU?
LIKE ABOUT THAT BIRTHRIGHT THING, AND ACTUALLY KNOWING WHO I AM?
HEH. I MIGHT BE A TEENSY BIT FUZZY ON THE DETAILS, BUT WE REALLY DID FIGHT EVIL TOGETHER.
...

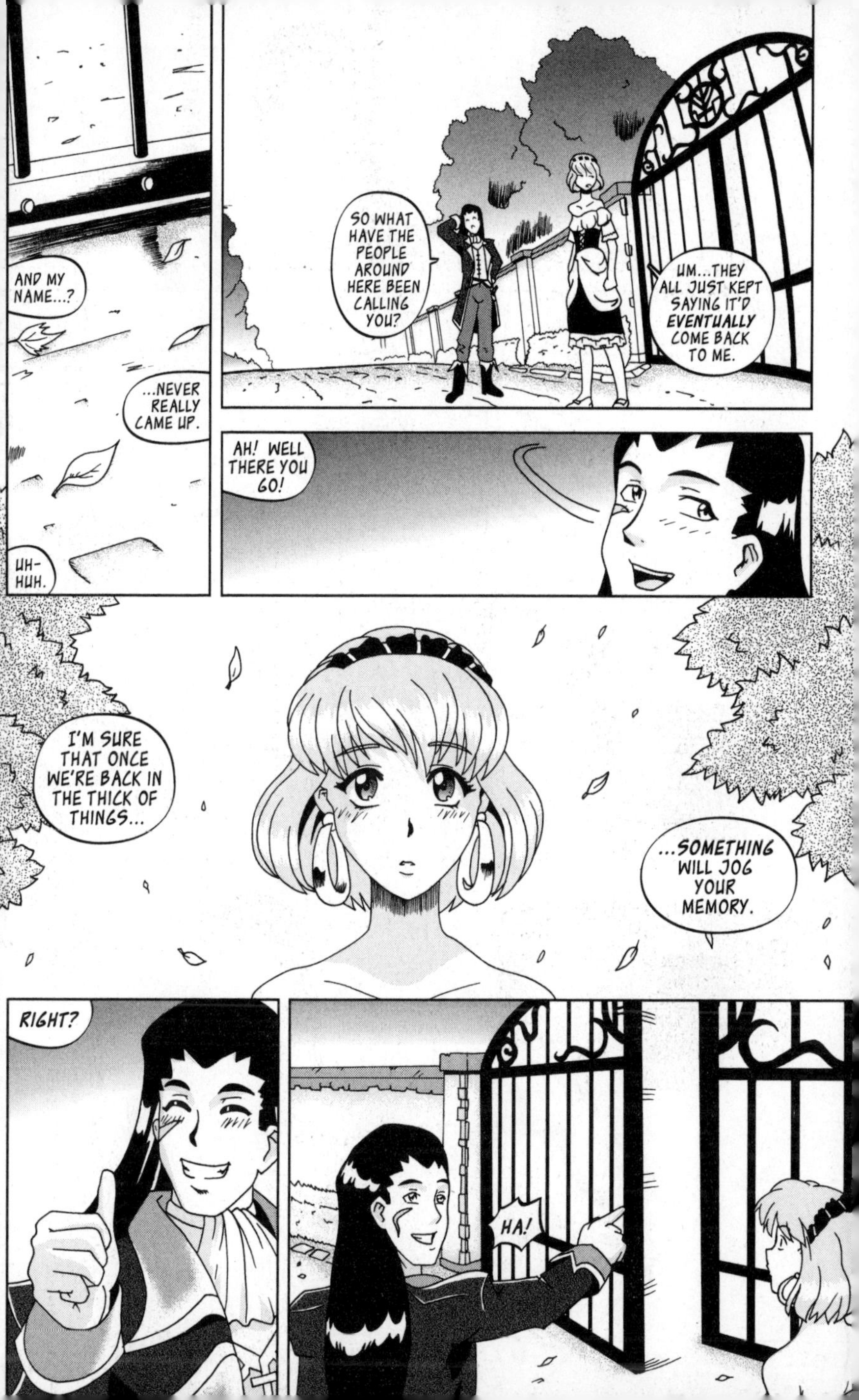

SO WHAT HAVE THE PEOPLE AROUND HERE BEEN CALLING YOU?
UM...THEY ALL JUST KEPT SAYING IT'D *EVENTUALLY* COME BACK TO ME.
AH! WELL THERE YOU GO!
AND MY NAME...?
...NEVER REALLY CAME UP.
UH-HUH.
I'M SURE THAT ONCE WE'RE BACK IN THE THICK OF THINGS...
...SOMETHING WILL JOG YOUR MEMORY.
HA!
RIGHT?

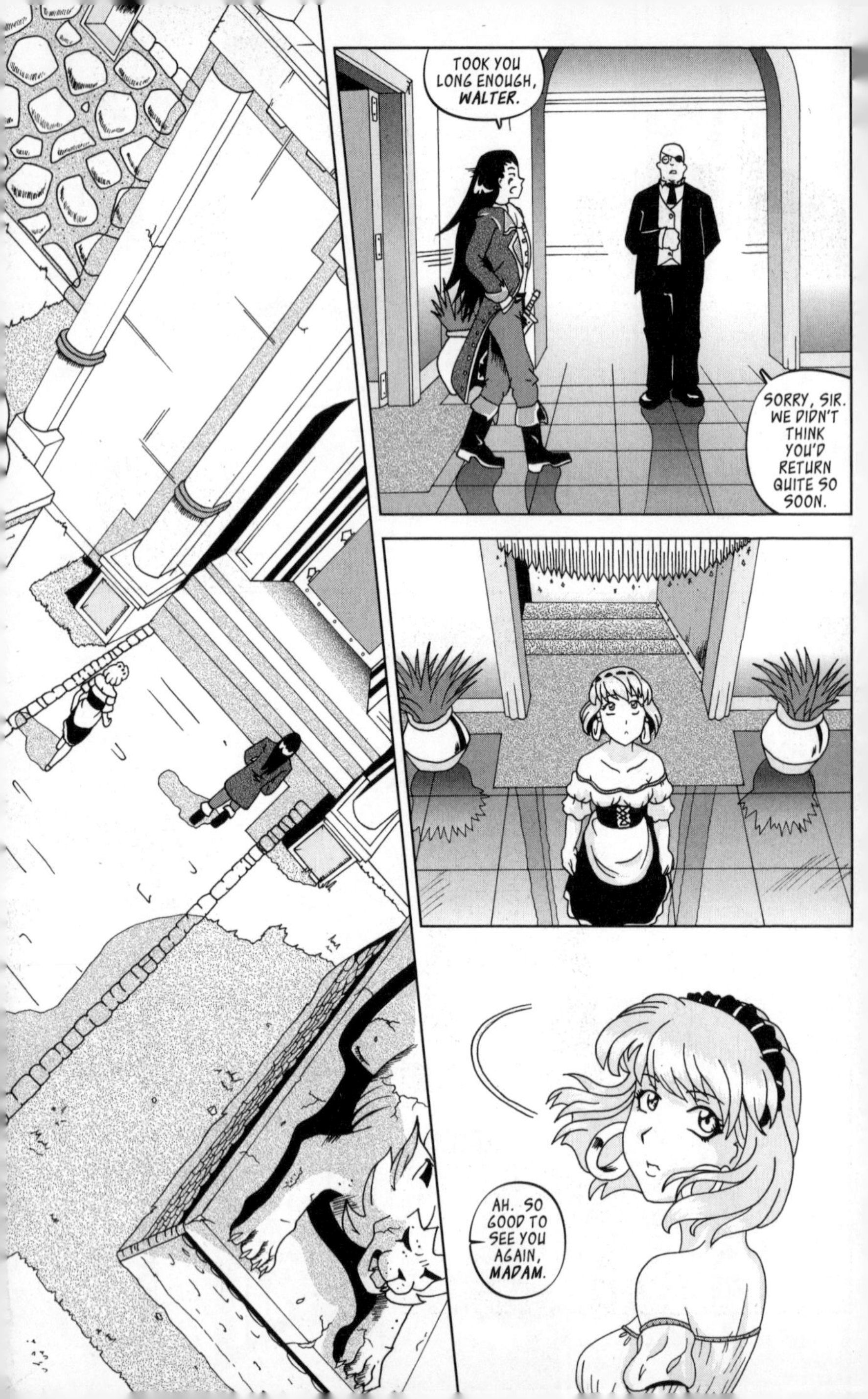
TOOK YOU LONG ENOUGH, WALTER.
SORRY, SIR. WE DIDN'T THINK YOU'D RETURN QUITE SO SOON.
AH. SO GOOD TO SEE YOU AGAIN, MADAM.

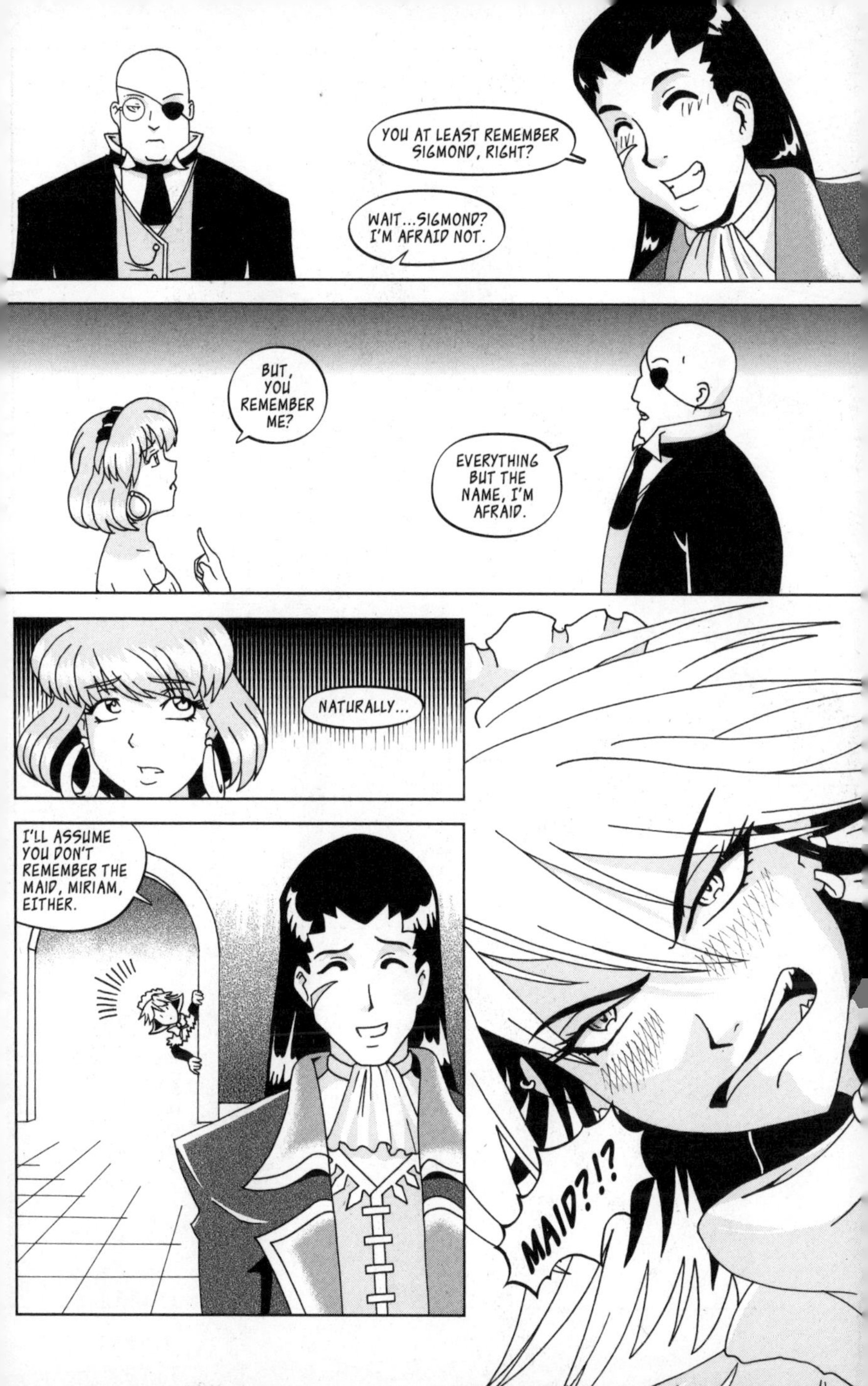
YOU AT LEAST REMEMBER SIGMOND, RIGHT?
WAIT...SIGMOND? I'M AFRAID NOT.
BUT, YOU REMEMBER ME?
EVERYTHING BUT THE NAME, I'M AFRAID.
NATURALLY...
I'LL ASSUME YOU DON'T REMEMBER THE MAID, MIRIAM, EITHER.
MAID?!?

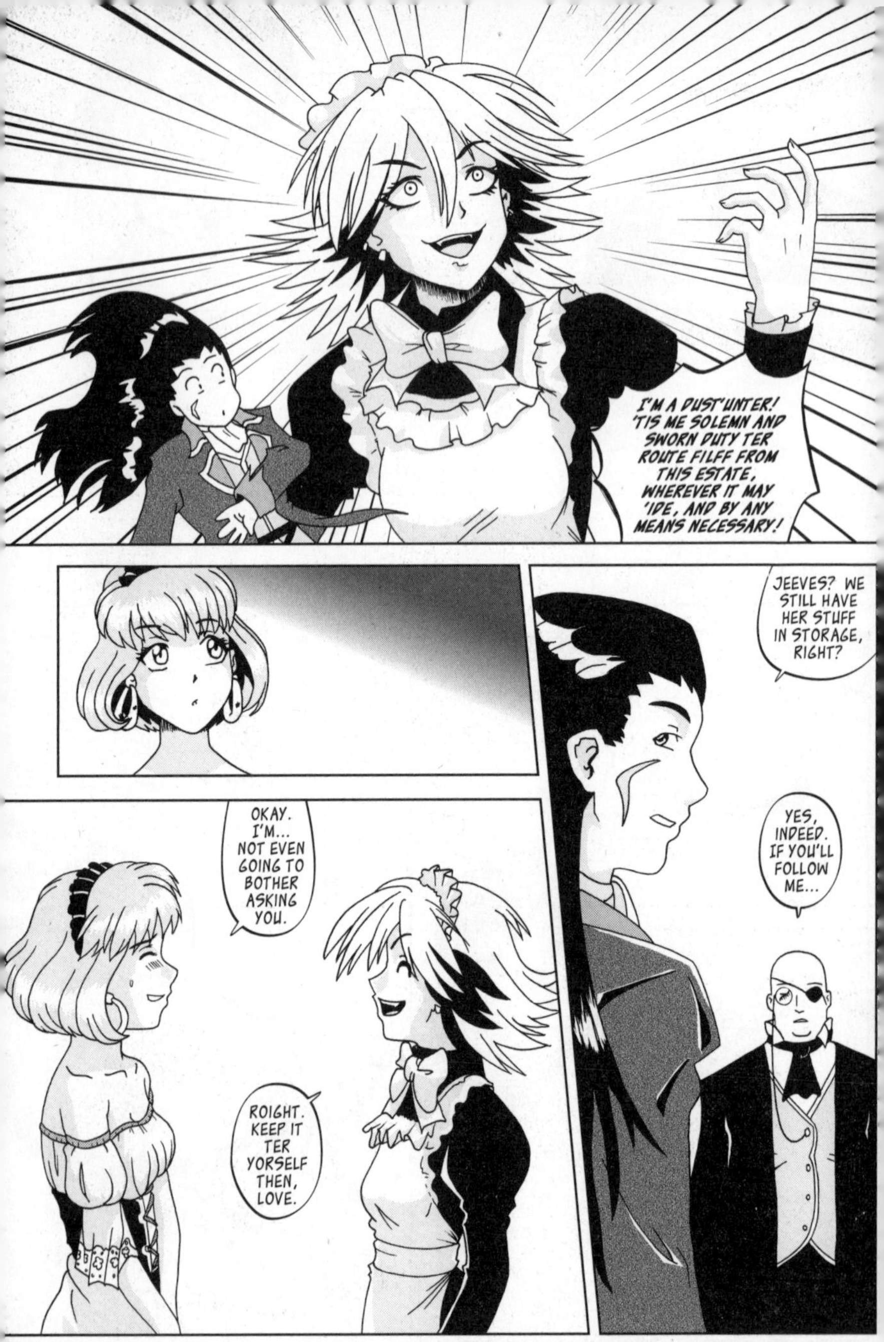
I'M A DUST'UNTER! 'TIS ME SOLEMN AND SWORN DUTY TER ROUTE FILFF FROM THIS ESTATE, WHEREVER IT MAY 'IDE, AND BY ANY MEANS NECESSARY!
JEEVES? WE STILL HAVE HER STUFF IN STORAGE, RIGHT?
YES, INDEED. IF YOU'LL FOLLOW ME...
OKAY. I'M... NOT EVEN GOING TO BOTHER ASKING YOU.
ROIGHT. KEEP IT TER YORSELF THEN, LOVE.

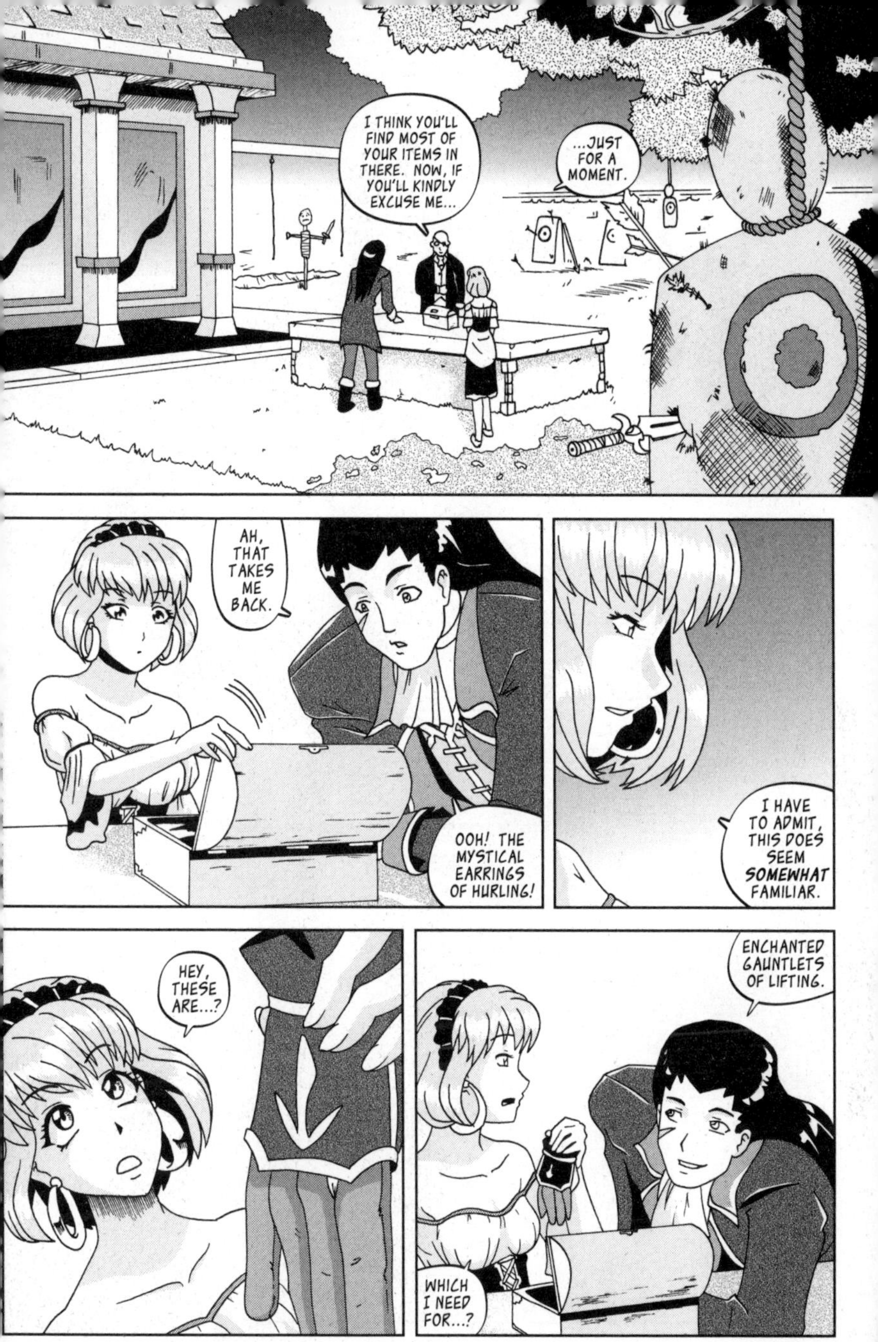
I THINK YOU'LL FIND MOST OF YOUR ITEMS IN THERE. NOW, IF YOU'LL KINDLY EXCUSE ME...
...JUST FOR A MOMENT.
I HAVE TO ADMIT, THIS DOES SEEM **SOMEWHAT** FAMILIAR.
AH, THAT TAKES ME BACK.
OOH! THE MYSTICAL EARRINGS OF HURLING!
ENCHANTED GAUNTLETS OF LIFTING.
WHICH I NEED FOR...?
HEY, THESE ARE...?

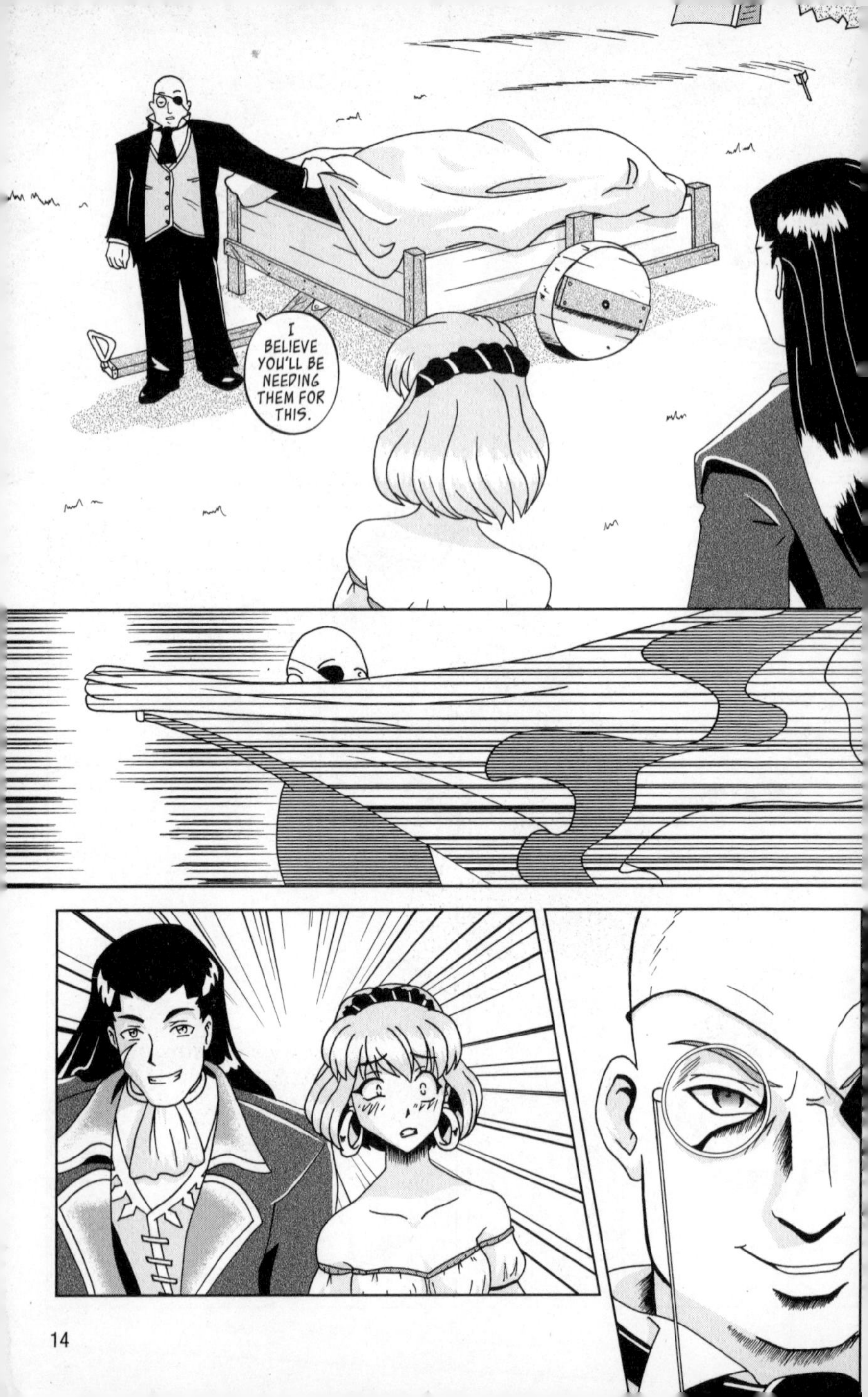
I BELIEVE YOU'LL BE NEEDING THEM FOR THIS.

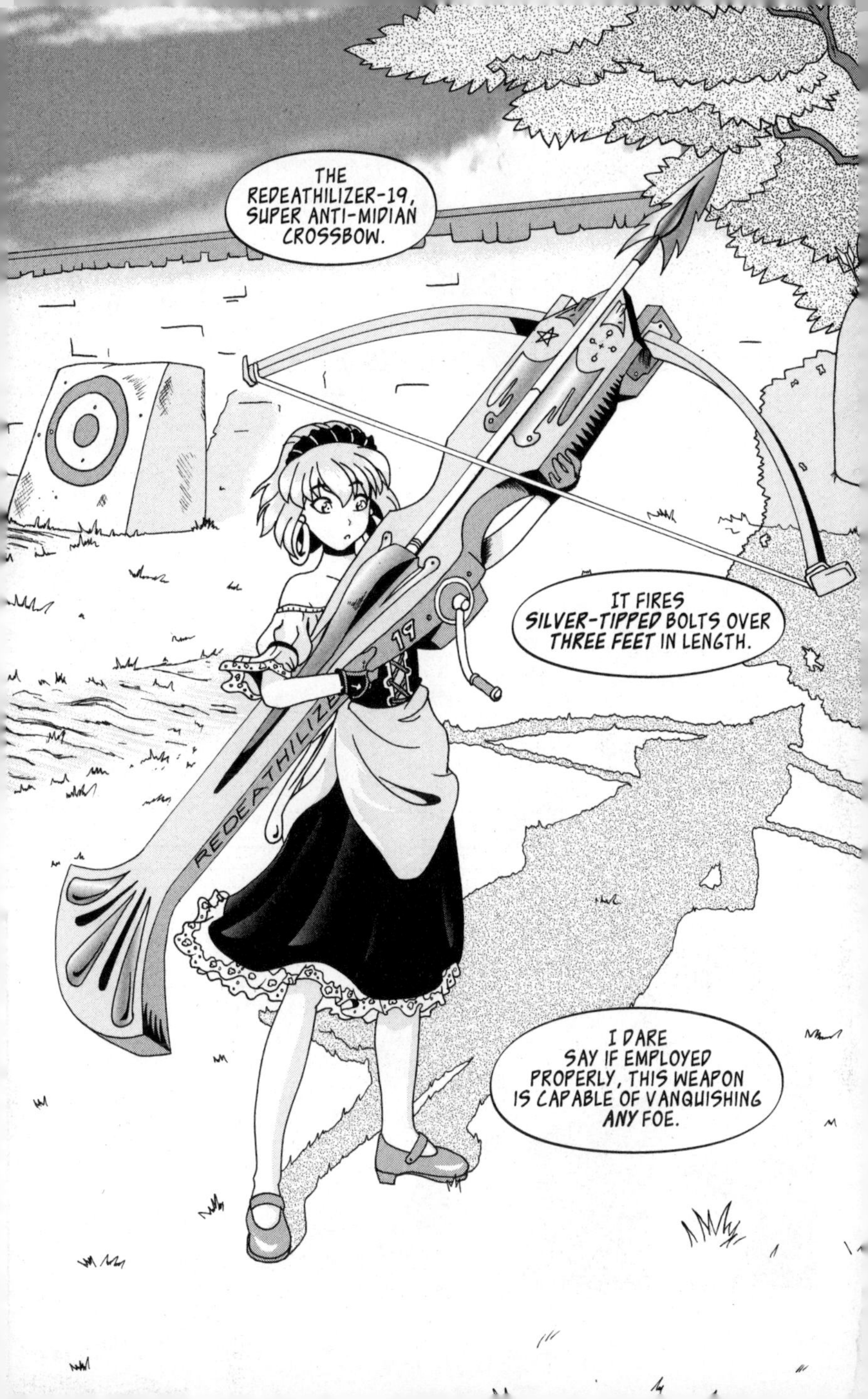
THE REDEATHILIZER-19, SUPER ANTI-MIDIAN CROSSBOW.
IT FIRES *SILVER-TIPPED* BOLTS OVER *THREE FEET* IN LENGTH.
I DARE SAY IF EMPLOYED PROPERLY, THIS WEAPON IS CAPABLE OF VANQUISHING *ANY* FOE.
REDEATHILIZER
19

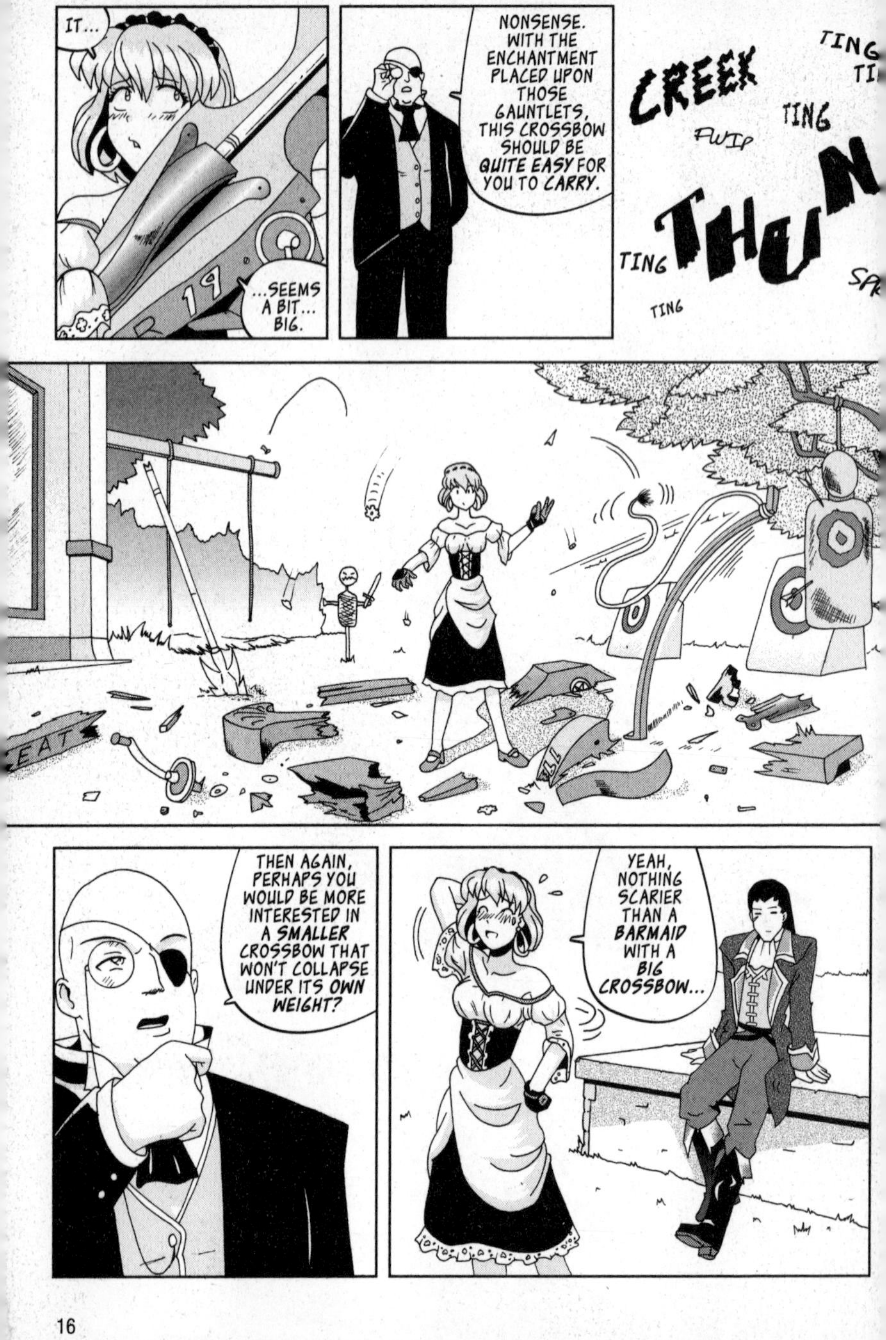
IT...
...SEEMS A BIT... BIG.
NONSENSE. WITH THE ENCHANTMENT PLACED UPON THOSE GAUNTLETS, THIS CROSSBOW SHOULD BE QUITE EASY FOR YOU TO CARRY.
CREEK
TING
TING
FWIP
THUN
TING
TING
EAT
THEN AGAIN, PERHAPS YOU WOULD BE MORE INTERESTED IN A SMALLER CROSSBOW THAT WON'T COLLAPSE UNDER ITS OWN WEIGHT?
YEAH, NOTHING SCARIER THAN A BARMAID WITH A BIG CROSSBOW...

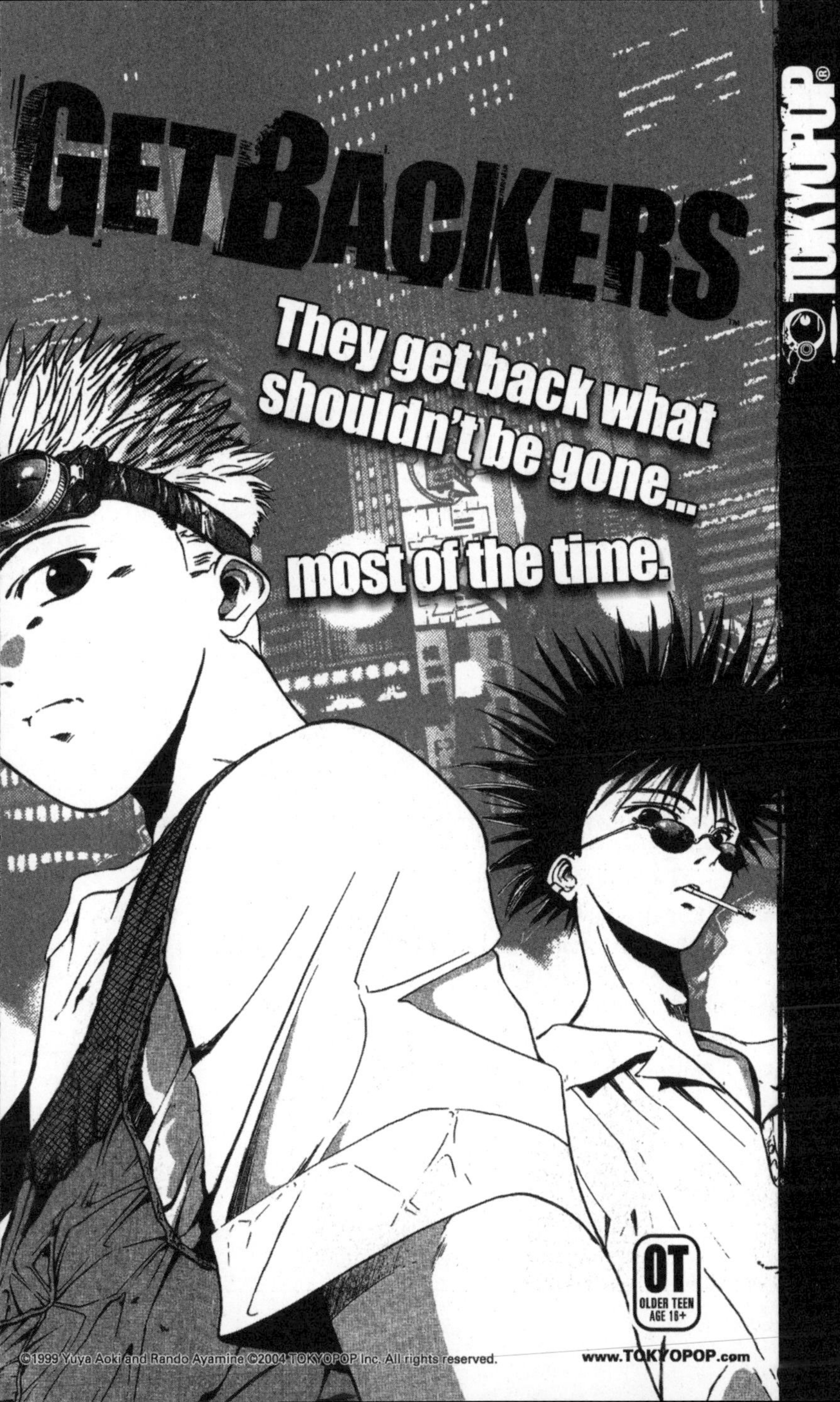
GETBACKERS™
They get back what shouldn't be gone...
...most of the time.
TOKYOPOP®
OT OLDER TEEN AGE 16+
©1999 Yuya Aoki and Rando Ayamine ©2004 TOKYOPOP Inc. All rights reserved.
www.TOKYOPOP.com

The Story:

Warcraft: The Sunwell Trilogy re-creates the world of Azeroth as you've
never seen it before: as a manga! The three-volume graphic novel series
follows the adventures of Kalec, a blue dragon who has taken human
form to escape the forces that seek to destroy his race, and Anveena, a
maiden with a mysterious power. What starts as a flight for survival
turns into a quest to save the entire High Elven Kingdom from the forces
of the Undead Scourge.

The Creators:

Richard Knaak and Jae-Hwan Kim

Behind the Manga:

- Set in the rich universe of Blizzard's online role-playing game World
  of Warcraft.
- Jae-Hwan Kim is the illustrator of *King of Hell*.
- Richard Knaak adapted TOKYOPOP's *Ragnarok* and is also the
  author of *Dragonlance*, *Diablo*, *Dragonrealm* and *Warcraft* novels.

Genre:

Action / Fantasy

SRP:

£ 6.99

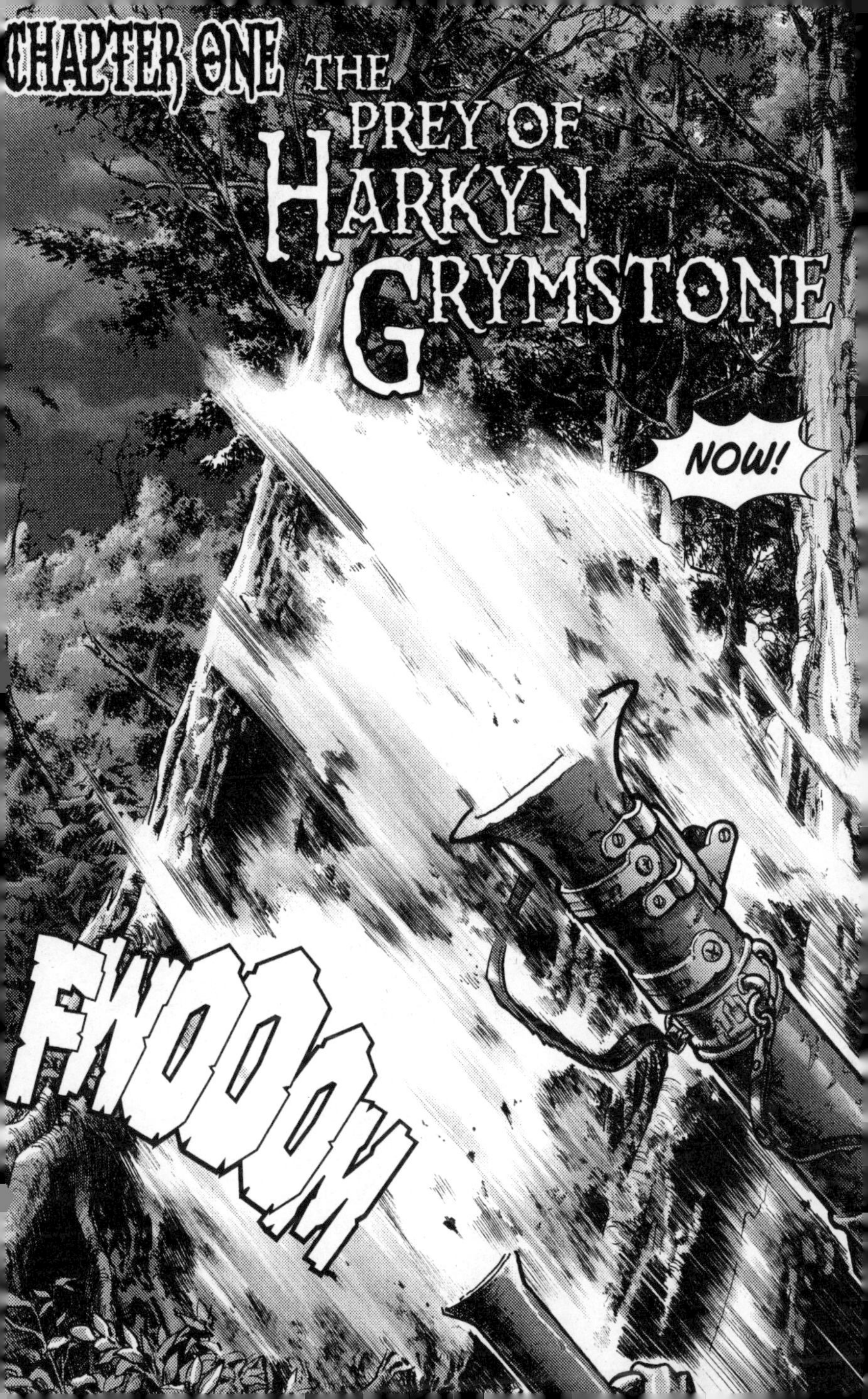
CHAPTER ONE THE PREY OF HARKYN GRYMSTONE
NOW!
FWOOOM

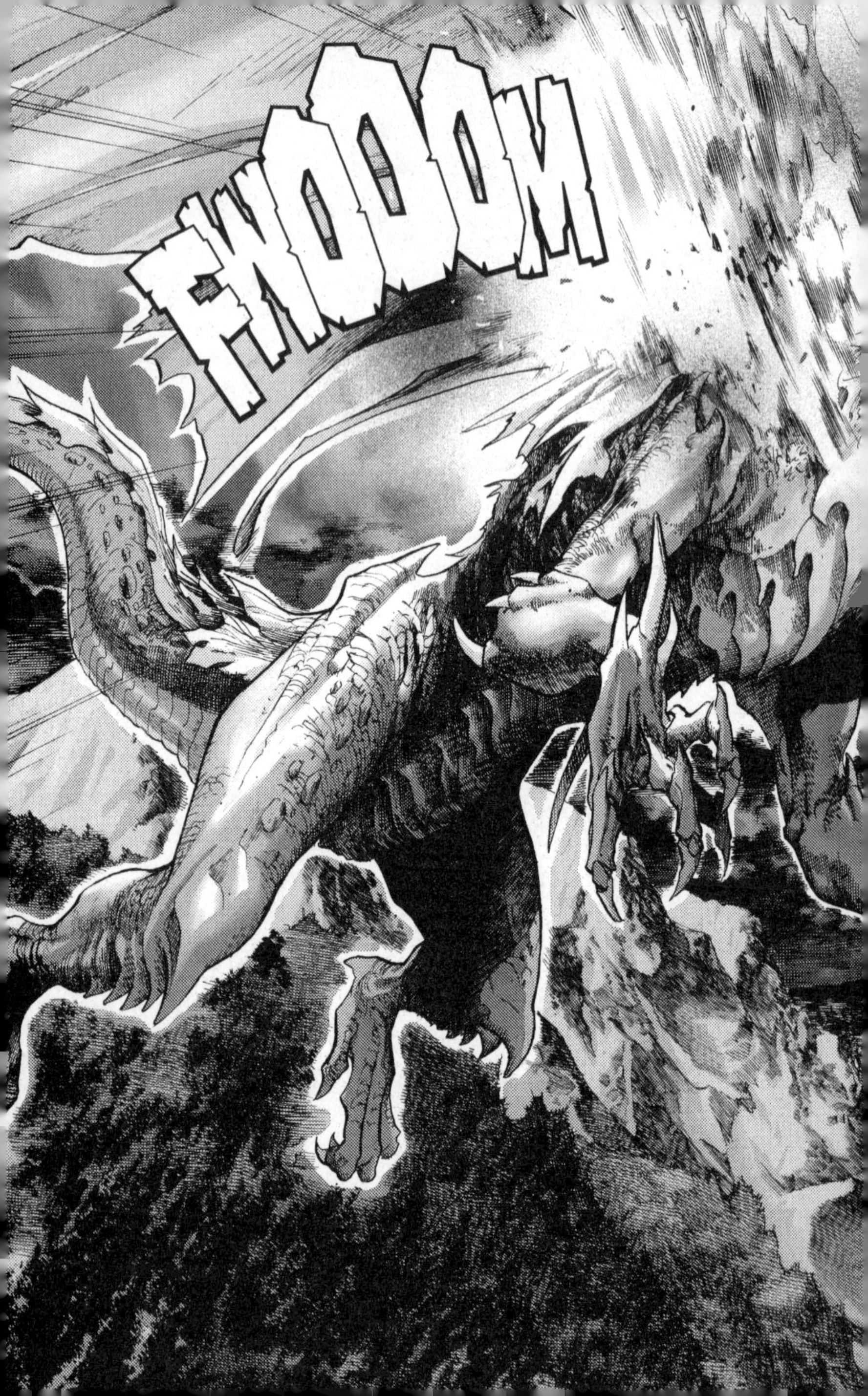
FWOOOM

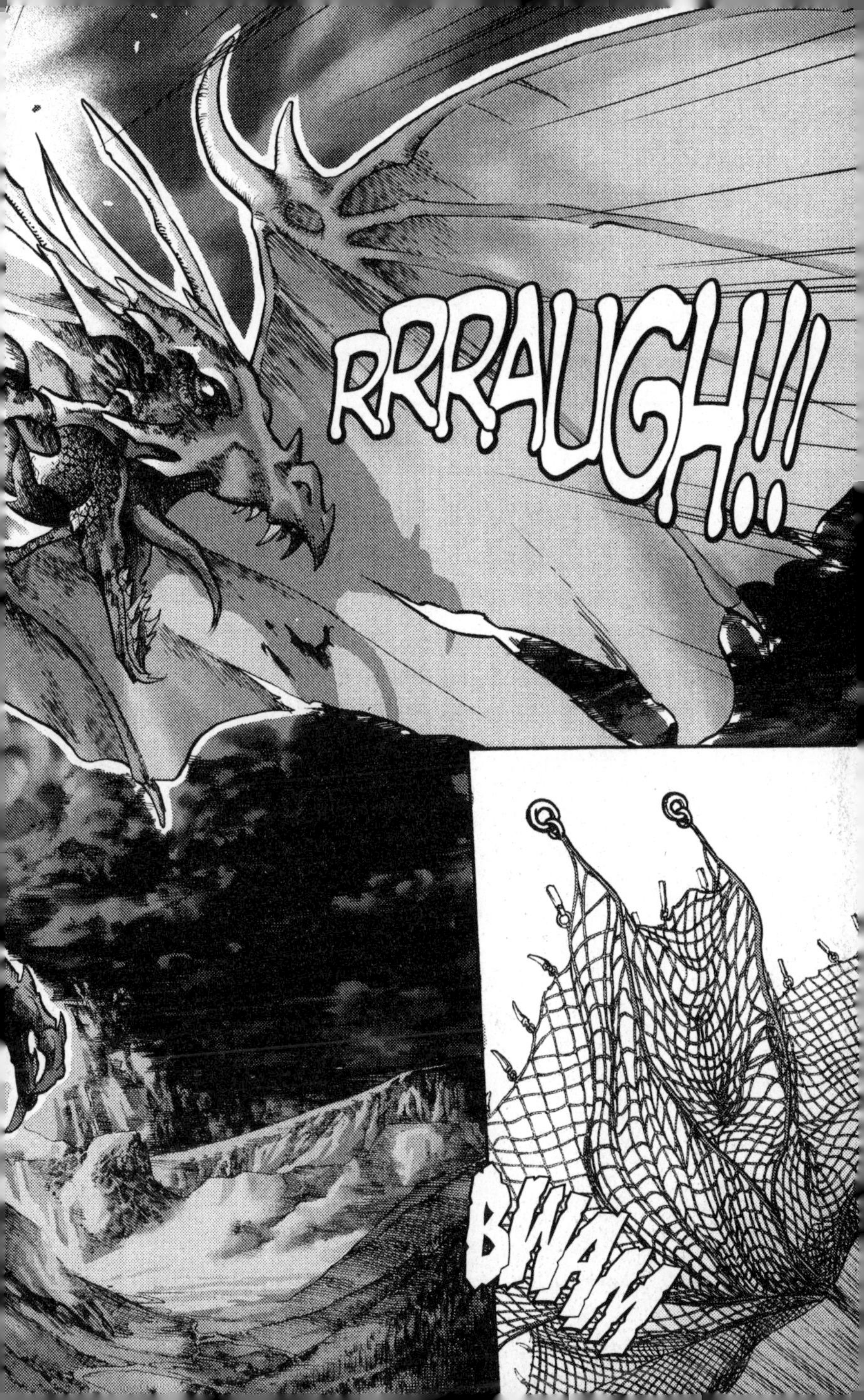
RRRAUGH!!!
BWAM

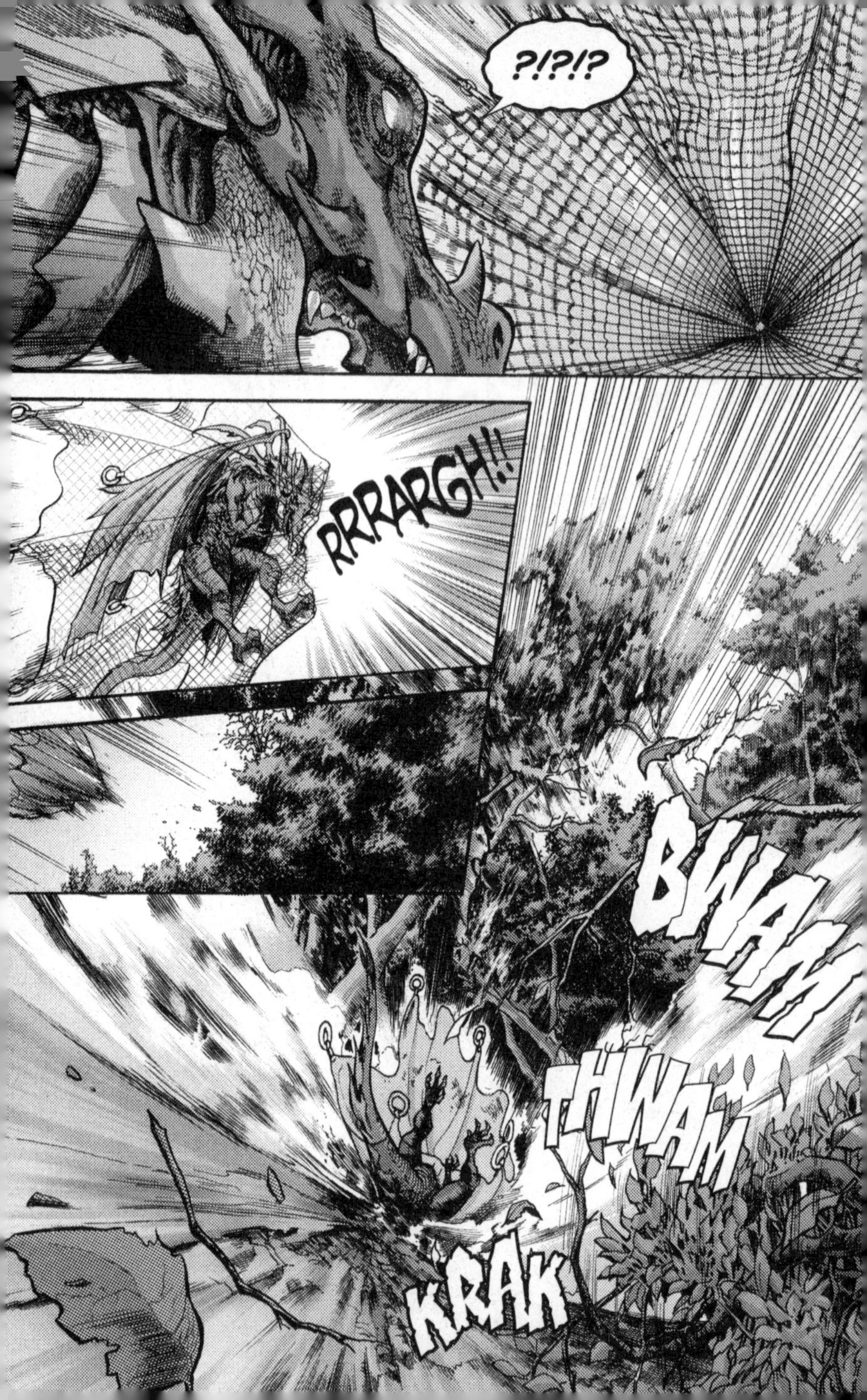
?!?!?
RRRARGH!!
BWAM
THWAM
KRAK

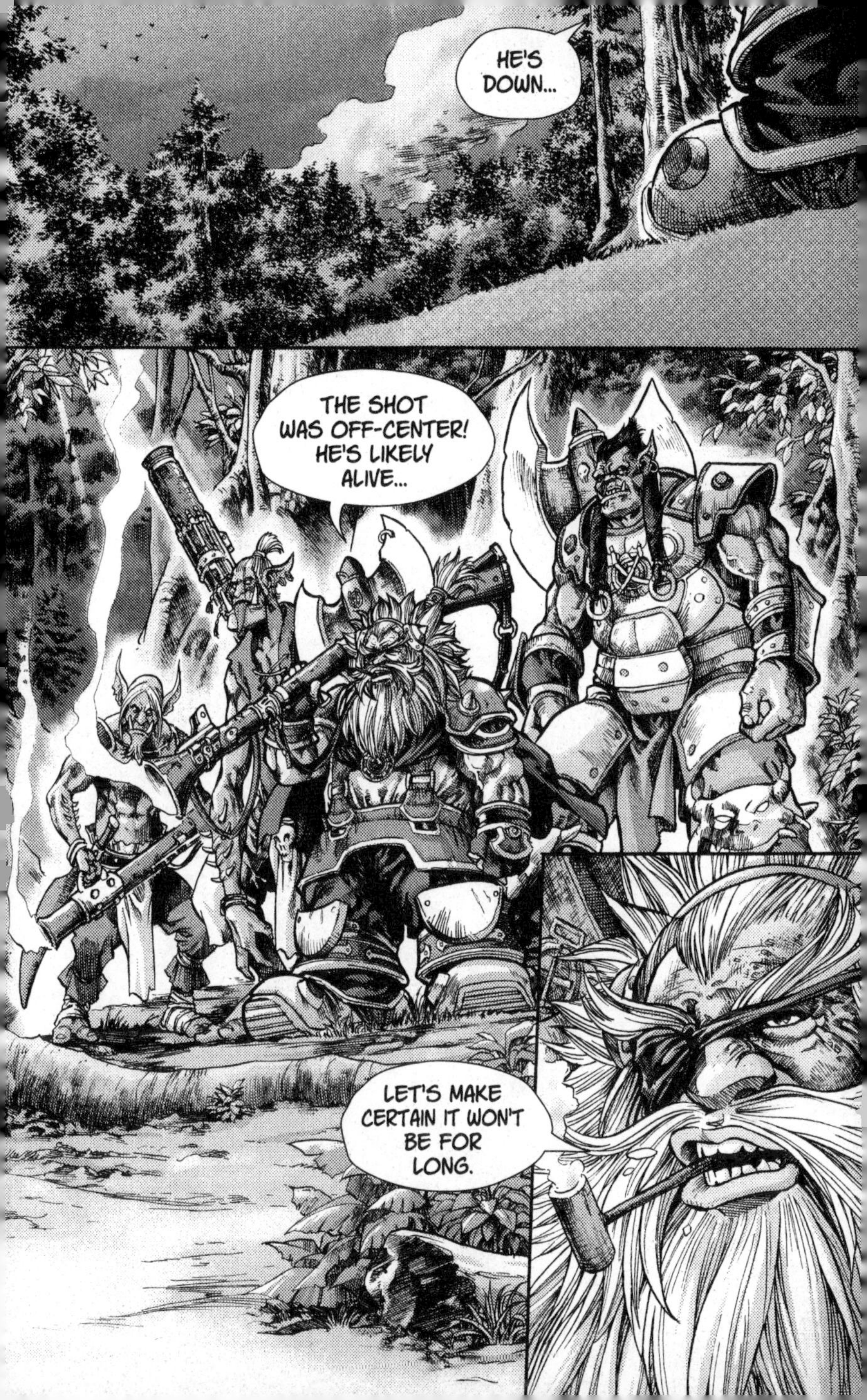
HE'S DOWN...
THE SHOT WAS OFF-CENTER! HE'S LIKELY ALIVE...
LET'S MAKE CERTAIN IT WON'T BE FOR LONG.

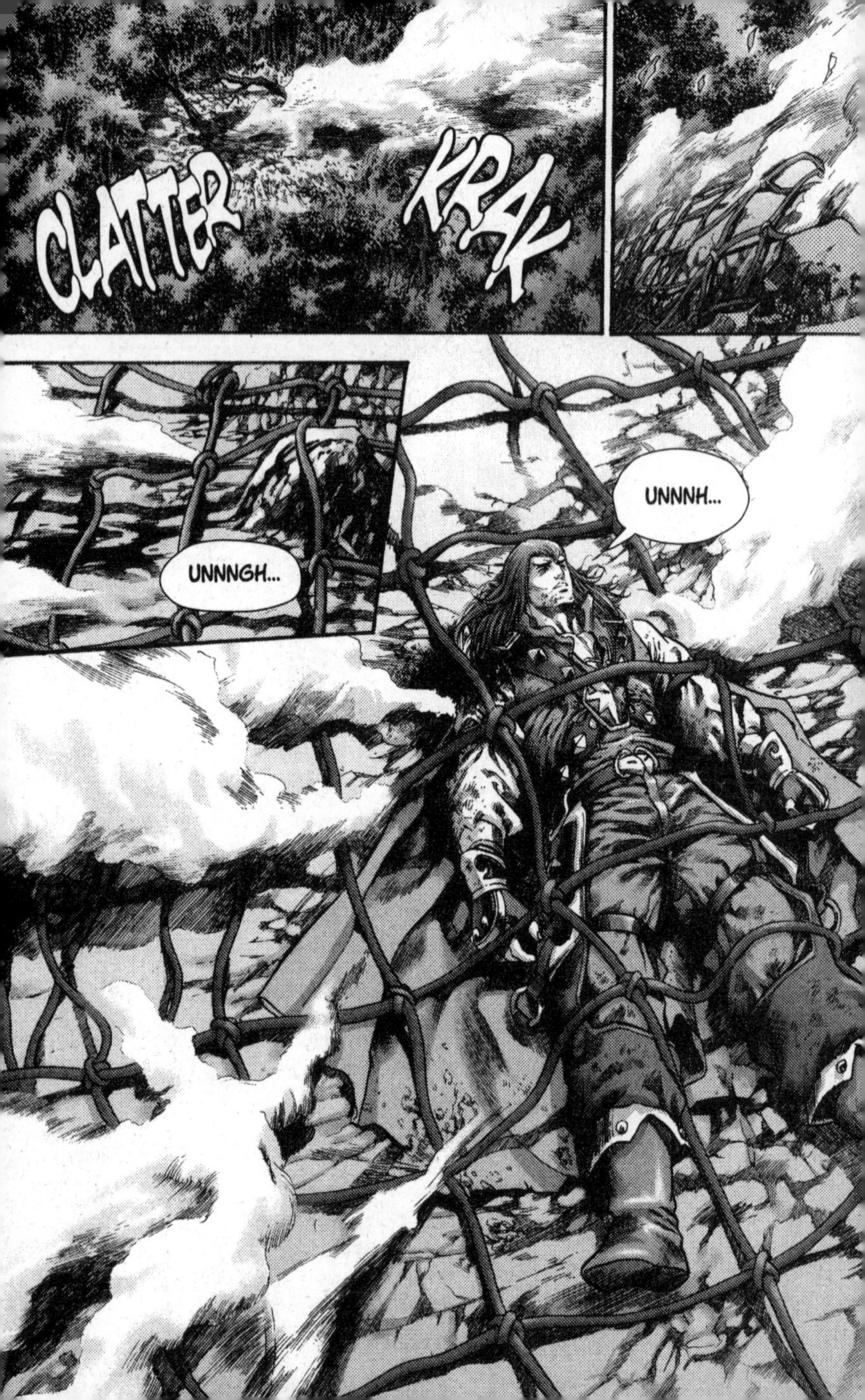
KRAK
CLATTER
UNNNH...
UNNNGH...

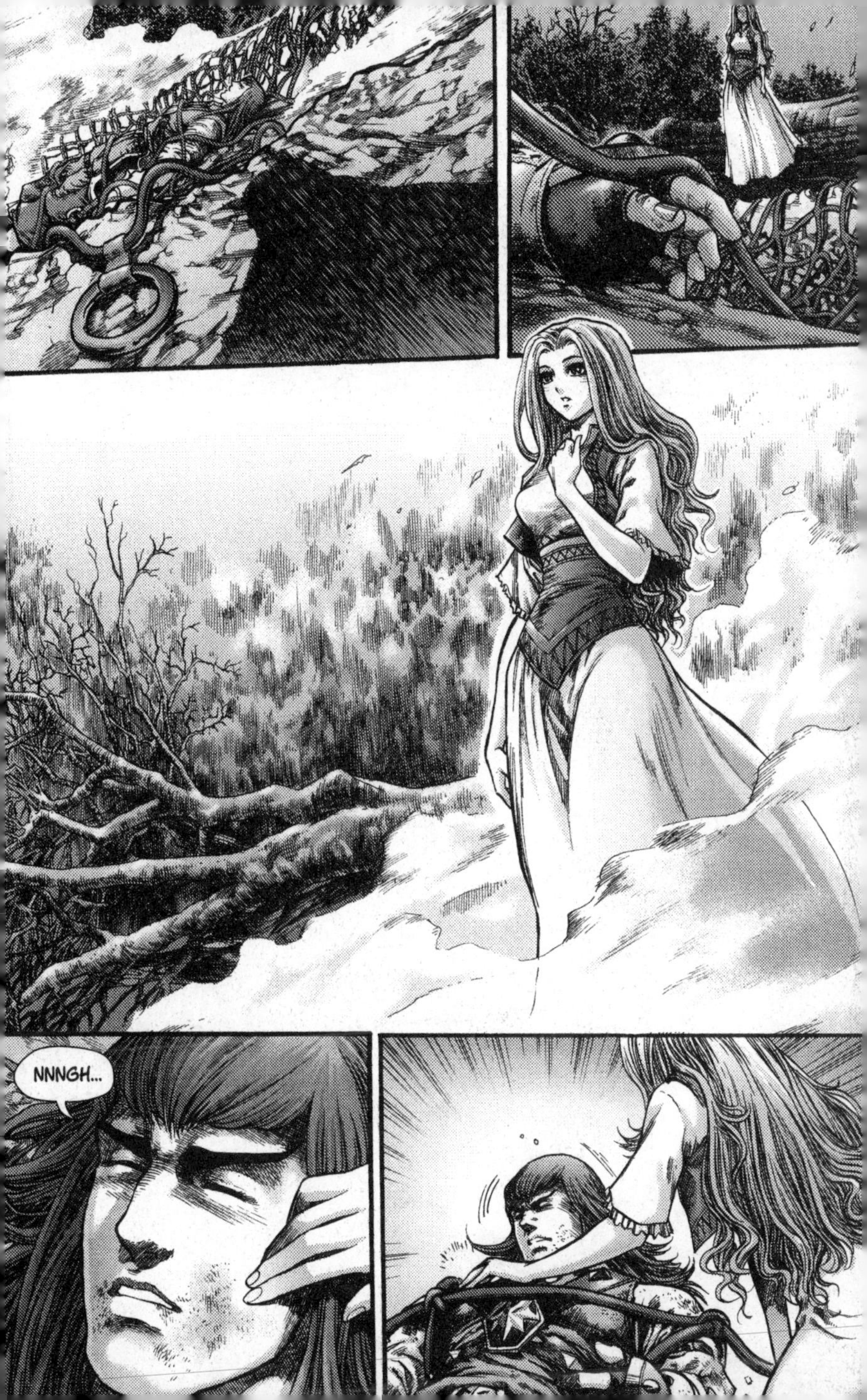
NNNGH...

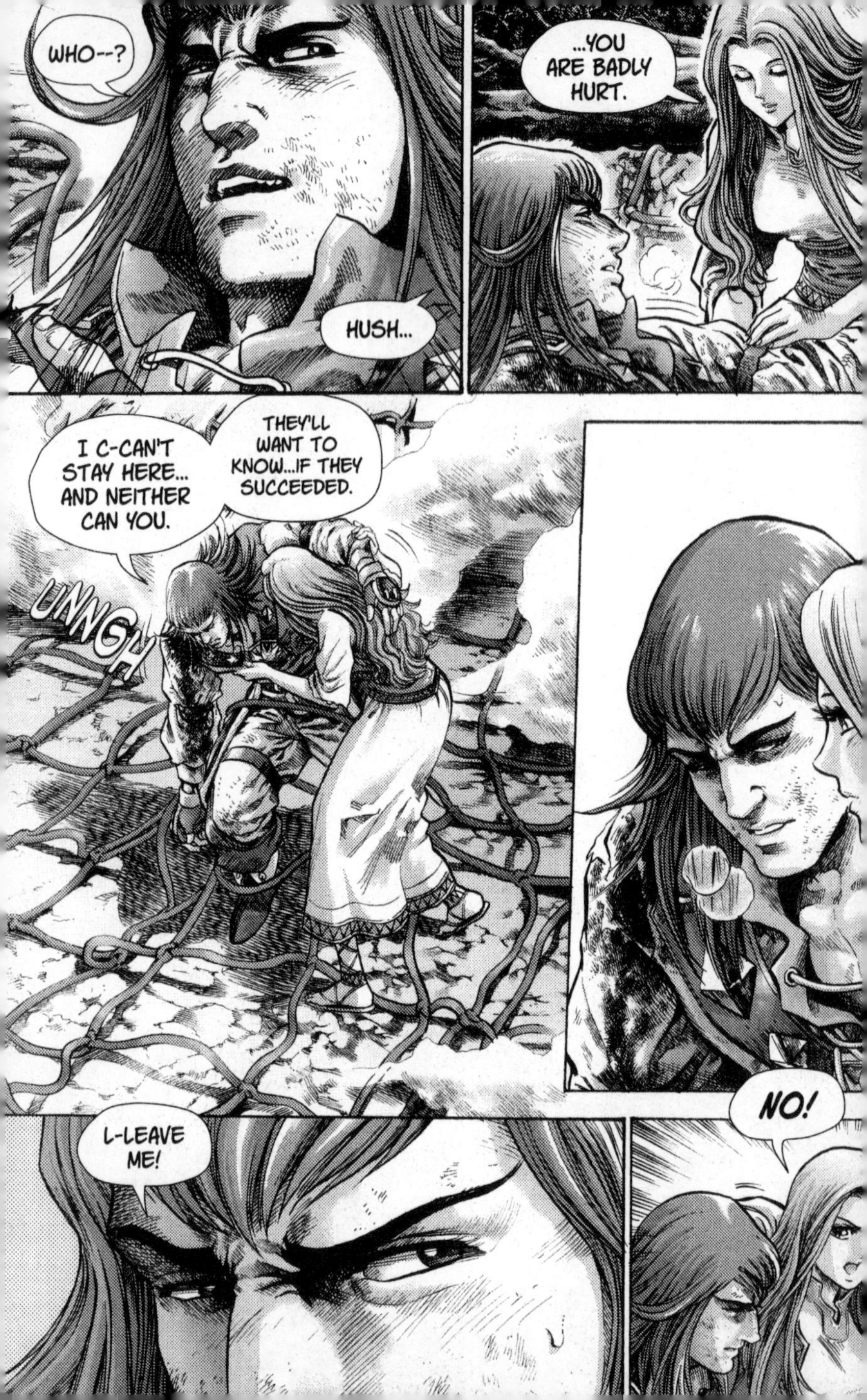
...YOU ARE BADLY HURT.
WHO--?
HUSH...
THEY'LL WANT TO KNOW...IF THEY SUCCEEDED.
I C-CAN'T STAY HERE... AND NEITHER CAN YOU.
UNNGH
NO!
L-LEAVE ME!

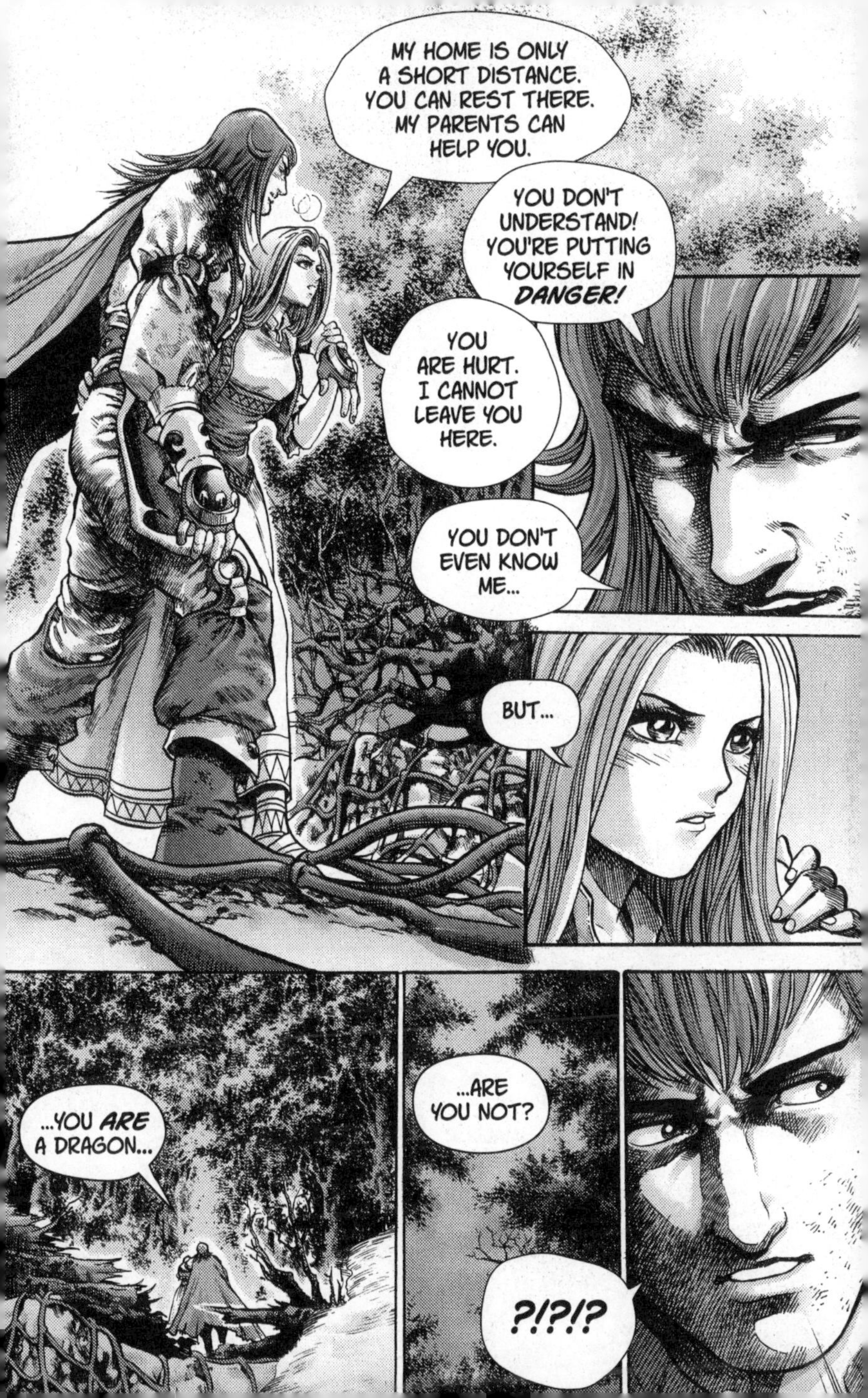
MY HOME IS ONLY A SHORT DISTANCE. YOU CAN REST THERE. MY PARENTS CAN HELP YOU.
YOU DON'T UNDERSTAND! YOU'RE PUTTING YOURSELF IN *DANGER!*
YOU ARE HURT. I CANNOT LEAVE YOU HERE.
YOU DON'T EVEN KNOW ME...
BUT...
...YOU *ARE* A DRAGON...
...ARE YOU NOT?
?!?!?

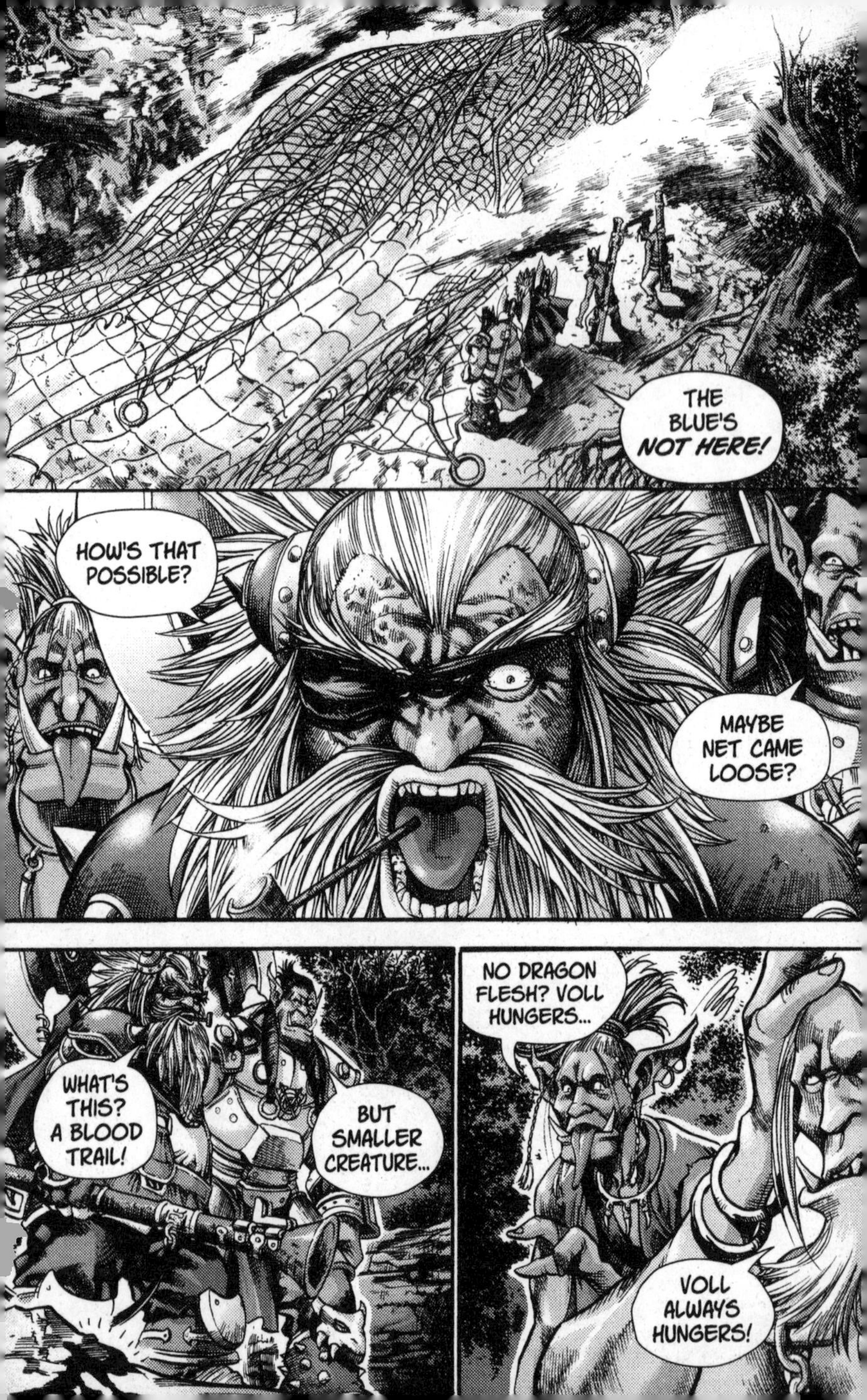
THE BLUE'S *NOT HERE!*
HOW'S THAT POSSIBLE?
MAYBE NET CAME LOOSE?
NO DRAGON FLESH? VOLL HUNGERS...
VOLL ALWAYS HUNGERS!
WHAT'S THIS? A BLOOD TRAIL!
BUT SMALLER CREATURE...

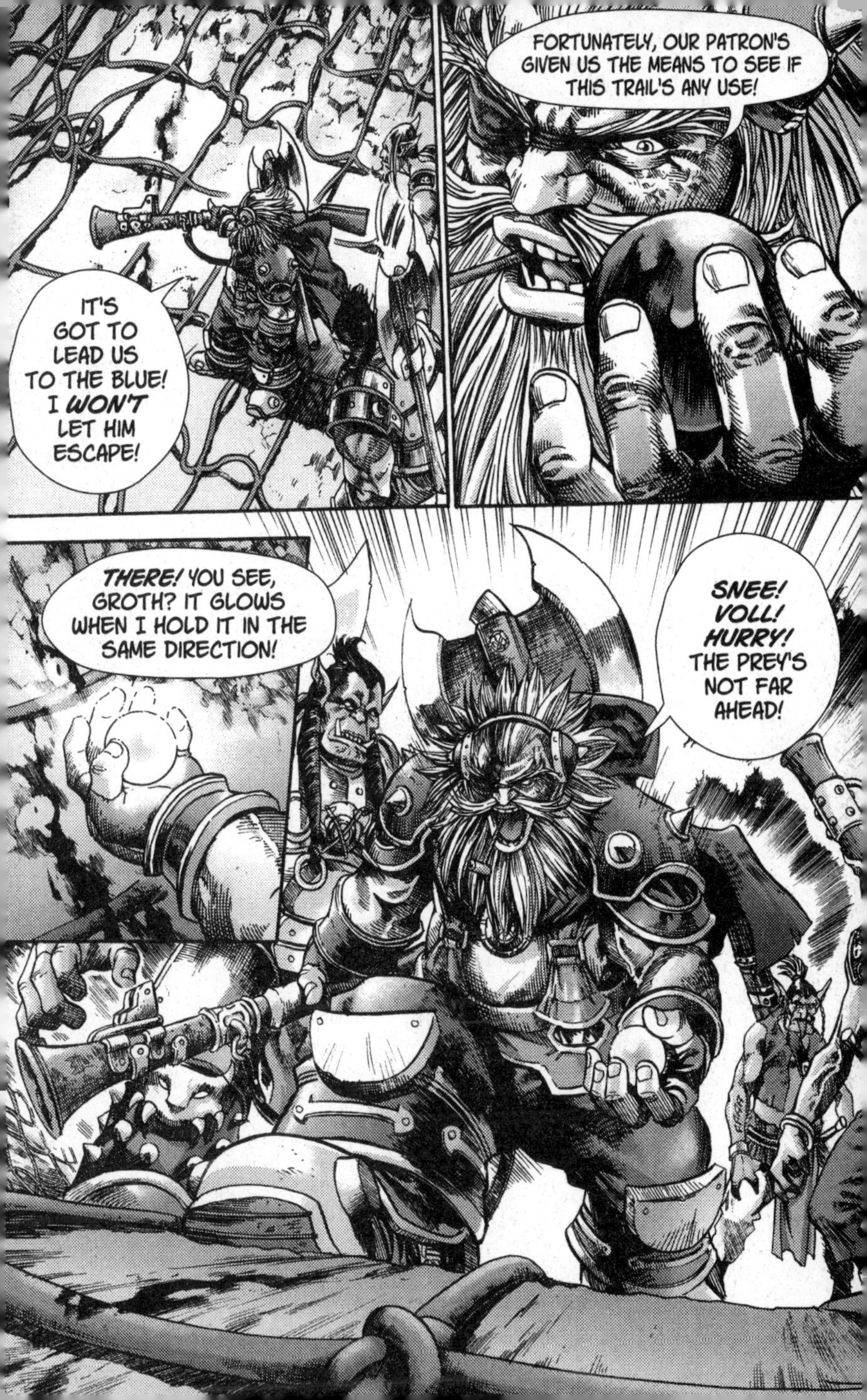
FORTUNATELY, OUR PATRON'S GIVEN US THE MEANS TO SEE IF THIS TRAIL'S ANY USE!
IT'S GOT TO LEAD US TO THE BLUE! I WON'T LET HIM ESCAPE!
SNEE! VOLL! HURRY! THE PREY'S NOT FAR AHEAD!
THERE! YOU SEE, GROTH? IT GLOWS WHEN I HOLD IT IN THE SAME DIRECTION!

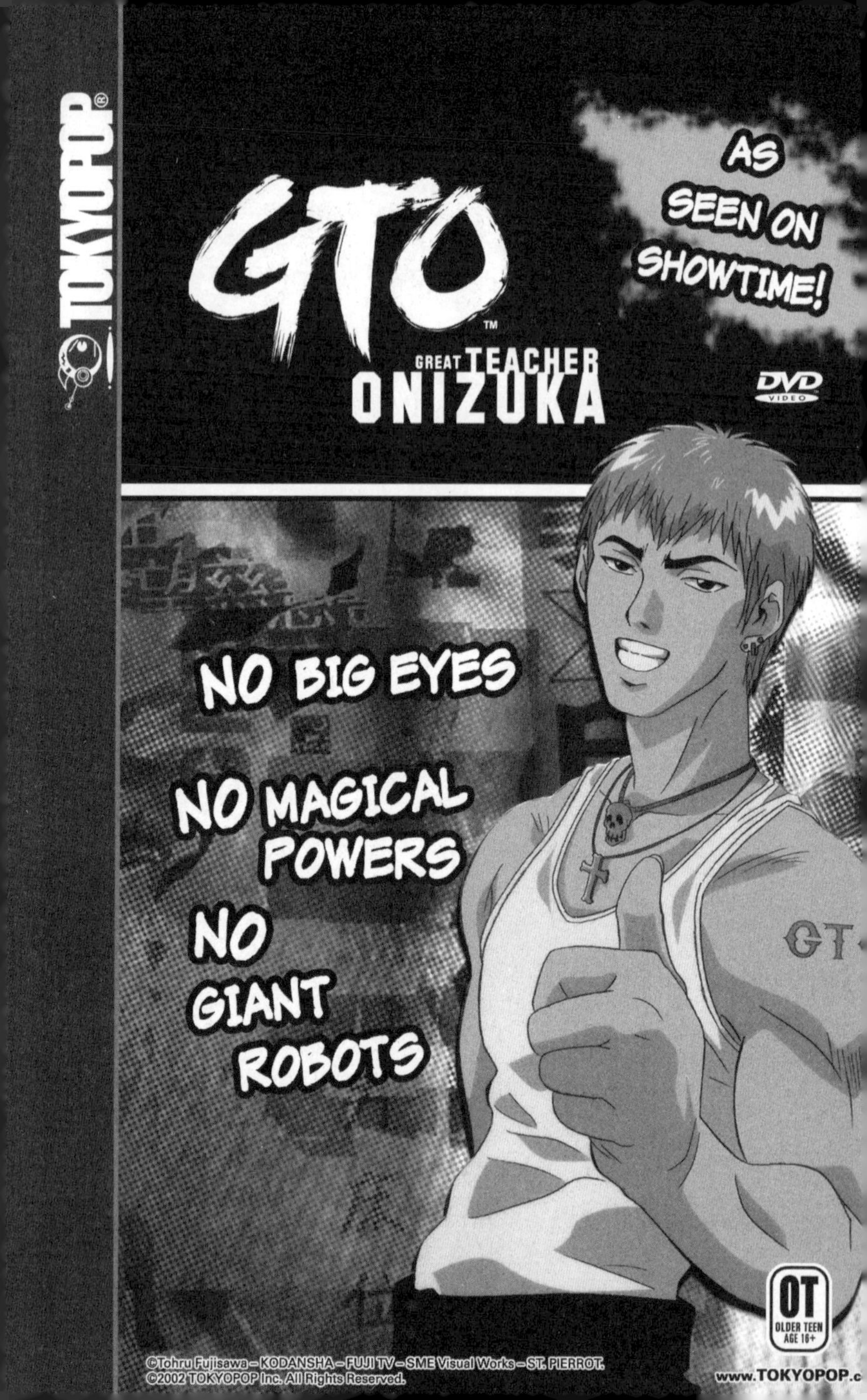
TOKYOPOP®
GTO™
GREAT TEACHER ONIZUKA
AS SEEN ON SHOWTIME!
DVD VIDEO
NO BIG EYES
NO MAGICAL POWERS
NO GIANT ROBOTS
OT OLDER TEEN AGE 16+
©Tohru Fujisawa – KODANSHA – FUJI TV – SME Visual Works – ST. PIERROT.
©2002 TOKYOPOP Inc. All Rights Reserved.
www.TOKYOPOP.c

STOP!

This is the back of the book.
You wouldn't want to spoil a great ending!

This book is printed "manga-style," in the authentic Japanese right-to-left format. Since none of the artwork has been flipped or altered, readers get to experience the story just as the creator intended. You've been asking for it, so TOKYOPOP® delivered: authentic, hot-off-the-press, and far more fun!

DIRECTIONS

If this is your first time reading manga-style, here's a quick guide to help you understand how it works.

It's easy... just start in the top right panel and follow the numbers. Have fun, and look for more 100% authentic manga from TOKYOPOP®!

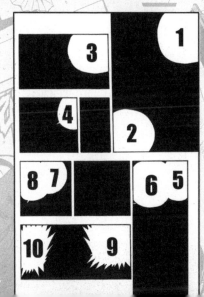

STOP!

This is the back of the book.
You wouldn't want to spoil a great ending!

The rest of the stories in this
volume were created to read
from left to right.

Turn to the other end of
the book to enjoy more
TOKYOPOP manga.

Whether it's left to right or right to left,
TOKYOPOP has manga covered
in all directions!

TOKYOPOP® SNEAKS™

Introduction

Welcome to the latest installment of TOKYOPOP Sneaks – your insider's guide to the wild and wonderful world of manga!

As you may already know, manga – the Japanese word for comics – has become a truly global phenomenon. Kids all over the world can't get enough of its irresistible visual storytelling and bleeding-edge graphic design. There's manga for every taste, too: science fiction, romance, comedy, fantasy, action...you name it and manga's got it covered!

Within the pages of this book you will find an extraordinary selection of TOKYOPOP's latest titles that are sure to fire your imagination like nothing you have ever read before. Once you pick out your favorites, remember that manga is available everywhere books are sold.

Check your local book or comic shop, go to your favorite e-commerce site, or visit TOKYOPOP's online store at www.TOKYOPOP.com/shop to buy the latest and greatest TOKYOPOP manga.

And, as always, for the freshest news and info, please visit us online at www.TOKYOPOP.com.

From all of us here at TOKYOPOP, thank you for your support – and welcome to the Manga Revolution!

Cover Art - Raymond Makowski
Graphic Design - Bowen Park
Project Coordinators - Rob Tokar, Seamus Tierney
Digital Imaging Manager - Chris Buford
Production Managers - Jennifer Miller, Mutsumi Miyazaki
Managing Editors - Jill Freshney, Lindsey Johnston
VP of Production - Ron Klamert
Publisher and E.I.C.- Mike Kiley
President & C.O.O. - John Parker
C.E.O. - Stuart Levy

E-mail: info@TOKYOPOP.com
Come visit us online at www.TOKYOPOP.com

A  Manga

5900 Wilshire Blvd., Suite 2000, Los Angeles, CA 90036

Alichino
© 1998 Kouyu Shurei

DearS
© 2002 PEACH-PIT

Erica Sakurazawa: Between the Sheets
© 2003 Erica Sakurazawa

Immortal Rain
© 2002 Kaori Ozaki

Lament of the Lamb
© 1994 KEI TOUME

Mahoromatic
© 1997 Bunjuro Nakayama/Bow Ditama

Pita-Ten
© 2005 Koge-Donbo

Princess Ai
© 2003 TOKYOPOP Inc. & Kitty Radio, Inc.

Qwan
© 2003 Aki Shimizu

Sorcerer Hunters
© 1995 Satoru Akahori and Ray Omishi.

Tokyo Tribes
© Santa Inoue

Warcraft
© 2005 Blizzard Entertainment

Van Von Hunter
© 2005 Tokyopop Inc.

English text © 2005 TOKYOPOP Inc.
TOKYOPOP Sneaks is published for promotional use only.

ISBN: 1-59532-741-X

First TOKYOPOP printing: September 2005

Printed in Italy

TOKYOPOP® SNEAKS™

right to left right to left right to l

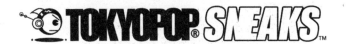

TABLE OF CONTENTS

Available on DVD from September 2005
from MVM Entertainment
Character art © Yuji Shiozaki

www.mvm-films.com

The Story:

Beautiful creatures called Alichino grant wishes to those in need—
but at a price! A young lady searching for an Alichino wants to bring
her brother back to life. She meets Tsugiri, a handsome young man who
she thinks is an Alichino. Tsugiri turns out to be a mere mortal, but he
does have a mysterious connection with these rare creatures—
a connection that will bring danger to those around him.

The Creator:

Kouyu Shurei

Behind the Manga:

• Kouyu Shurei is a winner of the prestigious Cobalt Illustrator's
  Award.
• Bonus full-color foldout.

Genre:

Fantasy

SRP:

£ 6.99

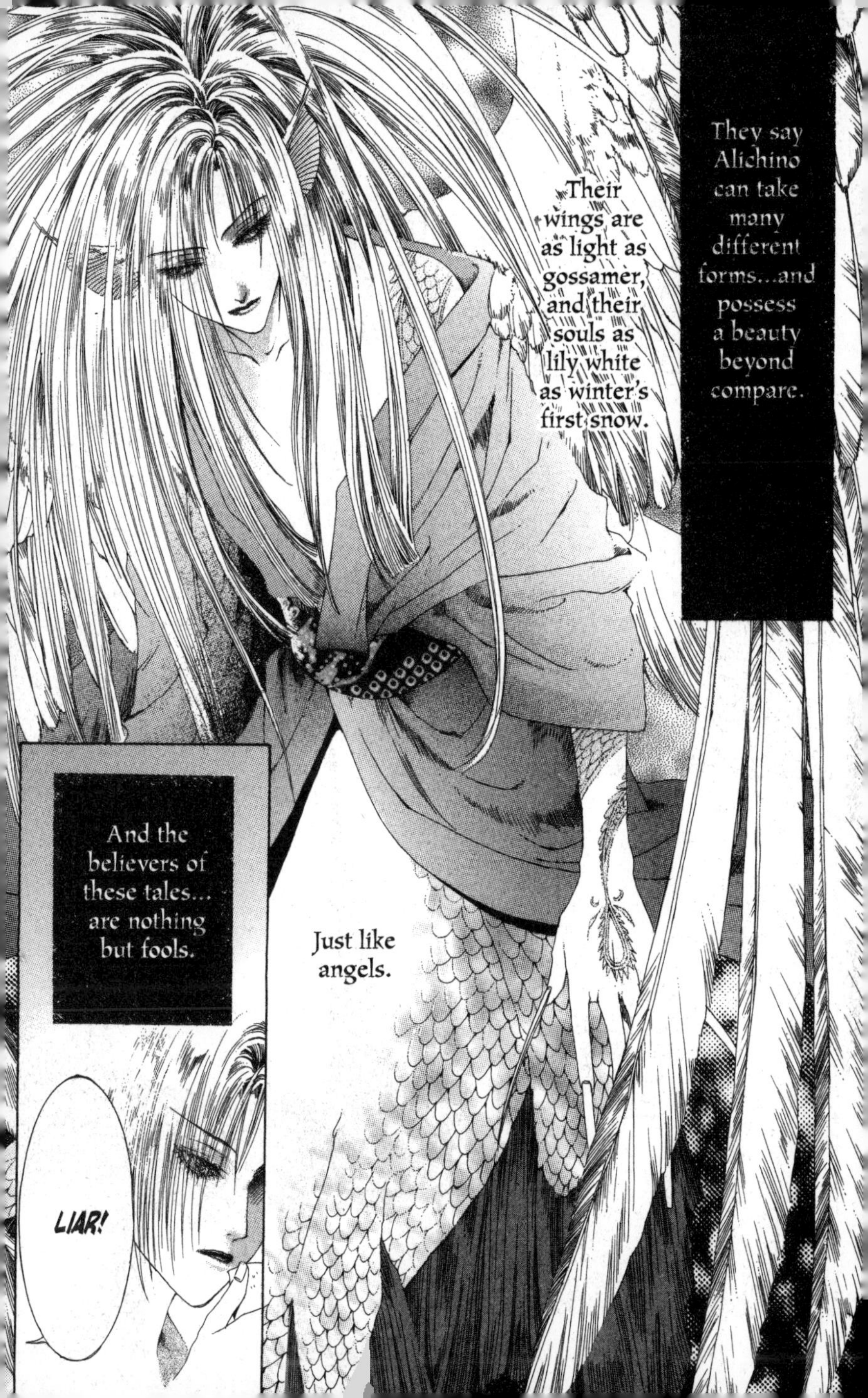
They say Alichino can take many different forms...and possess a beauty beyond compare.
Their wings are as light as gossamer, and their souls as lily white as winter's first snow.
Just like angels.
And the believers of these tales... are nothing but fools.
LIAR!

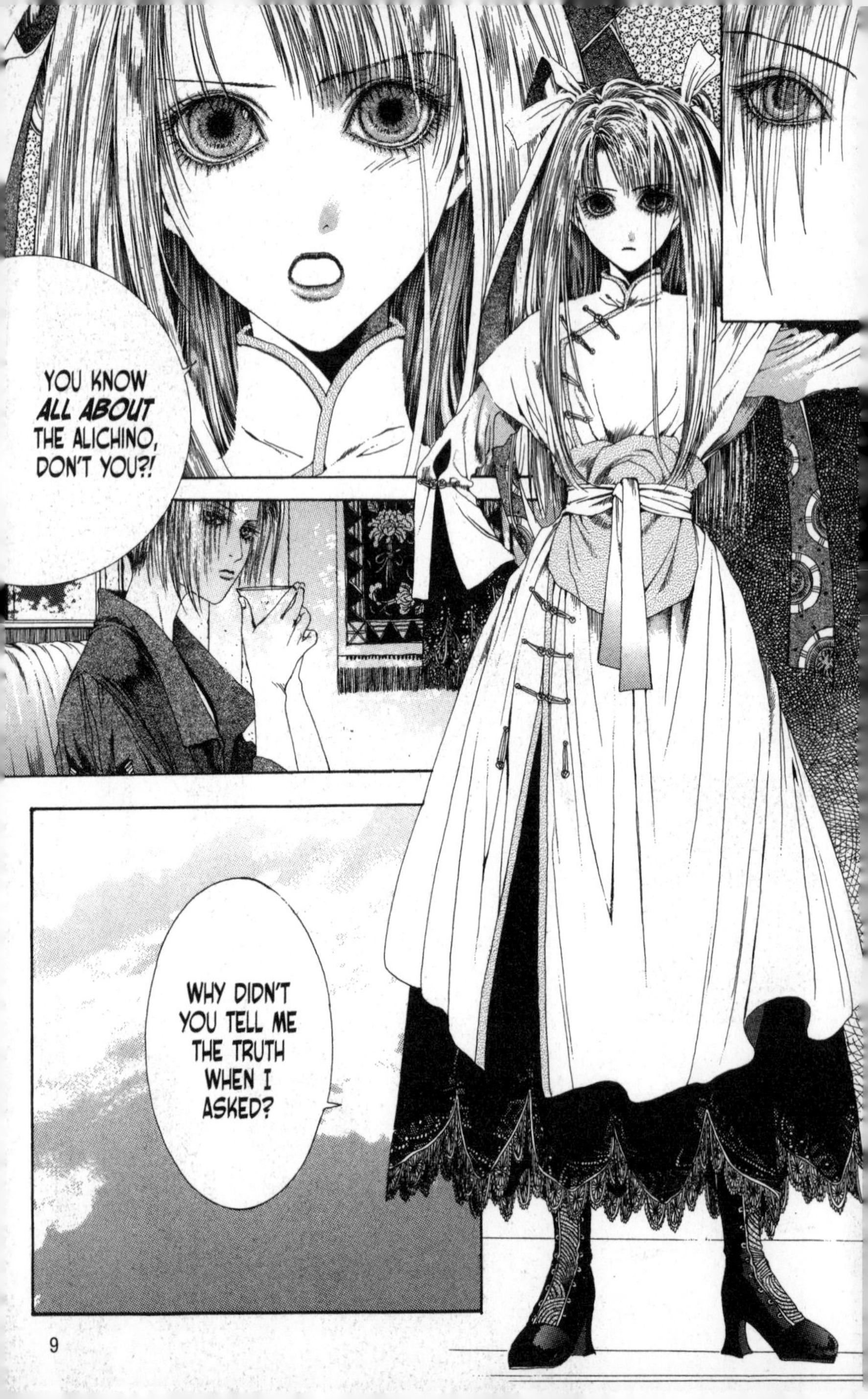
YOU KNOW **ALL ABOUT** THE ALICHINO, DON'T YOU?!
WHY DIDN'T YOU TELL ME THE TRUTH WHEN I ASKED?

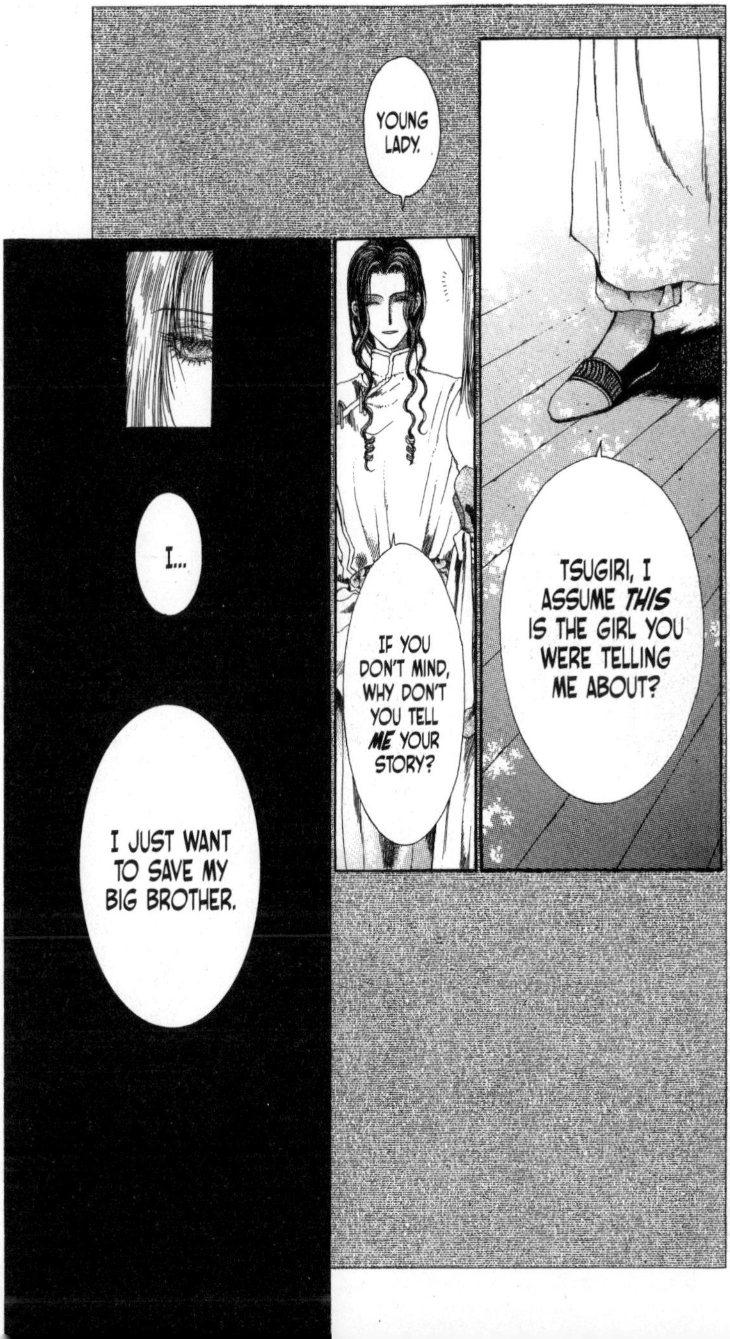

TSUGIRI, I ASSUME *THIS* IS THE GIRL YOU WERE TELLING ME ABOUT?
YOUNG LADY.
IF YOU DON'T MIND, WHY DON'T YOU TELL *ME* YOUR STORY?
I...
I JUST WANT TO SAVE MY BIG BROTHER.

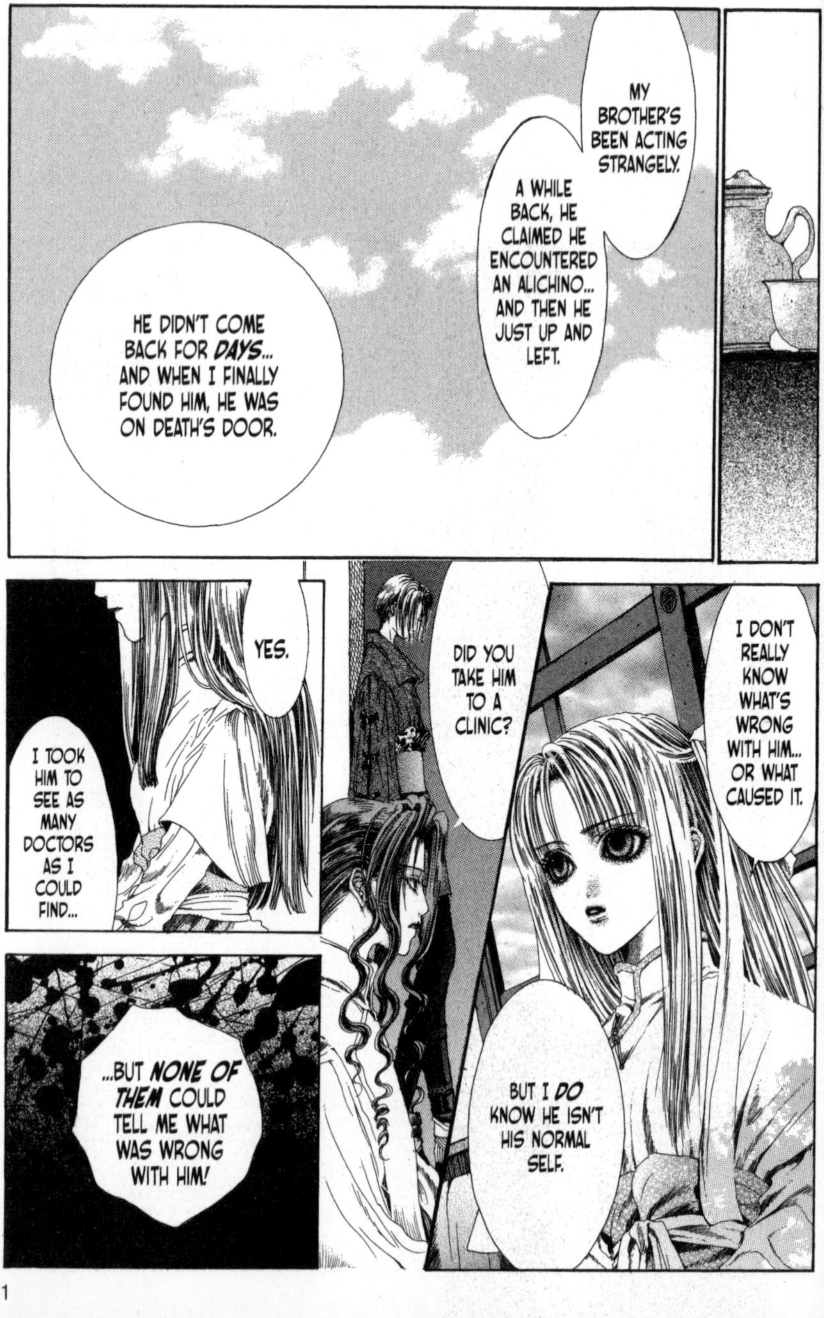
MY BROTHER'S BEEN ACTING STRANGELY.
A WHILE BACK, HE CLAIMED HE ENCOUNTERED AN ALICHINO... AND THEN HE JUST UP AND LEFT.
HE DIDN'T COME BACK FOR *DAYS*... AND WHEN I FINALLY FOUND HIM, HE WAS ON DEATH'S DOOR.
I DON'T REALLY KNOW WHAT'S WRONG WITH HIM... OR WHAT CAUSED IT.
BUT I *DO* KNOW HE ISN'T HIS NORMAL SELF.
DID YOU TAKE HIM TO A CLINIC?
YES.
I TOOK HIM TO SEE AS MANY DOCTORS AS I COULD FIND...
...BUT *NONE OF THEM* COULD TELL ME WHAT WAS WRONG WITH HIM!

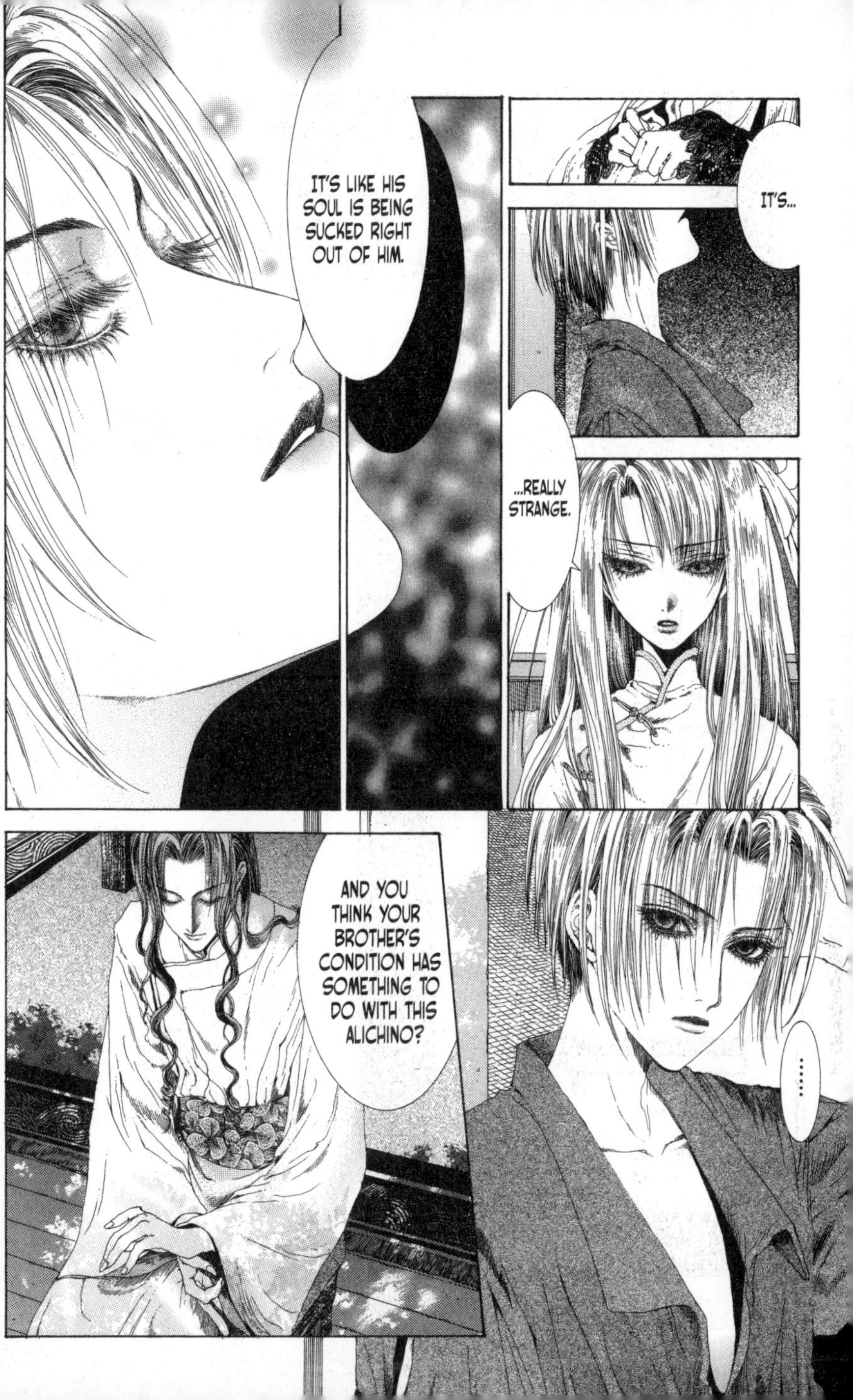
IT'S...
...REALLY STRANGE.
IT'S LIKE HIS SOUL IS BEING SUCKED RIGHT OUT OF HIM.
......
AND YOU THINK YOUR BROTHER'S CONDITION HAS SOMETHING TO DO WITH THIS ALICHINO?

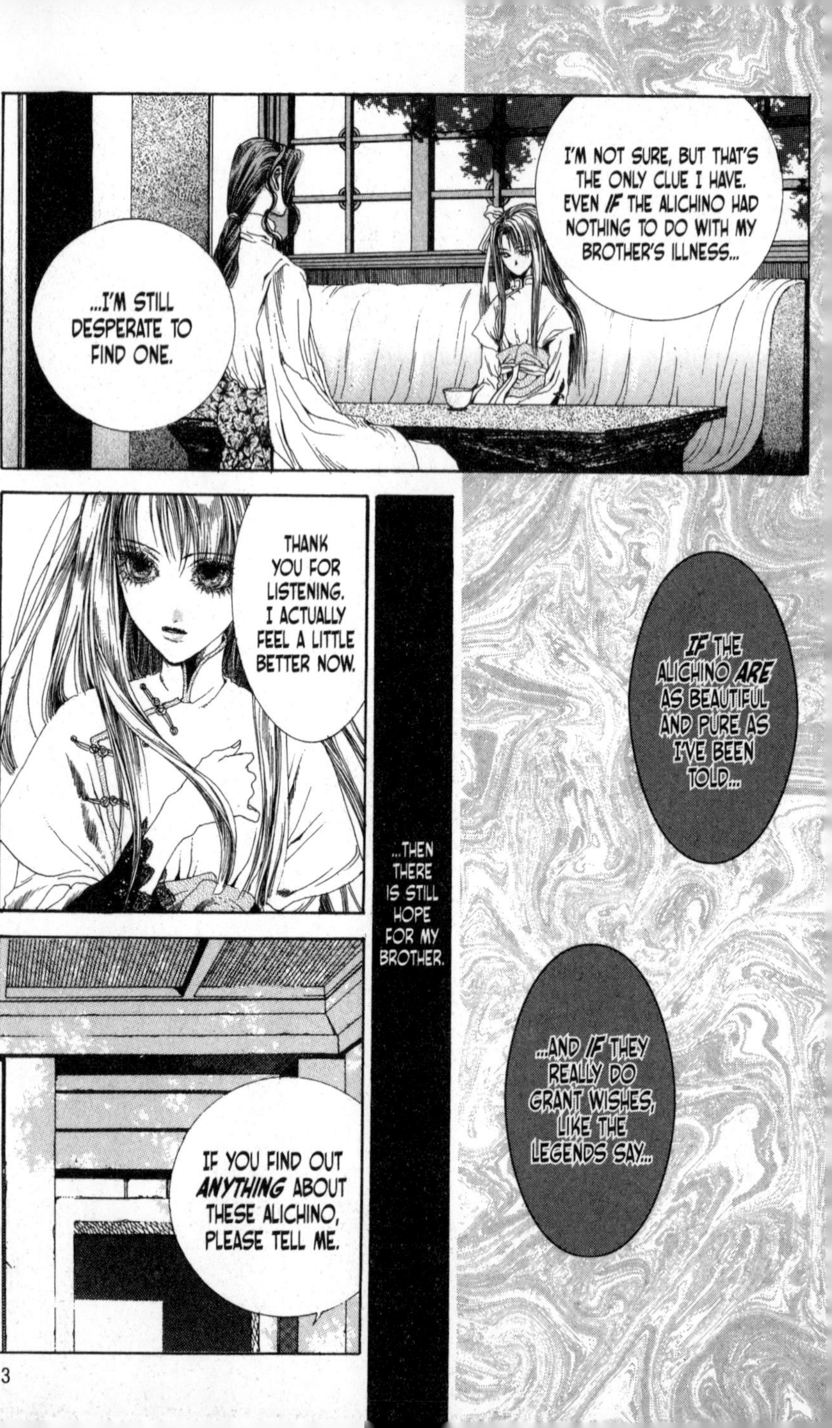
I'M NOT SURE, BUT THAT'S THE ONLY CLUE I HAVE. EVEN *IF* THE ALICHINO HAD NOTHING TO DO WITH MY BROTHER'S ILLNESS...
...I'M STILL DESPERATE TO FIND ONE.
IF THE ALICHINO *ARE* AS BEAUTIFUL AND PURE AS I'VE BEEN TOLD...
...AND *IF* THEY REALLY DO GRANT WISHES, LIKE THE LEGENDS SAY...
...THEN THERE IS STILL HOPE FOR MY BROTHER.
THANK YOU FOR LISTENING. I ACTUALLY FEEL A LITTLE BETTER NOW.
IF YOU FIND OUT *ANYTHING* ABOUT THESE ALICHINO, PLEASE TELL ME.

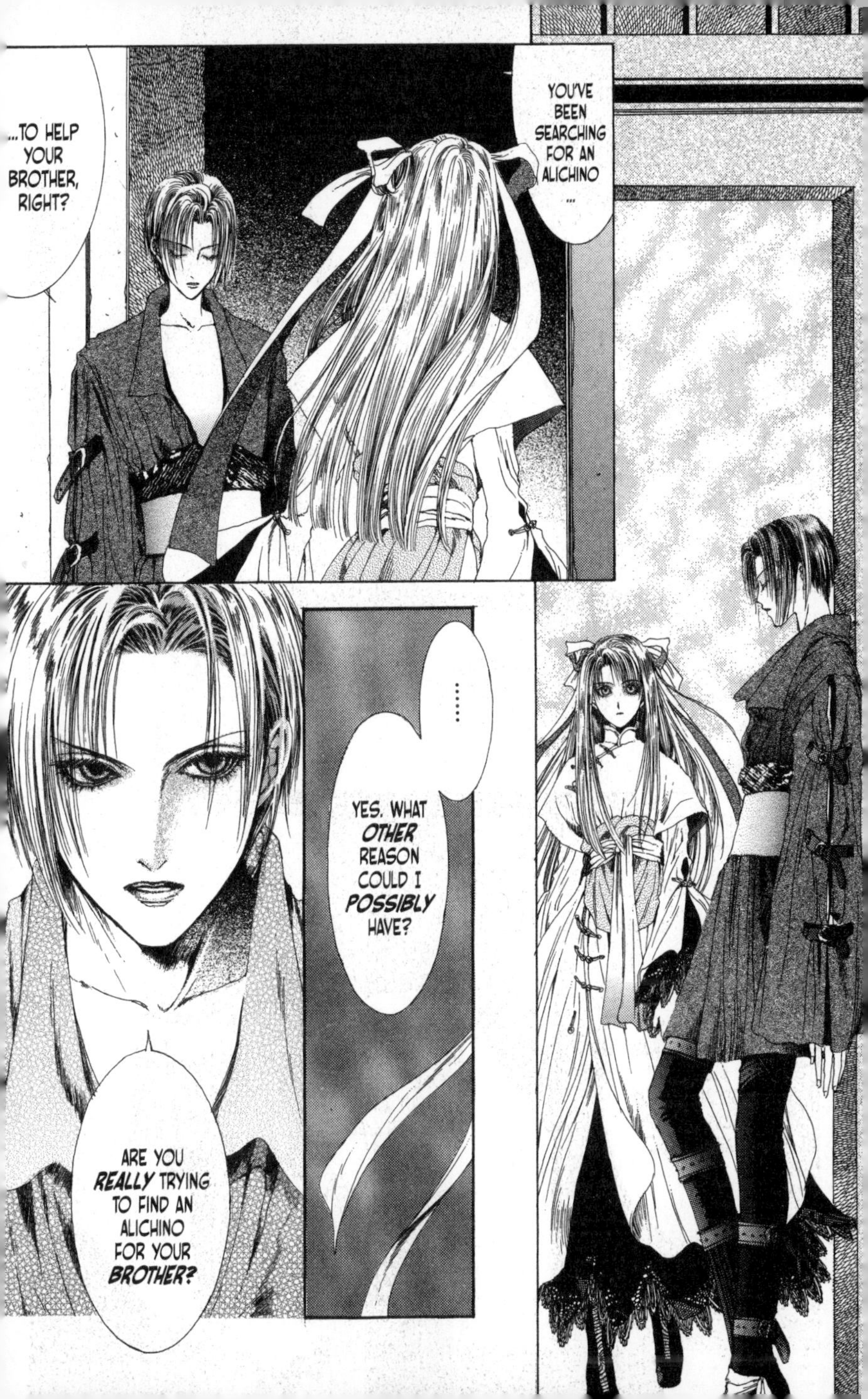
YOU'VE BEEN SEARCHING FOR AN ALICHINO ...
...TO HELP YOUR BROTHER, RIGHT?
......
YES. WHAT *OTHER* REASON COULD I *POSSIBLY* HAVE?
ARE YOU *REALLY* TRYING TO FIND AN ALICHINO FOR YOUR *BROTHER?*

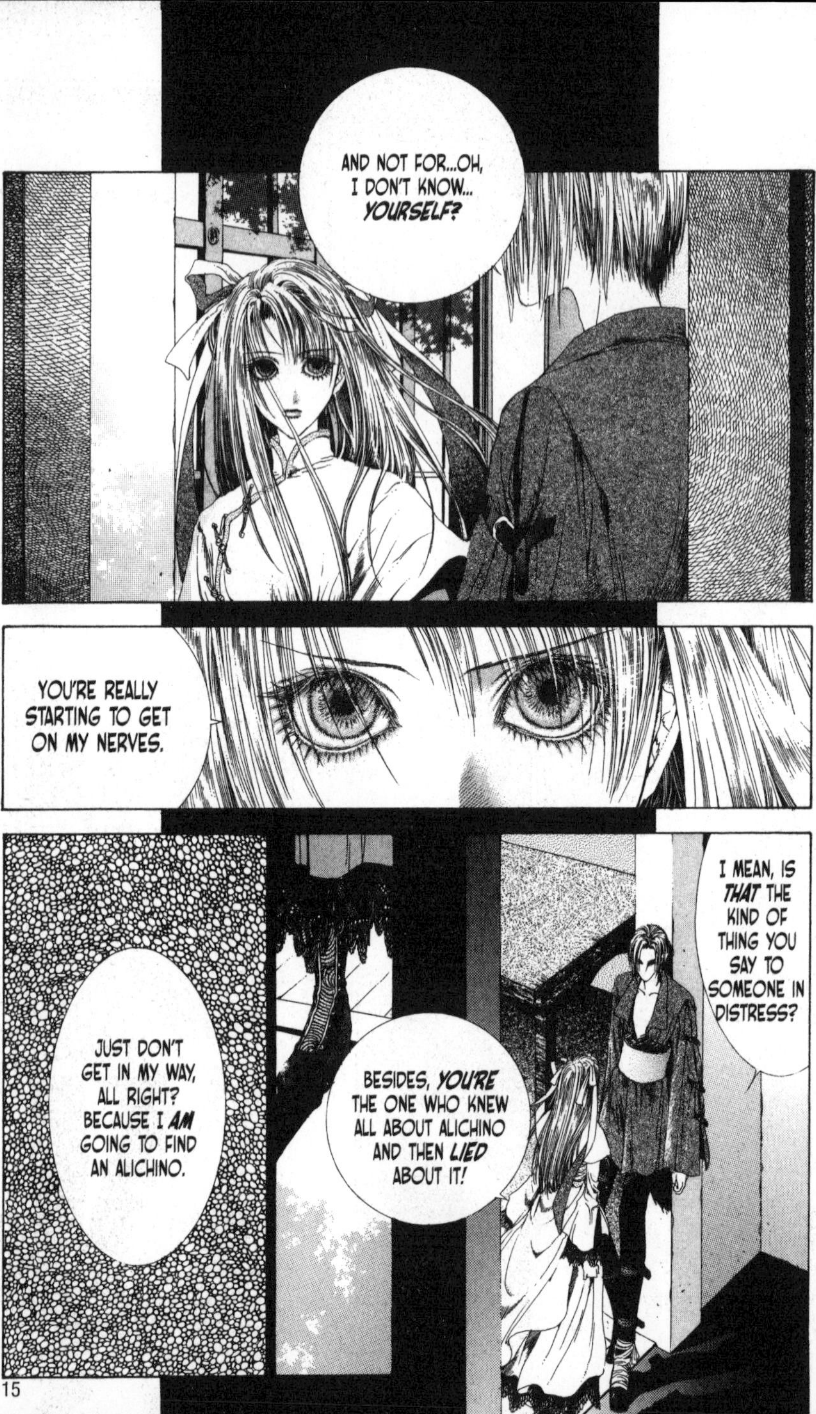
AND NOT FOR...OH, I DON'T KNOW... *YOURSELF?*
YOU'RE REALLY STARTING TO GET ON MY NERVES.
I MEAN, IS *THAT* THE KIND OF THING YOU SAY TO SOMEONE IN DISTRESS?
BESIDES, *YOU'RE* THE ONE WHO KNEW ALL ABOUT ALICHINO AND THEN *LIED* ABOUT IT!
JUST DON'T GET IN MY WAY, ALL RIGHT? BECAUSE I *AM* GOING TO FIND AN ALICHINO.

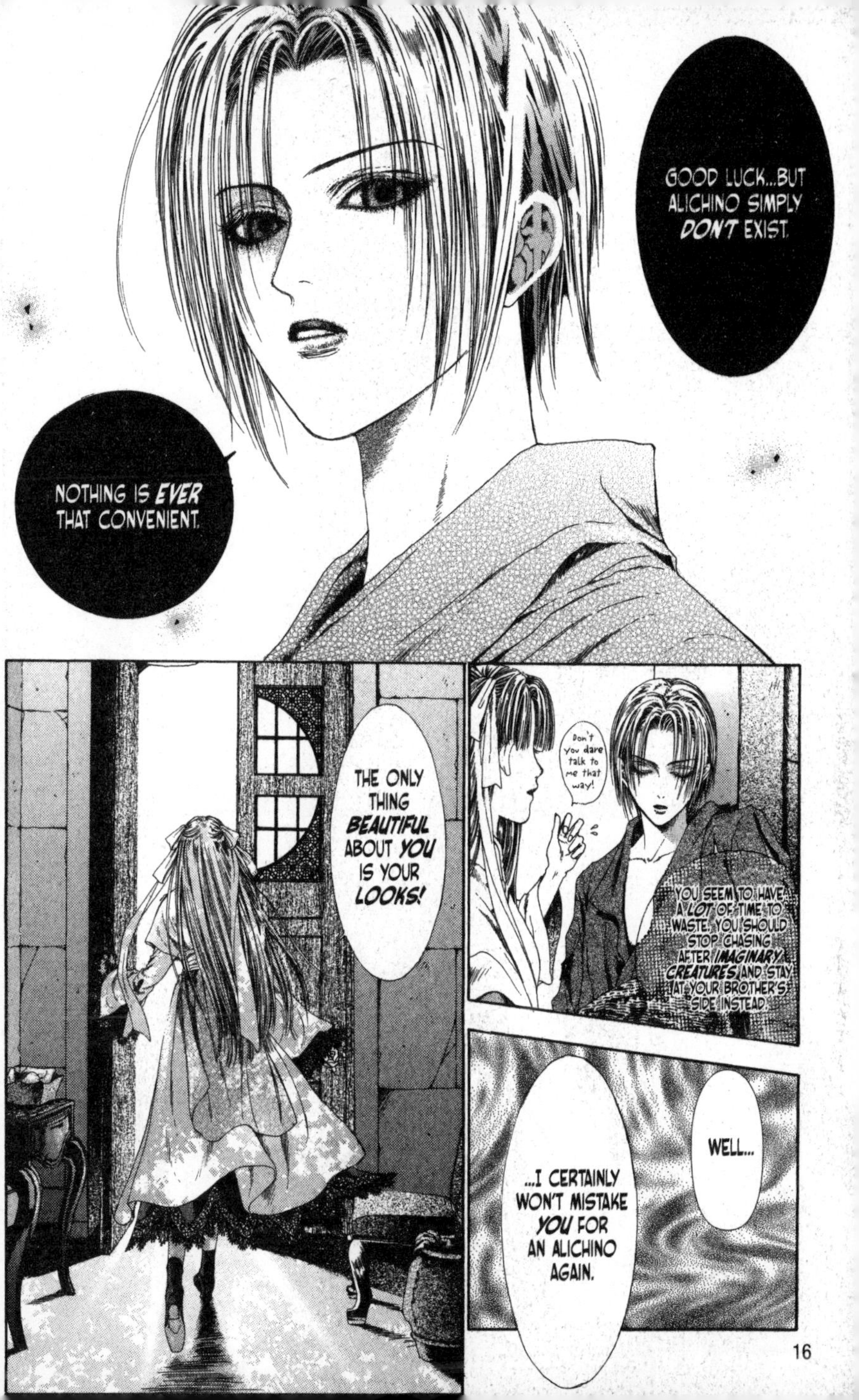
GOOD LUCK...BUT ALICHINO SIMPLY DON'T EXIST.
NOTHING IS EVER THAT CONVENIENT.
YOU SEEM TO HAVE A LOT OF TIME TO WASTE. YOU SHOULD STOP CHASING AFTER IMAGINARY CREATURES AND STAY AT YOUR BROTHER'S SIDE INSTEAD.
Don't you dare talk to me that way!
WELL...
...I CERTAINLY WON'T MISTAKE YOU FOR AN ALICHINO AGAIN.
THE ONLY THING BEAUTIFUL ABOUT YOU IS YOUR LOOKS!

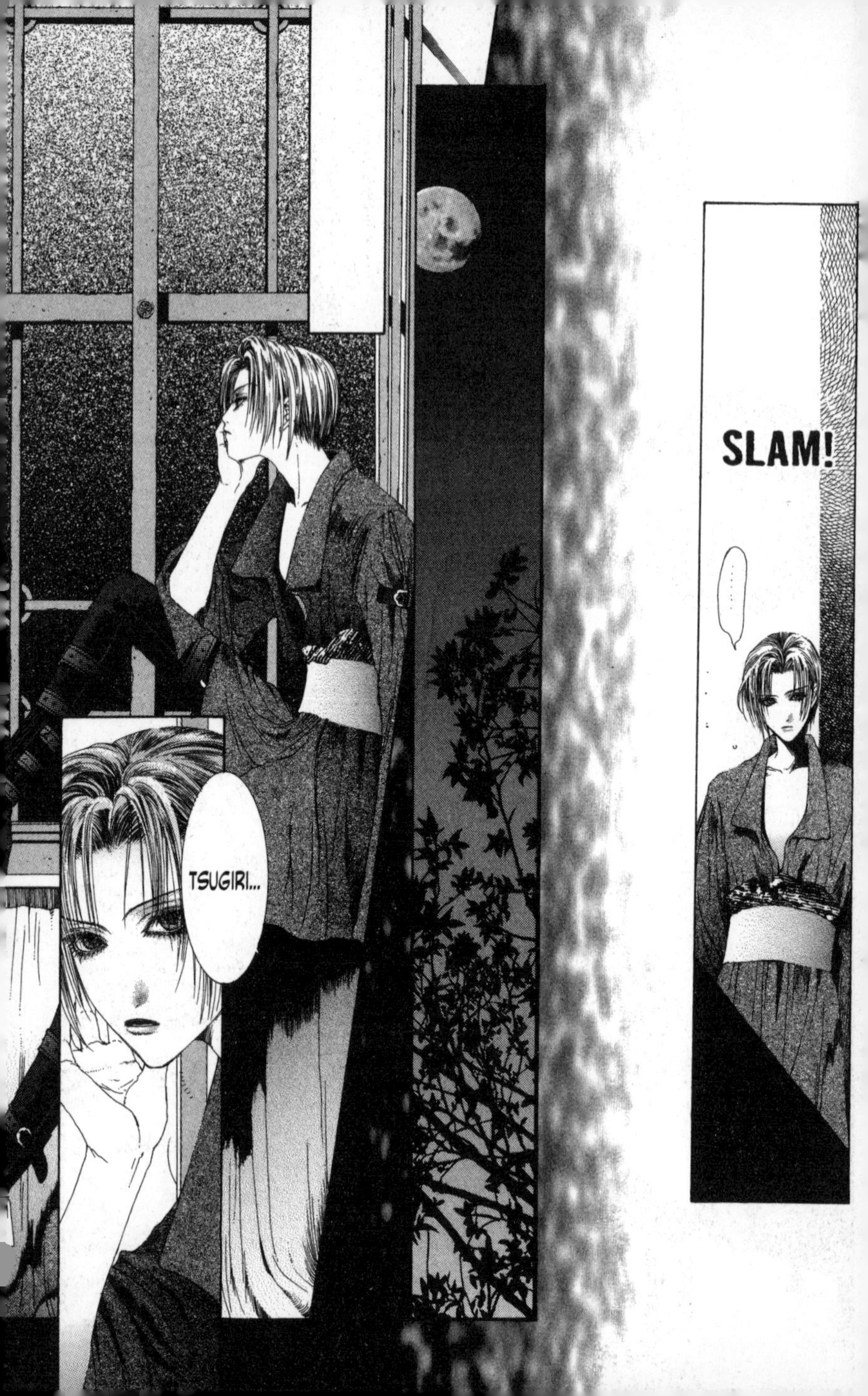
SLAM!
......
TSUGIRI...

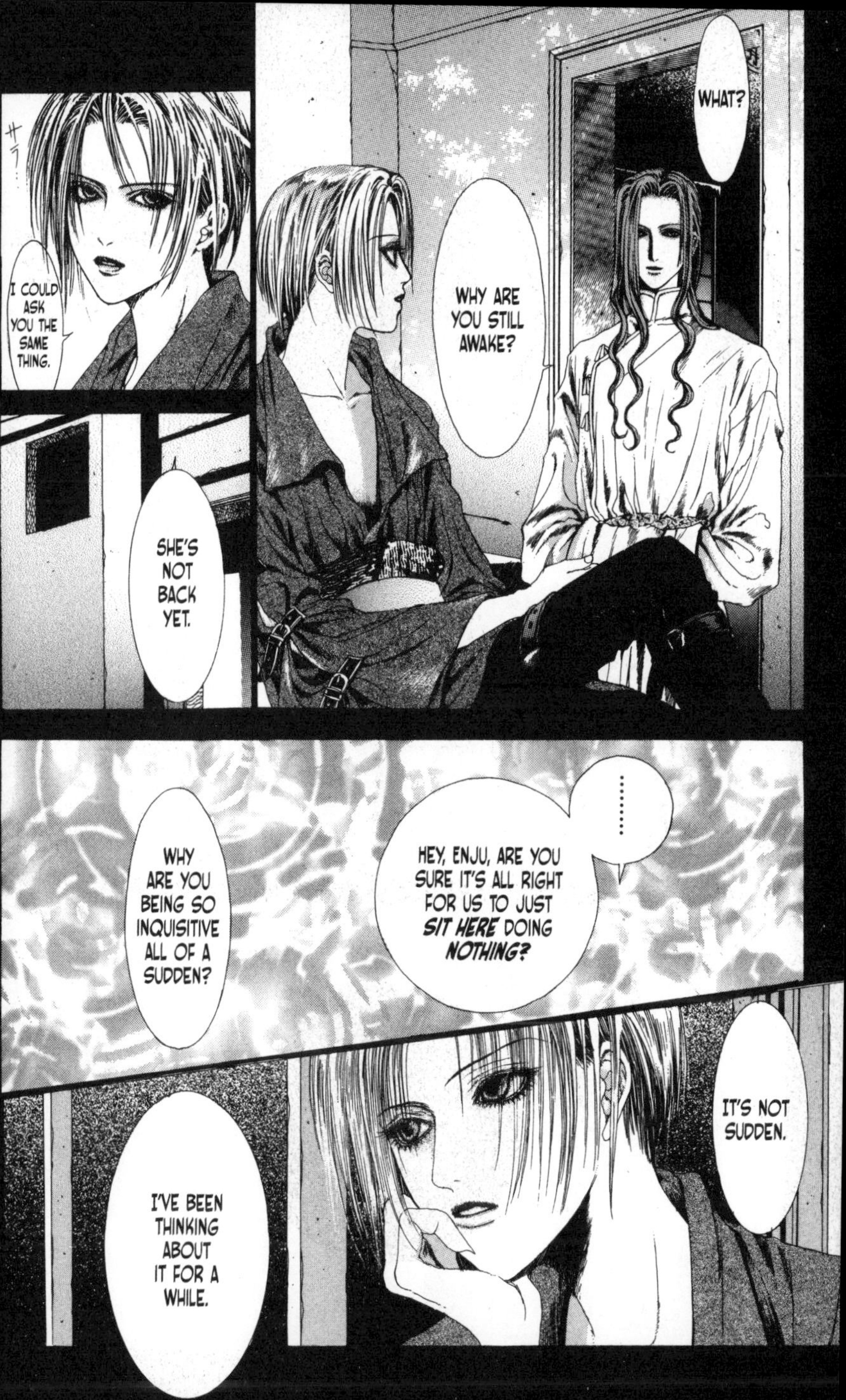
WHAT?
WHY ARE YOU STILL AWAKE?
サラ…
I COULD ASK YOU THE SAME THING.
SHE'S NOT BACK YET.
......
HEY, ENJU, ARE YOU SURE IT'S ALL RIGHT FOR US TO JUST *SIT HERE* DOING *NOTHING?*
WHY ARE YOU BEING SO INQUISITIVE ALL OF A SUDDEN?
IT'S NOT SUDDEN.
I'VE BEEN THINKING ABOUT IT FOR A WHILE.

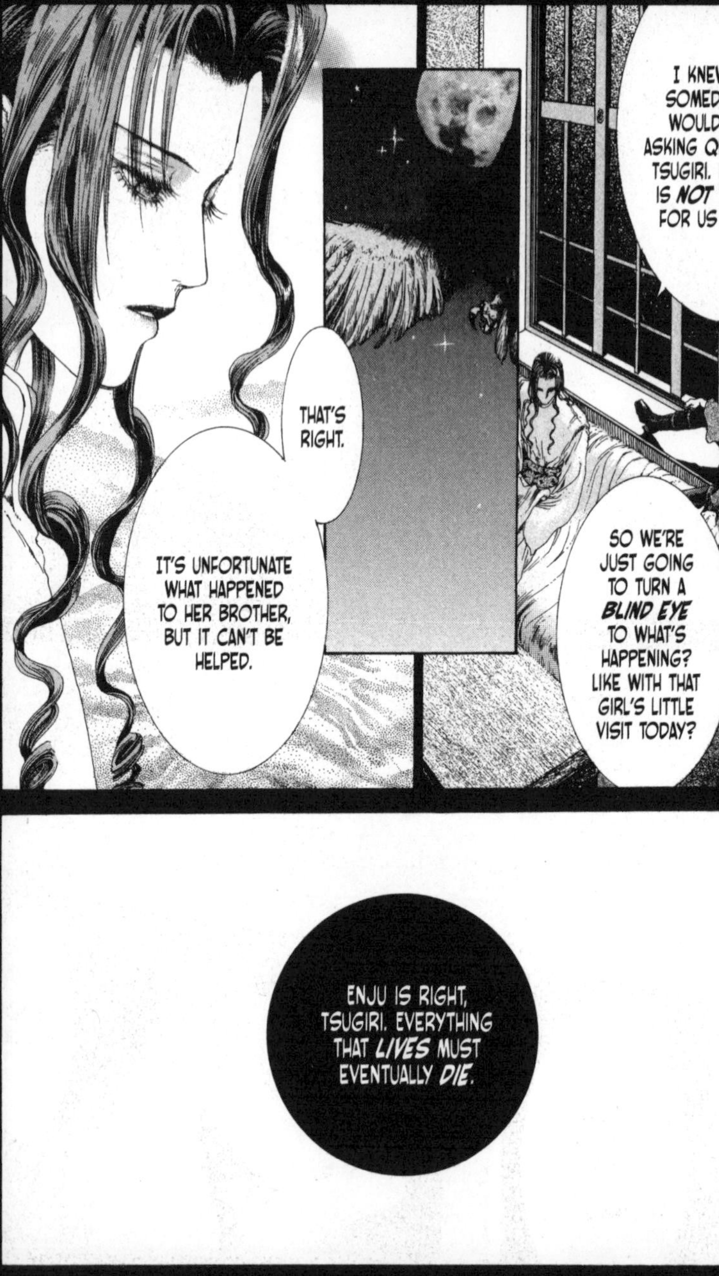
I KNEW THAT SOMEDAY YOU WOULD START ASKING QUESTIONS, TSUGIRI. BUT NOW IS *NOT* THE TIME FOR US TO ACT.
SO WE'RE JUST GOING TO TURN A *BLIND EYE* TO WHAT'S HAPPENING? LIKE WITH THAT GIRL'S LITTLE VISIT TODAY?
THAT'S RIGHT.
IT'S UNFORTUNATE WHAT HAPPENED TO HER BROTHER, BUT IT CAN'T BE HELPED.
ENJU IS RIGHT, TSUGIRI. EVERYTHING THAT *LIVES* MUST EVENTUALLY *DIE*.

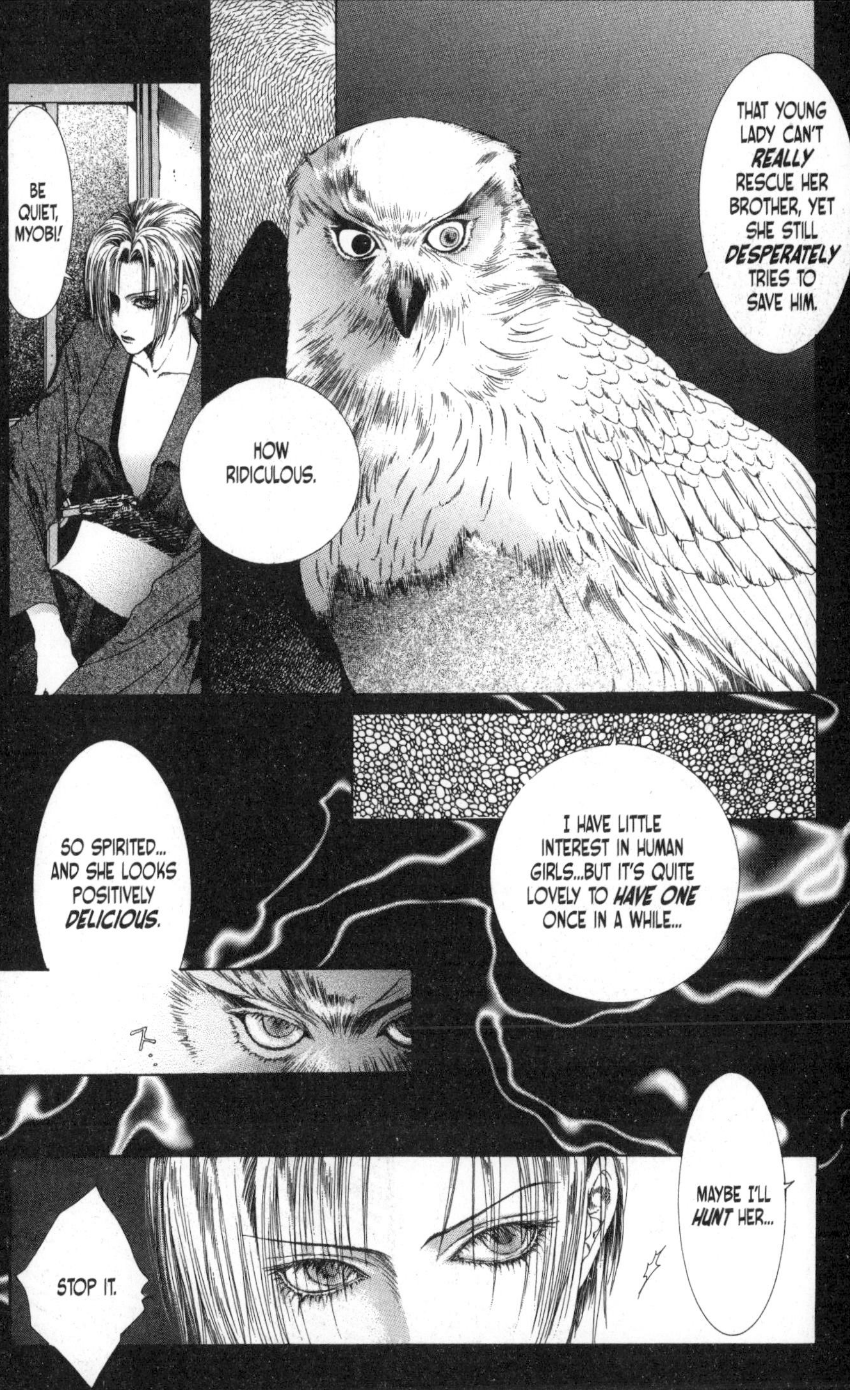
THAT YOUNG LADY CAN'T *REALLY* RESCUE HER BROTHER, YET SHE STILL *DESPERATELY* TRIES TO SAVE HIM.
HOW RIDICULOUS.
BE QUIET, MYOBI!
I HAVE LITTLE INTEREST IN HUMAN GIRLS...BUT IT'S QUITE LOVELY TO *HAVE ONE* ONCE IN A WHILE...
SO SPIRITED... AND SHE LOOKS POSITIVELY *DELICIOUS*.
MAYBE I'LL *HUNT* HER...
STOP IT.

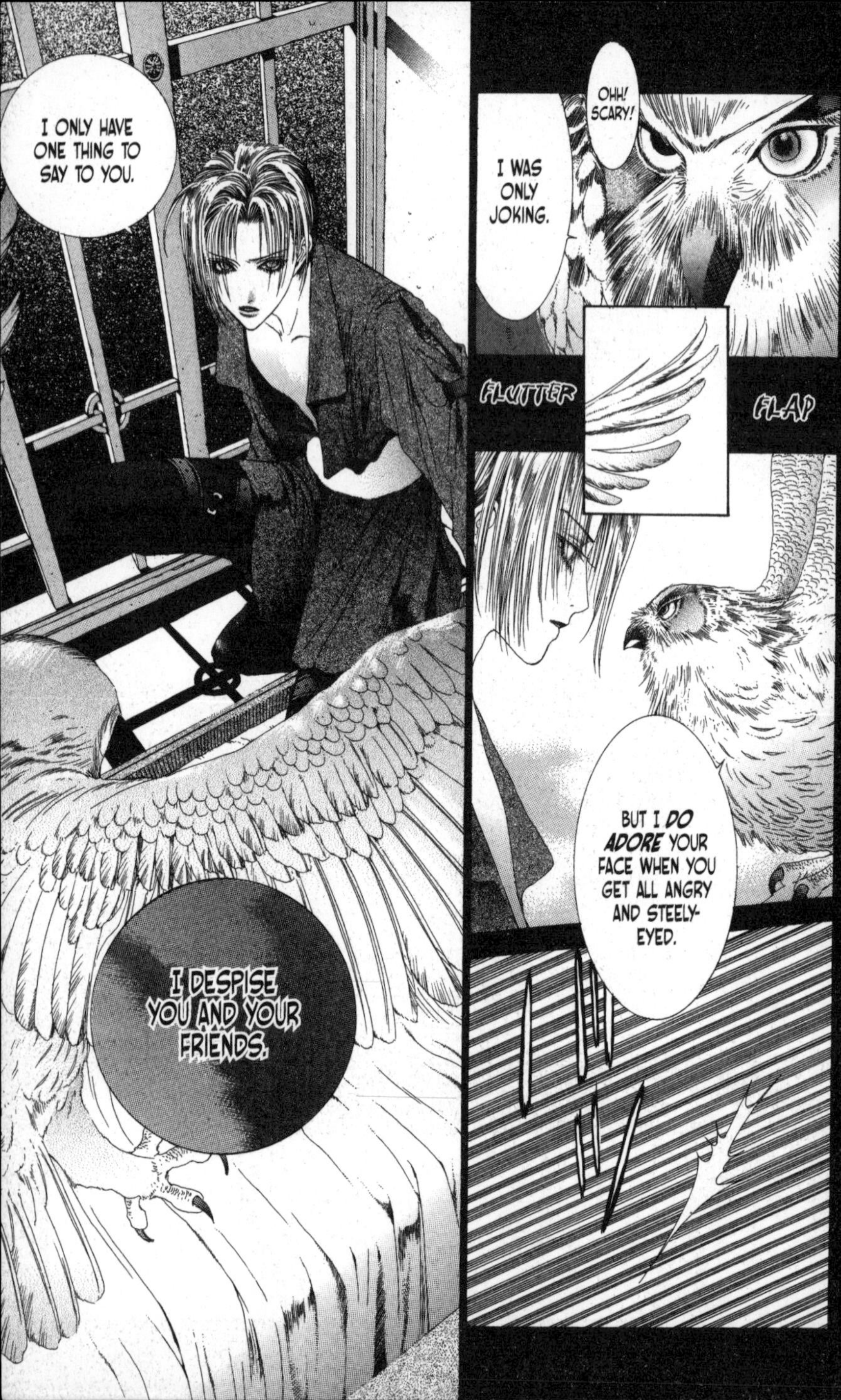
OHH! SCARY!
I WAS ONLY JOKING.
FLAP
FLUTTER
BUT I *DO ADORE* YOUR FACE WHEN YOU GET ALL ANGRY AND STEELY-EYED.
I ONLY HAVE ONE THING TO SAY TO YOU.
I DESPISE YOU AND YOUR FRIENDS.

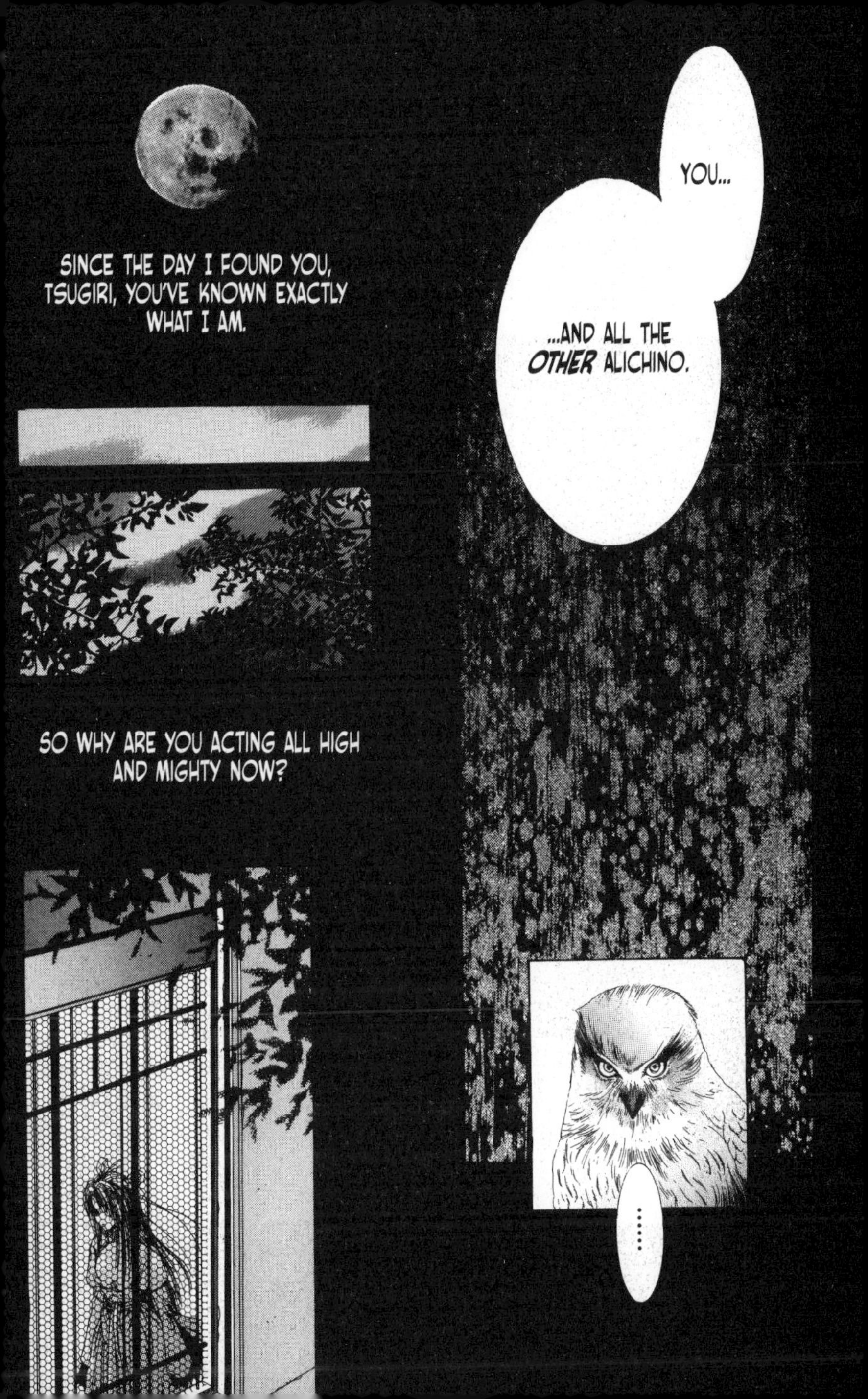
YOU...
...AND ALL THE *OTHER* ALICHINO.
......
SINCE THE DAY I FOUND YOU, TSUGIRI, YOU'VE KNOWN EXACTLY WHAT I AM.
SO WHY ARE YOU ACTING ALL HIGH AND MIGHTY NOW?

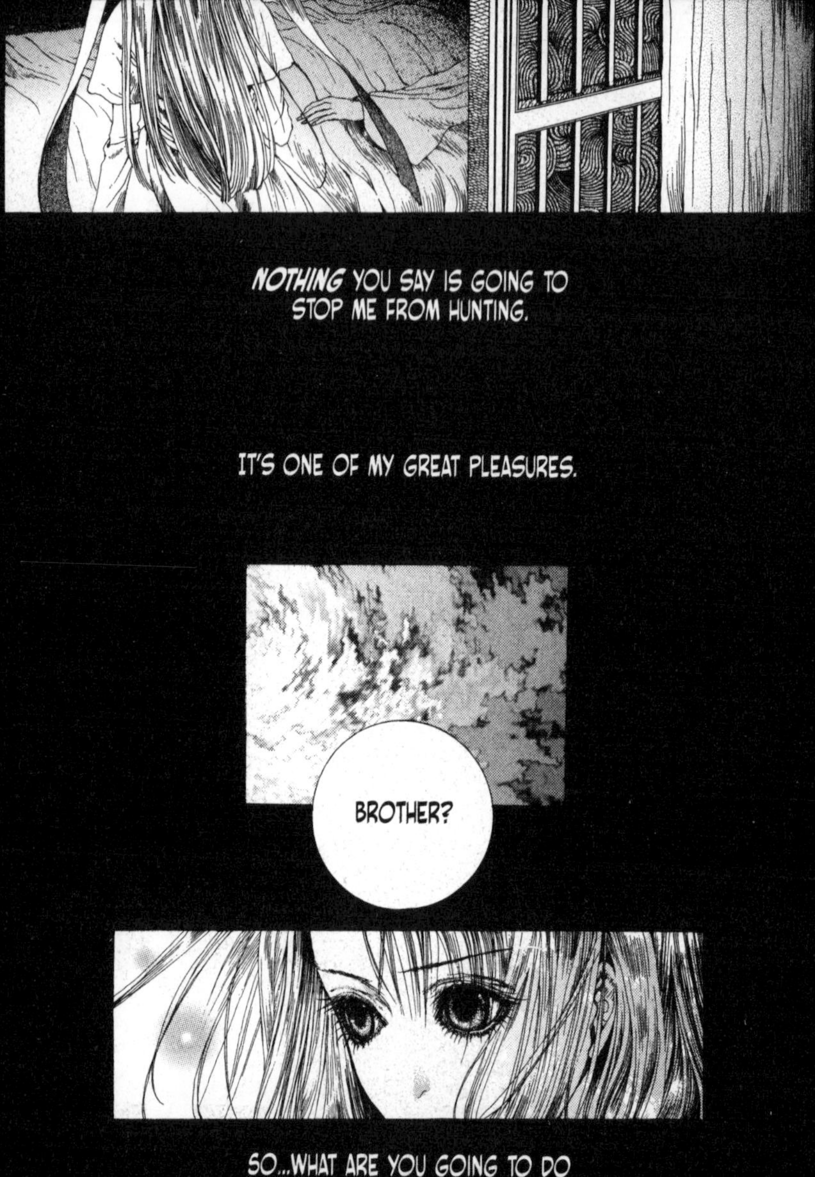
NOTHING YOU SAY IS GOING TO STOP ME FROM HUNTING.
IT'S ONE OF MY GREAT PLEASURES.
BROTHER?
SO...WHAT ARE YOU GOING TO DO

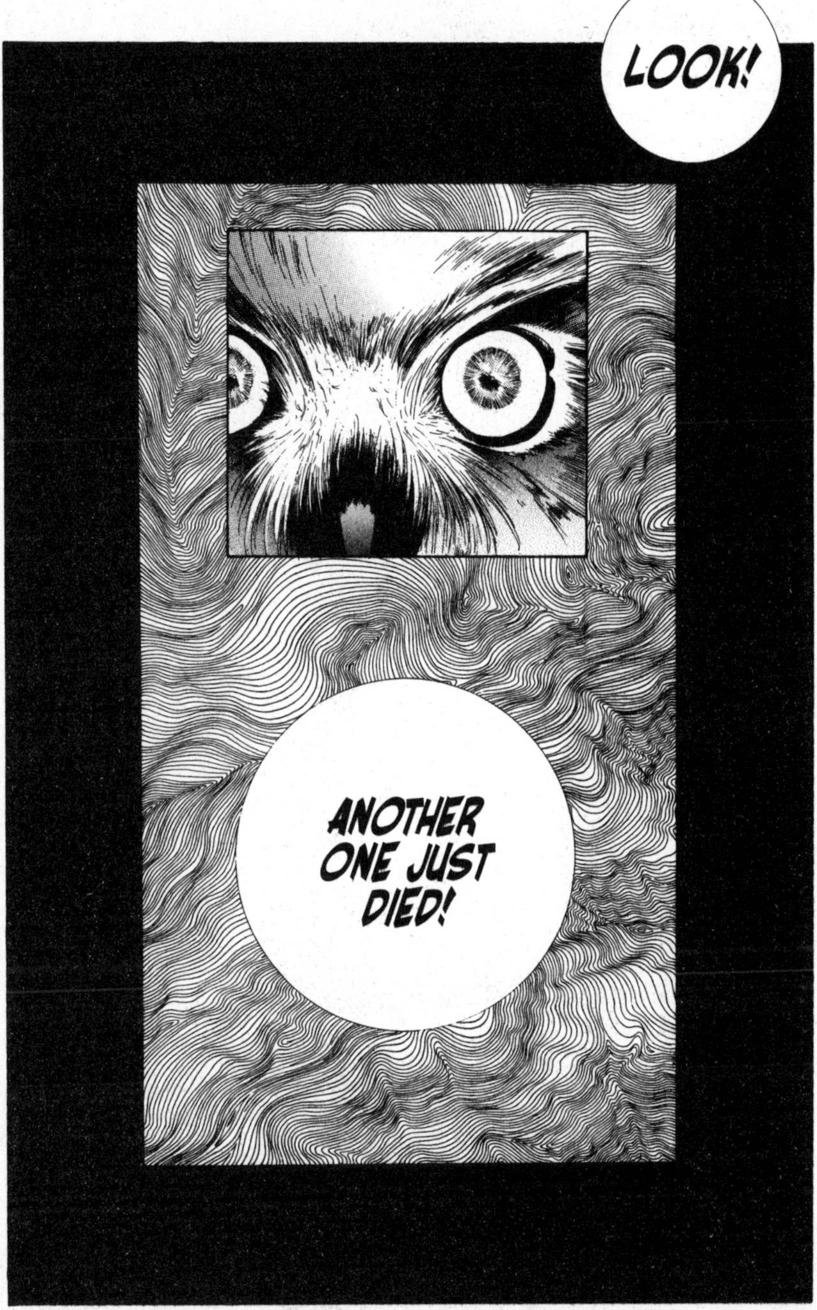
LOOK!
ANOTHER ONE JUST DIED!

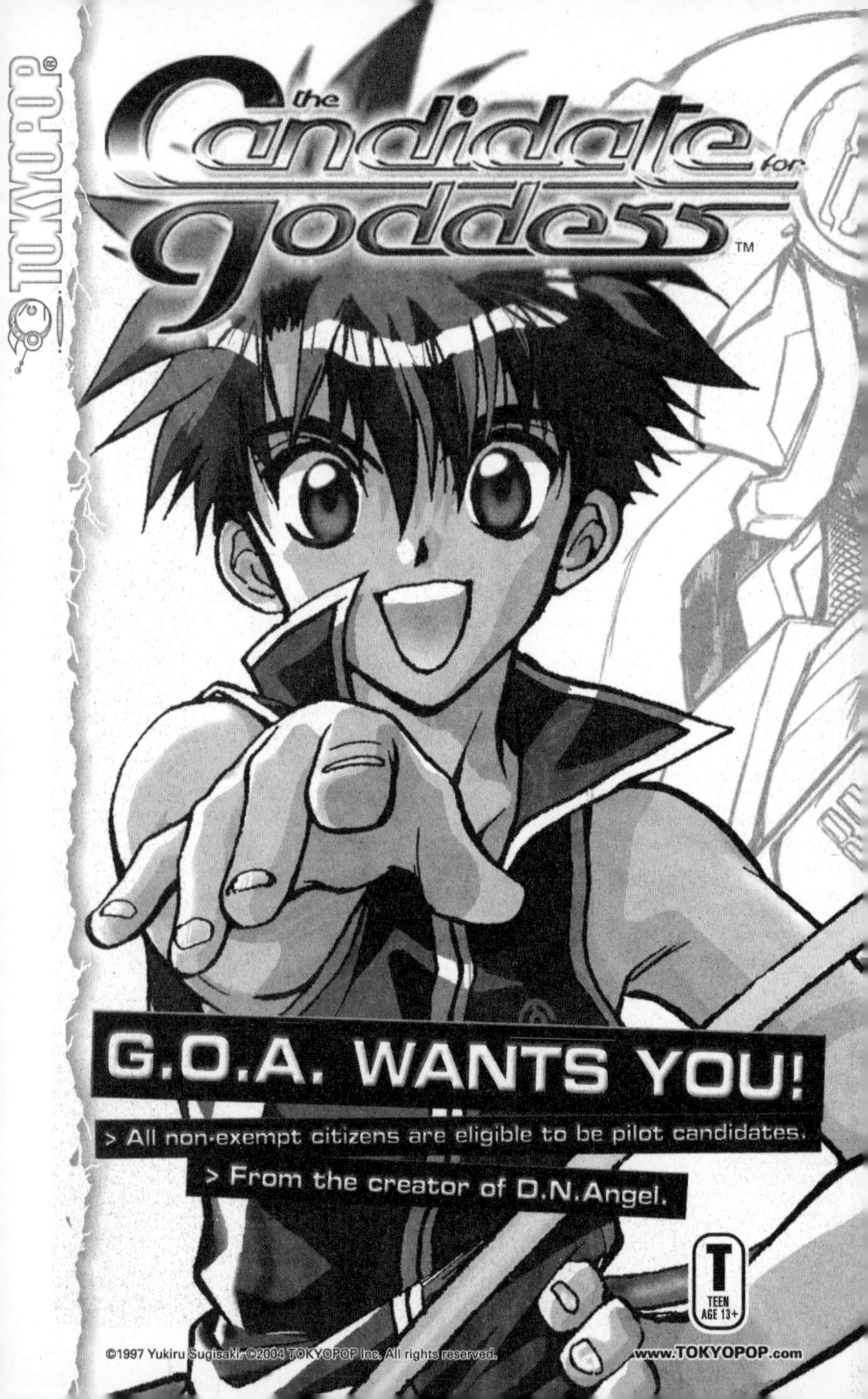
TOKYOPOP
the Candidate for Goddess™
G.O.A. WANTS YOU!
> All non-exempt citizens are eligible to be pilot candidates.
> From the creator of D.N.Angel.
T TEEN AGE 13+
©1997 Yukiru Sugisaki. ©2004 TOKYOPOP Inc. All rights reserved.
www.TOKYOPOP.com

DearS

The Story:

Aliens have landed on Earth and are now a normal part of society. These beautiful beings have been given the name "DearS" and are trusted and welcomed by most humans. In order for the DearS to learn Earth's customs, they are sent to random high schools for "home-stay." When Takeya helps a DearS on the way home from his school, she calls him "Master." Thus begins the humorous life of Takeya and his sexy alien follower, Ren, who tries to figure out the wacky customs of this place called Earth!

The Creator:

Peach-Pit

Behind the Manga:

· Bonus full-color, foldout.
· The PS2 adventure game, anime and collectible figures are all the rage in Japan.

Genre:

Comedy

SRP:

£ 6.99

2nd Contact

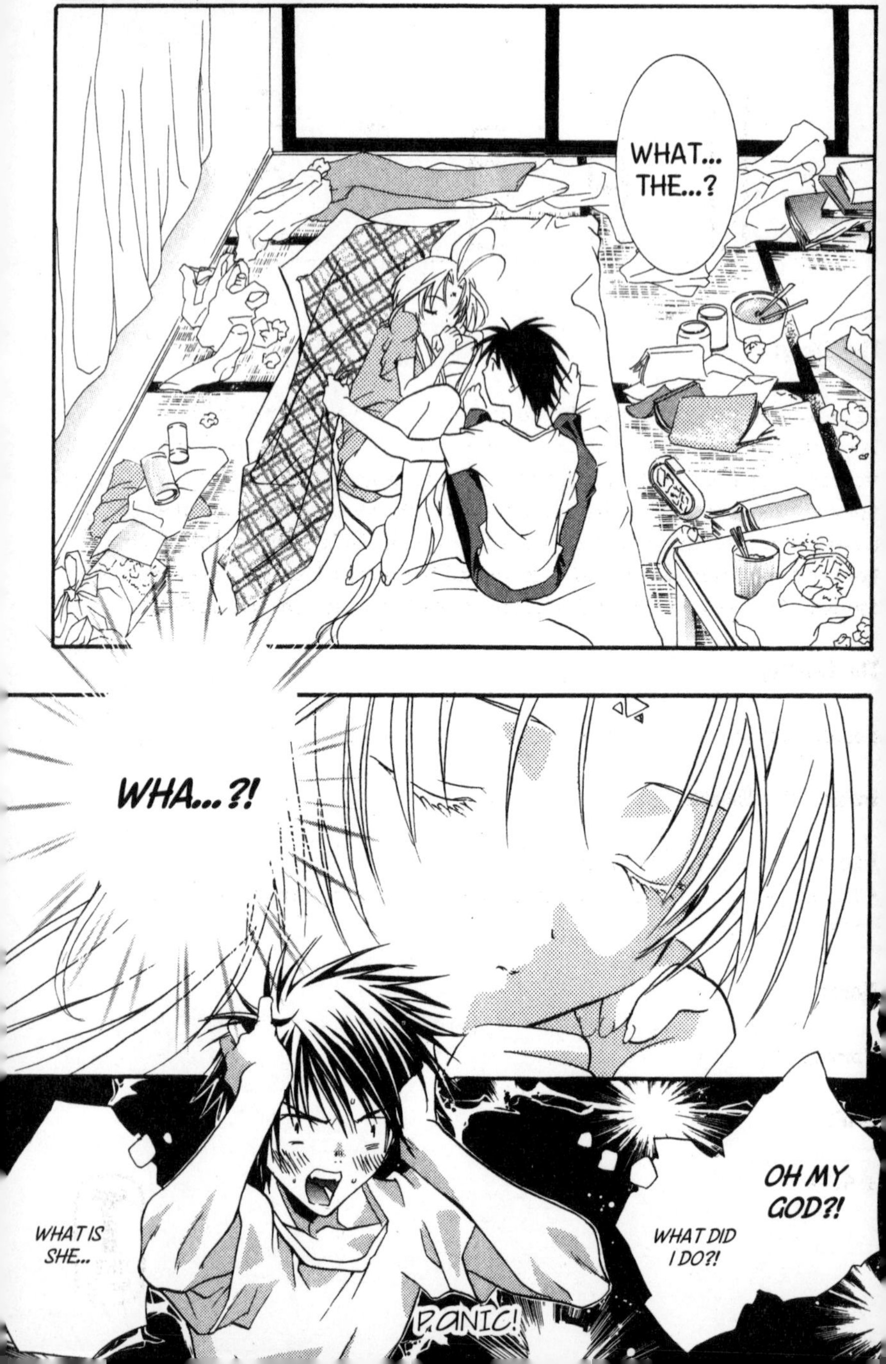
WHAT... THE...?
WHA...?!
OH MY GOD?!
WHAT DID I DO?!
WHAT IS SHE...
PANIC!

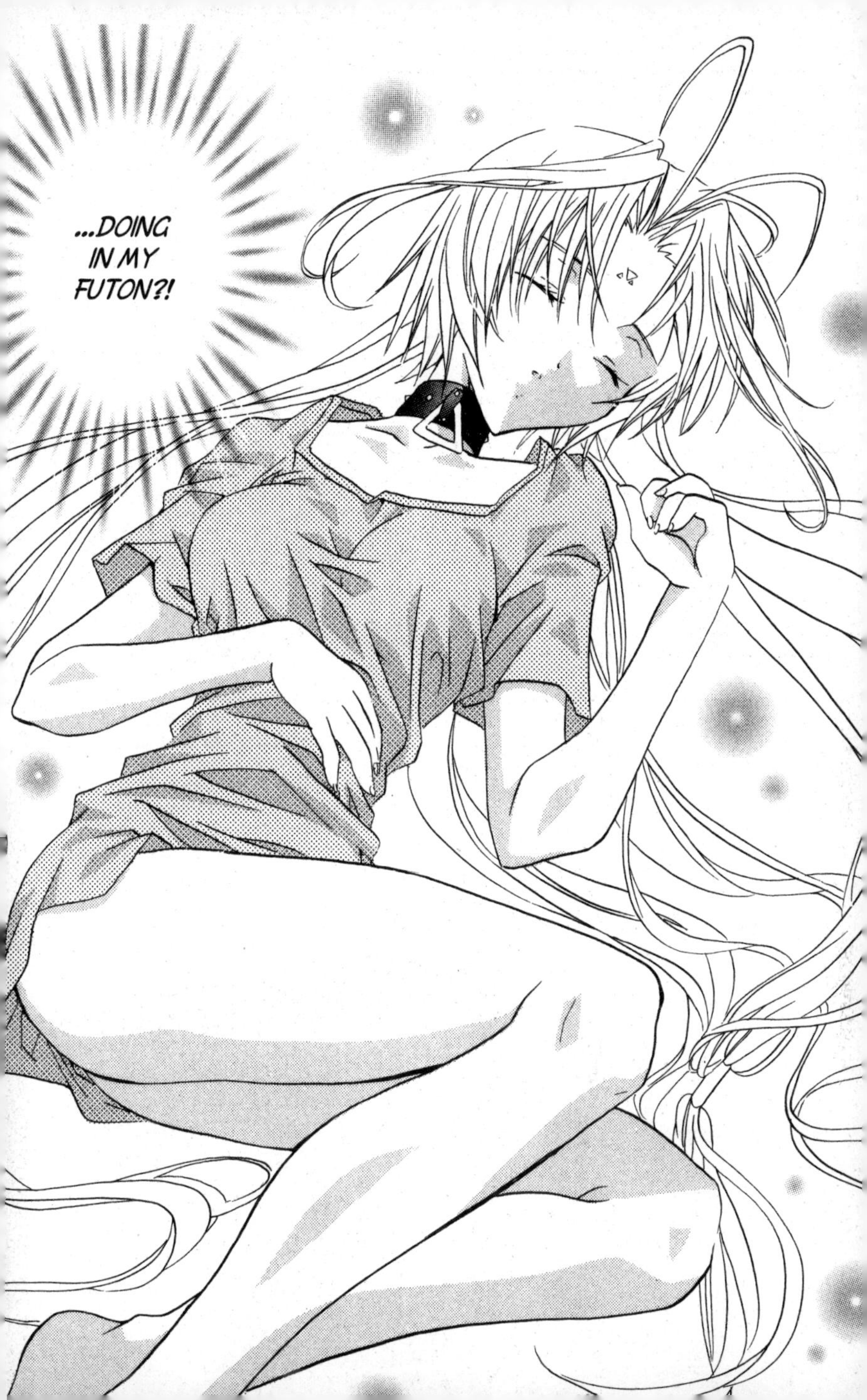
...DOING IN MY FUTON?!

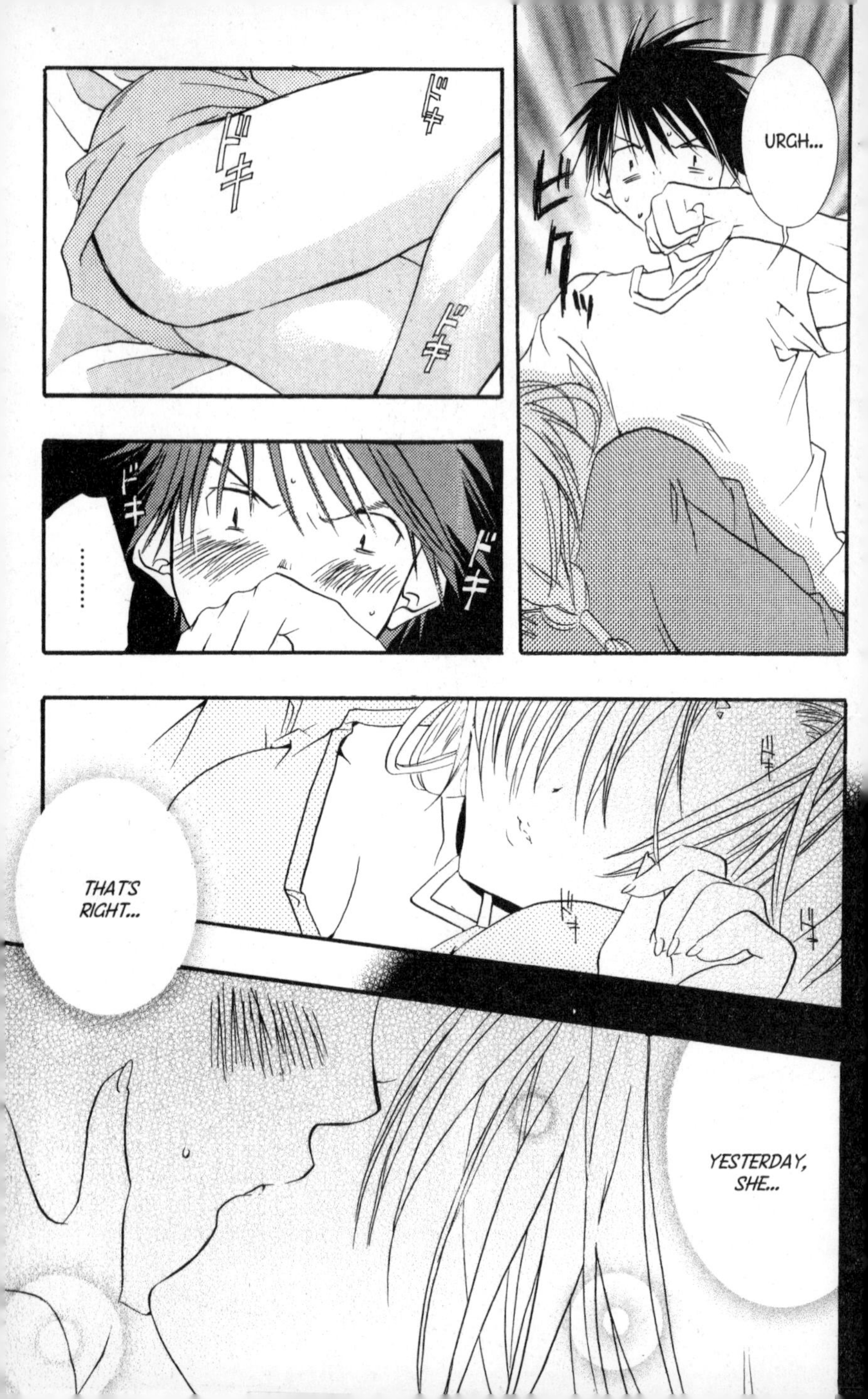
URGH...
ビクッ
ドキ
ドキ
ドキ
ドキ
ドキ
......
THAT'S RIGHT...
YESTERDAY, SHE...

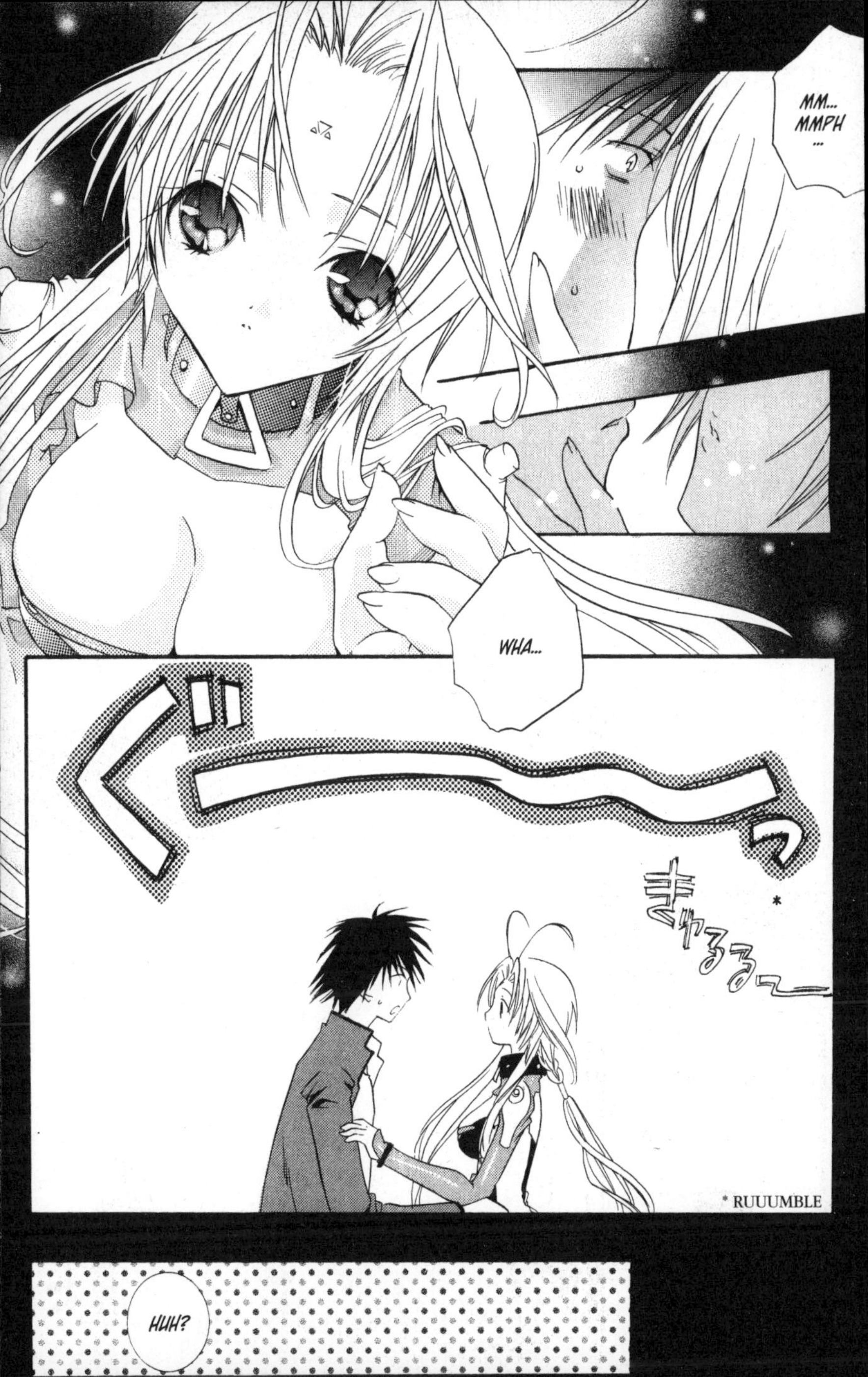
MM... MMPH ...
WHA...
ぐ〜〜っ
きゅるる〜 *
* RUUUMBLE
HUH?

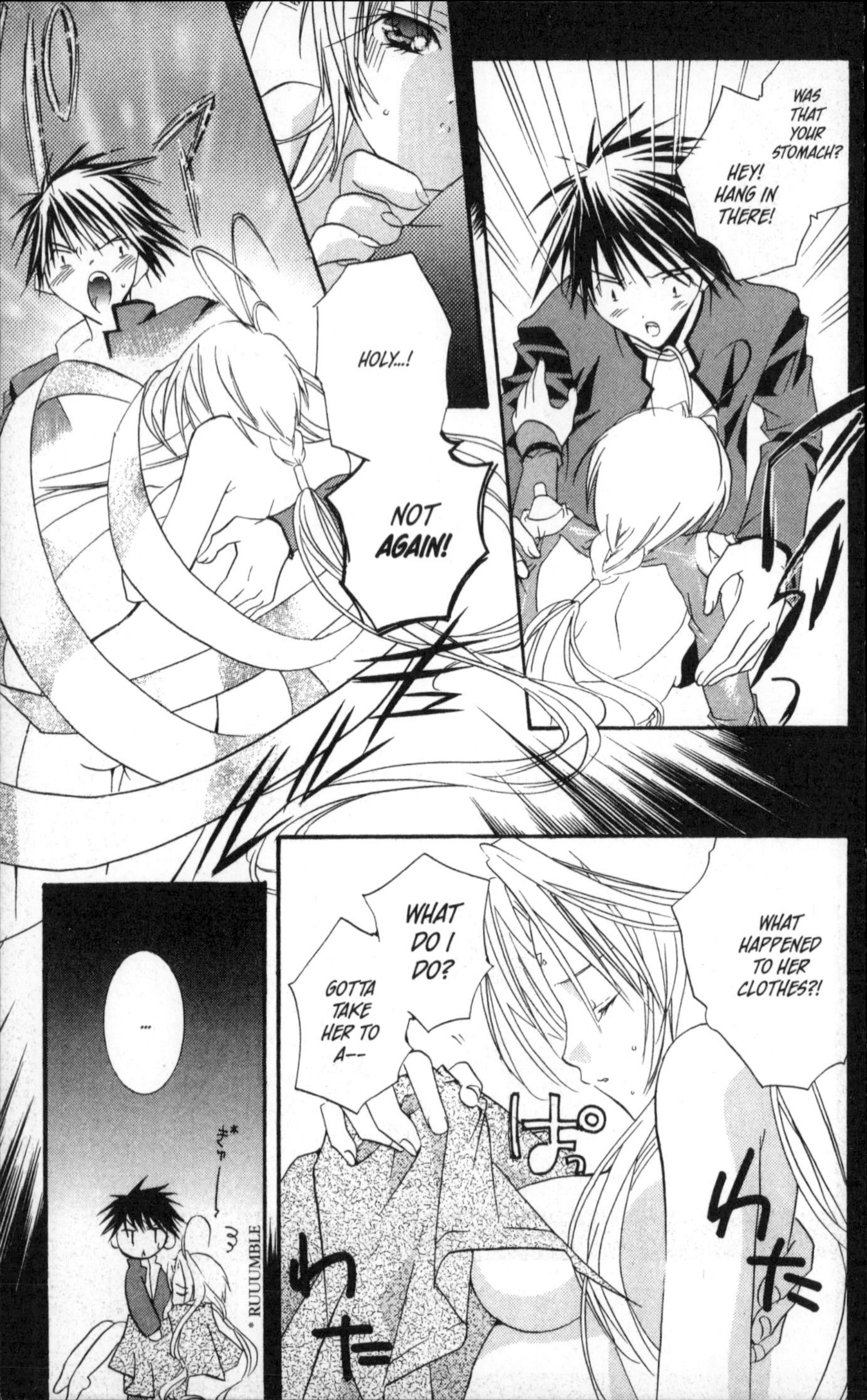
WAS THAT YOUR STOMACH?
HEY! HANG IN THERE!
HOLY...!
NOT AGAIN!
WHAT HAPPENED TO HER CLOTHES?!
WHAT DO I DO?
GOTTA TAKE HER TO A--
ぱっ
わた
わた
...
* RUUUMBLE

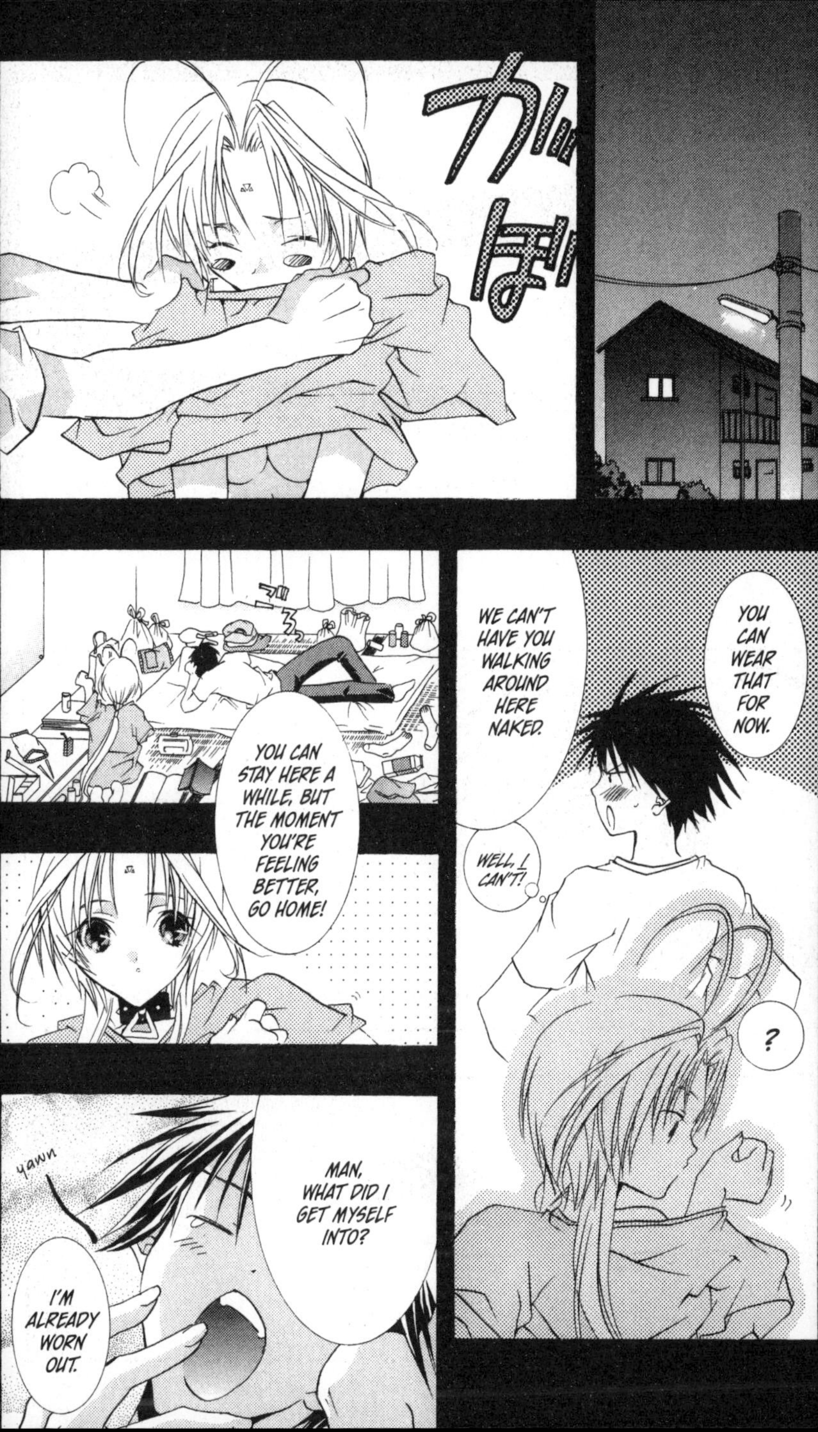
YOU CAN WEAR THAT FOR NOW.
WE CAN'T HAVE YOU WALKING AROUND HERE NAKED.
WELL, I CAN'T!
?
YOU CAN STAY HERE A WHILE, BUT THE MOMENT YOU'RE FEELING BETTER, GO HOME!
MAN, WHAT DID I GET MYSELF INTO?
yawn
I'M ALREADY WORN OUT.

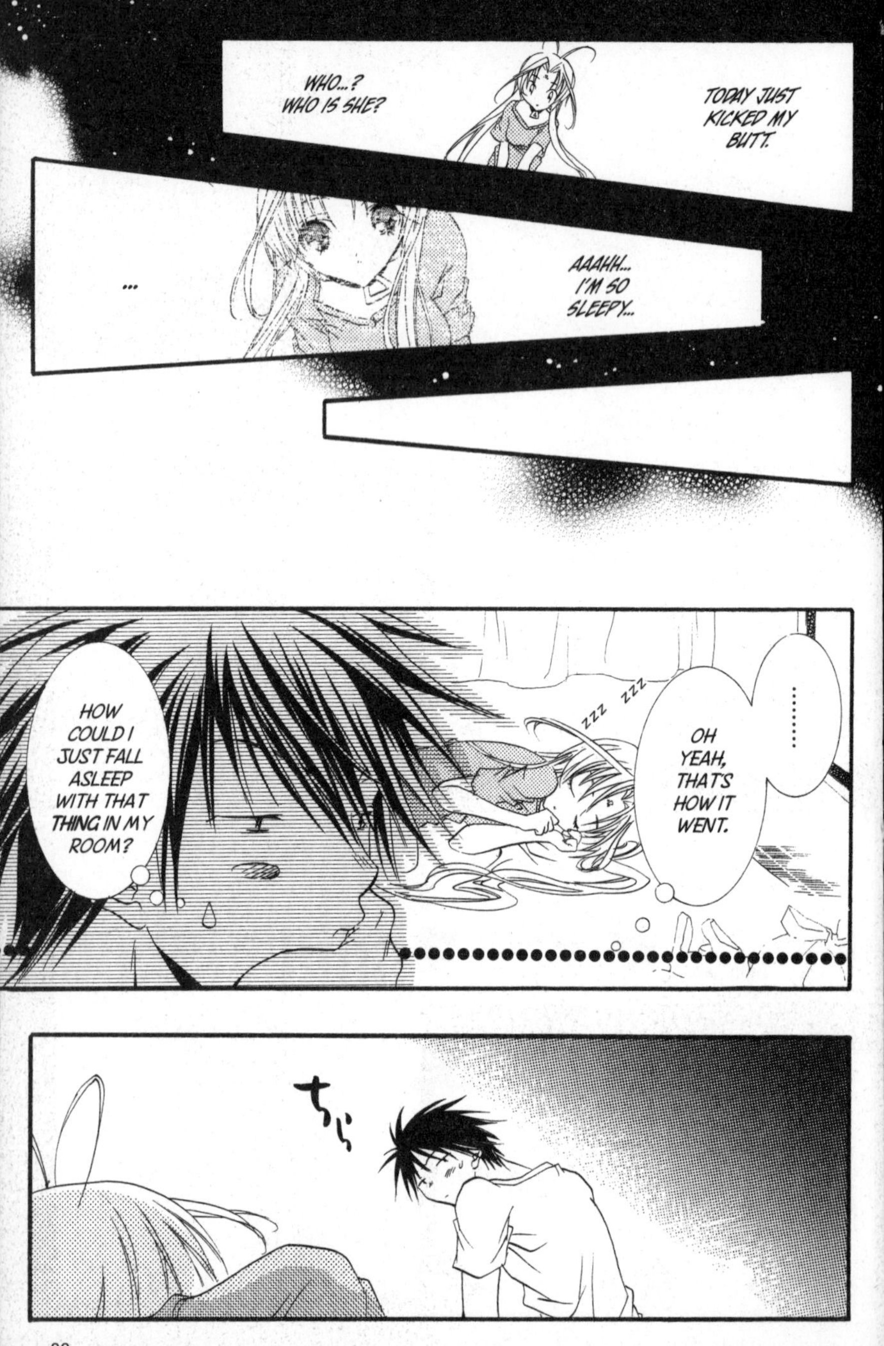
TODAY JUST KICKED MY BUTT.
WHO...? WHO IS SHE?
AAAHH... I'M SO SLEEPY...
...
......
OH YEAH, THAT'S HOW IT WENT.
ZZZ ZZZ
HOW COULD I JUST FALL ASLEEP WITH THAT THING IN MY ROOM?
ちら

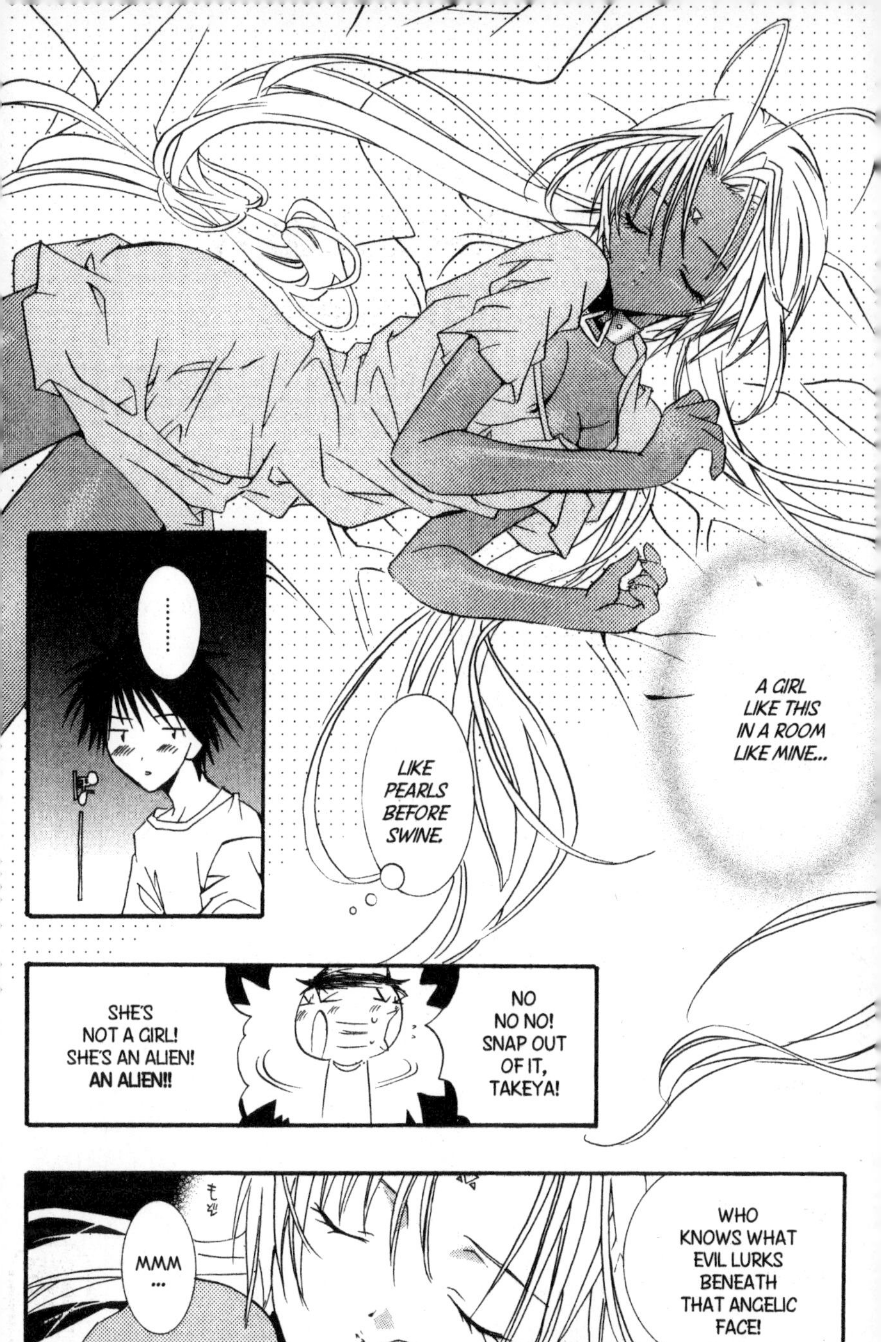
A GIRL LIKE THIS IN A ROOM LIKE MINE...
LIKE PEARLS BEFORE SWINE.
......
NO NO NO! SNAP OUT OF IT, TAKEYA!
SHE'S NOT A GIRL! SHE'S AN ALIEN! AN ALIEN!!
WHO KNOWS WHAT EVIL LURKS BENEATH THAT ANGELIC FACE!
もぞ
MMM ...

erica
SAKURAZAWA
Between the Sheets

The Story:

Saki and Minako are the best of friends, but where do they draw the line between friendship and something a little more? Hidden within Minako is the powerful desire to possess the beauty that Saki so freely shares with her male companions. *Between the Sheets* offers an in-depth glimpse into the world of female jealousy and betrayal between the closest of friends.

The Creator:

Erica Sakurazawa

Behind the Manga:

A fantastic story that crosses the line between love and obsession.

Genre:

Drama / Romance

SRP:

£ 6.99

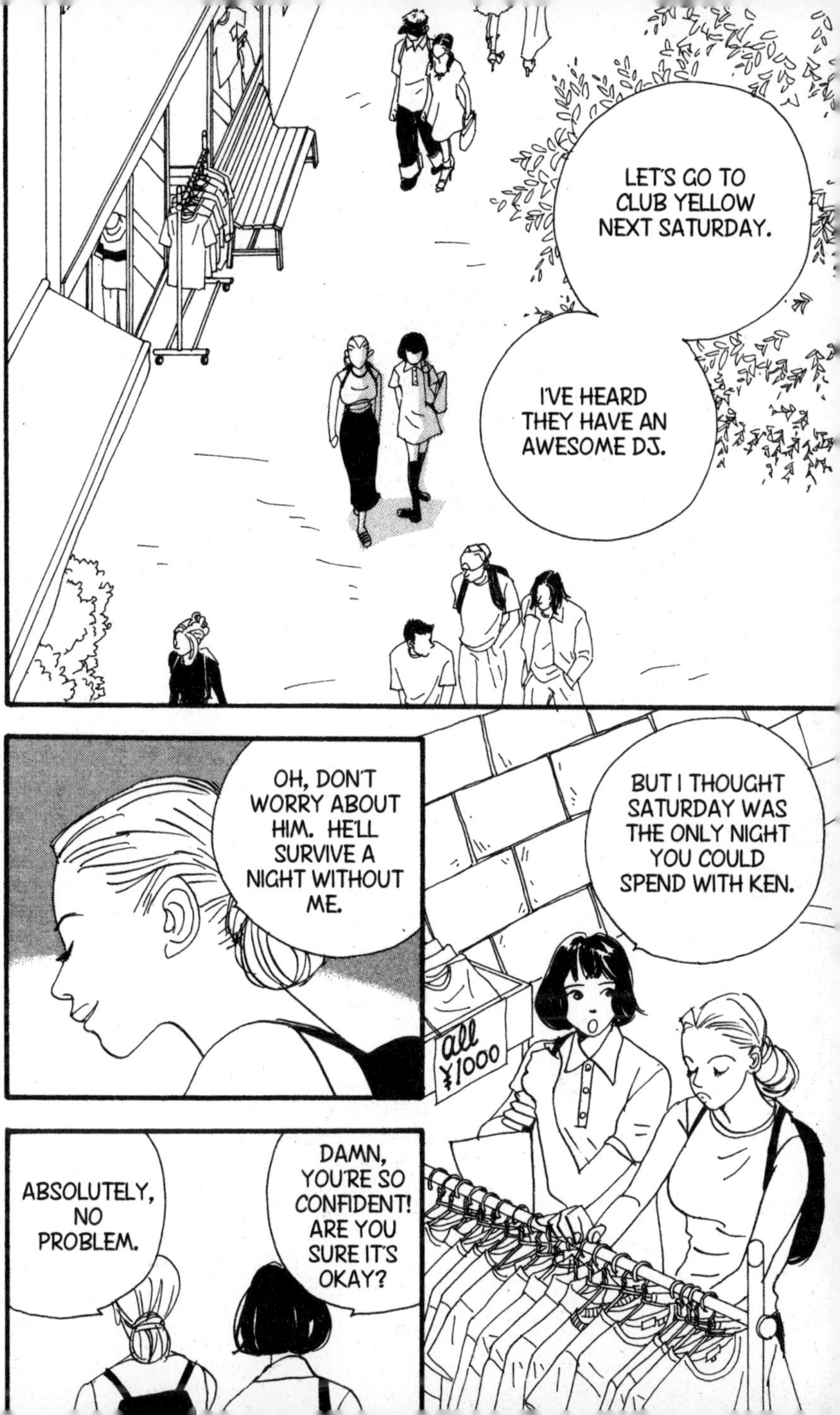
LET'S GO TO CLUB YELLOW NEXT SATURDAY.
I'VE HEARD THEY HAVE AN AWESOME DJ.
BUT I THOUGHT SATURDAY WAS THE ONLY NIGHT YOU COULD SPEND WITH KEN.
all ¥1000
OH, DON'T WORRY ABOUT HIM. HE'LL SURVIVE A NIGHT WITHOUT ME.
DAMN, YOU'RE SO CONFIDENT! ARE YOU SURE IT'S OKAY?
ABSOLUTELY, NO PROBLEM.

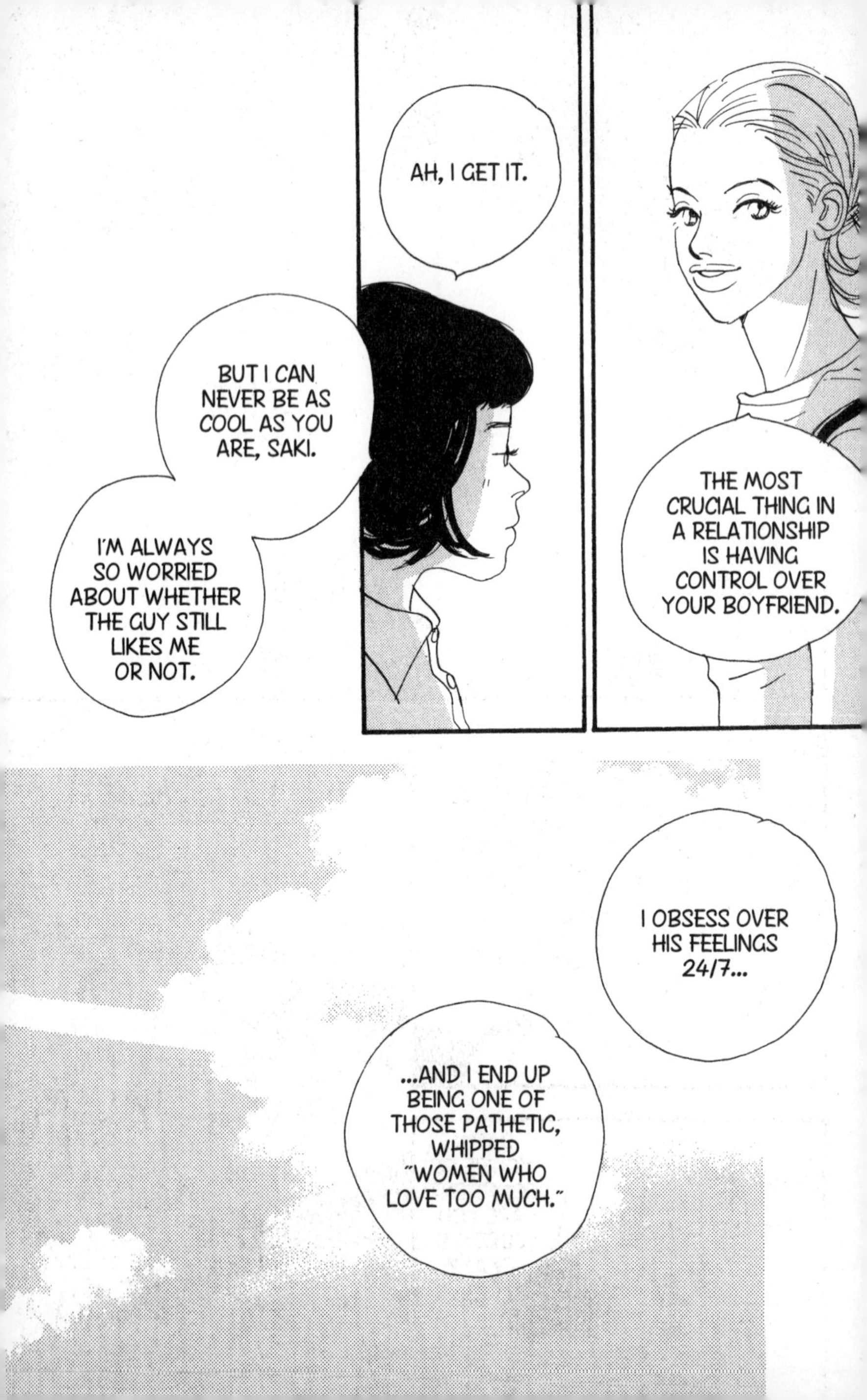
THE MOST CRUCIAL THING IN A RELATIONSHIP IS HAVING CONTROL OVER YOUR BOYFRIEND.
AH, I GET IT.
BUT I CAN NEVER BE AS COOL AS YOU ARE, SAKI.
I'M ALWAYS SO WORRIED ABOUT WHETHER THE GUY STILL LIKES ME OR NOT.
I OBSESS OVER HIS FEELINGS 24/7...
...AND I END UP BEING ONE OF THOSE PATHETIC, WHIPPED "WOMEN WHO LOVE TOO MUCH."

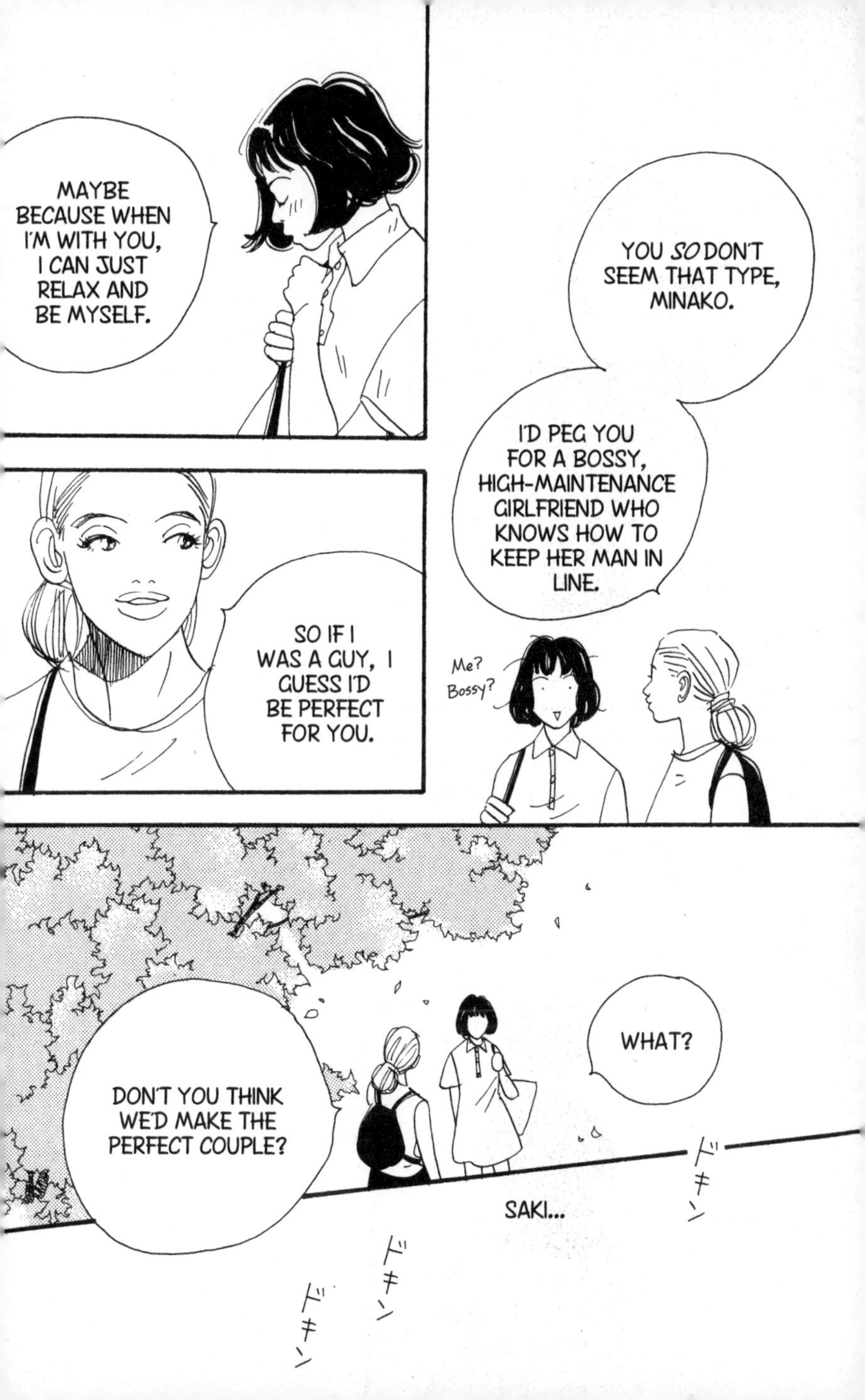
YOU SO DON'T SEEM THAT TYPE, MINAKO.
I'D PEG YOU FOR A BOSSY, HIGH-MAINTENANCE GIRLFRIEND WHO KNOWS HOW TO KEEP HER MAN IN LINE.
Me? Bossy?
MAYBE BECAUSE WHEN I'M WITH YOU, I CAN JUST RELAX AND BE MYSELF.
SO IF I WAS A GUY, I GUESS I'D BE PERFECT FOR YOU.
WHAT?
ドキン
SAKI...
DON'T YOU THINK WE'D MAKE THE PERFECT COUPLE?
ドキン
ドキン

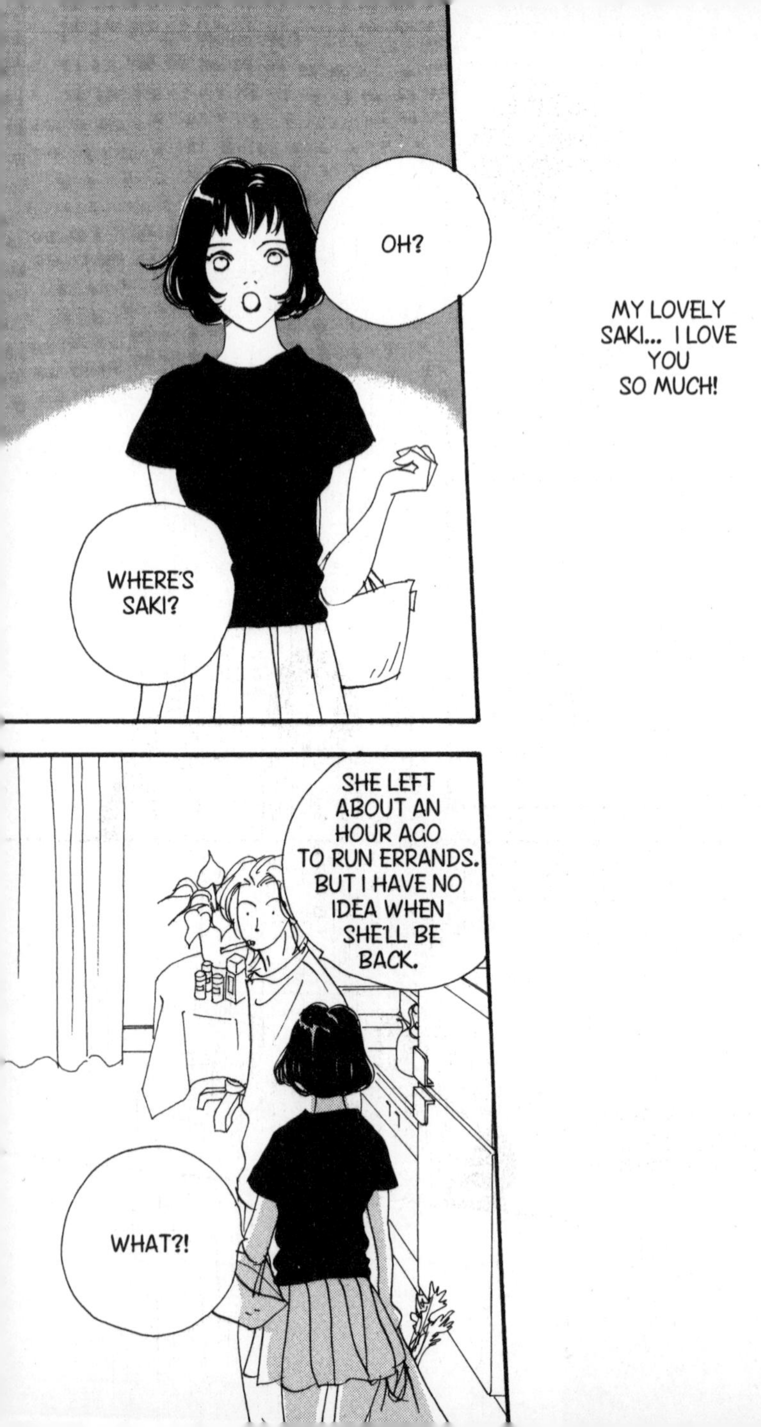
MY LOVELY SAKI... I LOVE YOU SO MUCH!
OH?
WHERE'S SAKI?
SHE LEFT ABOUT AN HOUR AGO TO RUN ERRANDS. BUT I HAVE NO IDEA WHEN SHE'LL BE BACK.
WHAT?!

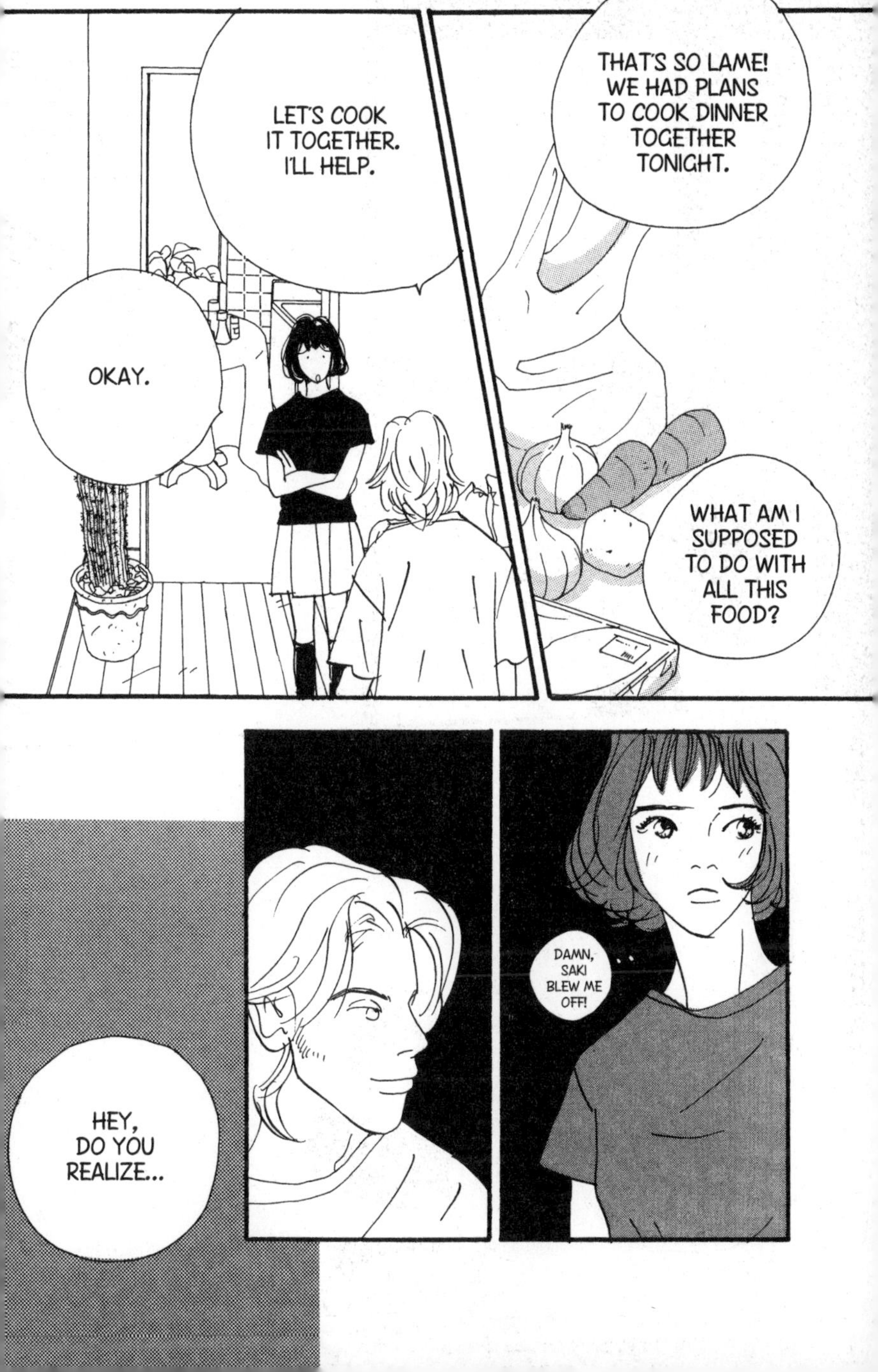
THAT'S SO LAME! WE HAD PLANS TO COOK DINNER TOGETHER TONIGHT.
WHAT AM I SUPPOSED TO DO WITH ALL THIS FOOD?
LET'S COOK IT TOGETHER. I'LL HELP.
OKAY.
DAMN, SAKI BLEW ME OFF!
HEY, DO YOU REALIZE...

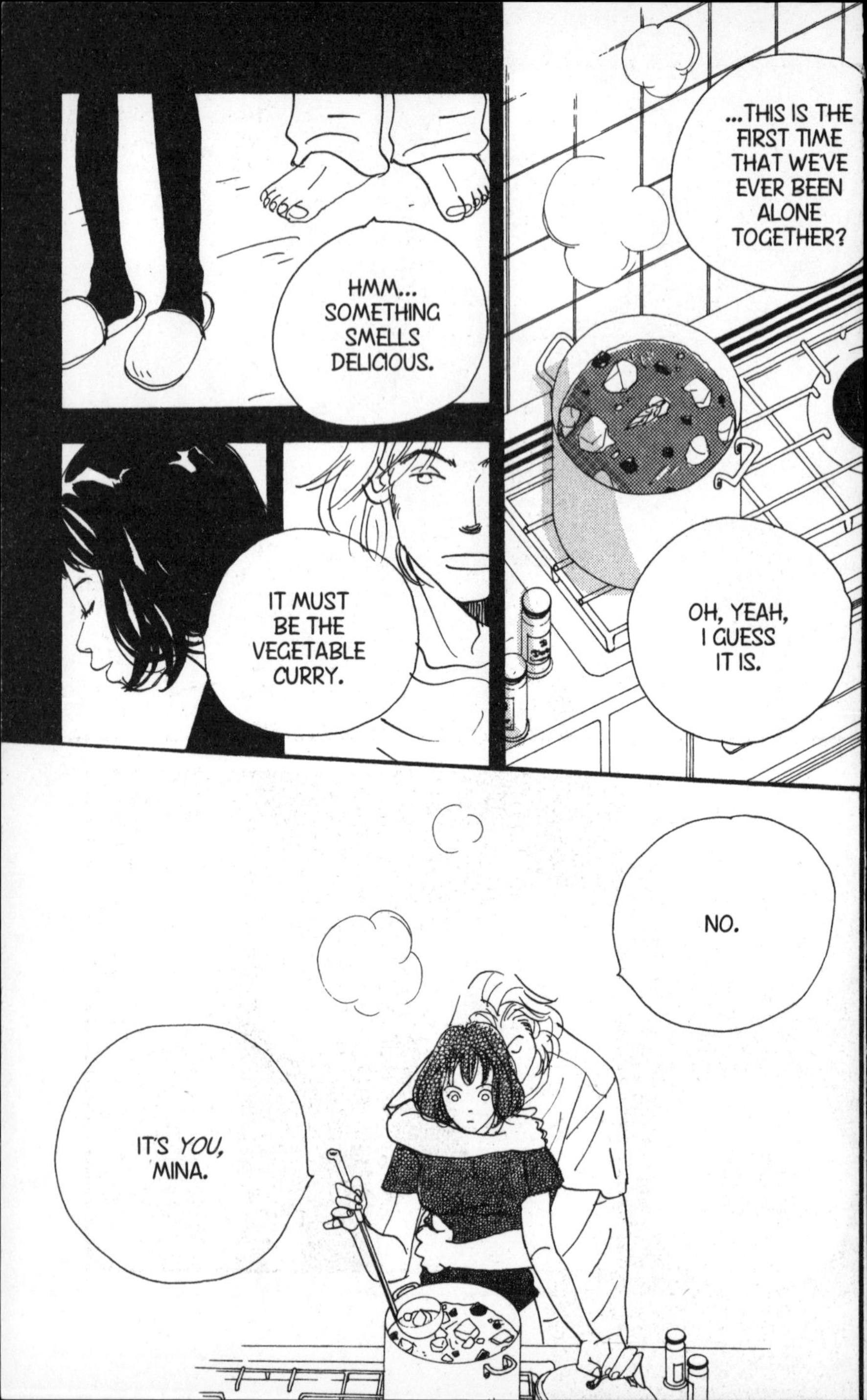
...THIS IS THE FIRST TIME THAT WE'VE EVER BEEN ALONE TOGETHER?
OH, YEAH, I GUESS IT IS.
HMM... SOMETHING SMELLS DELICIOUS.
IT MUST BE THE VEGETABLE CURRY.
NO.
IT'S *YOU,* MINA.

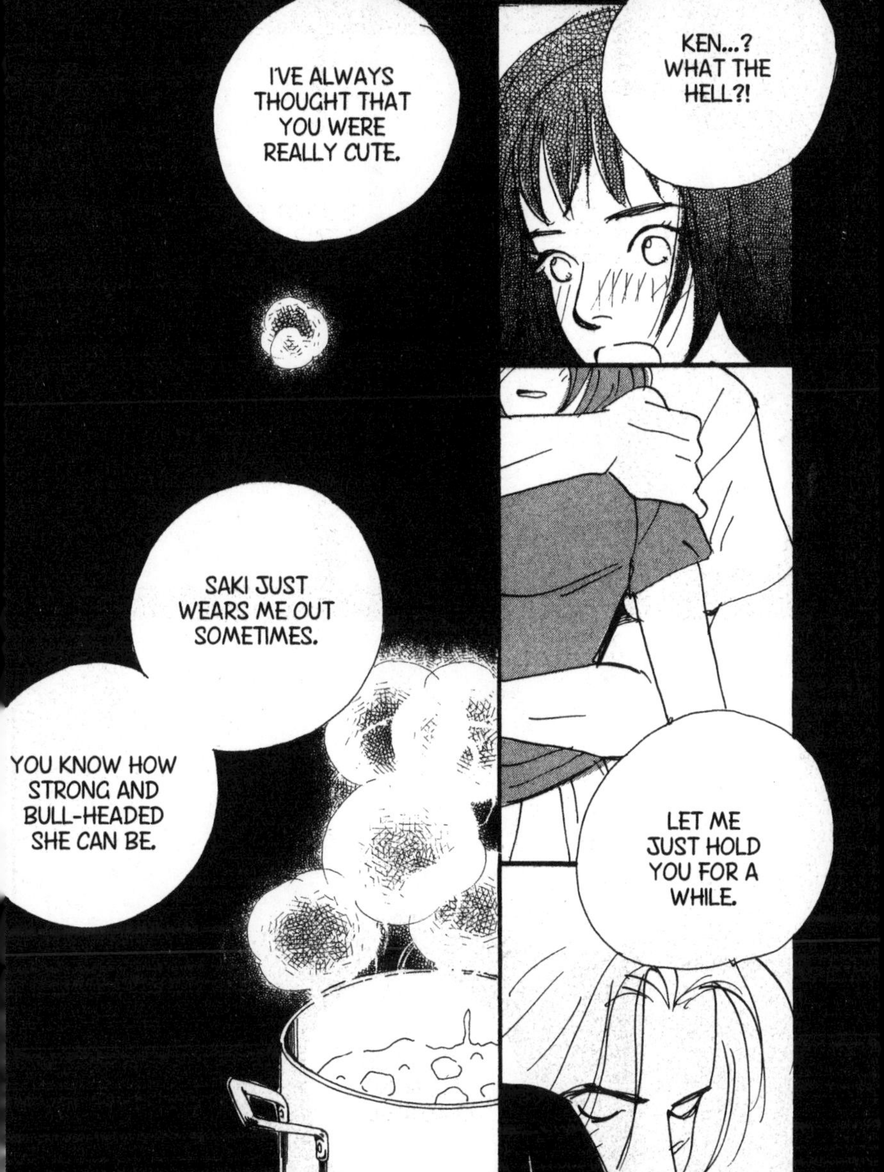
KEN...? WHAT THE HELL?!
LET ME JUST HOLD YOU FOR A WHILE.
I'VE ALWAYS THOUGHT THAT YOU WERE REALLY CUTE.
SAKI JUST WEARS ME OUT SOMETIMES.
YOU KNOW HOW STRONG AND BULL-HEADED SHE CAN BE.

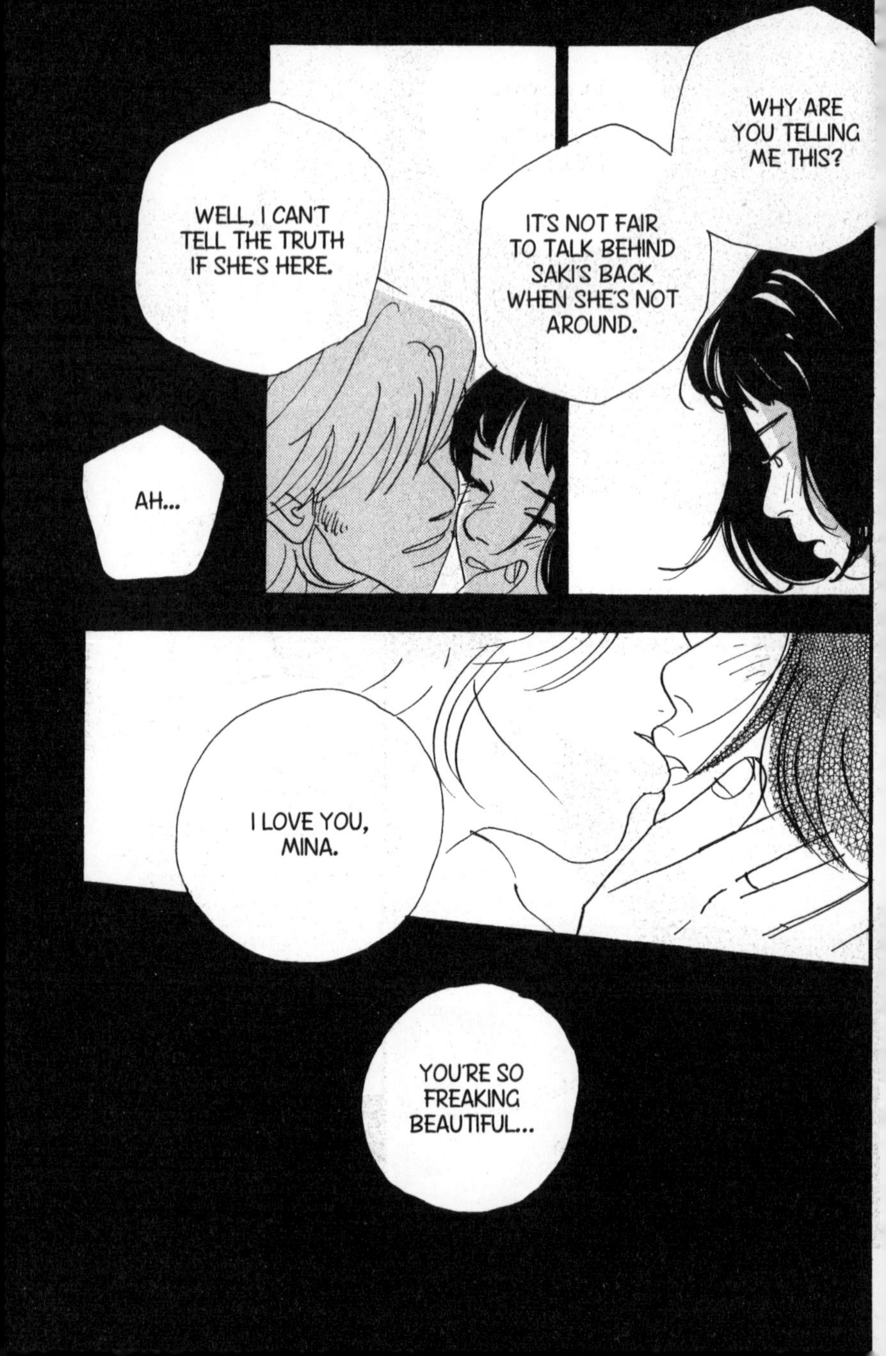
WHY ARE YOU TELLING ME THIS?
IT'S NOT FAIR TO TALK BEHIND SAKI'S BACK WHEN SHE'S NOT AROUND.
WELL, I CAN'T TELL THE TRUTH IF SHE'S HERE.
AH...
I LOVE YOU, MINA.
YOU'RE SO FREAKING BEAUTIFUL...

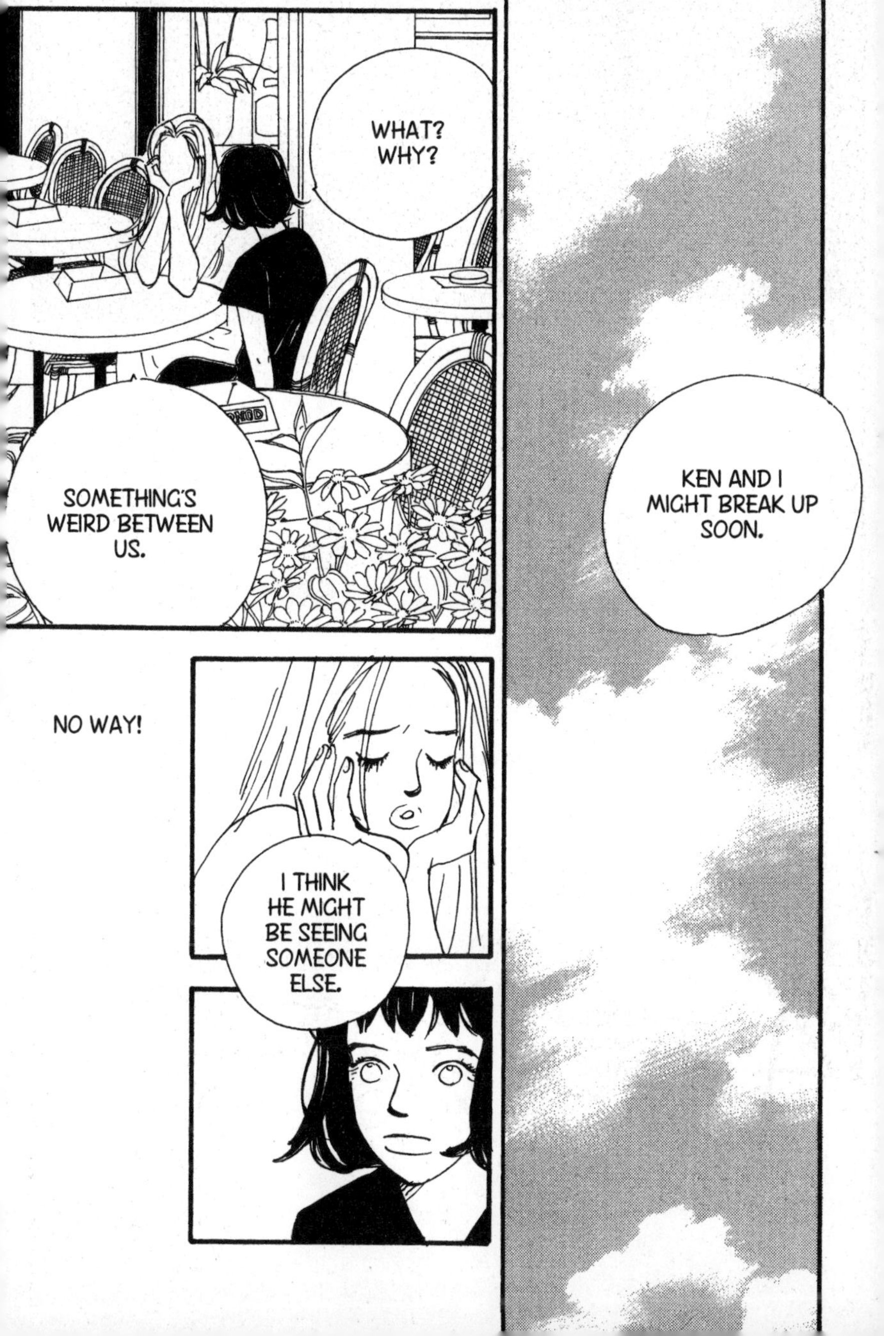
KEN AND I MIGHT BREAK UP SOON.
WHAT? WHY?
SOMETHING'S WEIRD BETWEEN US.
NO WAY!
I THINK HE MIGHT BE SEEING SOMEONE ELSE.

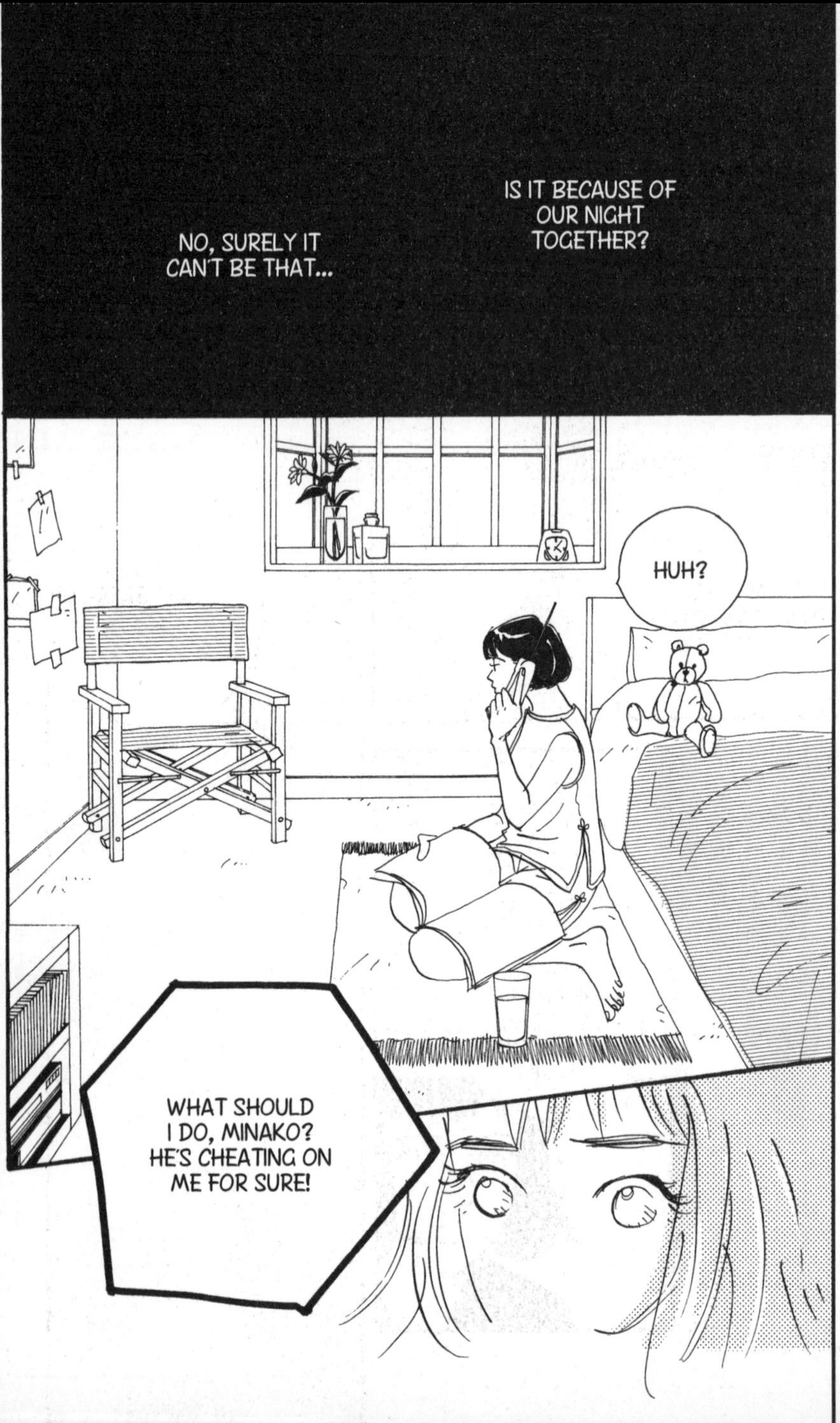
IS IT BECAUSE OF OUR NIGHT TOGETHER?
NO, SURELY IT CAN'T BE THAT...
HUH?
WHAT SHOULD I DO, MINAKO? HE'S CHEATING ON ME FOR SURE!

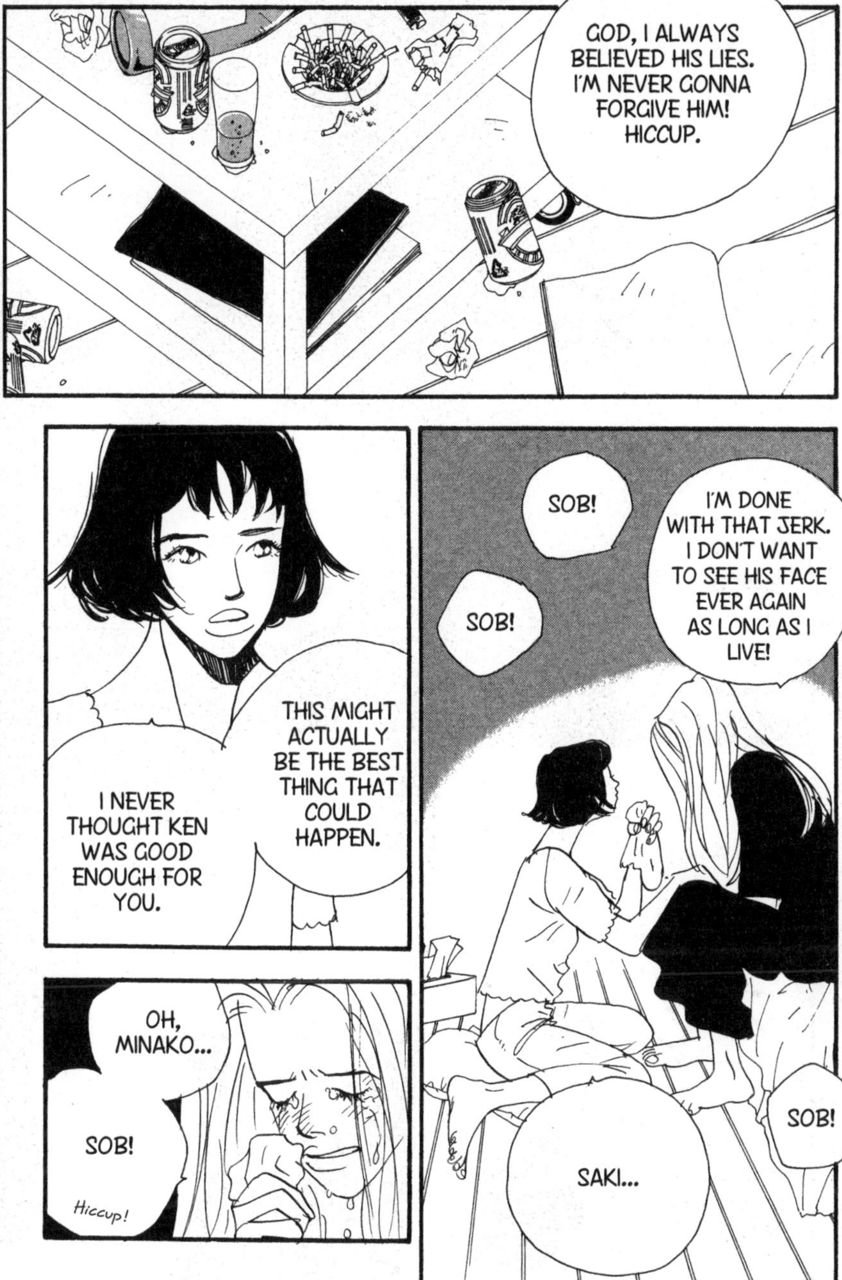
GOD, I ALWAYS BELIEVED HIS LIES. I'M NEVER GONNA FORGIVE HIM! HICCUP.
I'M DONE WITH THAT JERK. I DON'T WANT TO SEE HIS FACE EVER AGAIN AS LONG AS I LIVE!
SOB!
SOB!
SOB!
SAKI...
THIS MIGHT ACTUALLY BE THE BEST THING THAT COULD HAPPEN.
I NEVER THOUGHT KEN WAS GOOD ENOUGH FOR YOU.
OH, MINAKO...
SOB!
Hiccup!

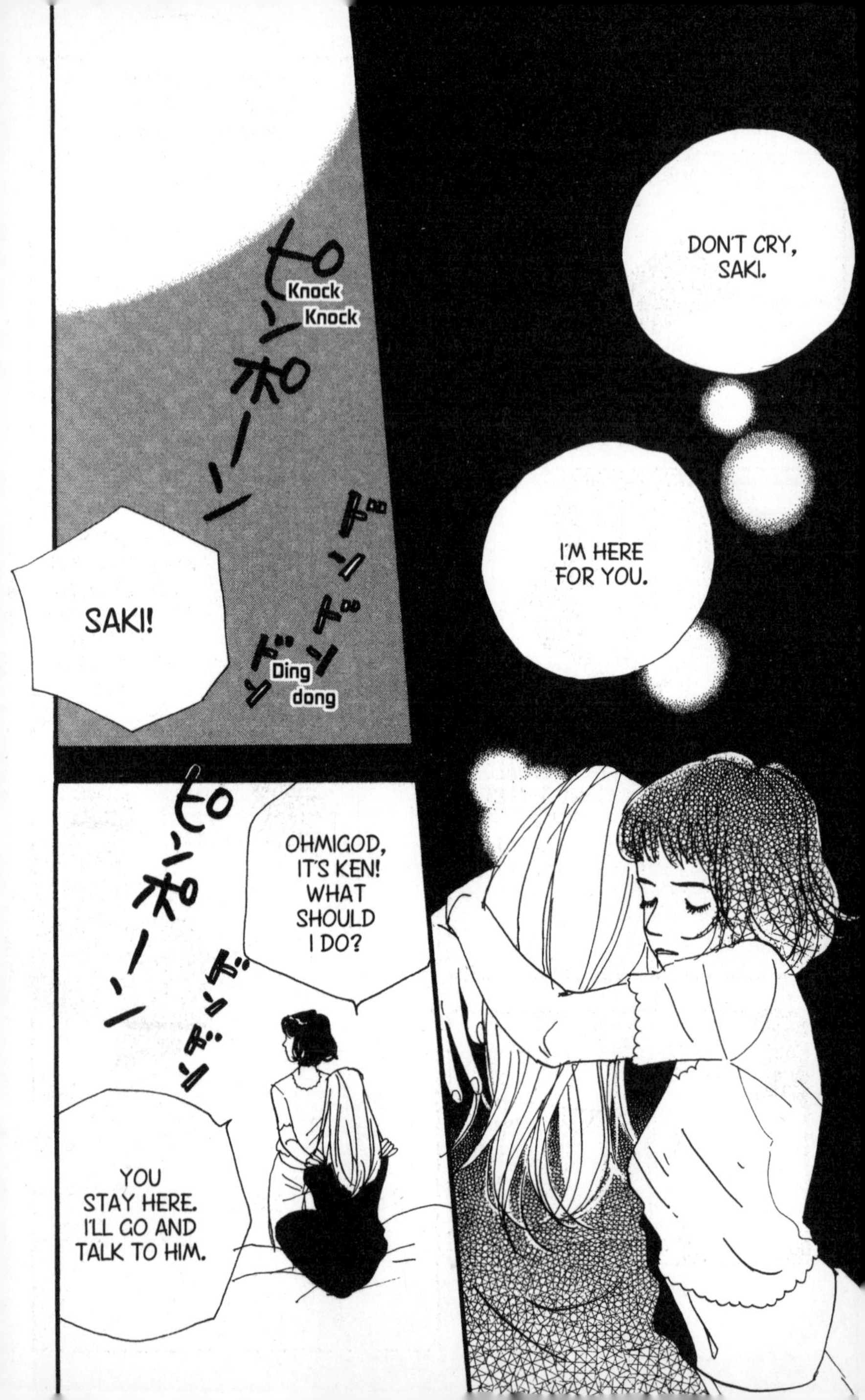
DON'T CRY, SAKI.
I'M HERE FOR YOU.
ピンポーン
Knock Knock
ドンドンドンドン
Ding dong
SAKI!
ピンポーン
OHMIGOD, IT'S KEN! WHAT SHOULD I DO?
ドンドン
YOU STAY HERE. I'LL GO AND TALK TO HIM.

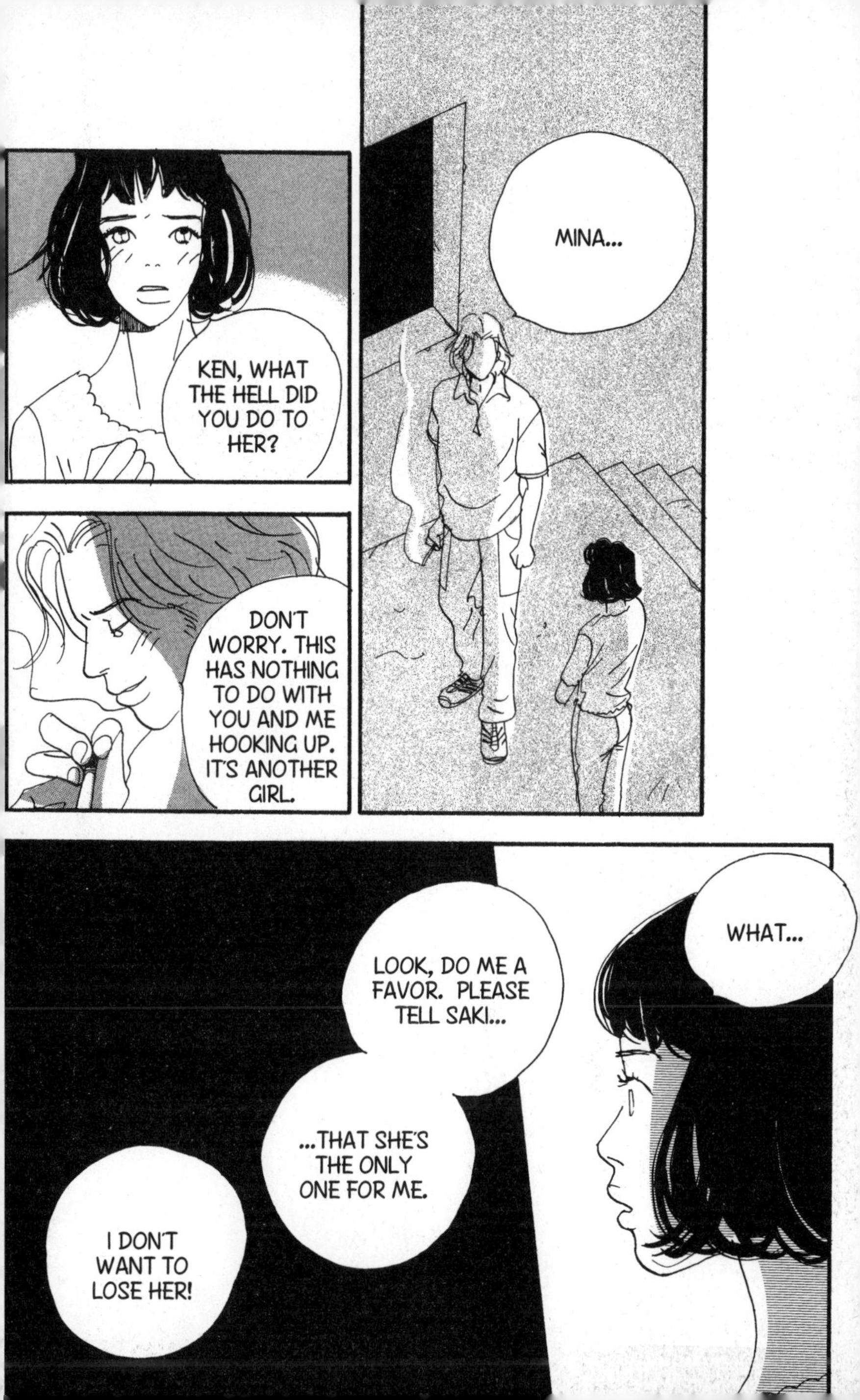
MINA...
KEN, WHAT THE HELL DID YOU DO TO HER?
DON'T WORRY. THIS HAS NOTHING TO DO WITH YOU AND ME HOOKING UP. IT'S ANOTHER GIRL.
WHAT...
LOOK, DO ME A FAVOR. PLEASE TELL SAKI...
...THAT SHE'S THE ONLY ONE FOR ME.
I DON'T WANT TO LOSE HER!

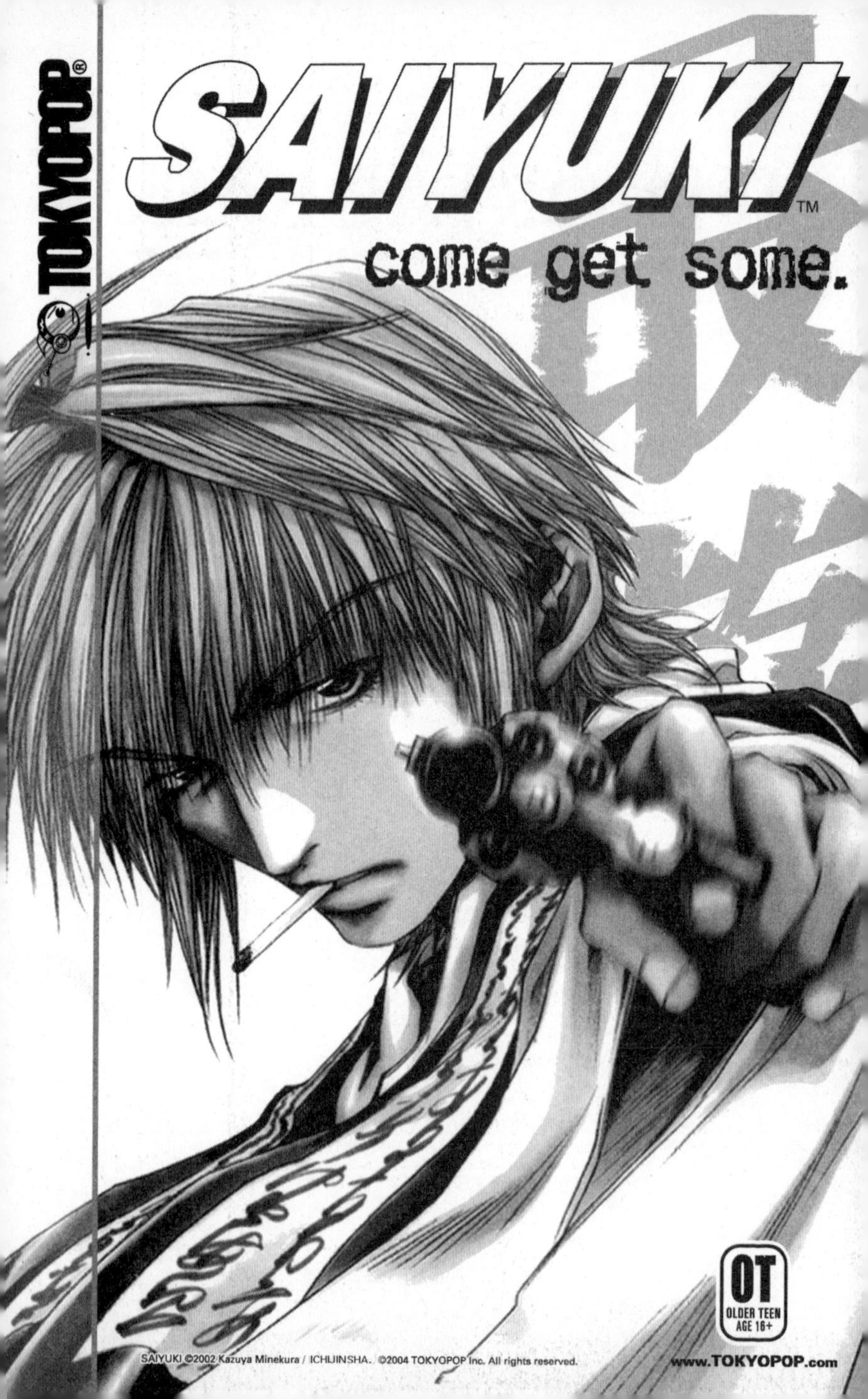
TOKYOPOP®
SAIYUKI™
come get some.
OT
OLDER TEEN
AGE 16+
SAIYUKI ©2002 Kazuya Minekura / ICHIJINSHA. ©2004 TOKYOPOP Inc. All rights reserved.
www.TOKYOPOP.com

IMMORTAL RAIN

The Story:

For centuries, the eternal Rain Jewlitt, known as Methuselah, has eluded assassins and bounty hunters out to uncover his timeless secret. One of his pursuers, the Grim Reaper Zol, never succeeded in killing Rain. In the wake of Zol's death, his 14-year-old granddaughter Machika vows to avenge her grandfather and put an end to Rain's immortality...but she soon realizes that the thin line between love and hate just might last forever.

The Creator:

Kaori Ozaki

Behind the Manga:

- From the creator of *Hitsuji-no-Hana* and *Honeymoon*.
- Originally published in the hugely popular *Wings* magazine— home to *Dragon Knights*, *RG Veda* and *Princess Ai*.

Genre:

Fantasy

SRP:

£ 6.99

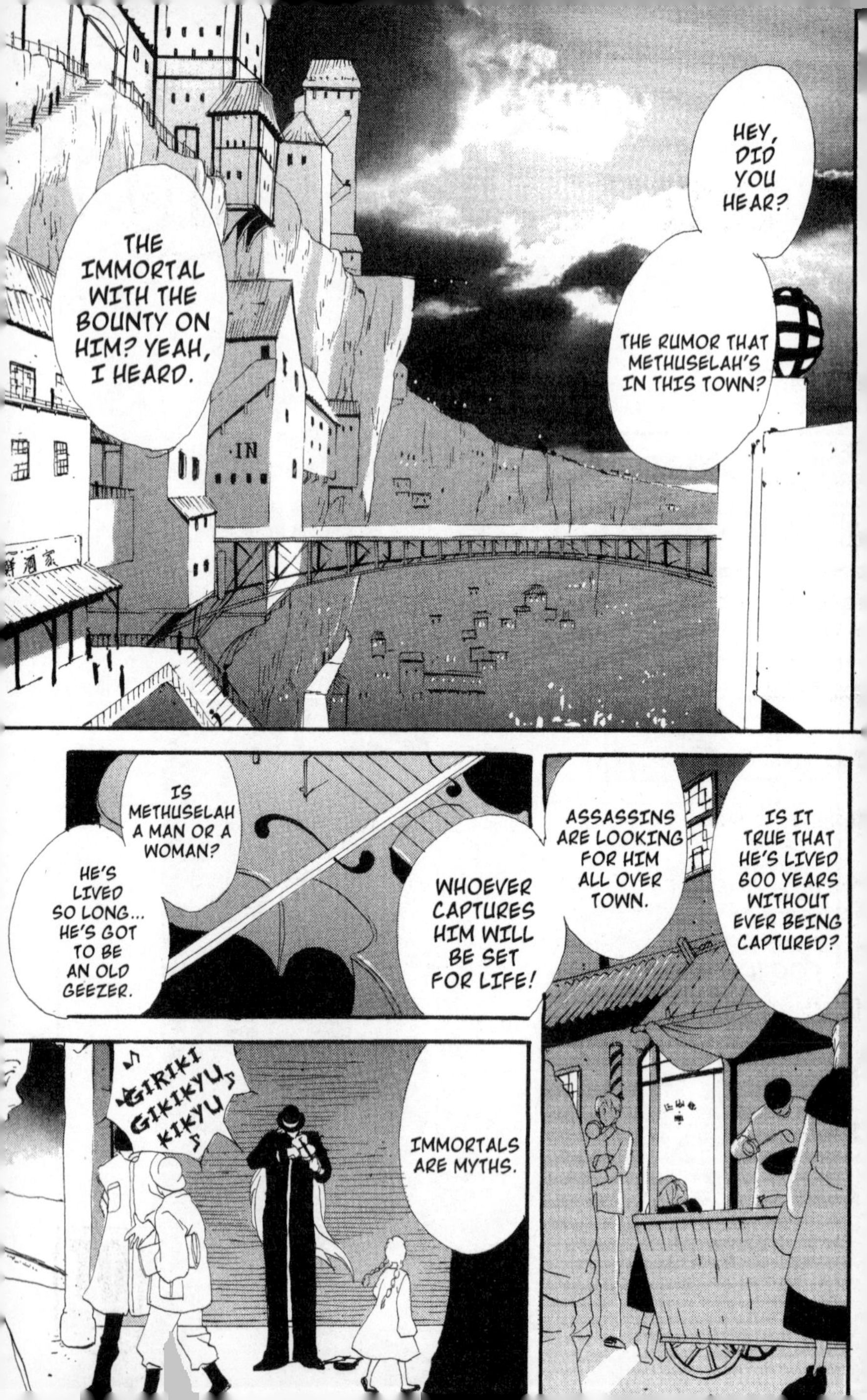
HEY, DID YOU HEAR?
THE RUMOR THAT METHUSELAH'S IN THIS TOWN?
THE IMMORTAL WITH THE BOUNTY ON HIM? YEAH, I HEARD.
IS IT TRUE THAT HE'S LIVED 600 YEARS WITHOUT EVER BEING CAPTURED?
ASSASSINS ARE LOOKING FOR HIM ALL OVER TOWN.
WHOEVER CAPTURES HIM WILL BE SET FOR LIFE!
IS METHUSELAH A MAN OR A WOMAN?
HE'S LIVED SO LONG... HE'S GOT TO BE AN OLD GEEZER.
IMMORTALS ARE MYTHS.
GIRIKI GIKIKYU KIKYU

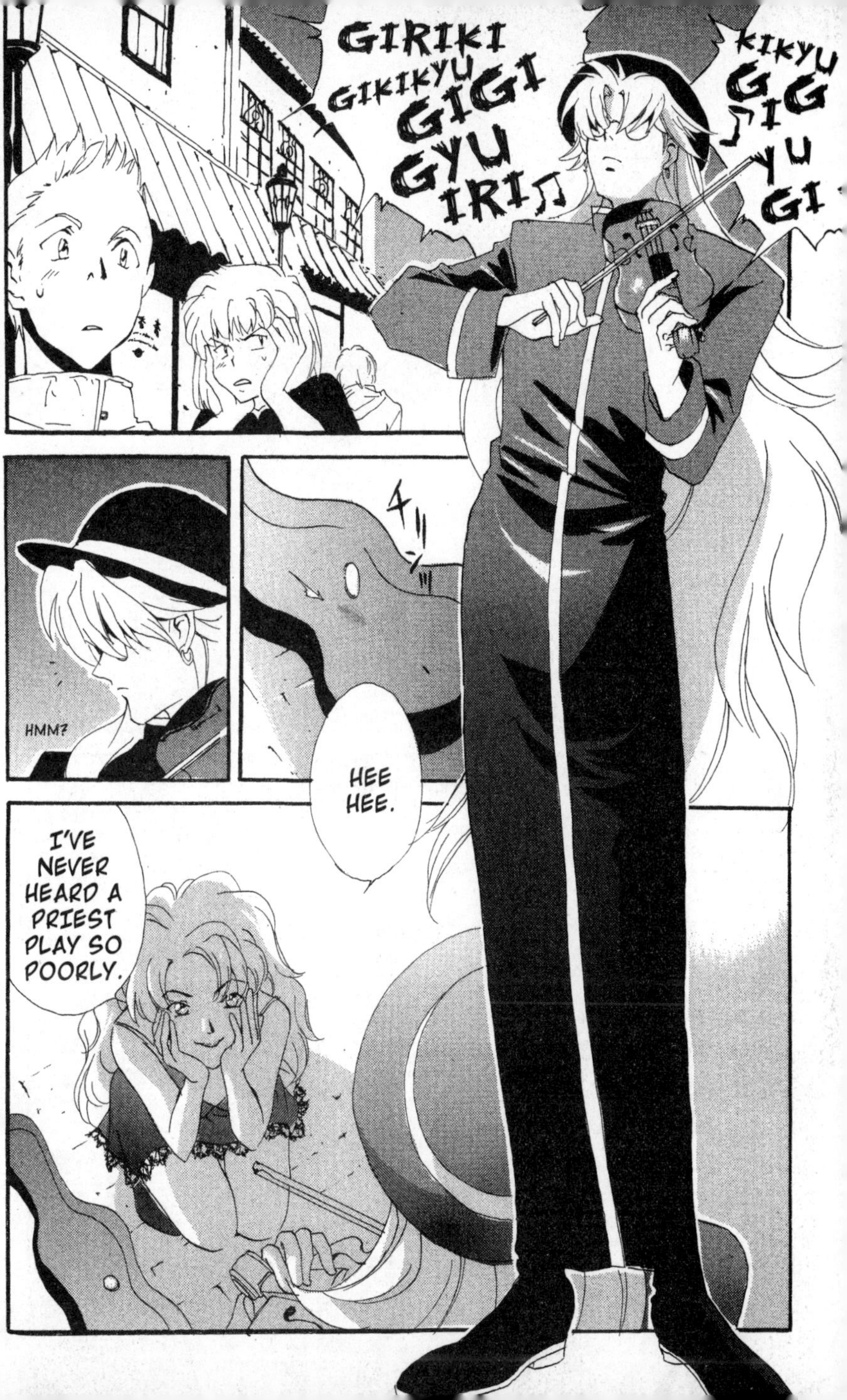
KIKYU GIGIYU GI
GIRIKI GIKIKYU GIGI GYU IRI♪
HMM?
HEE HEE.
I'VE NEVER HEARD A PRIEST PLAY SO POORLY.

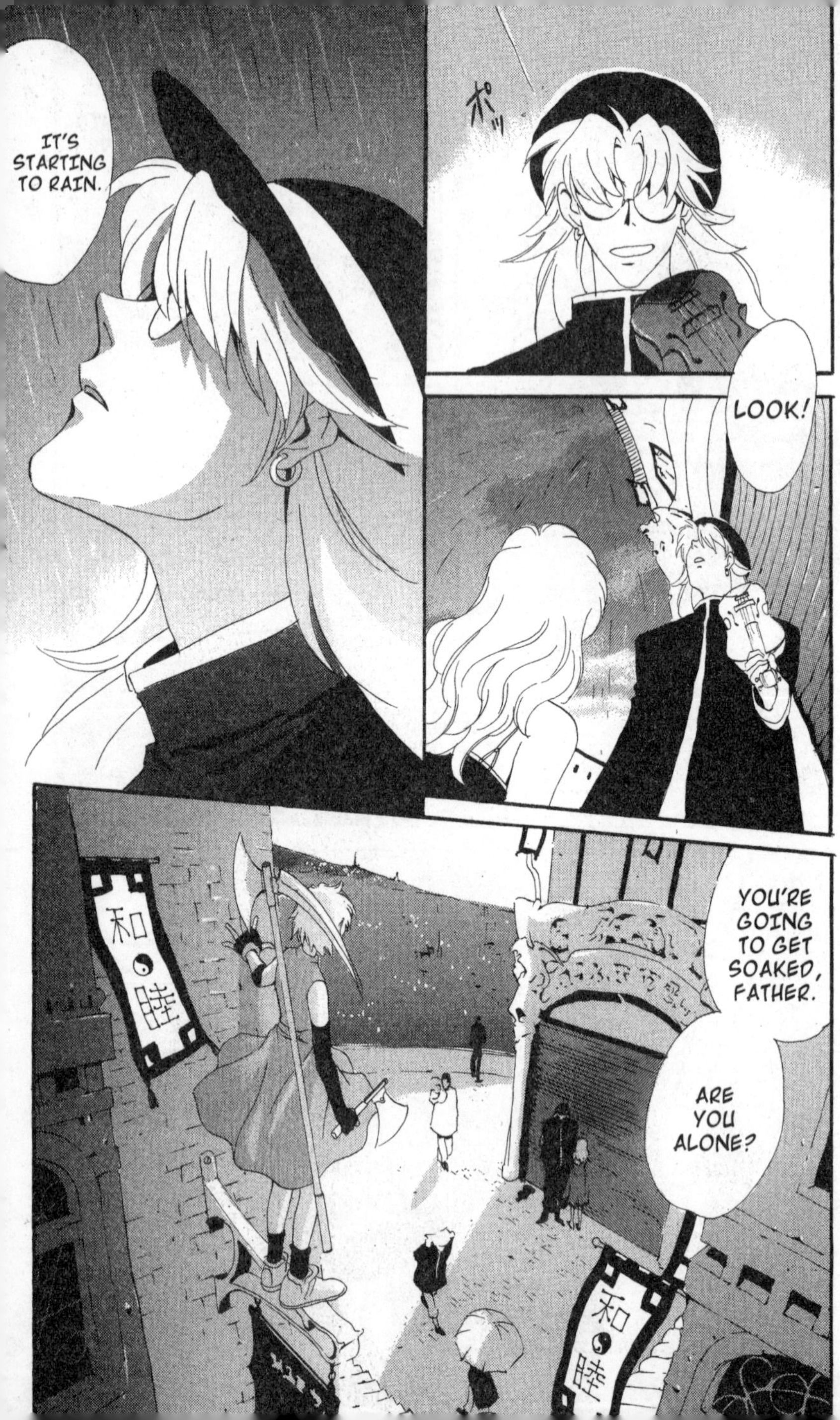
ポッ
LOOK!
IT'S STARTING TO RAIN.
YOU'RE GOING TO GET SOAKED, FATHER.
ARE YOU ALONE?
和睦
和睦

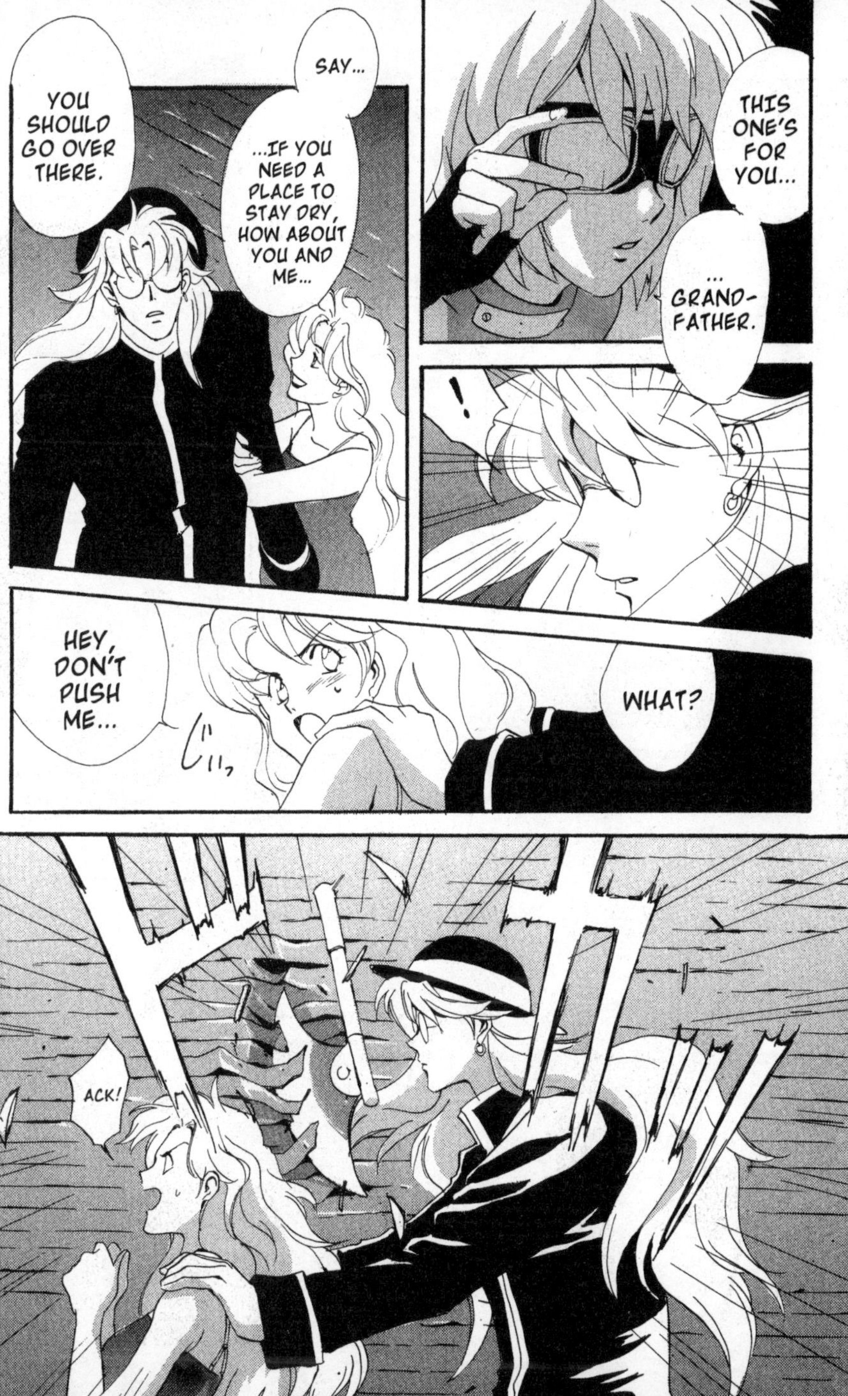
THIS ONE'S FOR YOU...
...GRANDFATHER.
!
SAY...
...IF YOU NEED A PLACE TO STAY DRY, HOW ABOUT YOU AND ME...
YOU SHOULD GO OVER THERE.
WHAT?
HEY, DON'T PUSH ME...
ACK!

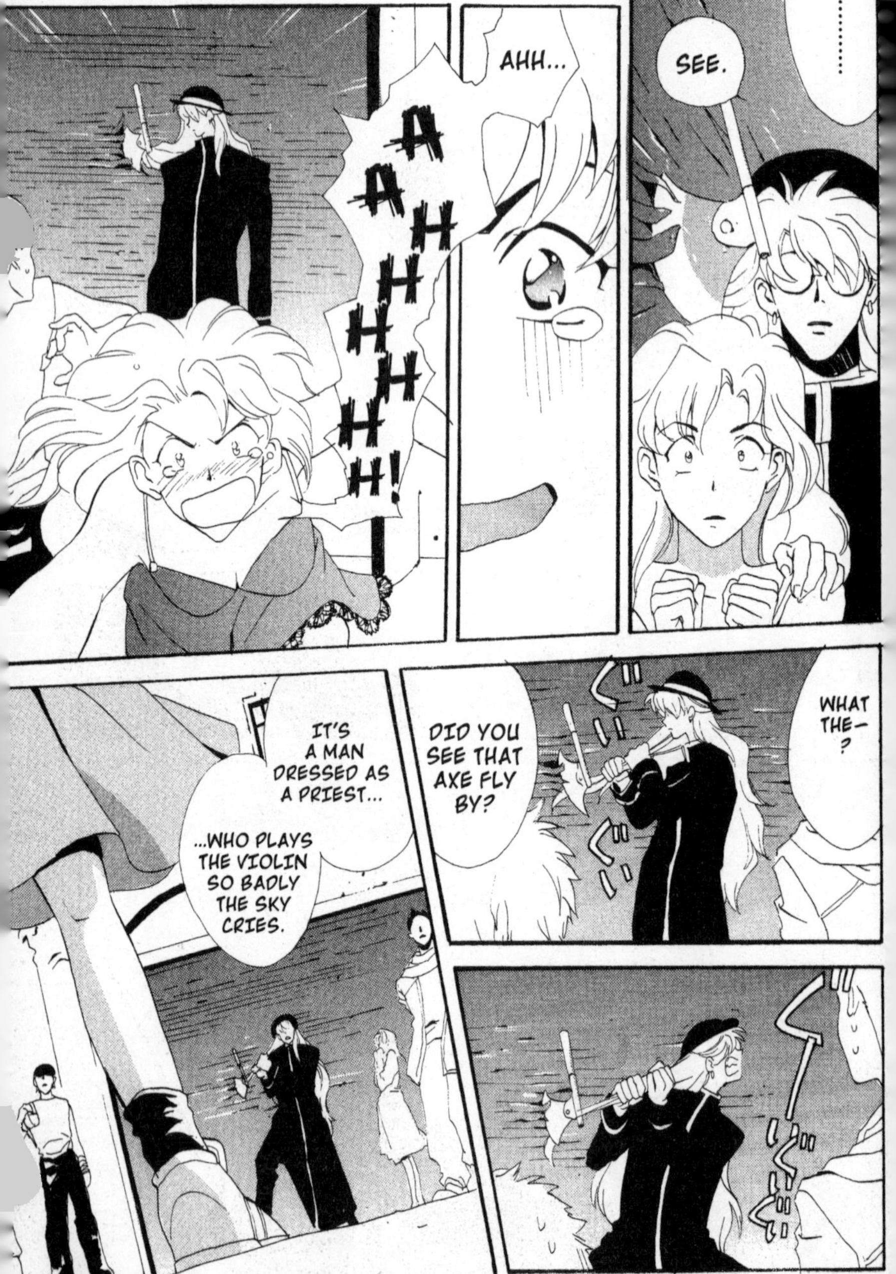
....
SEE.
AHH...
AAHHHHHHH!
WHAT THE—?
DID YOU SEE THAT AXE FLY BY?
IT'S A MAN DRESSED AS A PRIEST...
...WHO PLAYS THE VIOLIN SO BADLY THE SKY CRIES.

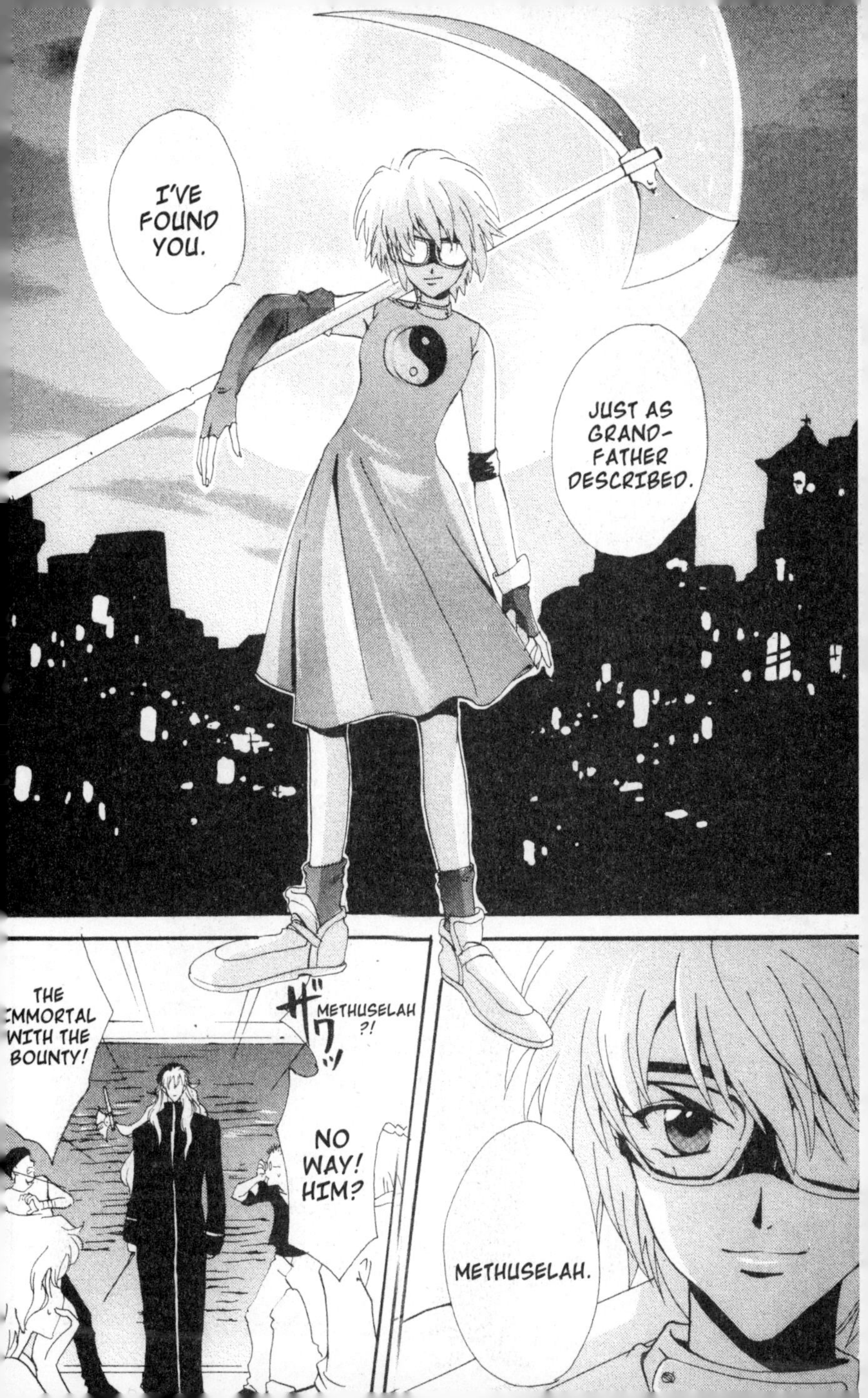
I'VE FOUND YOU.
JUST AS GRAND-FATHER DESCRIBED.
METHUSELAH.
ザワッ
METHUSELAH ?!
NO WAY! HIM?
THE IMMORTAL WITH THE BOUNTY!

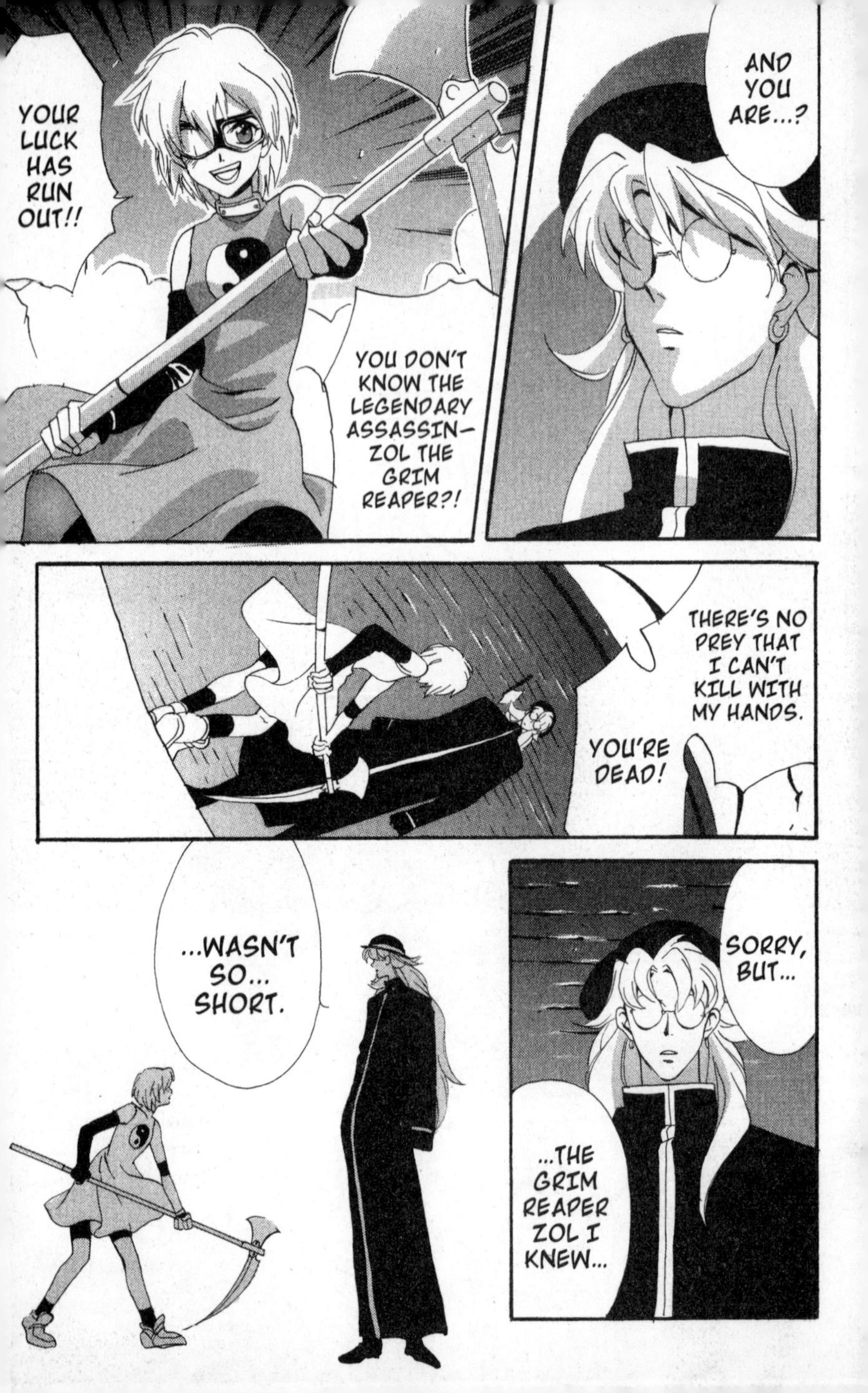
AND YOU ARE...?
YOUR LUCK HAS RUN OUT!!
YOU DON'T KNOW THE LEGENDARY ASSASSIN—ZOL THE GRIM REAPER?!
THERE'S NO PREY THAT I CAN'T KILL WITH MY HANDS.
YOU'RE DEAD!
SORRY, BUT...
...THE GRIM REAPER ZOL I KNEW...
...WASN'T SO... SHORT.

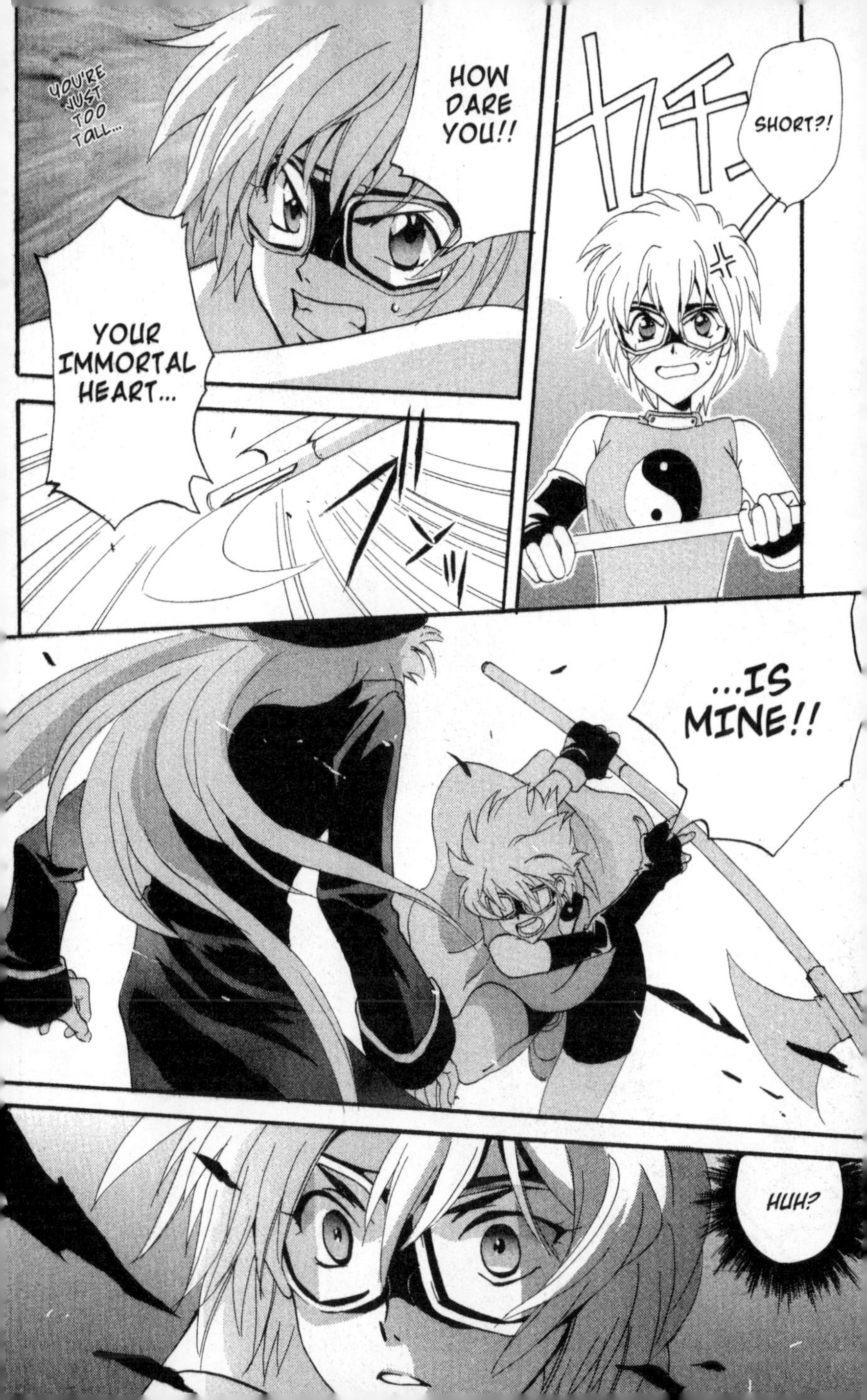
SHORT?!
HOW DARE YOU!!
YOU'RE JUST TOO TALL...
YOUR IMMORTAL HEART...
...IS MINE!!
HUH?

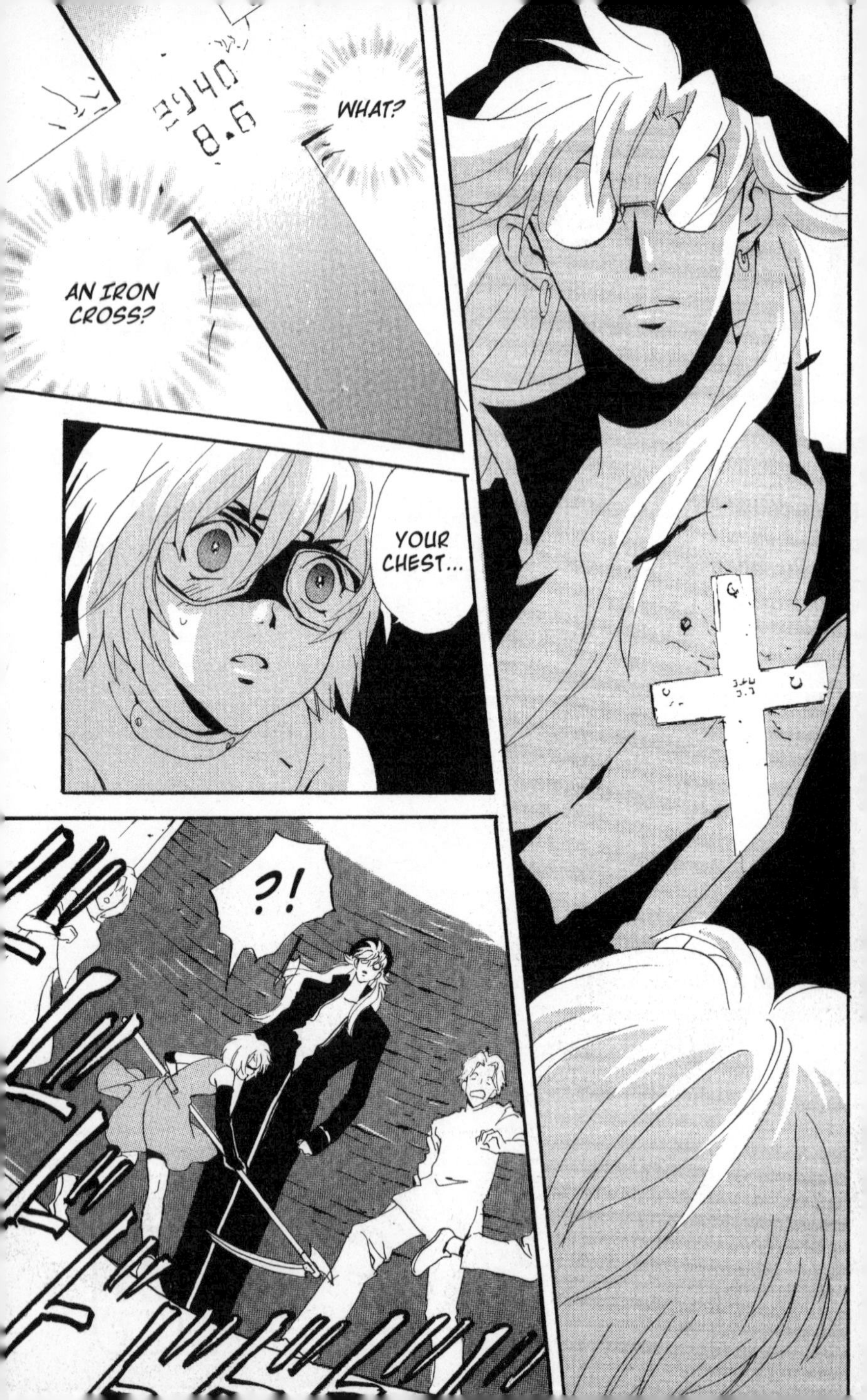
WHAT?
AN IRON CROSS?
YOUR CHEST...
?!

LAMENT *of the* LAMB™

The Story:

Kazuna Takashiro can't escape the pain of his past. Ever since his
mother died, nightmares and visions have been eating away at him. When
he finds his long-lost sister, Chizuna, the two discover they share
more than just a family name. The siblings are cursed with a disease of
the blood—a disease that will turn them into vampires! As they resist
accepting their destiny, Kazuna and Chizuna struggle to contain the
craving that is the very essence of what they will become...

The Creator:

Kei Toume

Behind the Manga:

- Appeals to fans of vampire stories and goth culture.
- Inspired a live-action film in Japan.
- Anime debuted in Japan in 2003.

Genre:

Drama / Horror

SRP:

£ 6.99

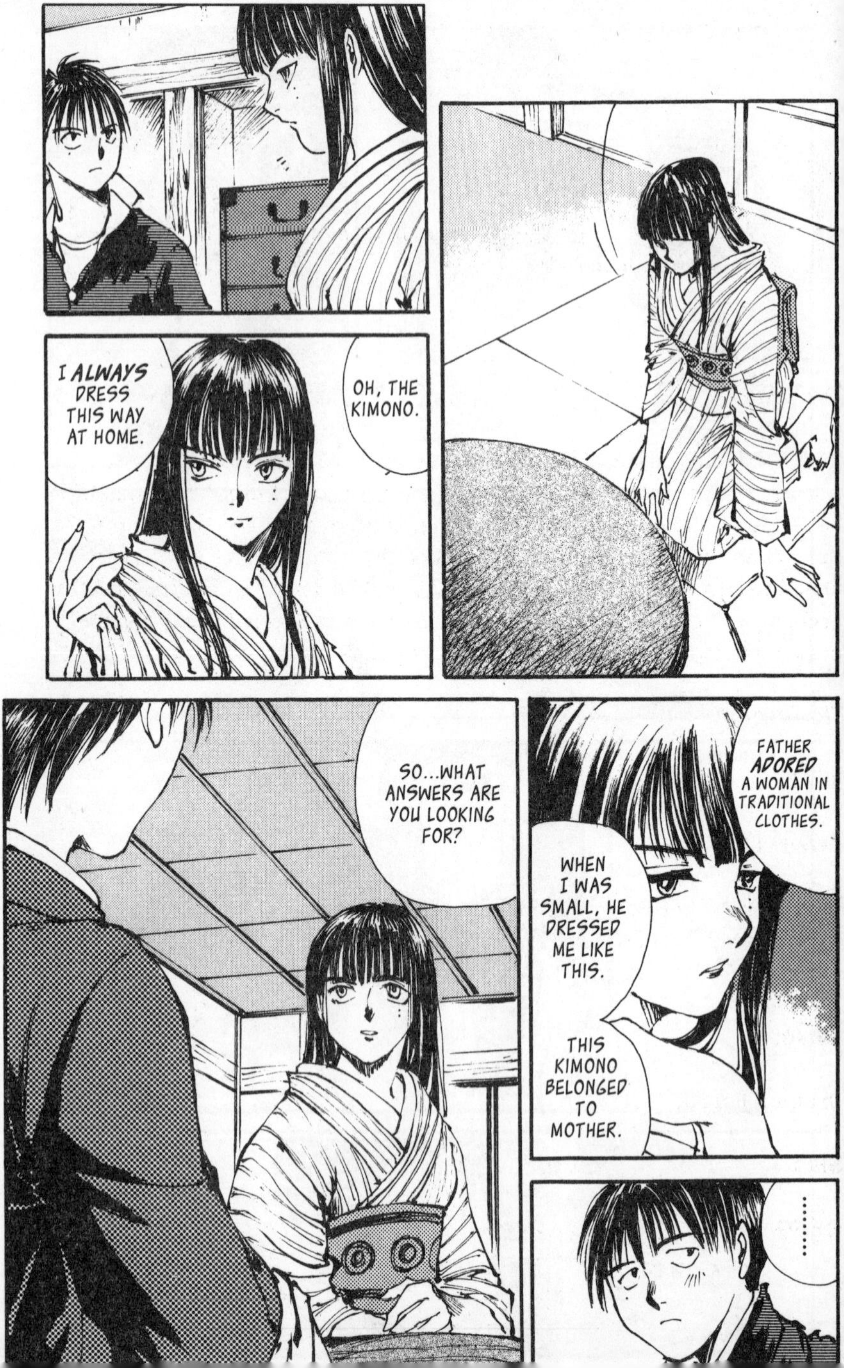
OH, THE KIMONO.
I *ALWAYS* DRESS THIS WAY AT HOME.
FATHER *ADORED* A WOMAN IN TRADITIONAL CLOTHES.
WHEN I WAS SMALL, HE DRESSED ME LIKE THIS.
THIS KIMONO BELONGED TO MOTHER.
....
SO...WHAT ANSWERS ARE YOU LOOKING FOR?

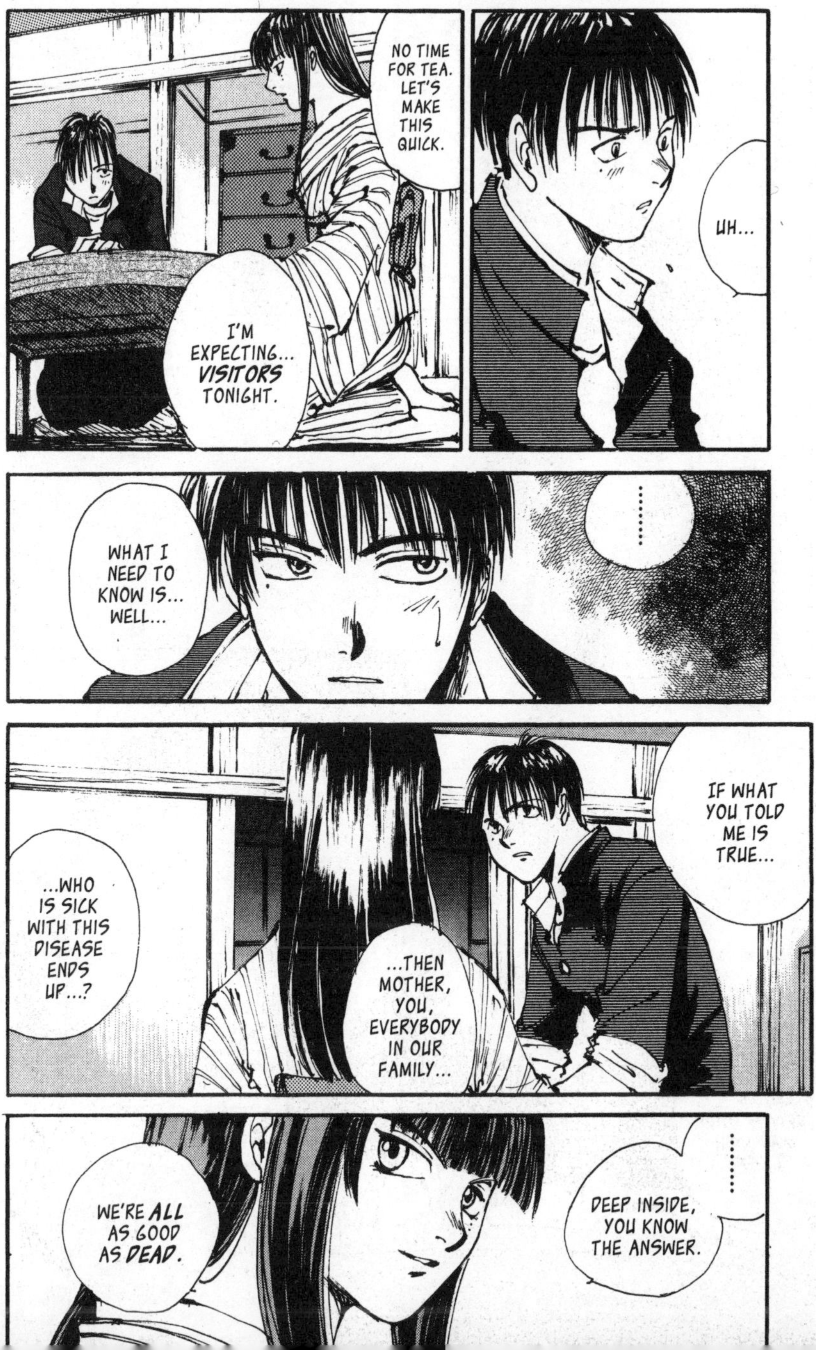
UH...
NO TIME FOR TEA. LET'S MAKE THIS QUICK.
I'M EXPECTING... VISITORS TONIGHT.
......
WHAT I NEED TO KNOW IS... WELL...
IF WHAT YOU TOLD ME IS TRUE...
...THEN MOTHER, YOU, EVERYBODY IN OUR FAMILY...
...WHO IS SICK WITH THIS DISEASE ENDS UP...?
......
DEEP INSIDE, YOU KNOW THE ANSWER.
WE'RE ALL AS GOOD AS DEAD.

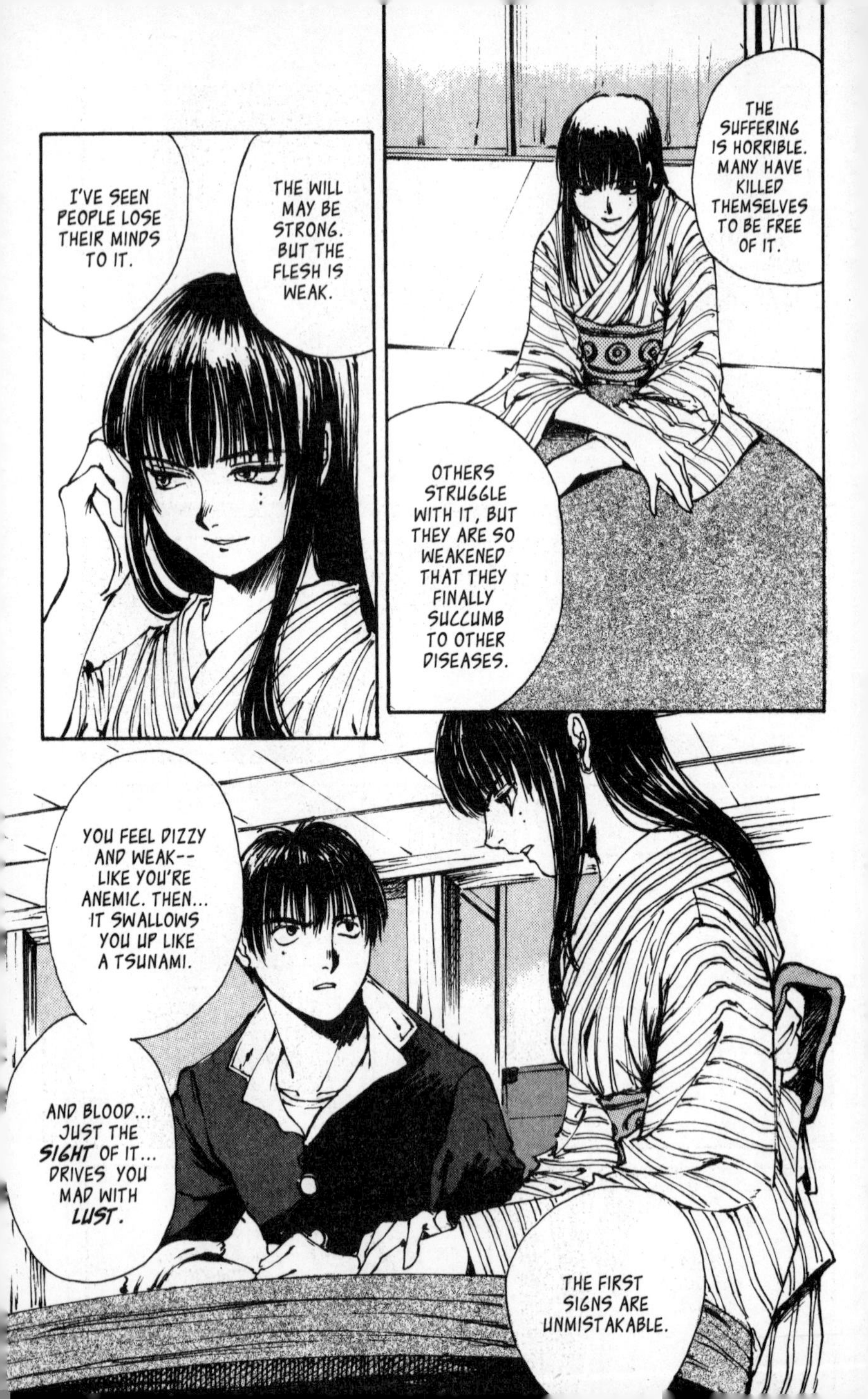
THE SUFFERING IS HORRIBLE. MANY HAVE KILLED THEMSELVES TO BE FREE OF IT.
OTHERS STRUGGLE WITH IT, BUT THEY ARE SO WEAKENED THAT THEY FINALLY SUCCUMB TO OTHER DISEASES.
THE WILL MAY BE STRONG. BUT THE FLESH IS WEAK.
I'VE SEEN PEOPLE LOSE THEIR MINDS TO IT.
THE FIRST SIGNS ARE UNMISTAKABLE.
YOU FEEL DIZZY AND WEAK-- LIKE YOU'RE ANEMIC. THEN... IT SWALLOWS YOU UP LIKE A TSUNAMI.
AND BLOOD... JUST THE ***SIGHT*** OF IT... DRIVES YOU MAD WITH ***LUST***.

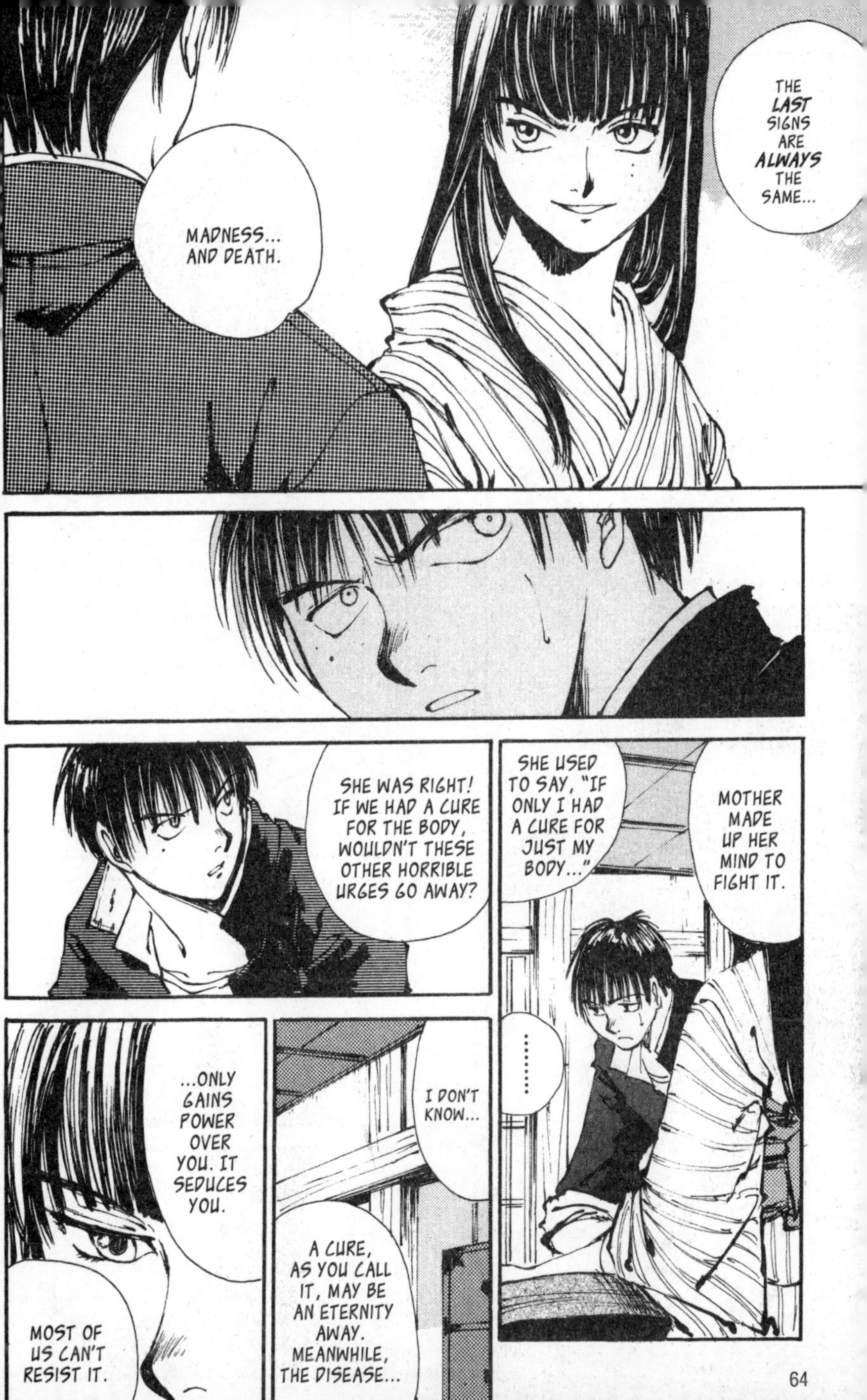
THE *LAST* SIGNS ARE *ALWAYS* THE SAME...
MADNESS... AND DEATH.
MOTHER MADE UP HER MIND TO FIGHT IT.
SHE USED TO SAY, "IF ONLY I HAD A CURE FOR JUST MY BODY..."
......
SHE WAS RIGHT! IF WE HAD A CURE FOR THE BODY, WOULDN'T THESE OTHER HORRIBLE URGES GO AWAY?
I DON'T KNOW...
A CURE, AS YOU CALL IT, MAY BE AN ETERNITY AWAY. MEANWHILE, THE DISEASE...
...ONLY GAINS POWER OVER YOU. IT SEDUCES YOU.
MOST OF US CAN'T RESIST IT.

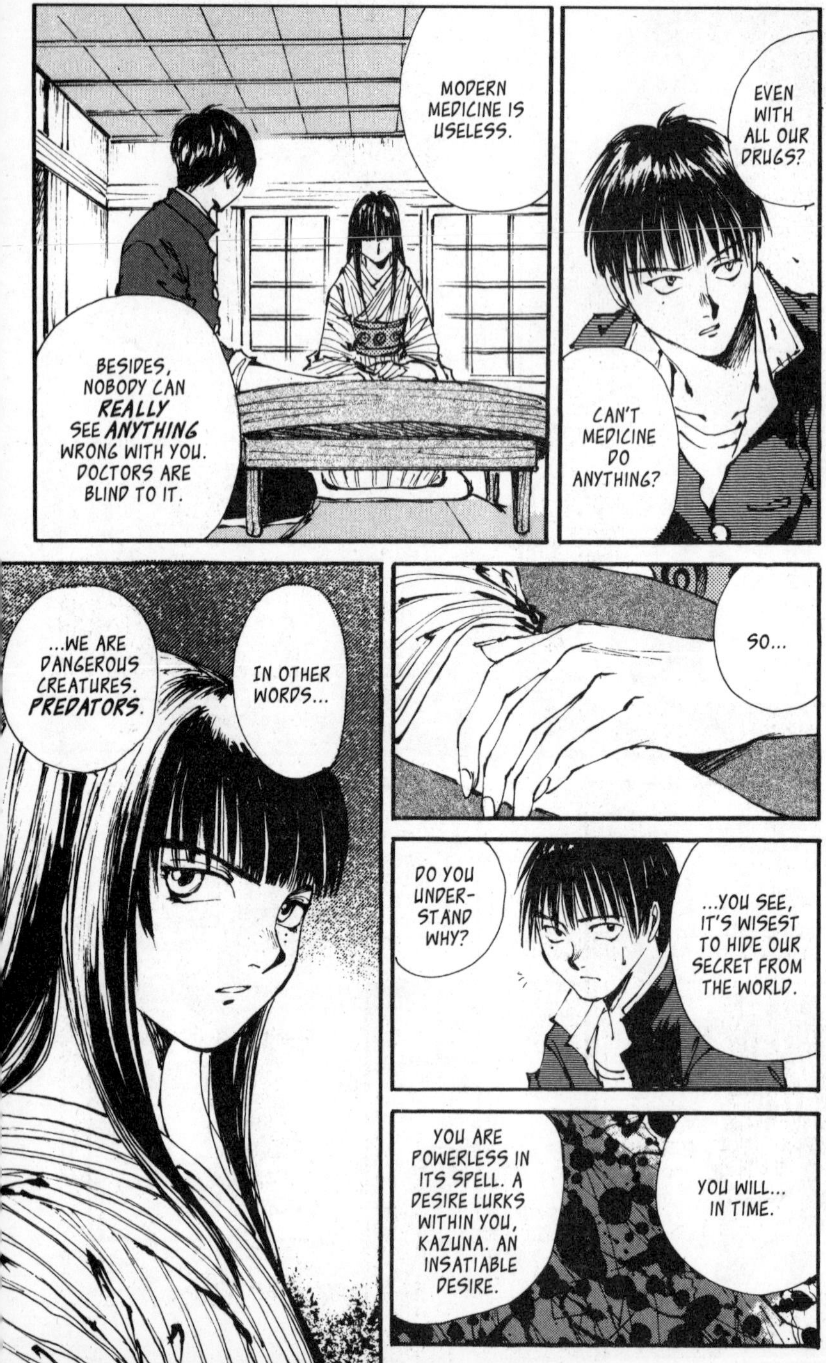
EVEN WITH ALL OUR DRUGS?
CAN'T MEDICINE DO ANYTHING?
MODERN MEDICINE IS USELESS.
BESIDES, NOBODY CAN *REALLY* SEE *ANYTHING* WRONG WITH YOU. DOCTORS ARE BLIND TO IT.
SO...
...YOU SEE, IT'S WISEST TO HIDE OUR SECRET FROM THE WORLD.
DO YOU UNDER-STAND WHY?
YOU WILL... IN TIME.
YOU ARE POWERLESS IN ITS SPELL. A DESIRE LURKS WITHIN YOU, KAZUNA. AN INSATIABLE DESIRE.
IN OTHER WORDS...
...WE ARE DANGEROUS CREATURES. **PREDATORS.**

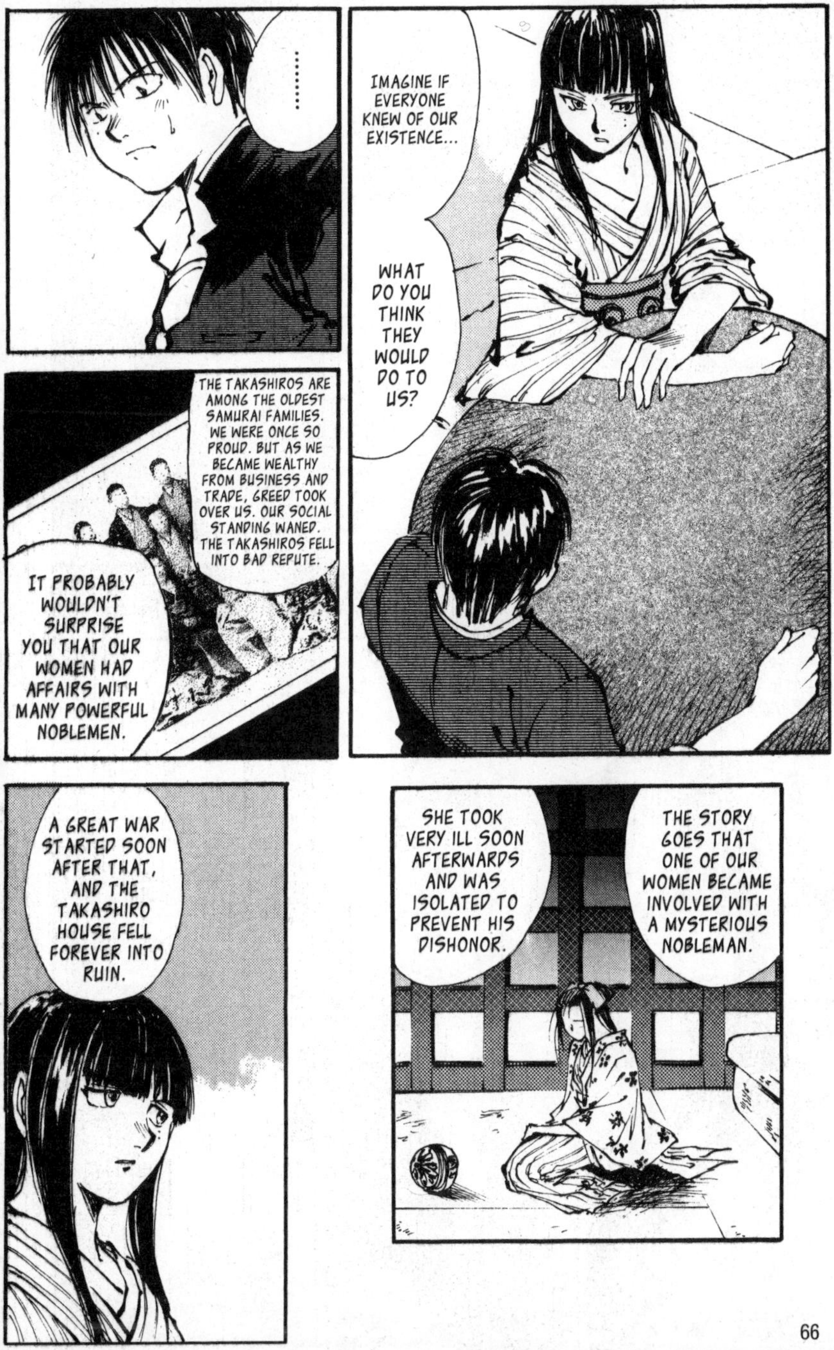
IMAGINE IF EVERYONE KNEW OF OUR EXISTENCE...
WHAT DO YOU THINK THEY WOULD DO TO US?
......
THE TAKASHIROS ARE AMONG THE OLDEST SAMURAI FAMILIES. WE WERE ONCE SO PROUD. BUT AS WE BECAME WEALTHY FROM BUSINESS AND TRADE, GREED TOOK OVER US. OUR SOCIAL STANDING WANED. THE TAKASHIROS FELL INTO BAD REPUTE.
IT PROBABLY WOULDN'T SURPRISE YOU THAT OUR WOMEN HAD AFFAIRS WITH MANY POWERFUL NOBLEMEN.
THE STORY GOES THAT ONE OF OUR WOMEN BECAME INVOLVED WITH A MYSTERIOUS NOBLEMAN.
SHE TOOK VERY ILL SOON AFTERWARDS AND WAS ISOLATED TO PREVENT HIS DISHONOR.
A GREAT WAR STARTED SOON AFTER THAT, AND THE TAKASHIRO HOUSE FELL FOREVER INTO RUIN.

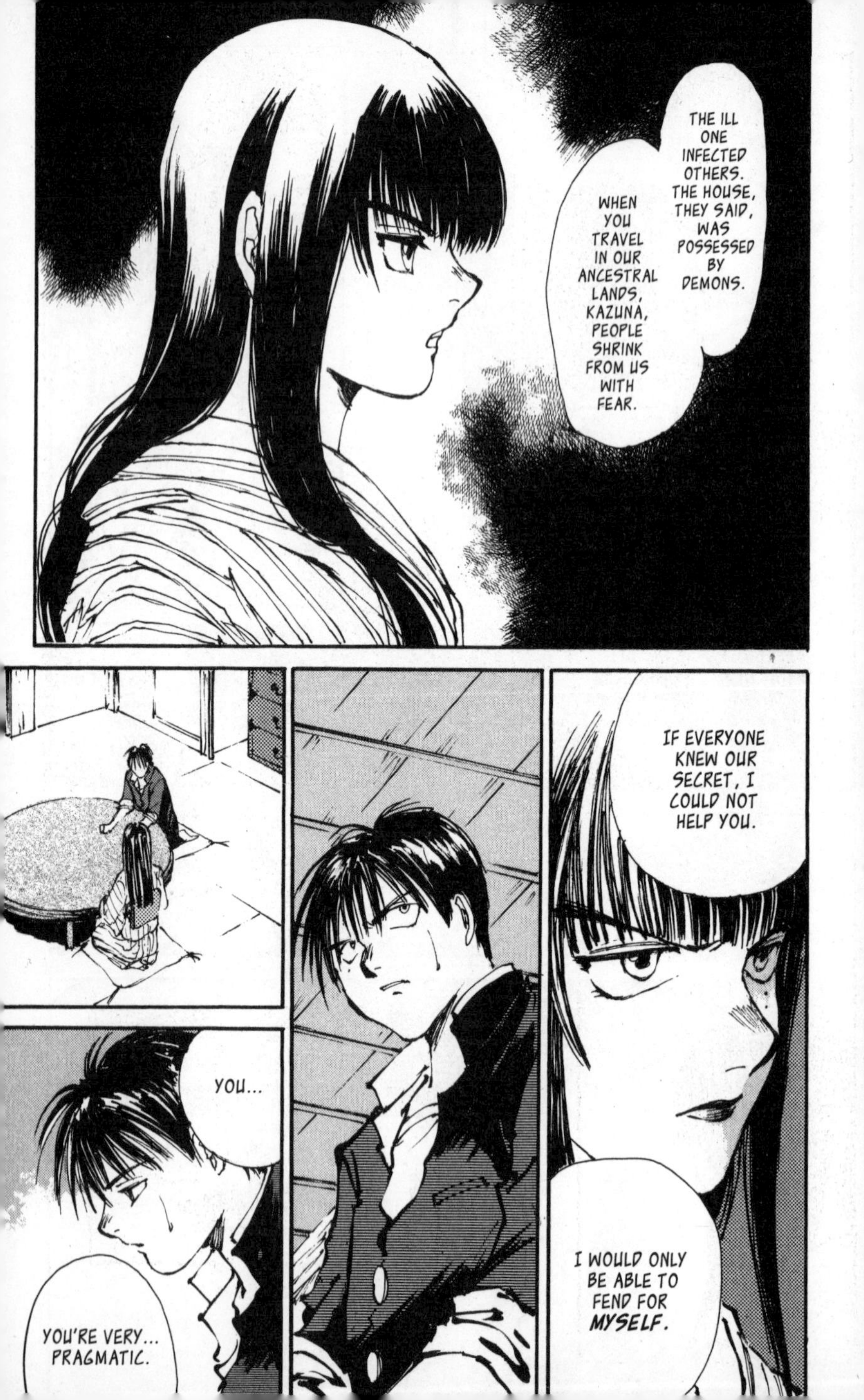
THE ILL ONE INFECTED OTHERS. THE HOUSE, THEY SAID, WAS POSSESSED BY DEMONS.
WHEN YOU TRAVEL IN OUR ANCESTRAL LANDS, KAZUNA, PEOPLE SHRINK FROM US WITH FEAR.
IF EVERYONE KNEW OUR SECRET, I COULD NOT HELP YOU.
I WOULD ONLY BE ABLE TO FEND FOR **MYSELF**.
YOU...
YOU'RE VERY... PRAGMATIC.

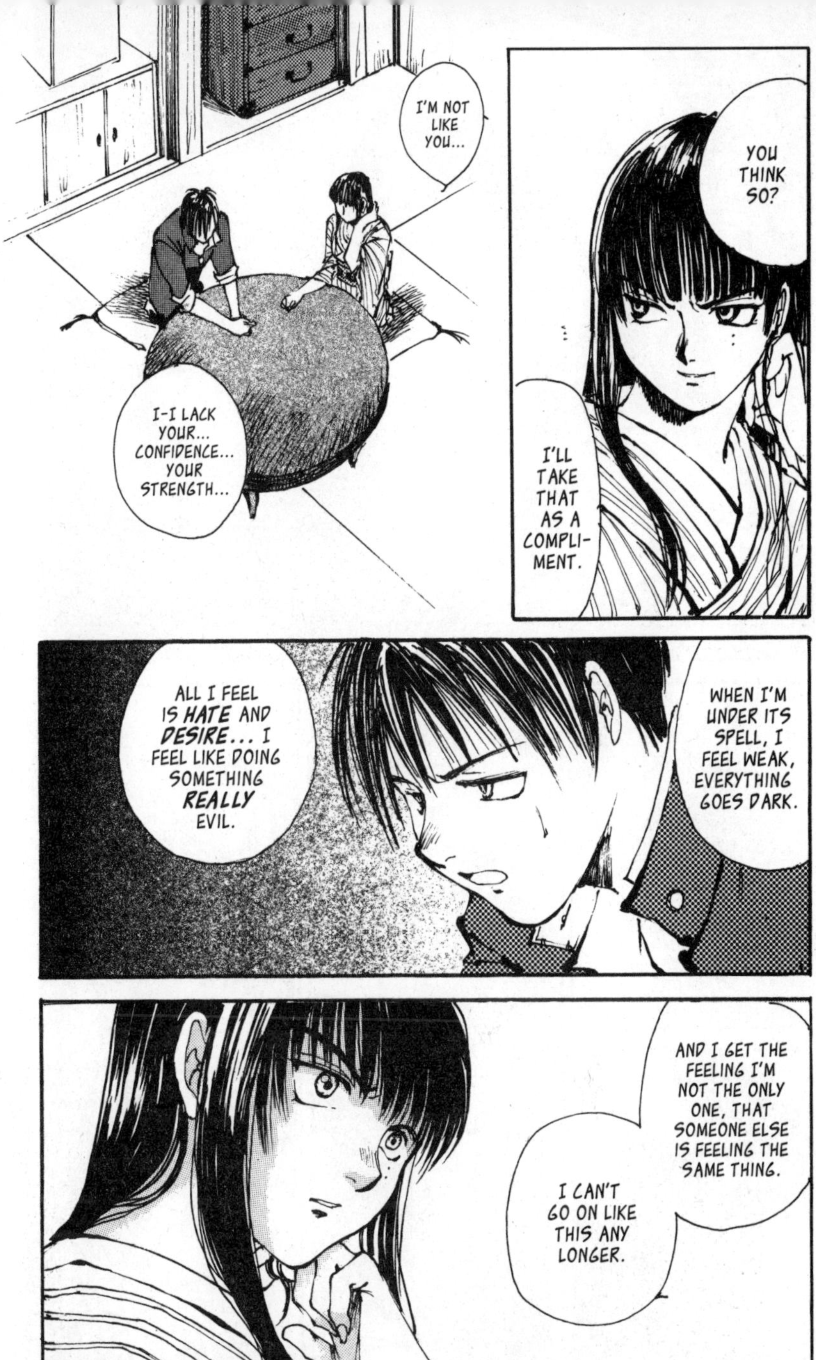
YOU THINK SO?
I'LL TAKE THAT AS A COMPLIMENT.
I'M NOT LIKE YOU...
I-I LACK YOUR... CONFIDENCE... YOUR STRENGTH...
WHEN I'M UNDER ITS SPELL, I FEEL WEAK, EVERYTHING GOES DARK.
ALL I FEEL IS **HATE** AND **DESIRE...** I FEEL LIKE DOING SOMETHING **REALLY** EVIL.
AND I GET THE FEELING I'M NOT THE ONLY ONE, THAT SOMEONE ELSE IS FEELING THE SAME THING.
I CAN'T GO ON LIKE THIS ANY LONGER.

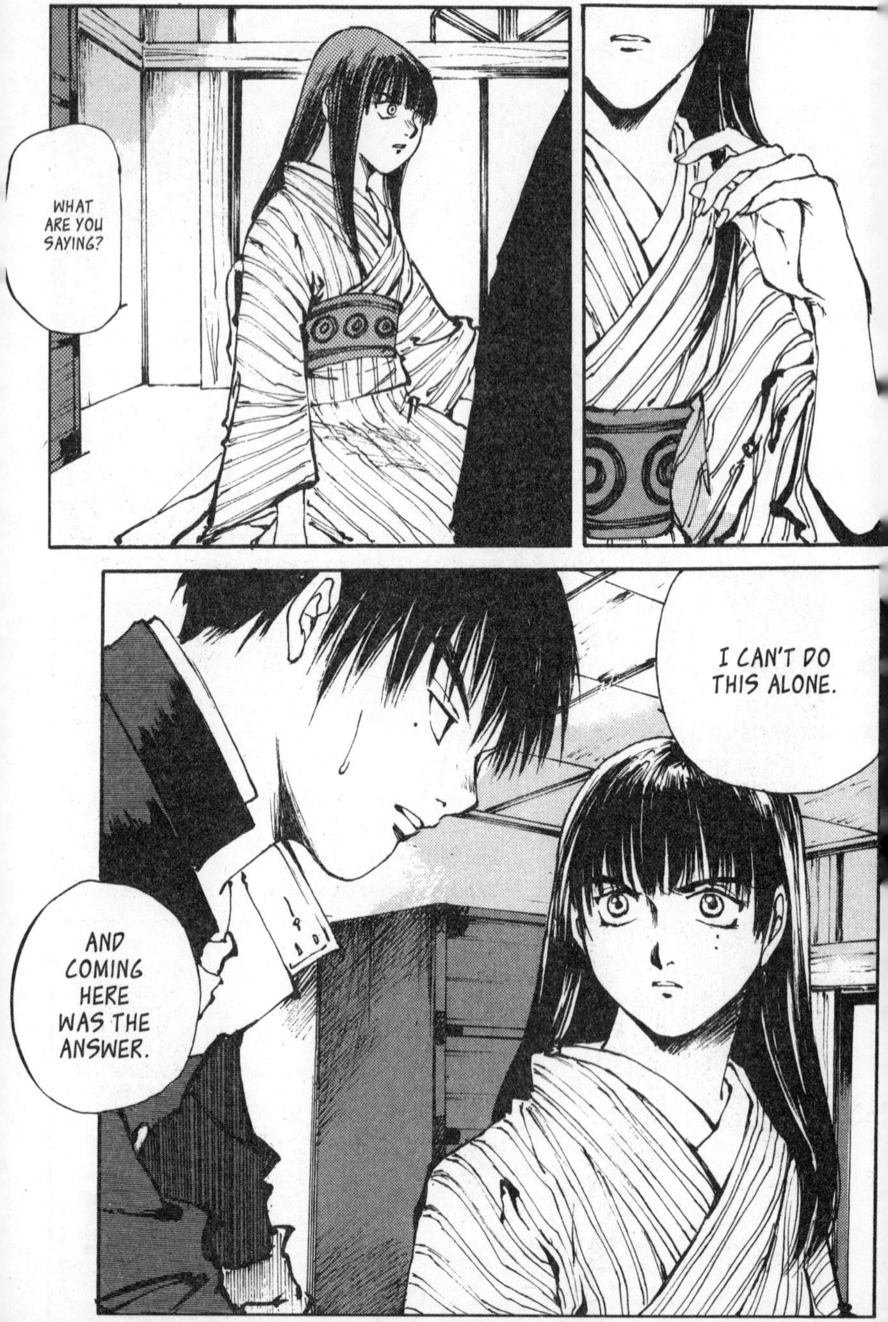
WHAT ARE YOU SAYING?
I CAN'T DO THIS ALONE.
AND COMING HERE WAS THE ANSWER.

AUTOMATIC MAIDEN

The Story:

Everybody oughtta have a maid...just ask Suguru Misato, a junior high school student who has been living by himself since his father's mysterious death. He would love a little companionship, not to mention someone to deal with the stacks of dishes and the ever-present family of dust bunnies. Enter Mahoro, a retired battle android who has been repurposed for domestic life. When Suguru meets his new maid, hilarity ensues, sexual tensions flare, and secret pasts become revealed in this quirky comedy about love, death, and robot nudity.

The Creators:

Bow Ditama and Bunjuro Nakayama

Behind the Manga:

• Inspired the hit anime available on DVD!
• A must-have series for fans of *Saber Marionette J*.
• From Gainax Studios, creators of *Evangelion* and *FLCL*.

Genre:

Action / Comedy

SRP:

£ 6.99

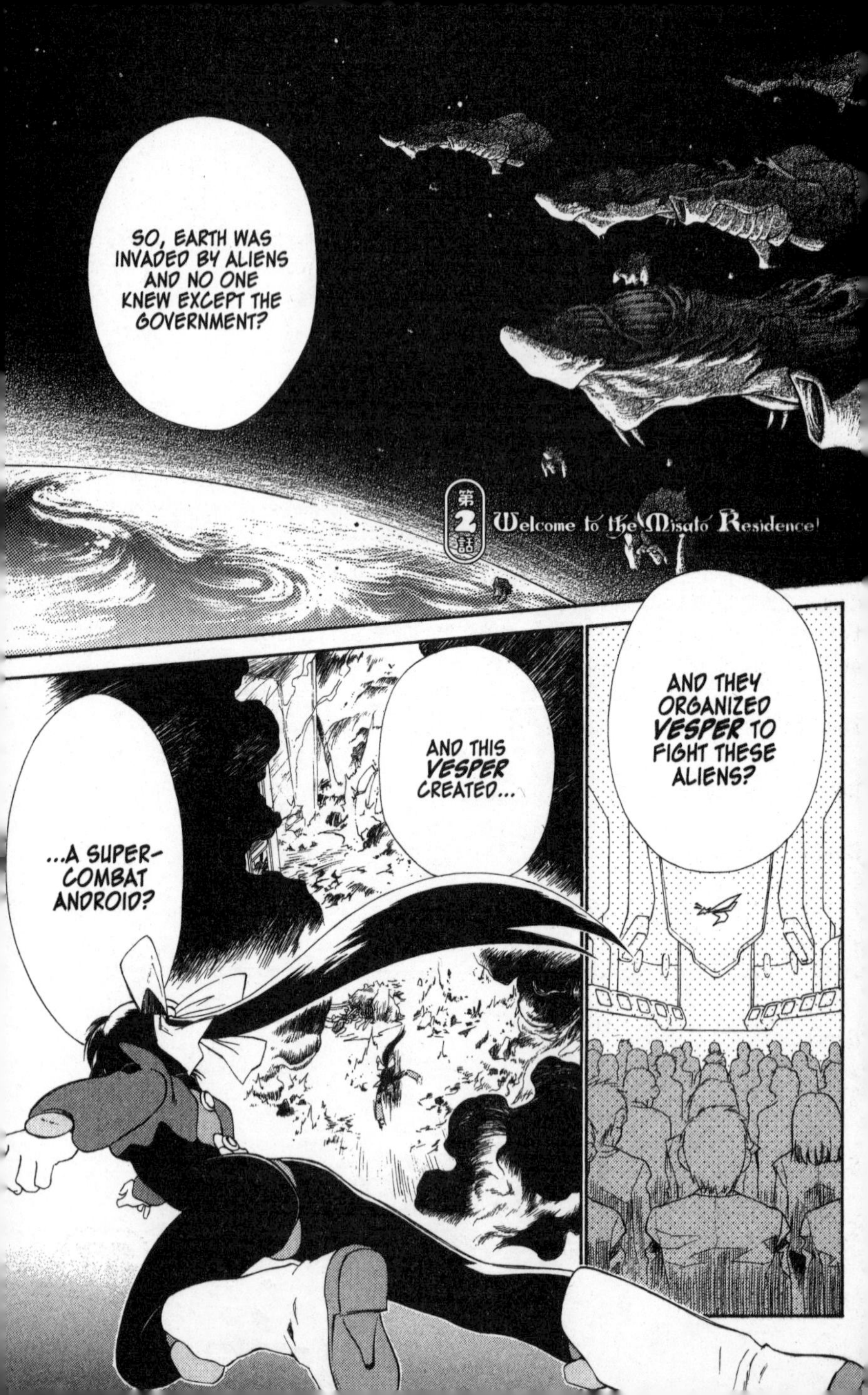
SO, EARTH WAS INVADED BY ALIENS AND NO ONE KNEW EXCEPT THE GOVERNMENT?
第2話 Welcome to the Misato Residence!
AND THEY ORGANIZED VESPER TO FIGHT THESE ALIENS?
AND THIS VESPER CREATED...
...A SUPER-COMBAT ANDROID?

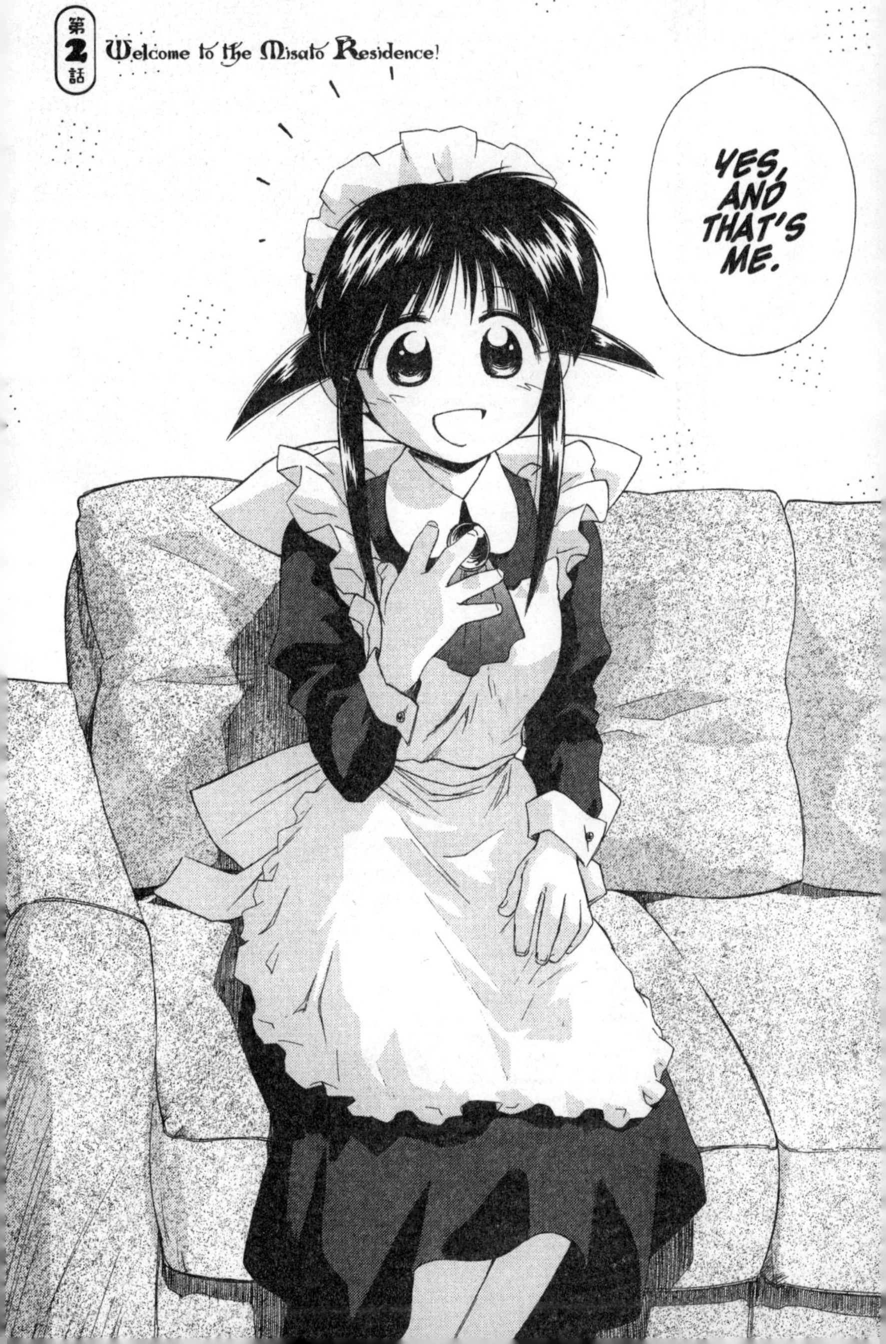
第2話
Welcome to the Misato Residence!
YES, AND THAT'S ME.

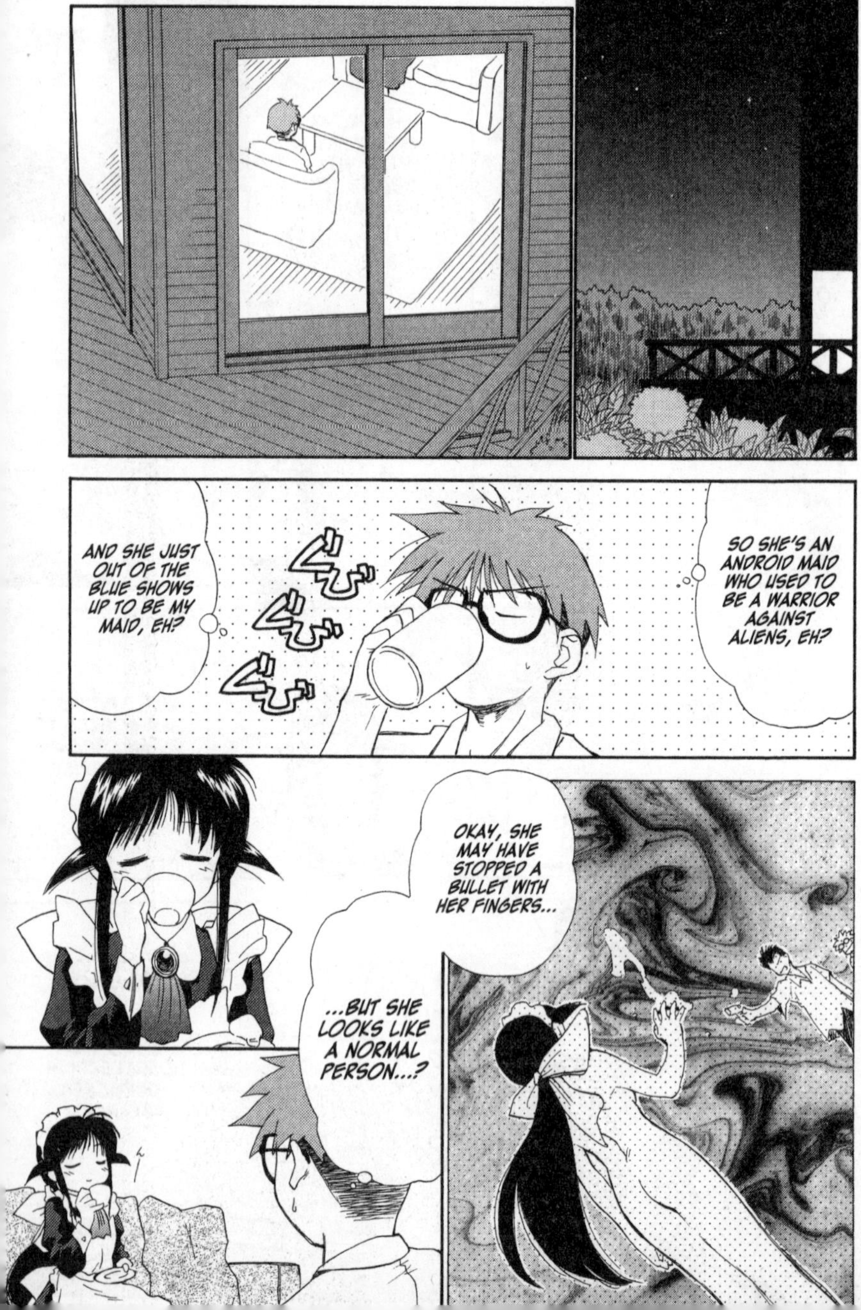
SO SHE'S AN ANDROID MAID WHO USED TO BE A WARRIOR AGAINST ALIENS, EH?
AND SHE JUST OUT OF THE BLUE SHOWS UP TO BE MY MAID, EH?
OKAY, SHE MAY HAVE STOPPED A BULLET WITH HER FINGERS...
...BUT SHE LOOKS LIKE A NORMAL PERSON...?

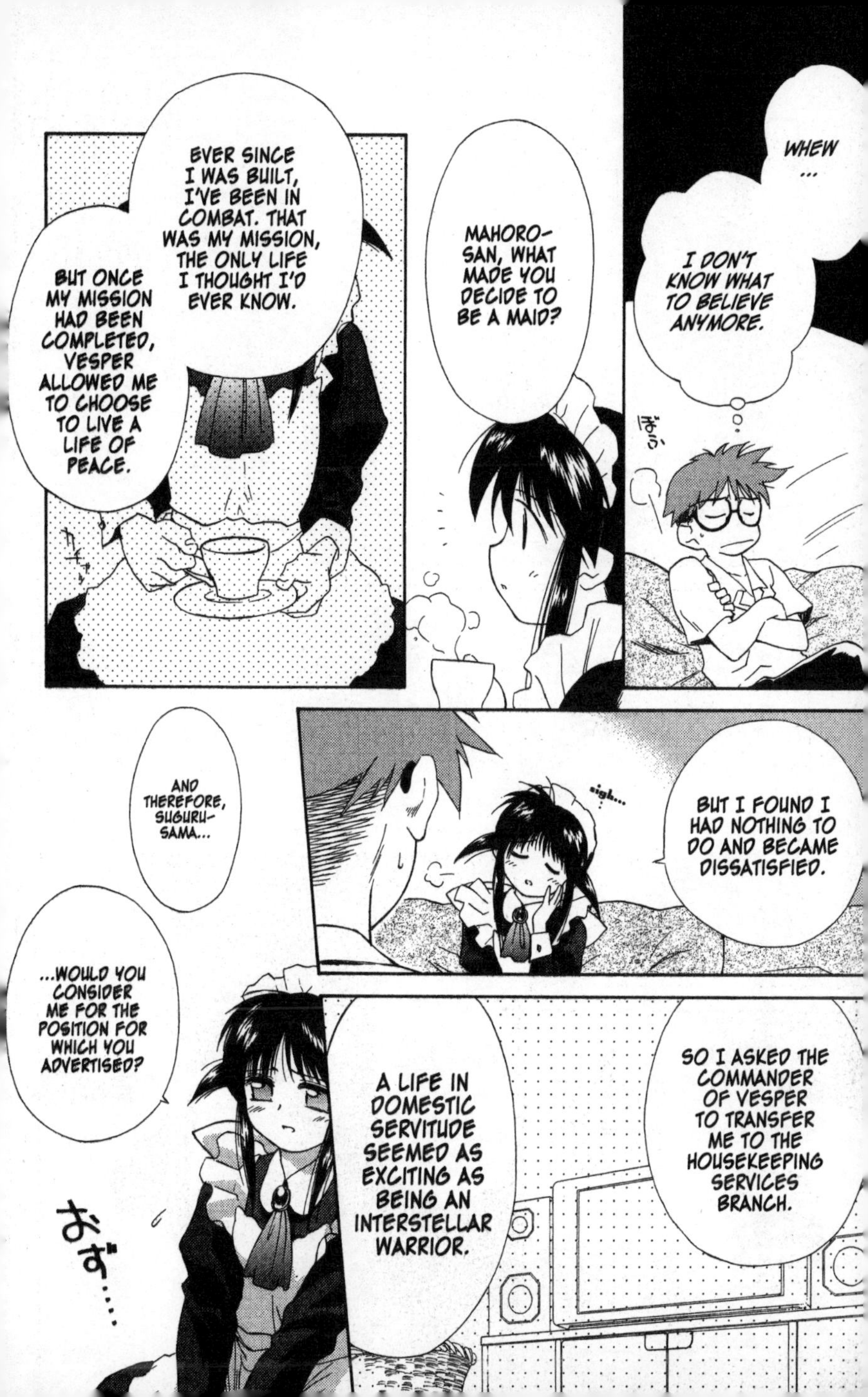
WHEW ...
I DON'T KNOW WHAT TO BELIEVE ANYMORE.
MAHORO-SAN, WHAT MADE YOU DECIDE TO BE A MAID?
EVER SINCE I WAS BUILT, I'VE BEEN IN COMBAT. THAT WAS MY MISSION, THE ONLY LIFE I THOUGHT I'D EVER KNOW.
BUT ONCE MY MISSION HAD BEEN COMPLETED, VESPER ALLOWED ME TO CHOOSE TO LIVE A LIFE OF PEACE.
sigh...
BUT I FOUND I HAD NOTHING TO DO AND BECAME DISSATISFIED.
SO I ASKED THE COMMANDER OF VESPER TO TRANSFER ME TO THE HOUSEKEEPING SERVICES BRANCH.
A LIFE IN DOMESTIC SERVITUDE SEEMED AS EXCITING AS BEING AN INTERSTELLAR WARRIOR.
AND THEREFORE, SUGURU-SAMA...
...WOULD YOU CONSIDER ME FOR THE POSITION FOR WHICH YOU ADVERTISED?
おず…

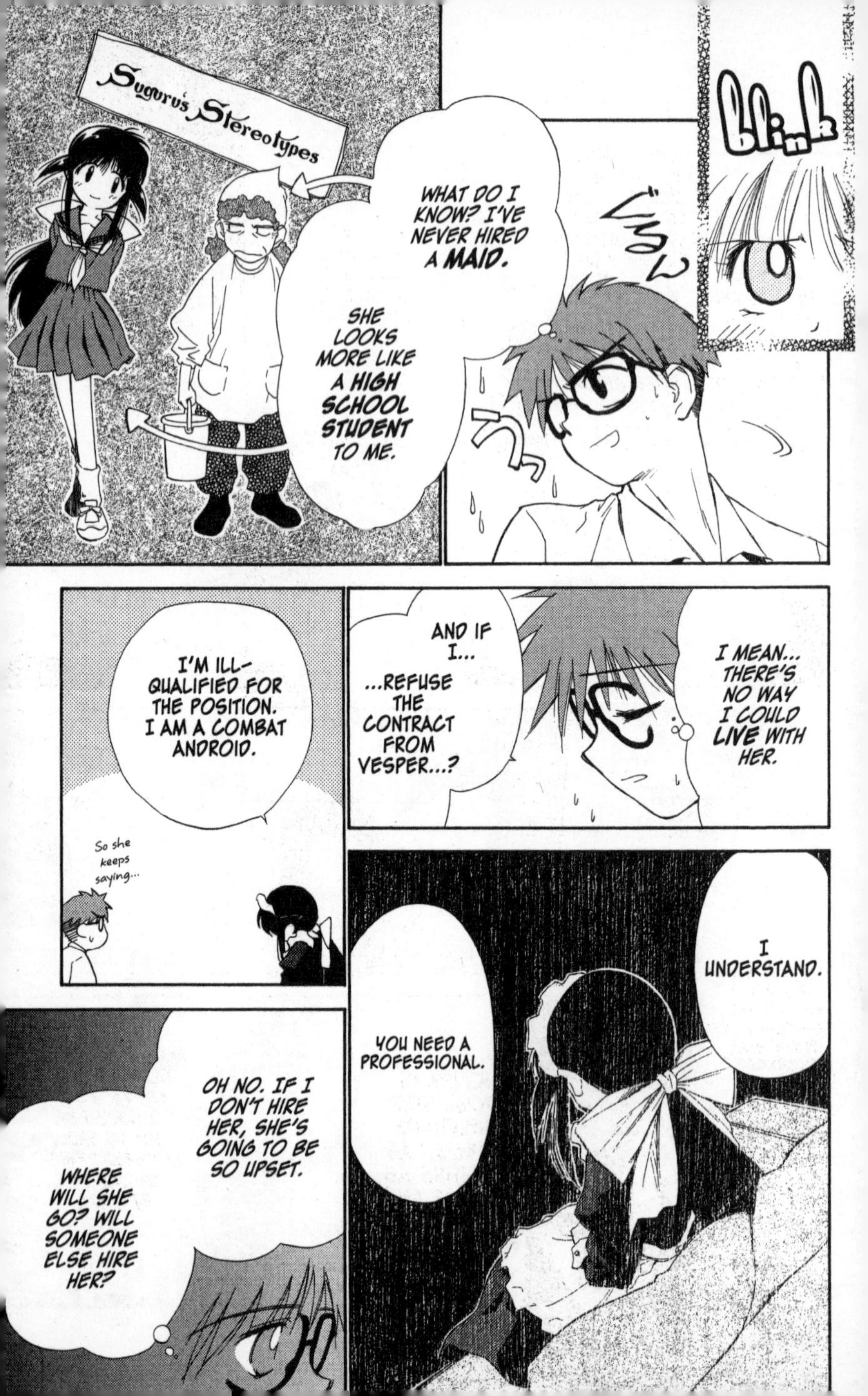
blink
Suguru's Stereotypes
WHAT DO I KNOW? I'VE NEVER HIRED A MAID.
SHE LOOKS MORE LIKE A HIGH SCHOOL STUDENT TO ME.
I MEAN... THERE'S NO WAY I COULD LIVE WITH HER.
AND IF I...
...REFUSE THE CONTRACT FROM VESPER...?
I'M ILL-QUALIFIED FOR THE POSITION. I AM A COMBAT ANDROID.
So she keeps saying...
I UNDERSTAND.
YOU NEED A PROFESSIONAL.
OH NO. IF I DON'T HIRE HER, SHE'S GOING TO BE SO UPSET.
WHERE WILL SHE GO? WILL SOMEONE ELSE HIRE HER?

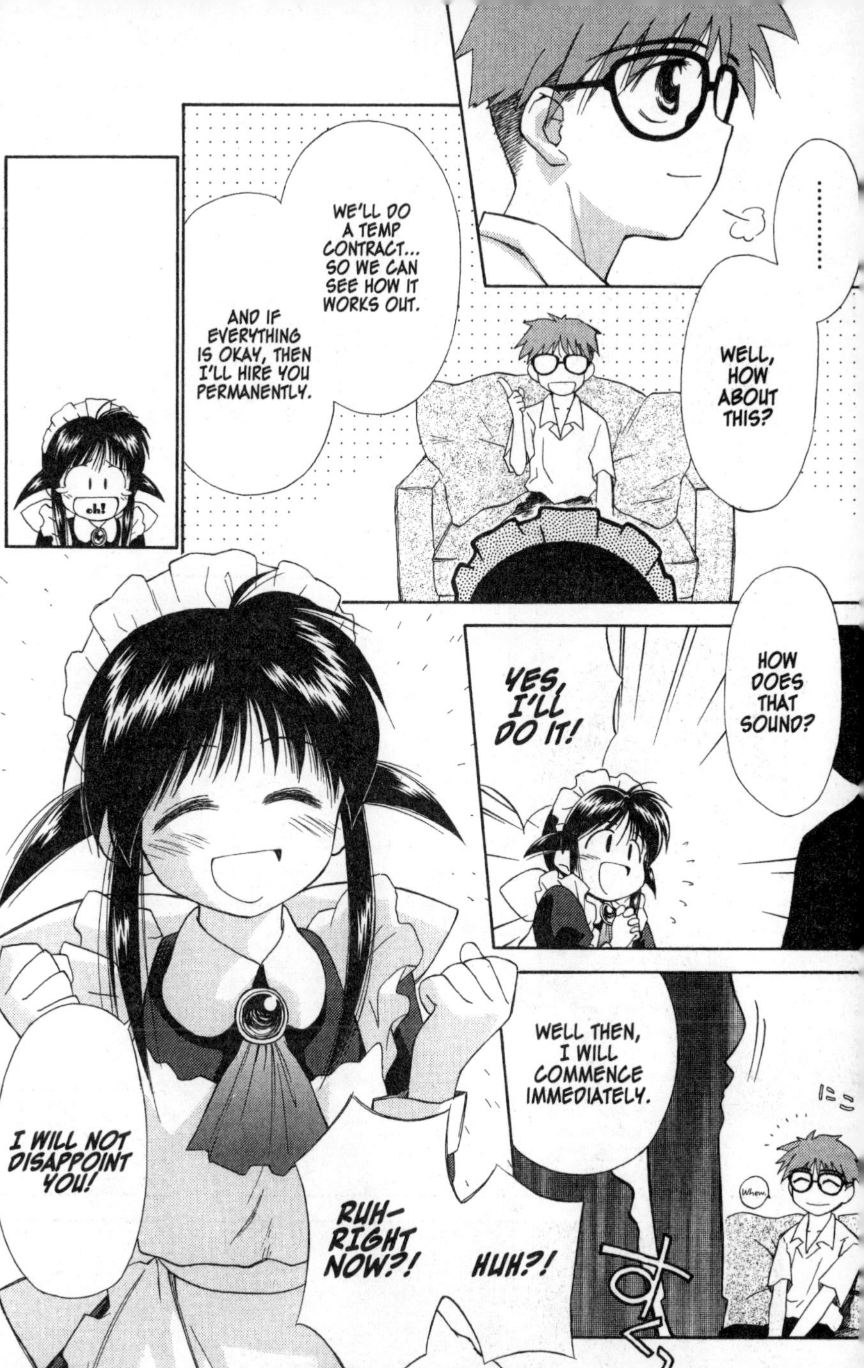
......
WELL, HOW ABOUT THIS?
WE'LL DO A TEMP CONTRACT... SO WE CAN SEE HOW IT WORKS OUT.
AND IF EVERYTHING IS OKAY, THEN I'LL HIRE YOU PERMANENTLY.
oh!
HOW DOES THAT SOUND?
YES, I'LL DO IT!
WELL THEN, I WILL COMMENCE IMMEDIATELY.
にこ
Whew.
HUH?!
RUH-RIGHT NOW?!
I WILL NOT DISAPPOINT YOU!

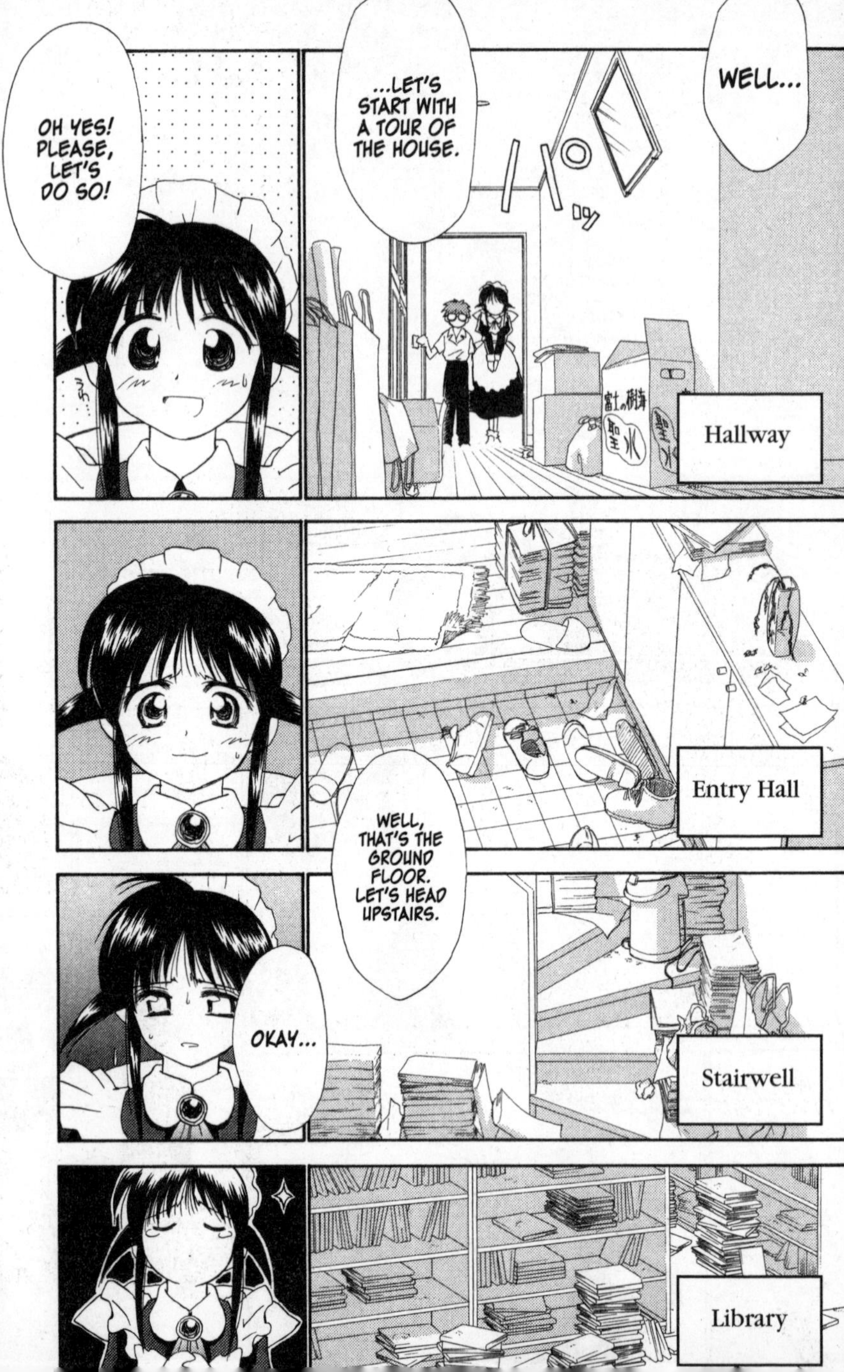
WELL...
...LET'S START WITH A TOUR OF THE HOUSE.
Hallway
OH YES! PLEASE, LET'S DO SO!
WELL, THAT'S THE GROUND FLOOR. LET'S HEAD UPSTAIRS.
Entry Hall
Stairwell
OKAY...
Library

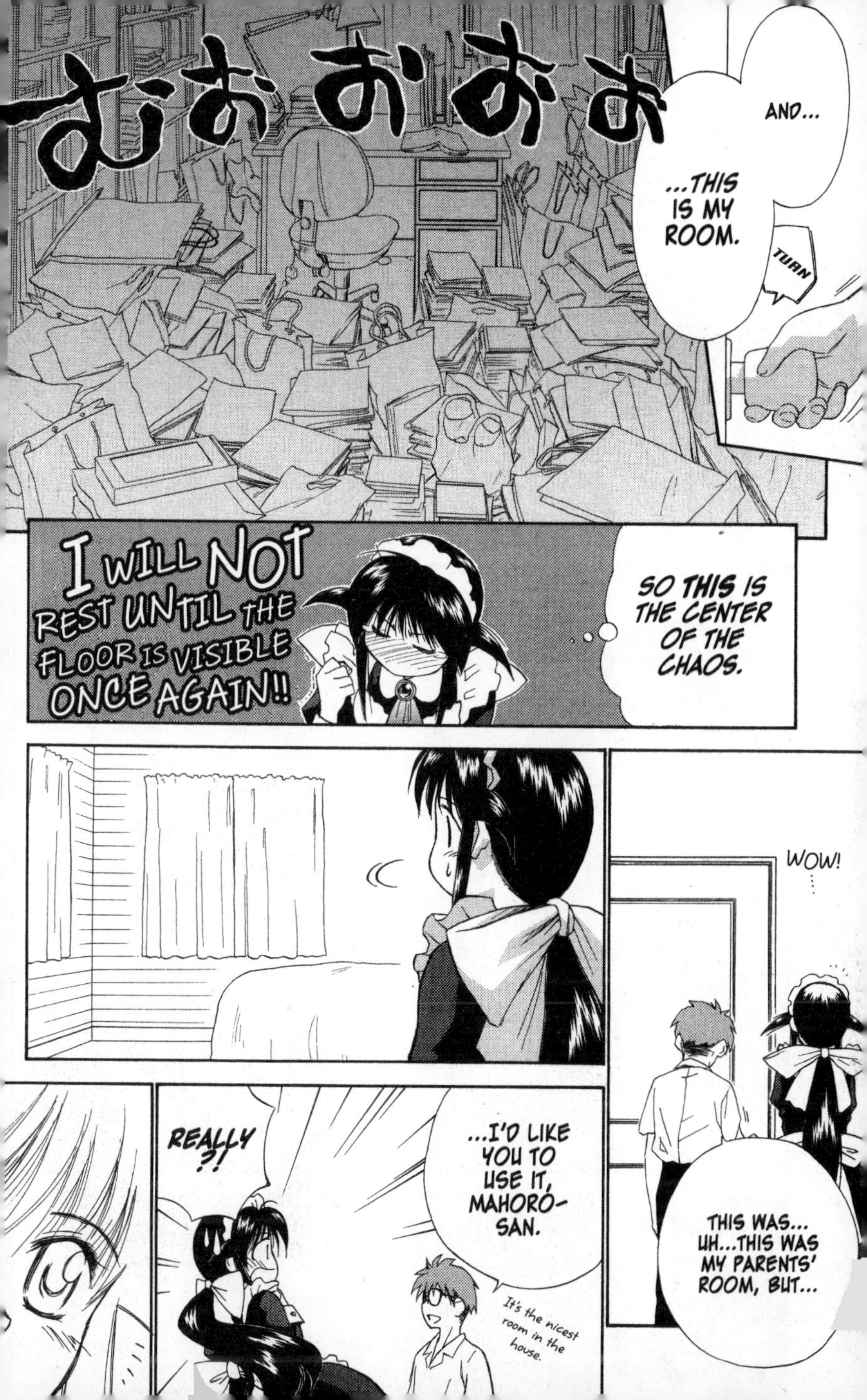
むぉおおお
AND...
...THIS IS MY ROOM.
TURN
SO THIS IS THE CENTER OF THE CHAOS.
I WILL NOT REST UNTIL THE FLOOR IS VISIBLE ONCE AGAIN!!
WOW! ...
THIS WAS... UH...THIS WAS MY PARENTS' ROOM, BUT...
...I'D LIKE YOU TO USE IT, MAHORO-SAN.
It's the nicest room in the house.
REALLY?!

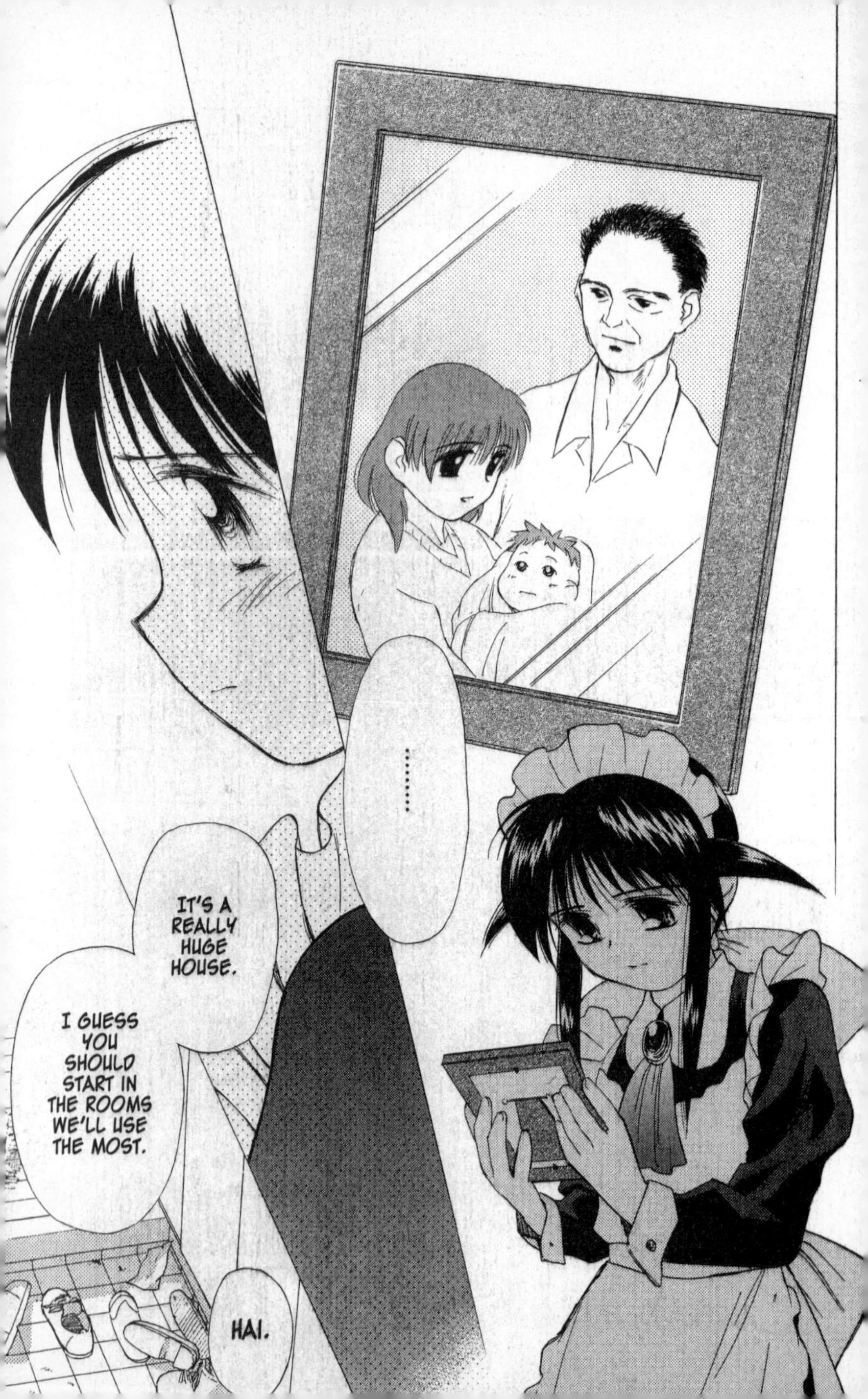
......
IT'S A REALLY HUGE HOUSE.
I GUESS YOU SHOULD START IN THE ROOMS WE'LL USE THE MOST.
HAI.

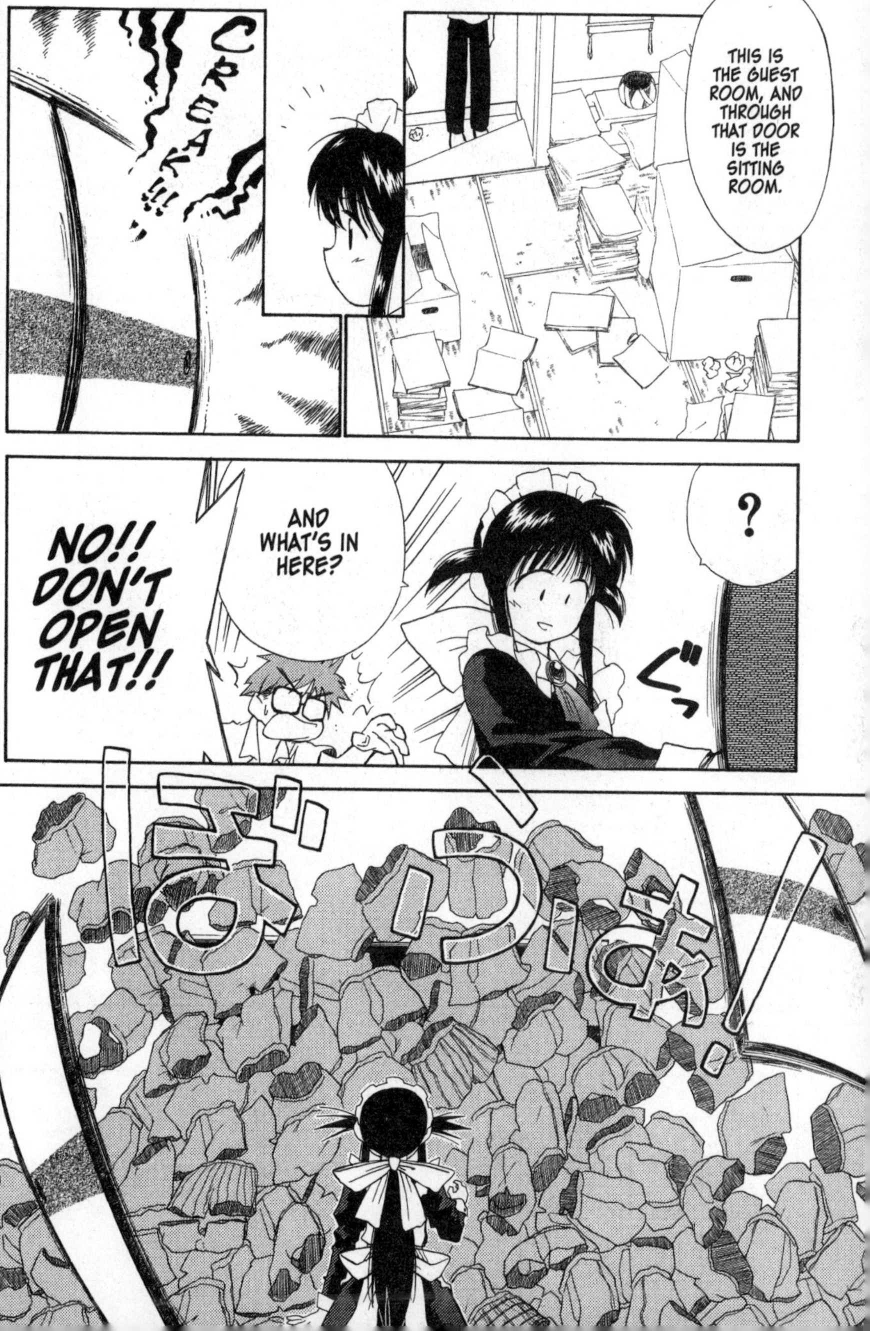
THIS IS THE GUEST ROOM, AND THROUGH THAT DOOR IS THE SITTING ROOM.
CREAK!!!
?
ぐっ
AND WHAT'S IN HERE?
NO!! DON'T OPEN THAT!!

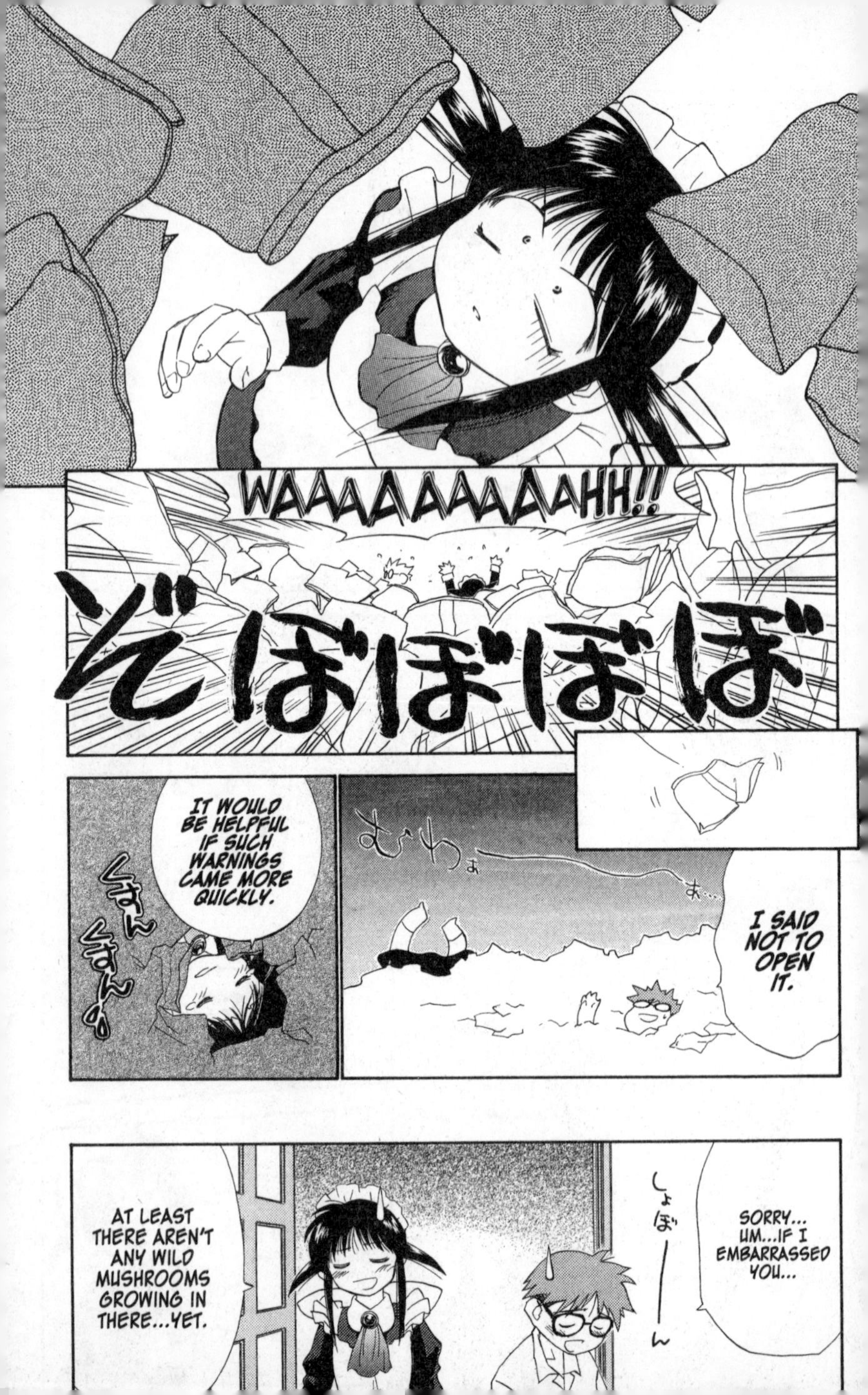
WAAAAAAAAAAHH!!
ぞぼぼぼぼ
むわぁ
ぁ…
I SAID NOT TO OPEN IT.
IT WOULD BE HELPFUL IF SUCH WARNINGS CAME MORE QUICKLY.
くすん くすん
しょぼーん
SORRY... UM...IF I EMBARRASSED YOU...
AT LEAST THERE AREN'T ANY WILD MUSHROOMS GROWING IN THERE...YET.

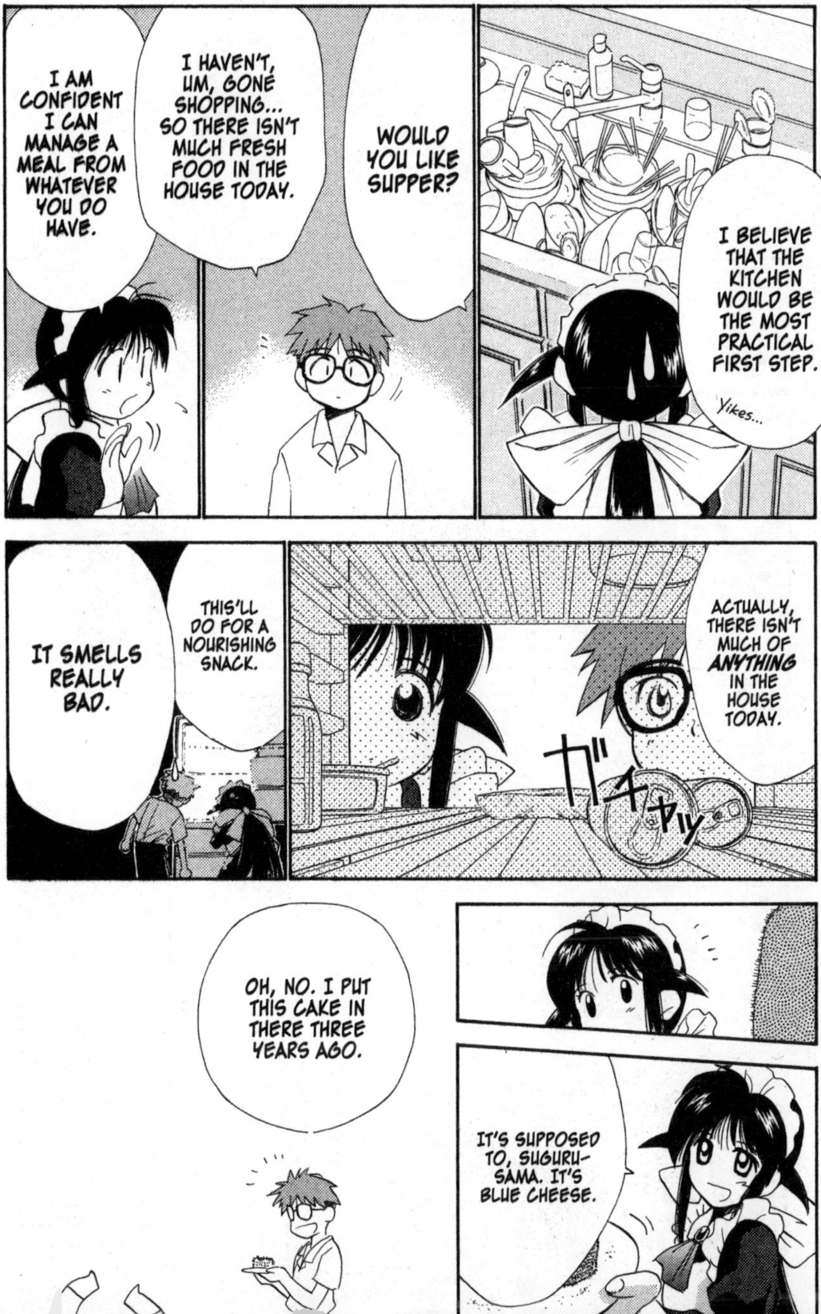
I BELIEVE THAT THE KITCHEN WOULD BE THE MOST PRACTICAL FIRST STEP.
Yikes...
WOULD YOU LIKE SUPPER?
I HAVEN'T, UM, GONE SHOPPING... SO THERE ISN'T MUCH FRESH FOOD IN THE HOUSE TODAY.
I AM CONFIDENT I CAN MANAGE A MEAL FROM WHATEVER YOU DO HAVE.
ACTUALLY, THERE ISN'T MUCH OF ANYTHING IN THE HOUSE TODAY.
THIS'LL DO FOR A NOURISHING SNACK.
IT SMELLS REALLY BAD.
OH, NO. I PUT THIS CAKE IN THERE THREE YEARS AGO.
IT'S SUPPOSED TO, SUGURU-SAMA. IT'S BLUE CHEESE.

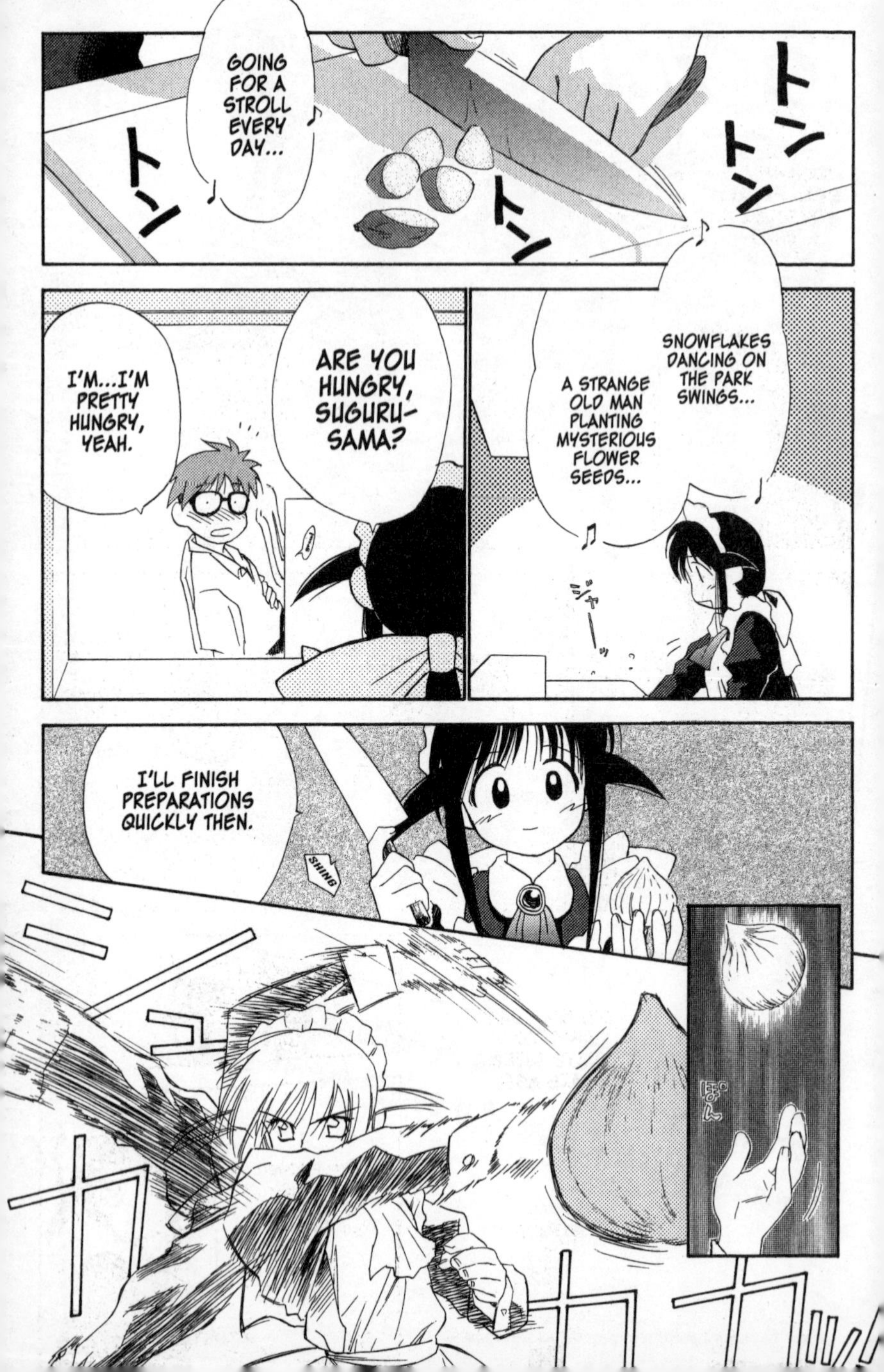
トン
トン
トン
トン
GOING FOR A STROLL EVERY DAY...
SNOWFLAKES DANCING ON THE PARK SWINGS...
A STRANGE OLD MAN PLANTING MYSTERIOUS FLOWER SEEDS...
ジャー
ARE YOU HUNGRY, SUGURU-SAMA?
I'M...I'M PRETTY HUNGRY, YEAH.
I'LL FINISH PREPARATIONS QUICKLY THEN.
SHING
ぽん

COMIC PARTY

Behind-the-scenes with artistic dreams and unconventional love at a comic convention

TEEN
AGE 13+

www.**TOKYOPOP**.com

The Story:

Kotarou Higuchi is an elementary school student whose mother died and whose father is often away on business. He is doing his best—and failing—on his exams, and his so-called life becomes even harder when his new neighbor Misha just won't leave him alone. She claims to be an angel...and she just might change his heart. Will Kotarou see that it's a wonderful life?

The Creator:

Koge-Donbo

Behind the Manga:

- A younger, cuter *Oh My Goddess!*
- From the best-selling creator of *DiGi Charat*.
- Inspired the hit anime.

Genre:

Romance

SRP:

€ 6.99

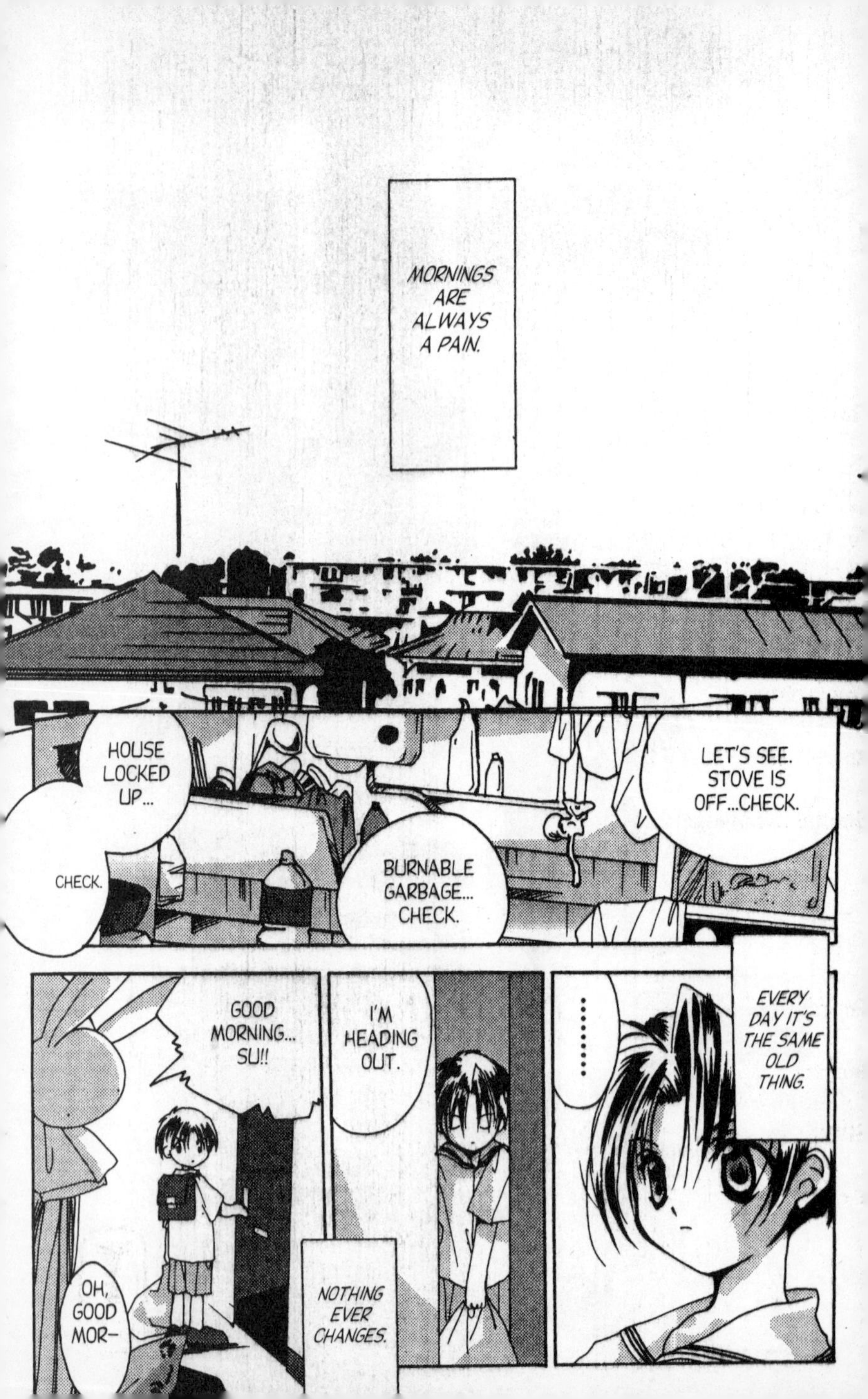
MORNINGS ARE ALWAYS A PAIN.
LET'S SEE. STOVE IS OFF...CHECK.
BURNABLE GARBAGE... CHECK.
HOUSE LOCKED UP...
CHECK.
EVERY DAY IT'S THE SAME OLD THING.
......
I'M HEADING OUT.
NOTHING EVER CHANGES.
GOOD MORNING... SU!!
OH, GOOD MOR–

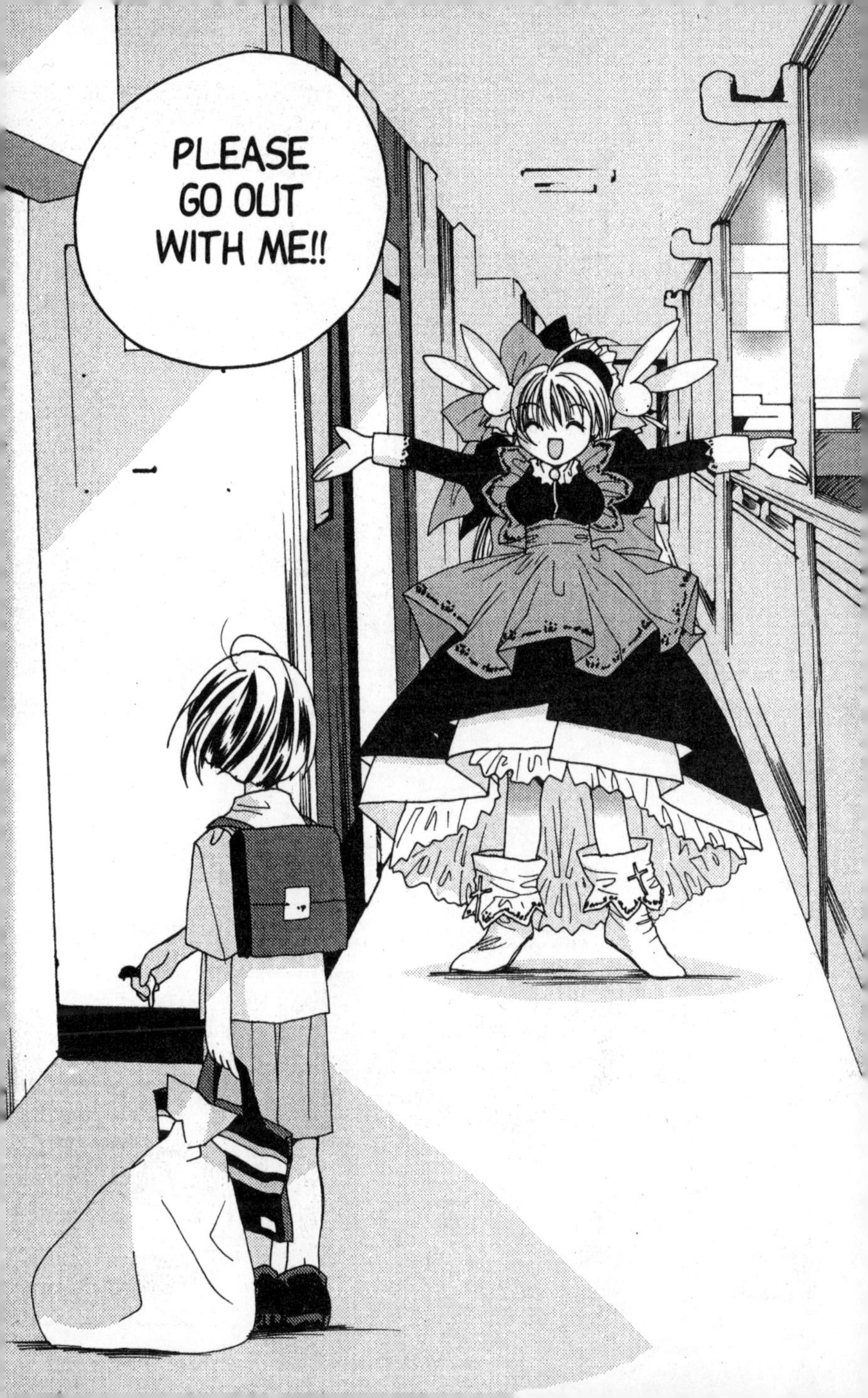
PLEASE GO OUT WITH ME!!

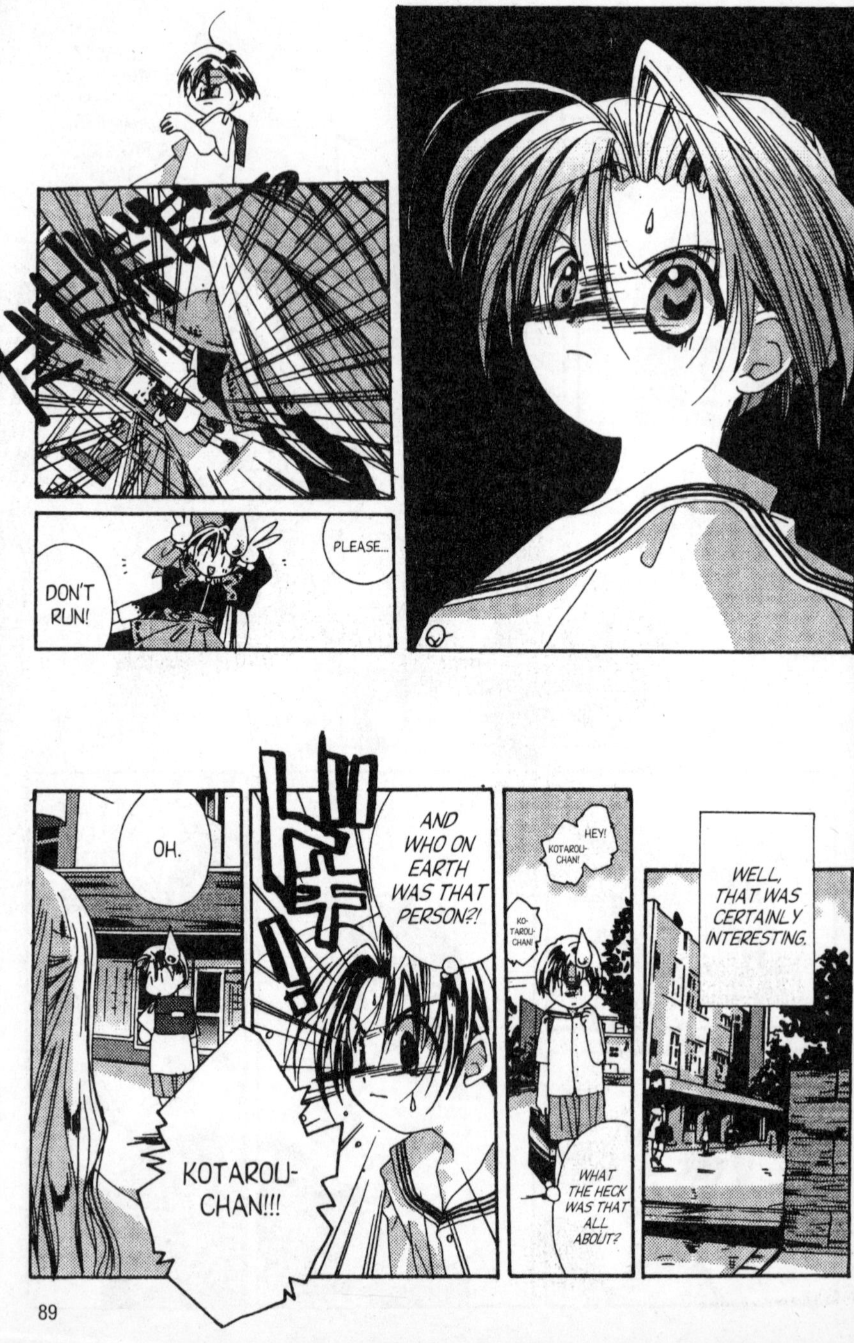
PLEASE...
DON'T RUN!
WELL, THAT WAS CERTAINLY INTERESTING.
HEY! KOTAROU-CHAN!
KO-TAROU-CHAN!
WHAT THE HECK WAS THAT ALL ABOUT?
AND WHO ON EARTH WAS THAT PERSON?!
OH.
KOTAROU-CHAN!!!

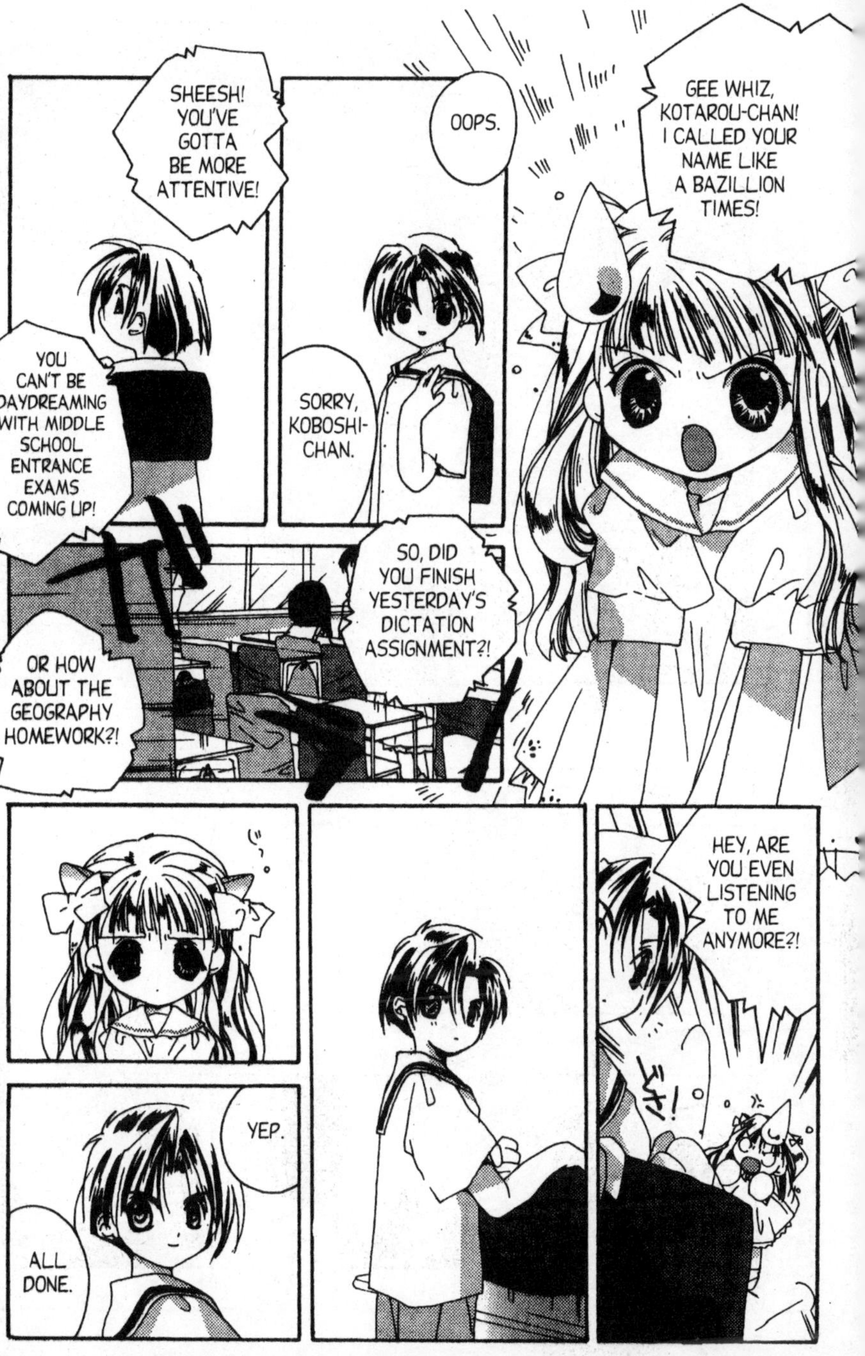
GEE WHIZ, KOTAROU-CHAN! I CALLED YOUR NAME LIKE A BAZILLION TIMES!
OOPS.
SORRY, KOBOSHI-CHAN.
SHEESH! YOU'VE GOTTA BE MORE ATTENTIVE!
YOU CAN'T BE DAYDREAMING WITH MIDDLE SCHOOL ENTRANCE EXAMS COMING UP!
SO, DID YOU FINISH YESTERDAY'S DICTATION ASSIGNMENT?!
OR HOW ABOUT THE GEOGRAPHY HOMEWORK?!
HEY, ARE YOU EVEN LISTENING TO ME ANYMORE?!
ドキ!
YEP.
ALL DONE.

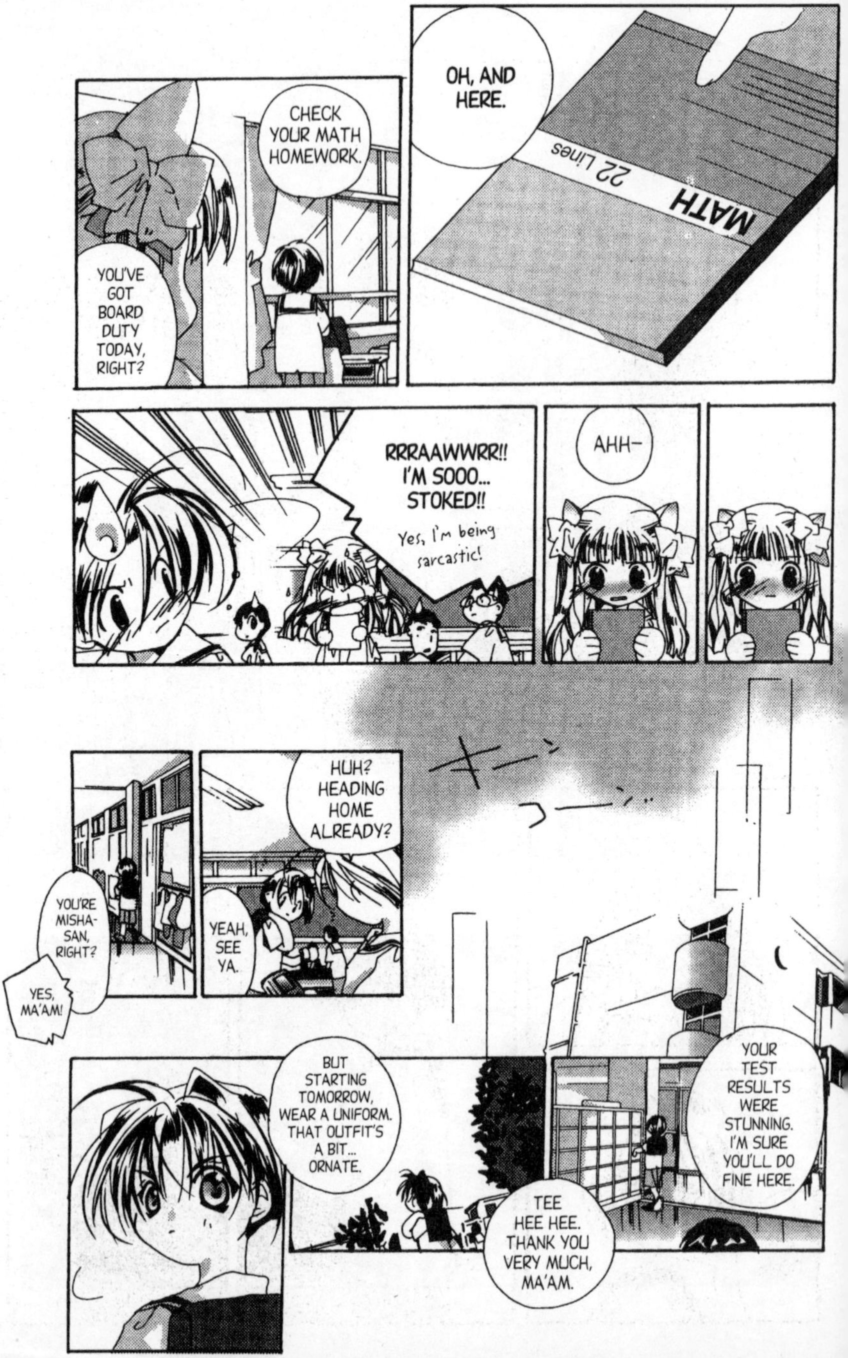
OH, AND HERE.
MATH
22 Lines
CHECK YOUR MATH HOMEWORK.
YOU'VE GOT BOARD DUTY TODAY, RIGHT?
AHH-
RRRAAWWRR!! I'M SOOO... STOKED!!
Yes, I'm being sarcastic!
HUH? HEADING HOME ALREADY?
YEAH, SEE YA.
YOU'RE MISHA-SAN, RIGHT?
YES, MA'AM!
YOUR TEST RESULTS WERE STUNNING. I'M SURE YOU'LL DO FINE HERE.
TEE HEE HEE. THANK YOU VERY MUCH, MA'AM.
BUT STARTING TOMORROW, WEAR A UNIFORM. THAT OUTFIT'S A BIT... ORNATE.

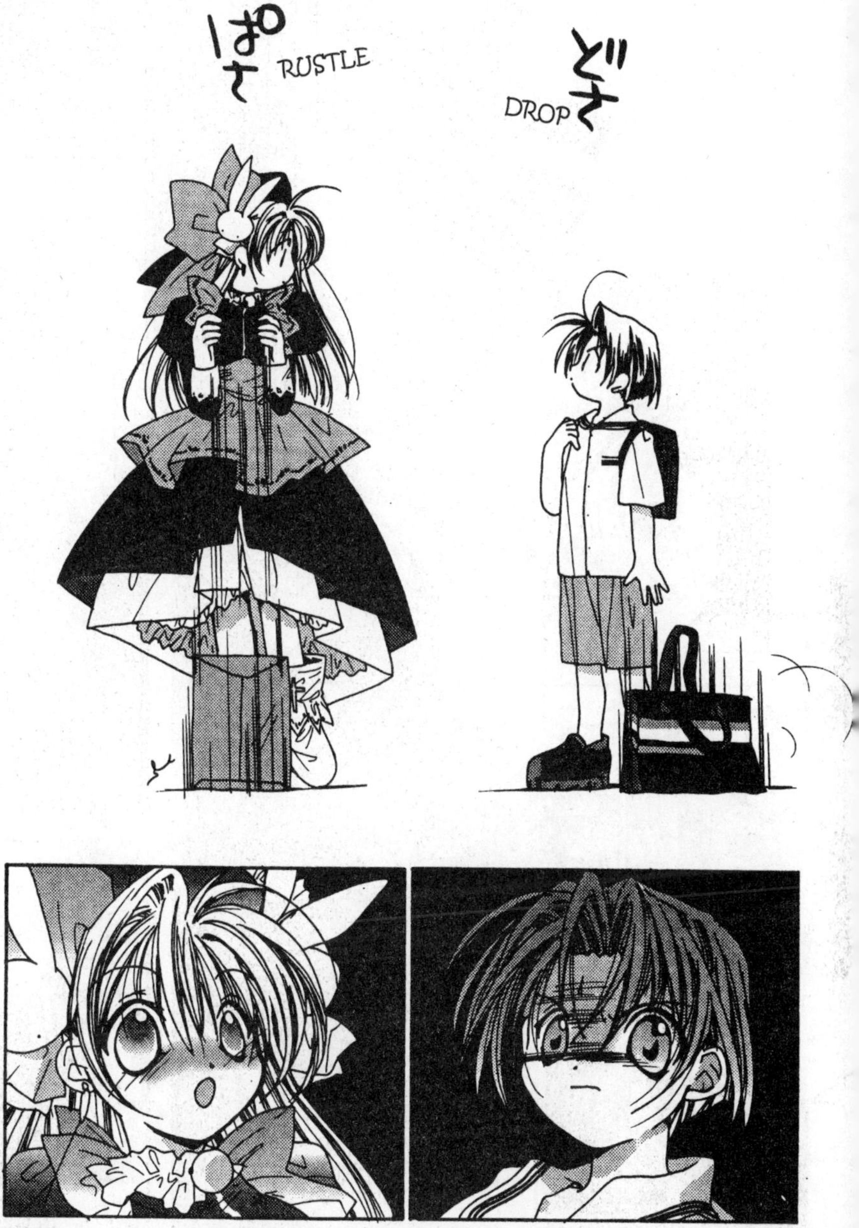
どさ
DROP
ぱさ
RUSTLE

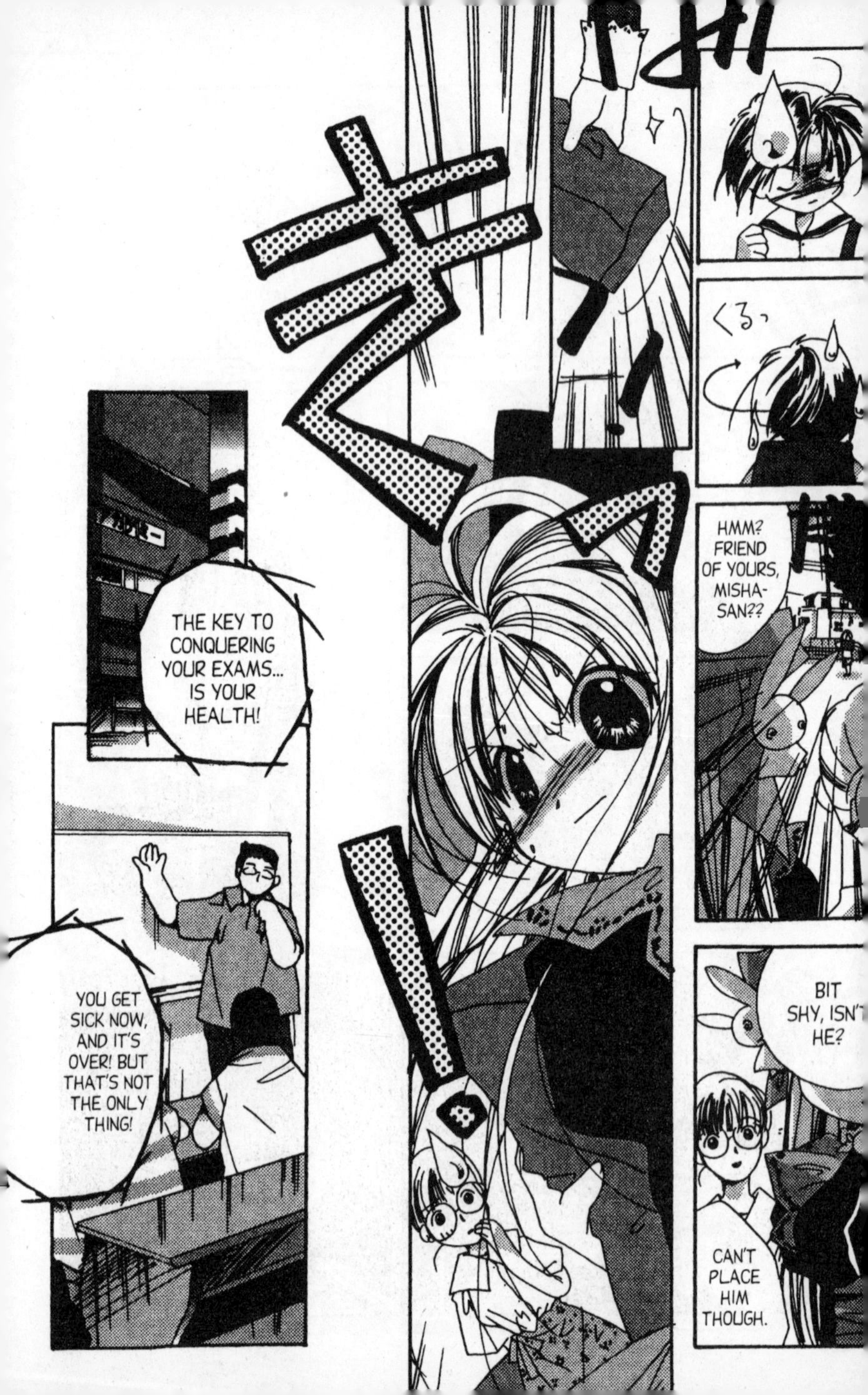
くるっ
HMM? FRIEND OF YOURS, MISHA-SAN??
BIT SHY, ISN'T HE?
CAN'T PLACE HIM THOUGH.
ギくッ!
THE KEY TO CONQUERING YOUR EXAMS... IS YOUR HEALTH!
YOU GET SICK NOW, AND IT'S OVER! BUT THAT'S NOT THE ONLY THING!

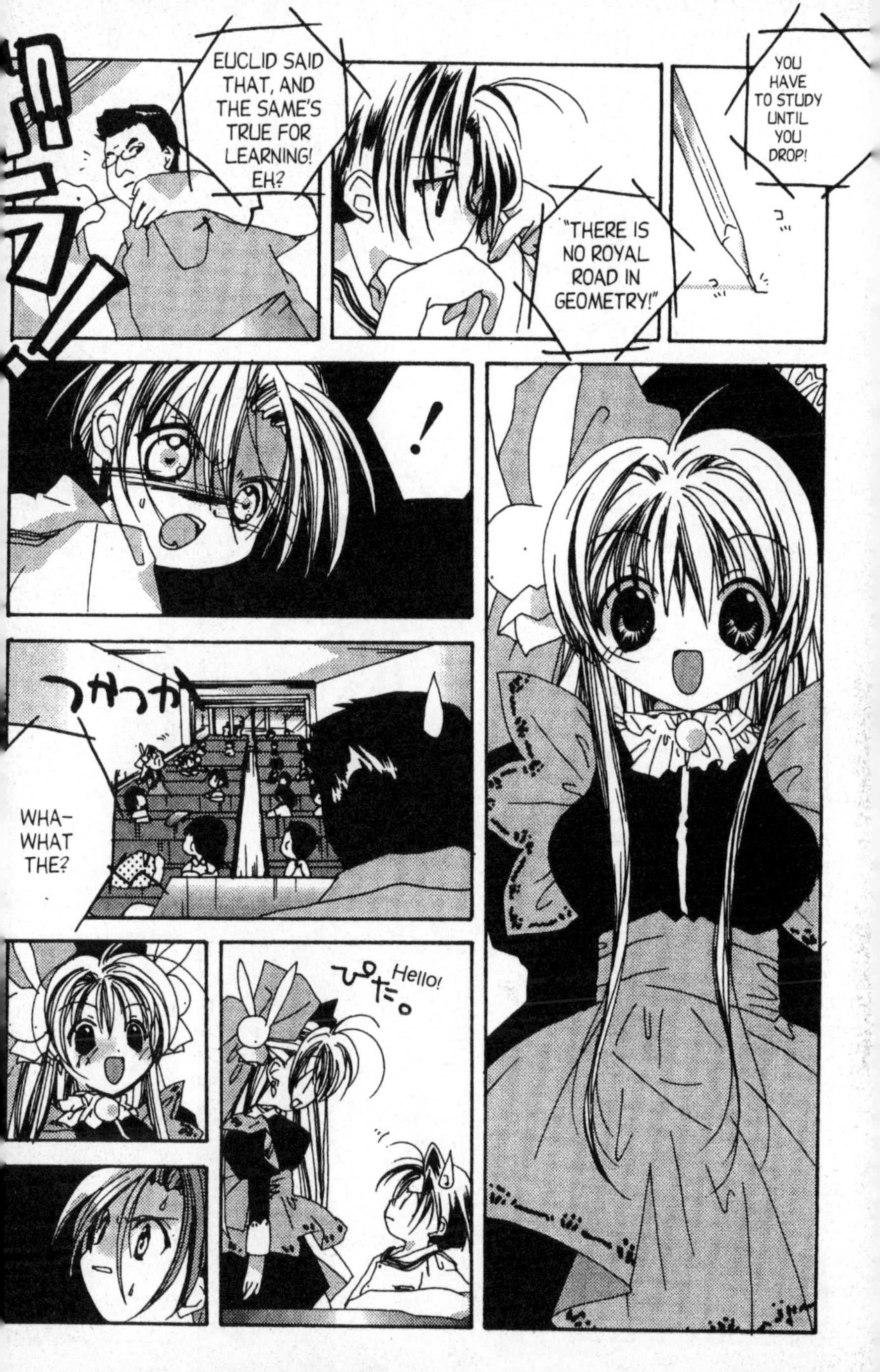
YOU HAVE TO STUDY UNTIL YOU DROP!
"THERE IS NO ROYAL ROAD IN GEOMETRY!"
EUCLID SAID THAT, AND THE SAME'S TRUE FOR LEARNING! EH?
!
つかつか
WHA- WHAT THE?
ぴた。
Hello!

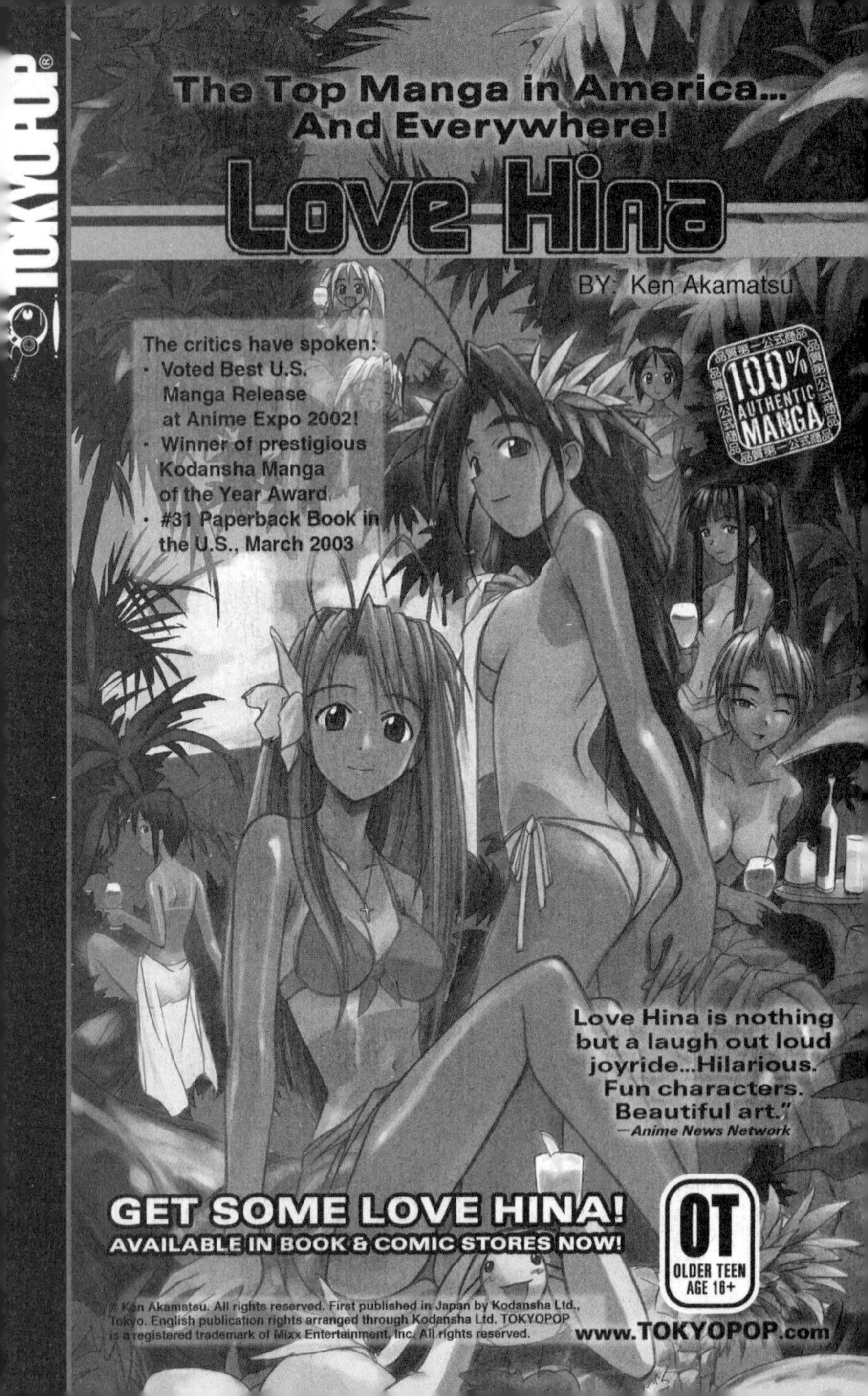
TOKYOPOP®
The Top Manga in America...
And Everywhere!
Love Hina
BY: Ken Akamatsu
The critics have spoken:
· Voted Best U.S. Manga Release at Anime Expo 2002!
· Winner of prestigious Kodansha Manga of the Year Award
· #31 Paperback Book in the U.S., March 2003
100% AUTHENTIC MANGA
Love Hina is nothing but a laugh out loud joyride...Hilarious. Fun characters. Beautiful art."
—Anime News Network
GET SOME LOVE HINA!
AVAILABLE IN BOOK & COMIC STORES NOW!
OT
OLDER TEEN AGE 16+
© Ken Akamatsu. All rights reserved. First published in Japan by Kodansha Ltd., Tokyo. English publication rights arranged through Kodansha Ltd. TOKYOPOP is a registered trademark of Mixx Entertainment, Inc. All rights reserved.
www.TOKYOPOP.com

The Story:

A Diva torn from Chaos; a Savior doomed to Love...
Take an amazing journey with a mysterious young woman who is
searching for identity and salvation in this world and beyond. Ai
finds herself lost, alone, and penniless on the cold, hard streets of
Tokyo. With flickers of memory, she must piece together clues about
who she is, how she ended up on Earth, and the secret of the ornate
heart-shaped box she carries with her. Sparks fly when Kent, a
complicated young college student, offers his help...and possibly
more. But time is running out as the clashing forces of love and
chaos close in around her.

The Creators:

Courtney Love, D.J. Milky and Misaho Kujiradou

Behind the Manga:

* Bonus 4 full-color pages.
* Character designs by Ai Yazawa, creator of *Paradise Kiss*.
* As serialized in *Wings* magazine, Japan.
* Reached #1 in Bookscan sales!

Genre:

Fantasy / Romance

SRP:

£ 6.99

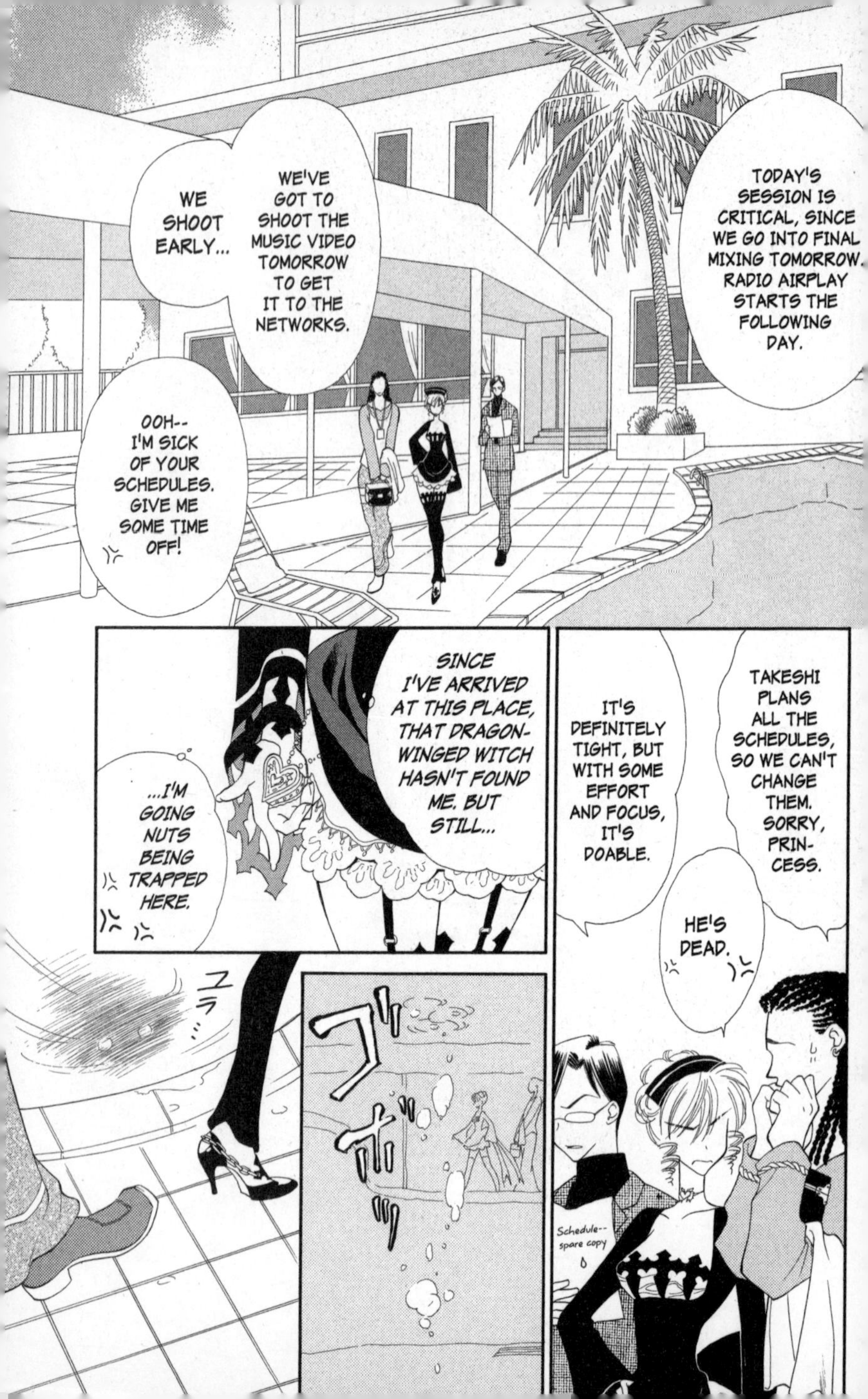
TODAY'S SESSION IS CRITICAL, SINCE WE GO INTO FINAL MIXING TOMORROW. RADIO AIRPLAY STARTS THE FOLLOWING DAY.
WE'VE GOT TO SHOOT THE MUSIC VIDEO TOMORROW TO GET IT TO THE NETWORKS.
WE SHOOT EARLY...
OOH-- I'M SICK OF YOUR SCHEDULES. GIVE ME SOME TIME OFF!
TAKESHI PLANS ALL THE SCHEDULES, SO WE CAN'T CHANGE THEM. SORRY, PRINCESS.
IT'S DEFINITELY TIGHT, BUT WITH SOME EFFORT AND FOCUS, IT'S DOABLE.
SINCE I'VE ARRIVED AT THIS PLACE, THAT DRAGON-WINGED WITCH HASN'T FOUND ME. BUT STILL...
...I'M GOING NUTS BEING TRAPPED HERE.
HE'S DEAD.
Schedule-- spare copy
ゴゴッ
ユラ...

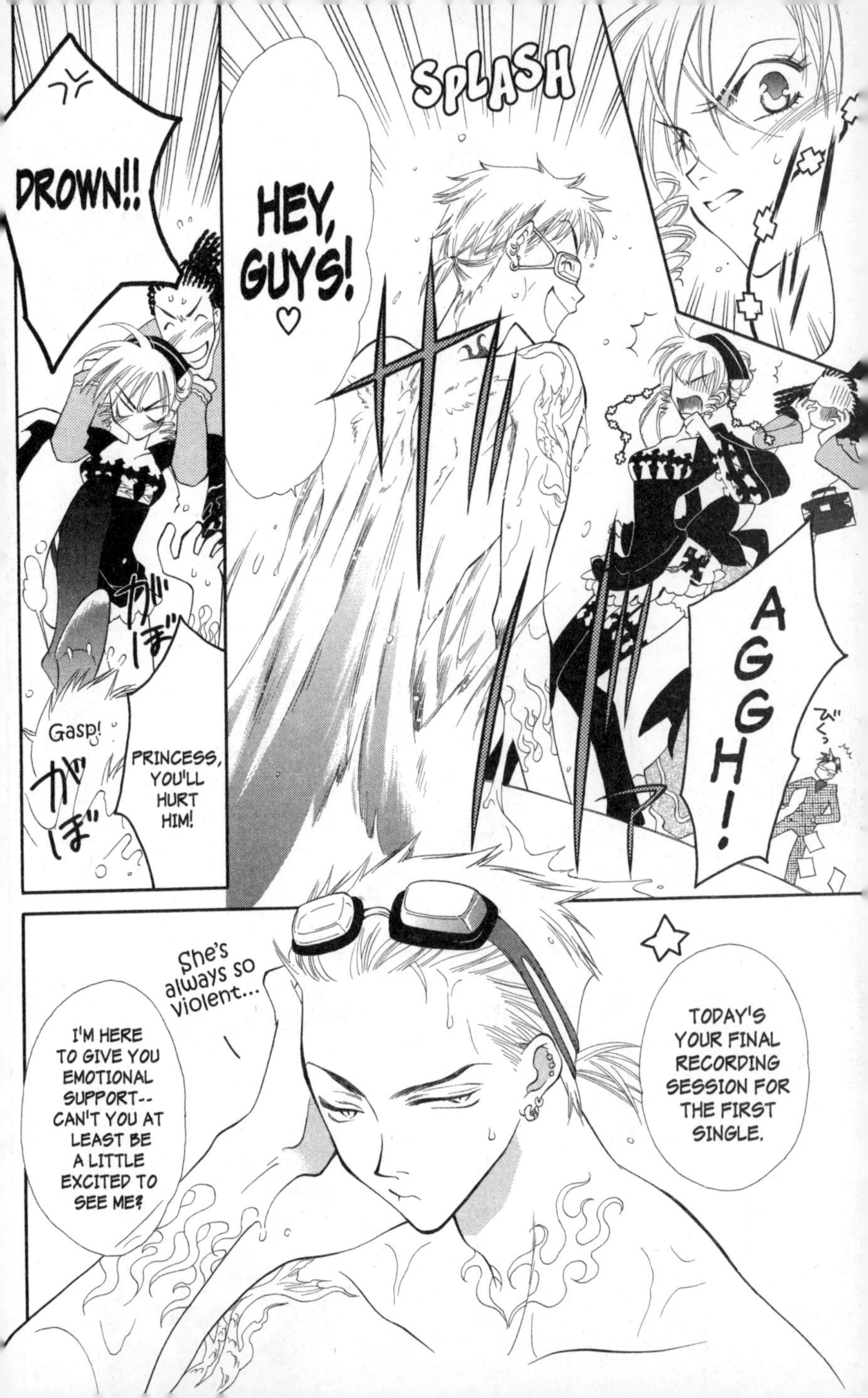
SPLASH
HEY, GUYS! ♡
AGGH!
びくっ
DROWN!!
がぼ
Gasp!
がぼ
PRINCESS, YOU'LL HURT HIM!
TODAY'S YOUR FINAL RECORDING SESSION FOR THE FIRST SINGLE.
She's always so violent...
I'M HERE TO GIVE YOU EMOTIONAL SUPPORT-- CAN'T YOU AT LEAST BE A LITTLE EXCITED TO SEE ME?

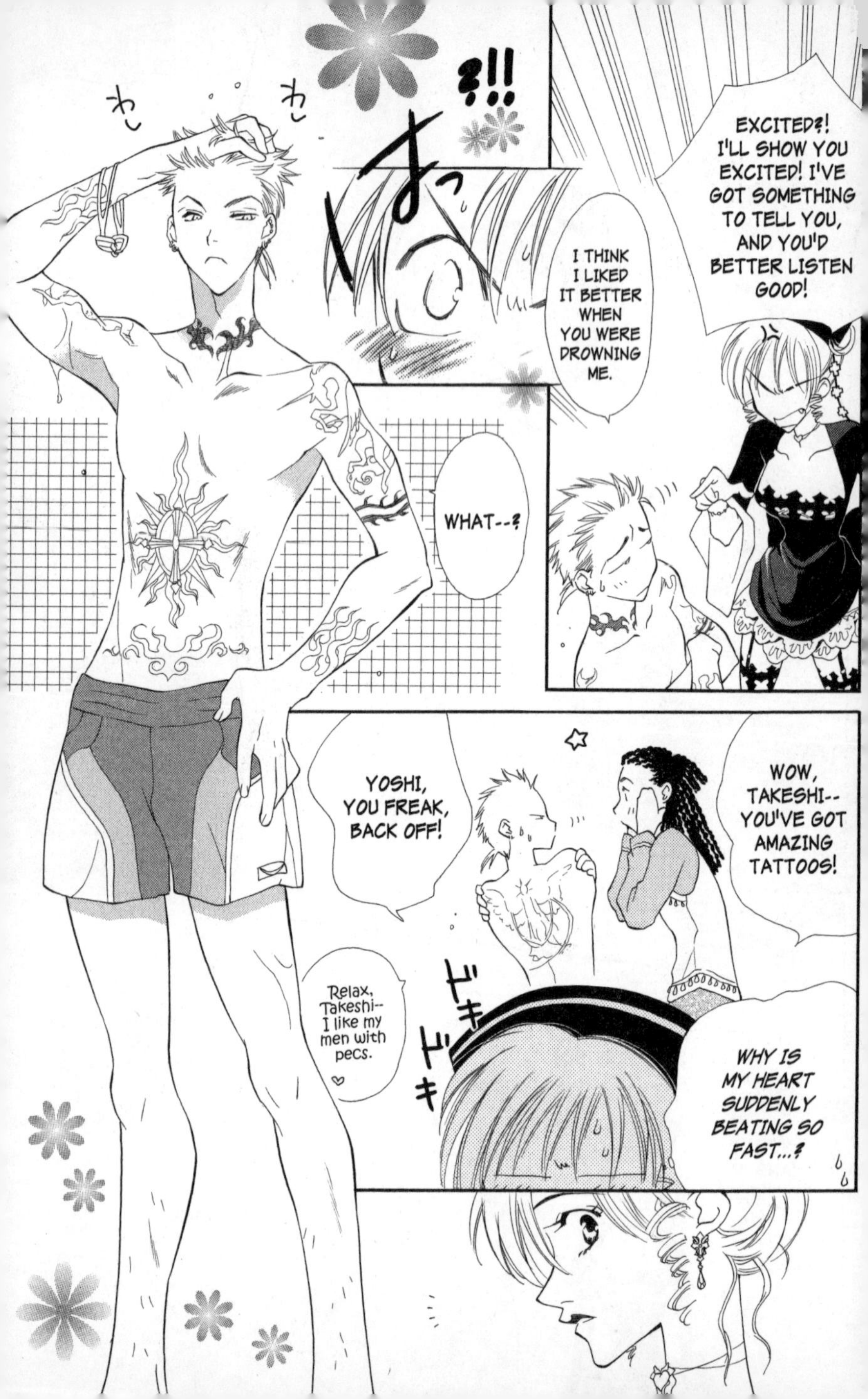
EXCITED?! I'LL SHOW YOU EXCITED! I'VE GOT SOMETHING TO TELL YOU, AND YOU'D BETTER LISTEN GOOD!
I THINK I LIKED IT BETTER WHEN YOU WERE DROWNING ME.
?!!
WHAT--?
WOW, TAKESHI-- YOU'VE GOT AMAZING TATTOOS!
YOSHI, YOU FREAK, BACK OFF!
Relax, Takeshi-- I like my men with pecs.
WHY IS MY HEART SUDDENLY BEATING SO FAST...?

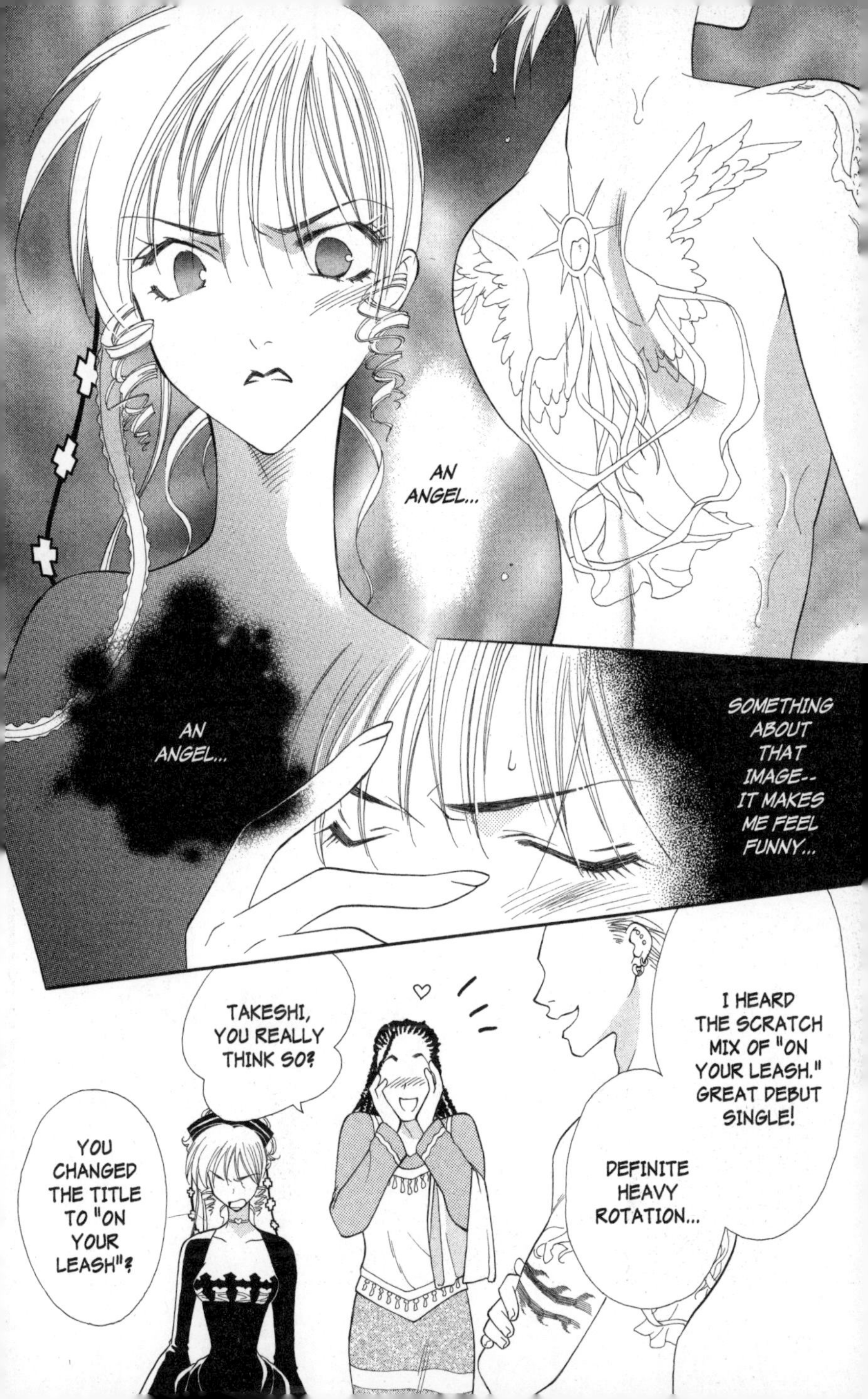
AN ANGEL...
AN ANGEL...
SOMETHING ABOUT THAT IMAGE-- IT MAKES ME FEEL FUNNY...
I HEARD THE SCRATCH MIX OF "ON YOUR LEASH." GREAT DEBUT SINGLE!
DEFINITE HEAVY ROTATION...
TAKESHI, YOU REALLY THINK SO?
YOU CHANGED THE TITLE TO "ON YOUR LEASH"?

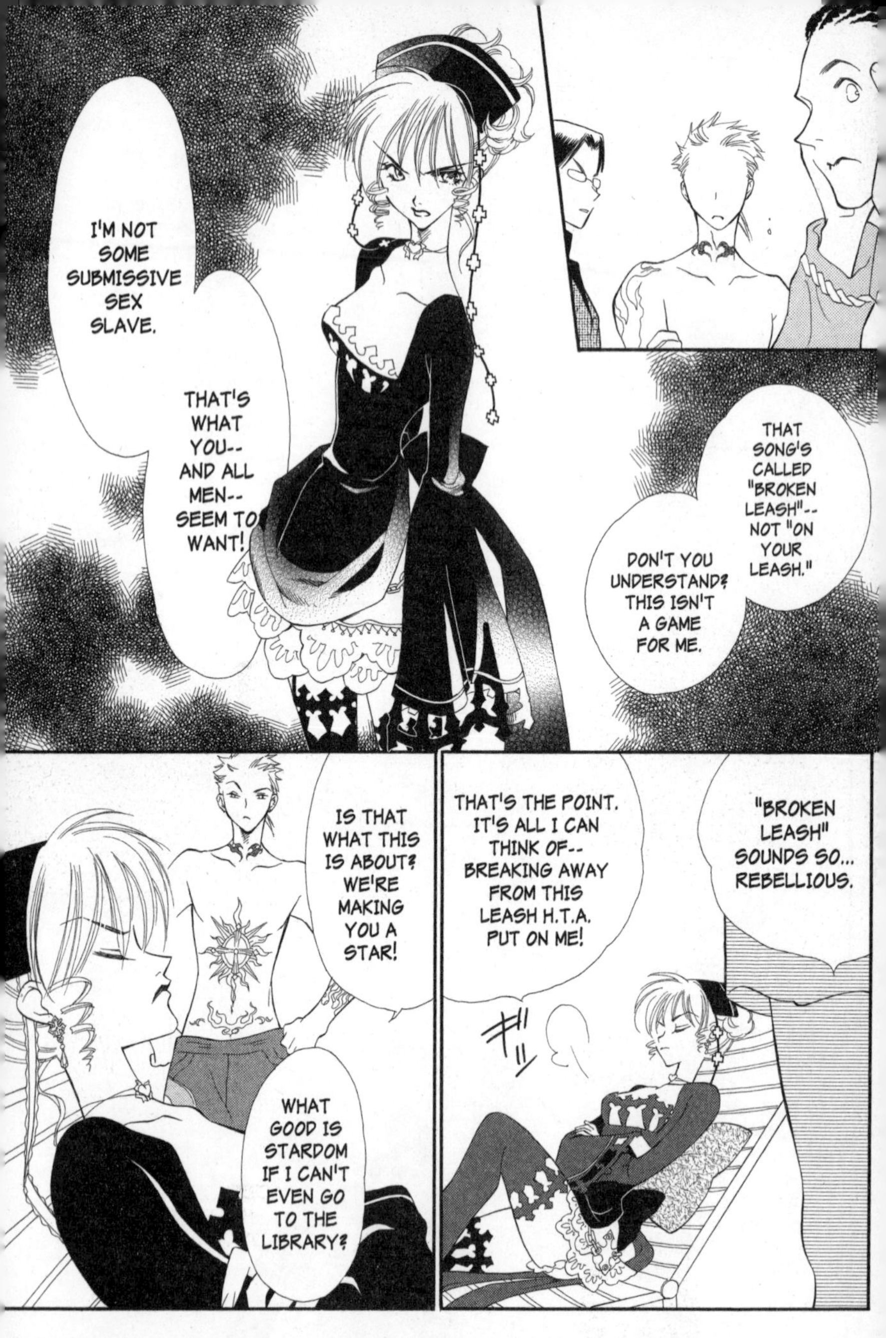
THAT SONG'S CALLED "BROKEN LEASH"-- NOT "ON YOUR LEASH."
DON'T YOU UNDERSTAND? THIS ISN'T A GAME FOR ME.
I'M NOT SOME SUBMISSIVE SEX SLAVE.
THAT'S WHAT YOU-- AND ALL MEN-- SEEM TO WANT!
"BROKEN LEASH" SOUNDS SO... REBELLIOUS.
THAT'S THE POINT. IT'S ALL I CAN THINK OF-- BREAKING AWAY FROM THIS LEASH H.T.A. PUT ON ME!
IS THAT WHAT THIS IS ABOUT? WE'RE MAKING YOU A STAR!
WHAT GOOD IS STARDOM IF I CAN'T EVEN GO TO THE LIBRARY?

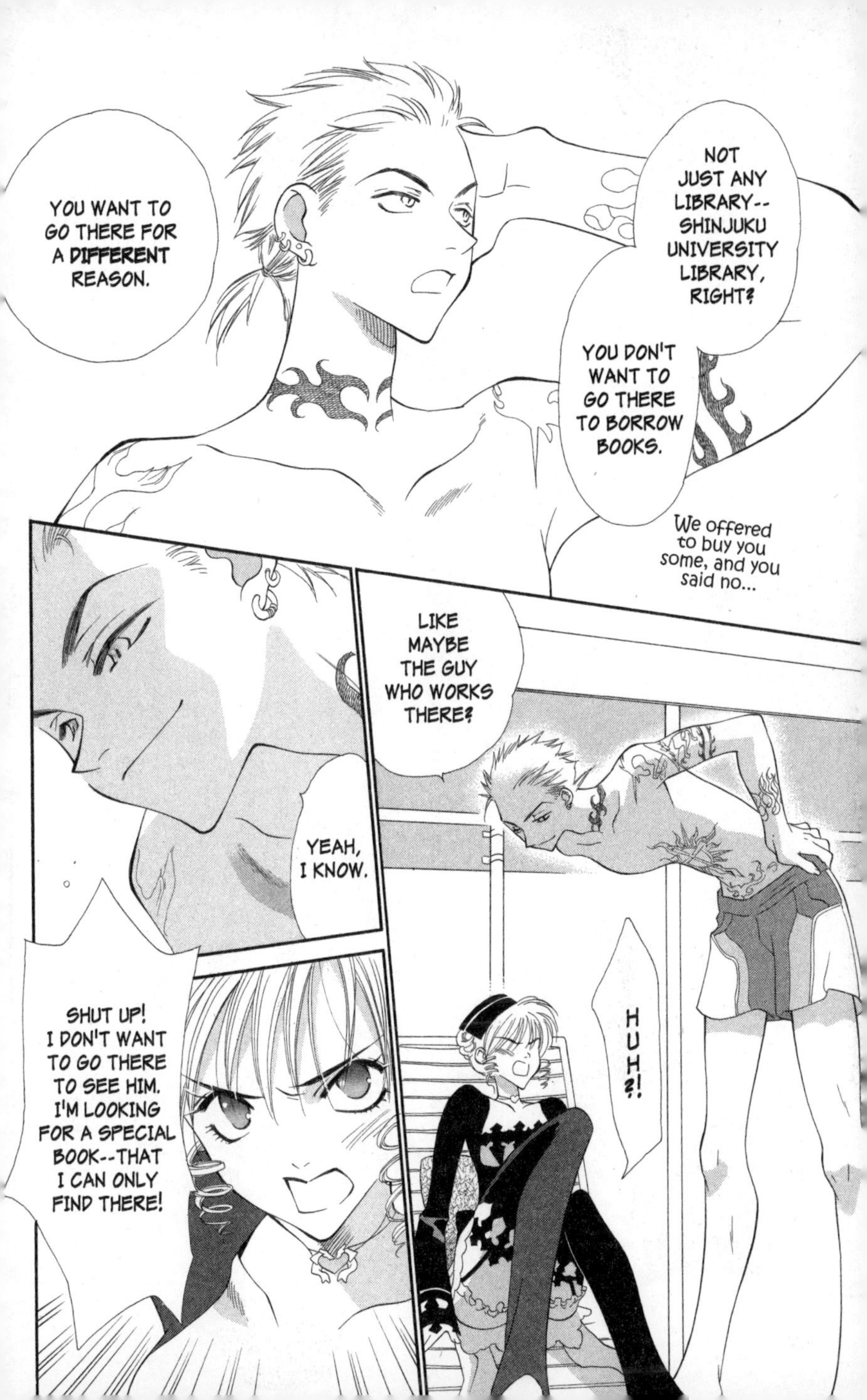

NOT JUST ANY LIBRARY--SHINJUKU UNIVERSITY LIBRARY, RIGHT?
YOU DON'T WANT TO GO THERE TO BORROW BOOKS.
YOU WANT TO GO THERE FOR A DIFFERENT REASON.
We offered to buy you some, and you said no...
LIKE MAYBE THE GUY WHO WORKS THERE?
HUH?!
YEAH, I KNOW.
SHUT UP! I DON'T WANT TO GO THERE TO SEE HIM. I'M LOOKING FOR A SPECIAL BOOK--THAT I CAN ONLY FIND THERE!

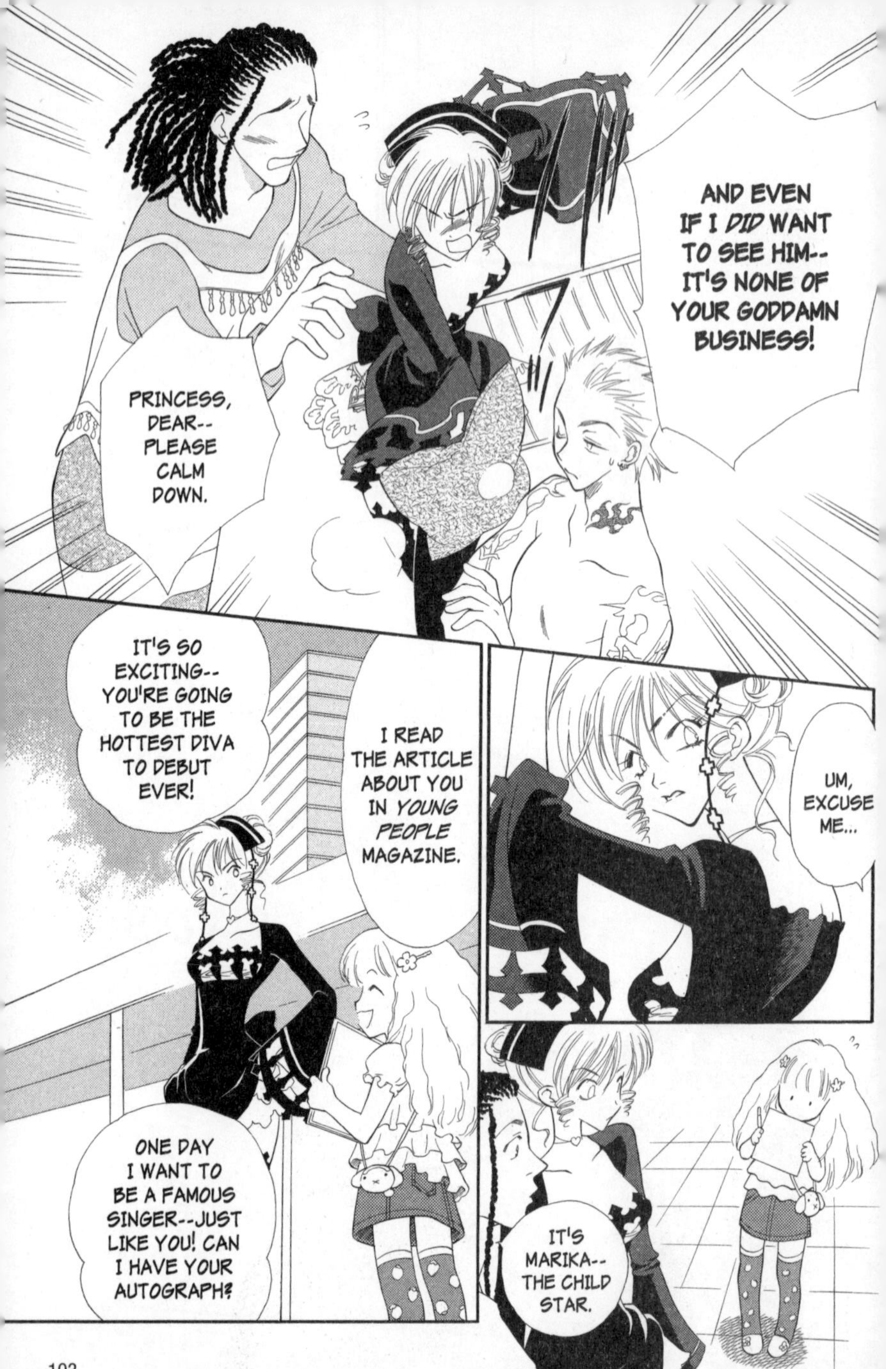
AND EVEN IF I *DID* WANT TO SEE HIM--IT'S NONE OF YOUR GODDAMN BUSINESS!
PRINCESS, DEAR--PLEASE CALM DOWN.
UM, EXCUSE ME...
IT'S MARIKA--THE CHILD STAR.
I READ THE ARTICLE ABOUT YOU IN *YOUNG PEOPLE* MAGAZINE.
IT'S SO EXCITING--YOU'RE GOING TO BE THE HOTTEST DIVA TO DEBUT EVER!
ONE DAY I WANT TO BE A FAMOUS SINGER--JUST LIKE YOU! CAN I HAVE YOUR AUTOGRAPH?

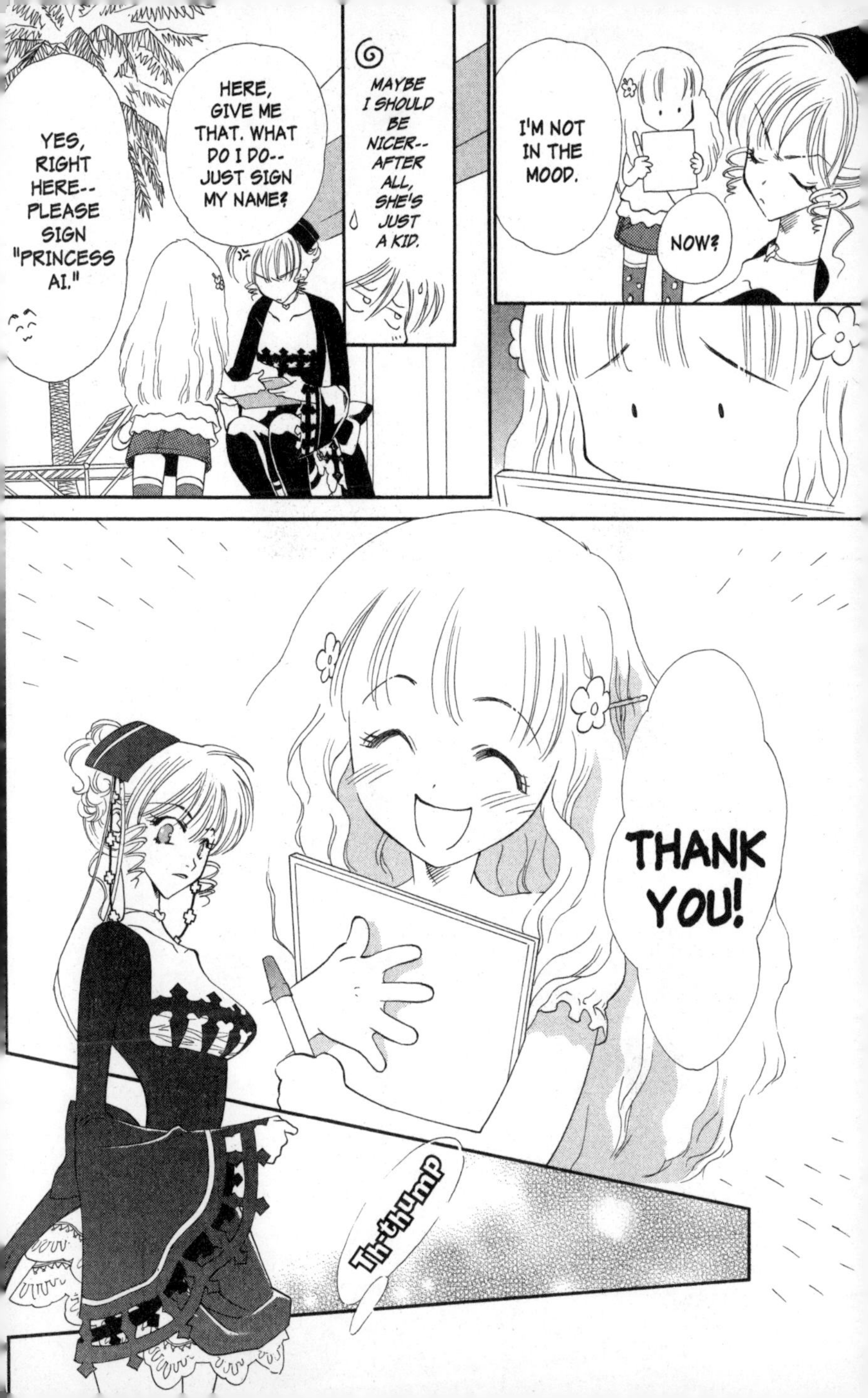
I'M NOT IN THE MOOD.
NOW?
MAYBE I SHOULD BE NICER-- AFTER ALL, SHE'S JUST A KID.
HERE, GIVE ME THAT. WHAT DO I DO-- JUST SIGN MY NAME?
YES, RIGHT HERE-- PLEASE SIGN "PRINCESS AI."
THANK YOU!
Th-thump

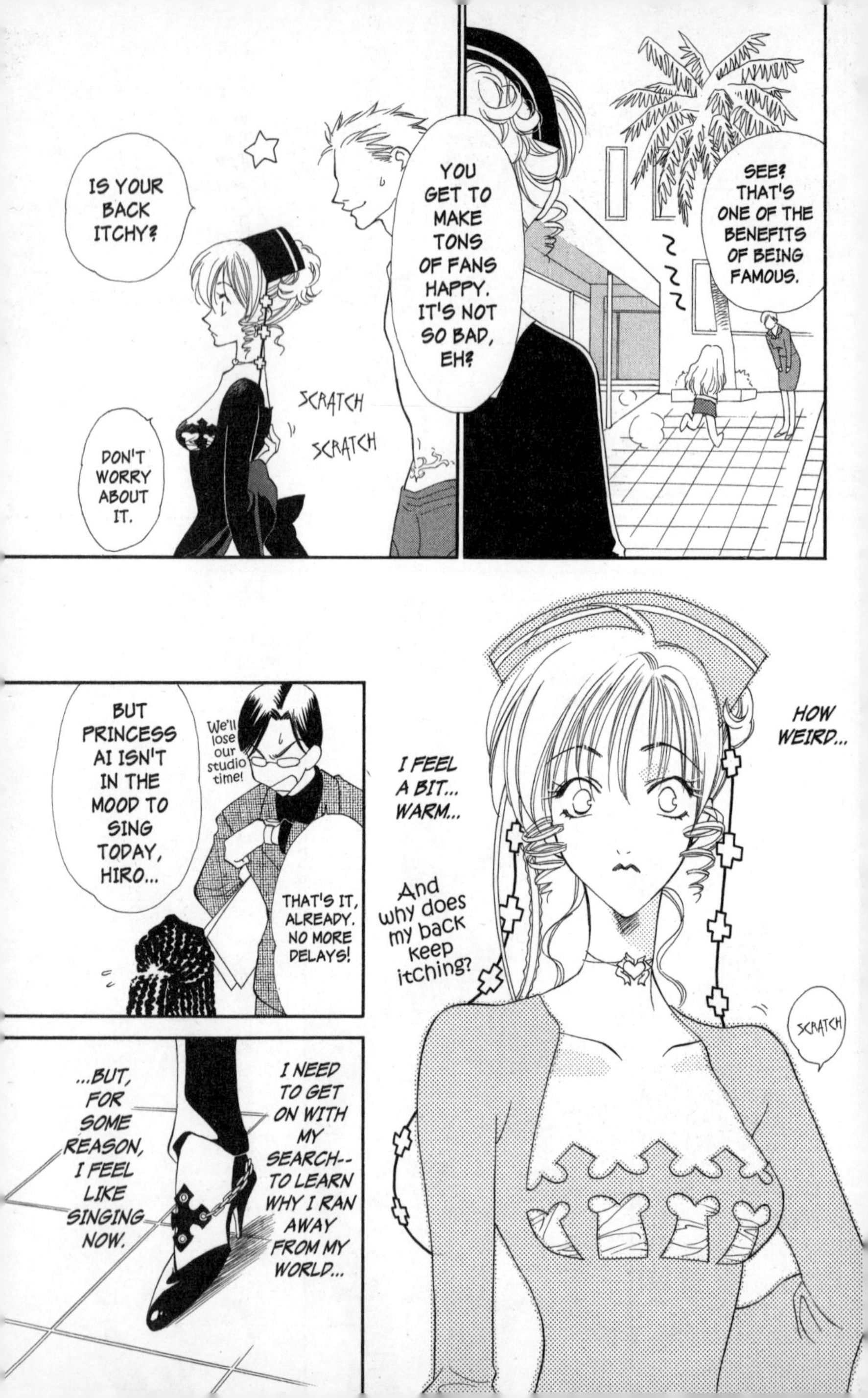
SEE? THAT'S ONE OF THE BENEFITS OF BEING FAMOUS.
YOU GET TO MAKE TONS OF FANS HAPPY. IT'S NOT SO BAD, EH?
IS YOUR BACK ITCHY?
SCRATCH
SCRATCH
DON'T WORRY ABOUT IT.
HOW WEIRD...
I FEEL A BIT... WARM...
And why does my back keep itching?
SCRATCH
BUT PRINCESS AI ISN'T IN THE MOOD TO SING TODAY, HIRO...
We'll lose our studio time!
THAT'S IT, ALREADY. NO MORE DELAYS!
I NEED TO GET ON WITH MY SEARCH-- TO LEARN WHY I RAN AWAY FROM MY WORLD...
...BUT, FOR SOME REASON, I FEEL LIKE SINGING NOW.

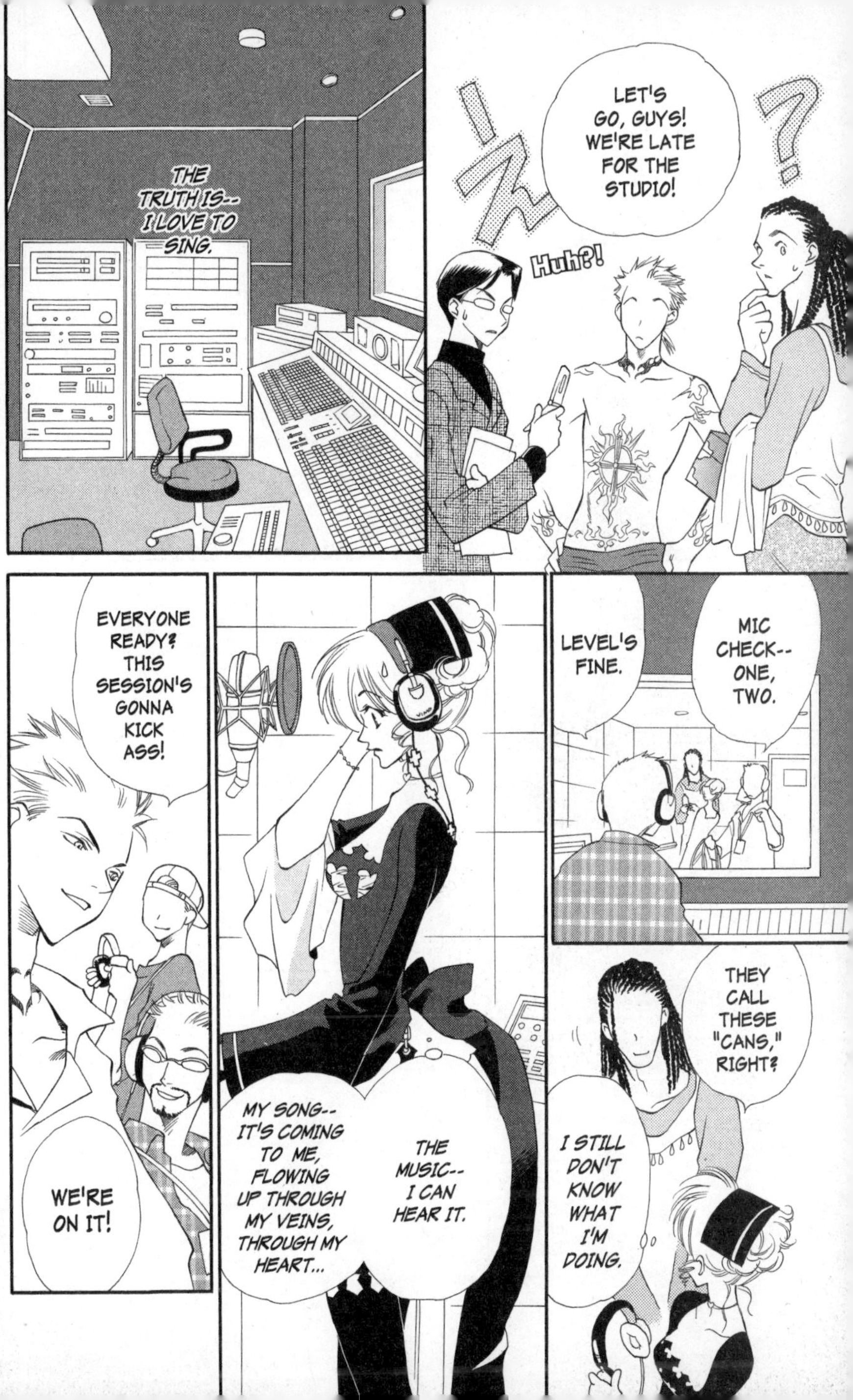
LET'S GO, GUYS! WE'RE LATE FOR THE STUDIO!
Huh?!
THE TRUTH IS-- I LOVE TO SING.
MIC CHECK-- ONE, TWO.
LEVEL'S FINE.
THEY CALL THESE "CANS," RIGHT?
I STILL DON'T KNOW WHAT I'M DOING.
THE MUSIC-- I CAN HEAR IT.
MY SONG-- IT'S COMING TO ME, FLOWING UP THROUGH MY VEINS, THROUGH MY HEART...
EVERYONE READY? THIS SESSION'S GONNA KICK ASS!
WE'RE ON IT!

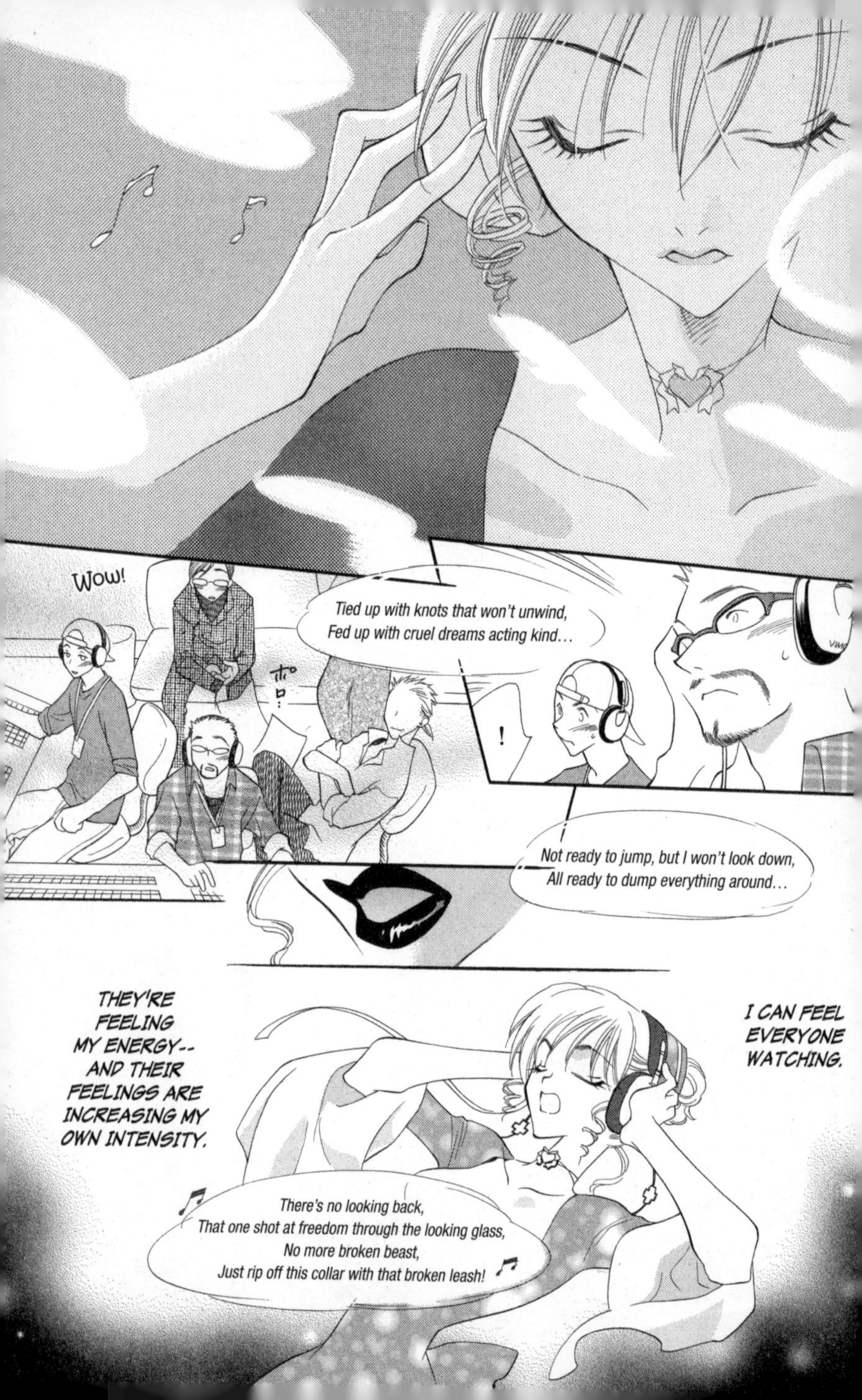
Tied up with knots that won't unwind, Fed up with cruel dreams acting kind...
!
WOW!
Not ready to jump, but I won't look down, All ready to dump everything around...
I CAN FEEL EVERYONE WATCHING.
THEY'RE FEELING MY ENERGY-- AND THEIR FEELINGS ARE INCREASING MY OWN INTENSITY.
There's no looking back, That one shot at freedom through the looking glass, No more broken beast, Just rip off this collar with that broken leash!

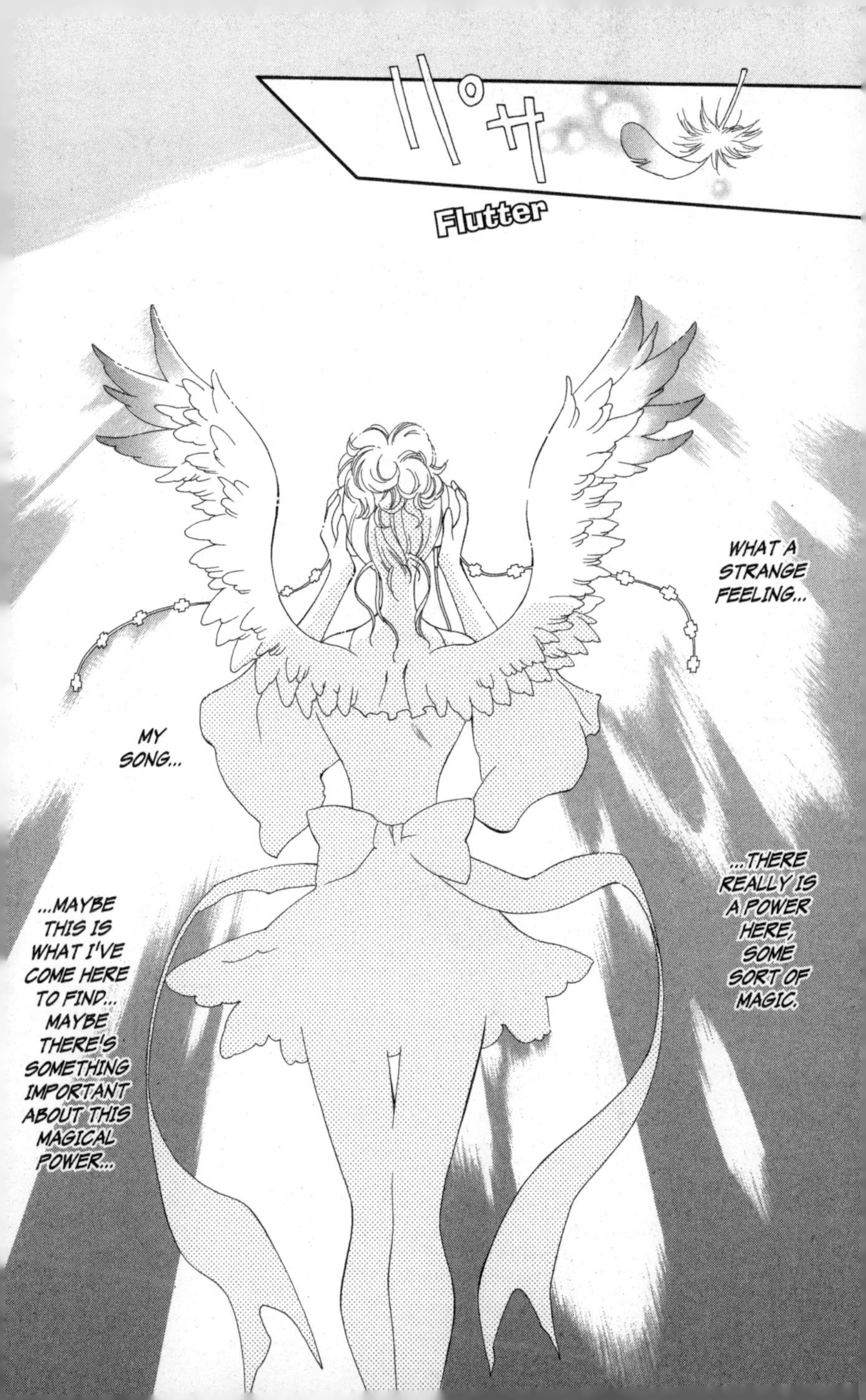
パサ
Flutter
WHAT A STRANGE FEELING...
...THERE REALLY IS A POWER HERE, SOME SORT OF MAGIC.
MY SONG...
...MAYBE THIS IS WHAT I'VE COME HERE TO FIND... MAYBE THERE'S SOMETHING IMPORTANT ABOUT THIS MAGICAL POWER...

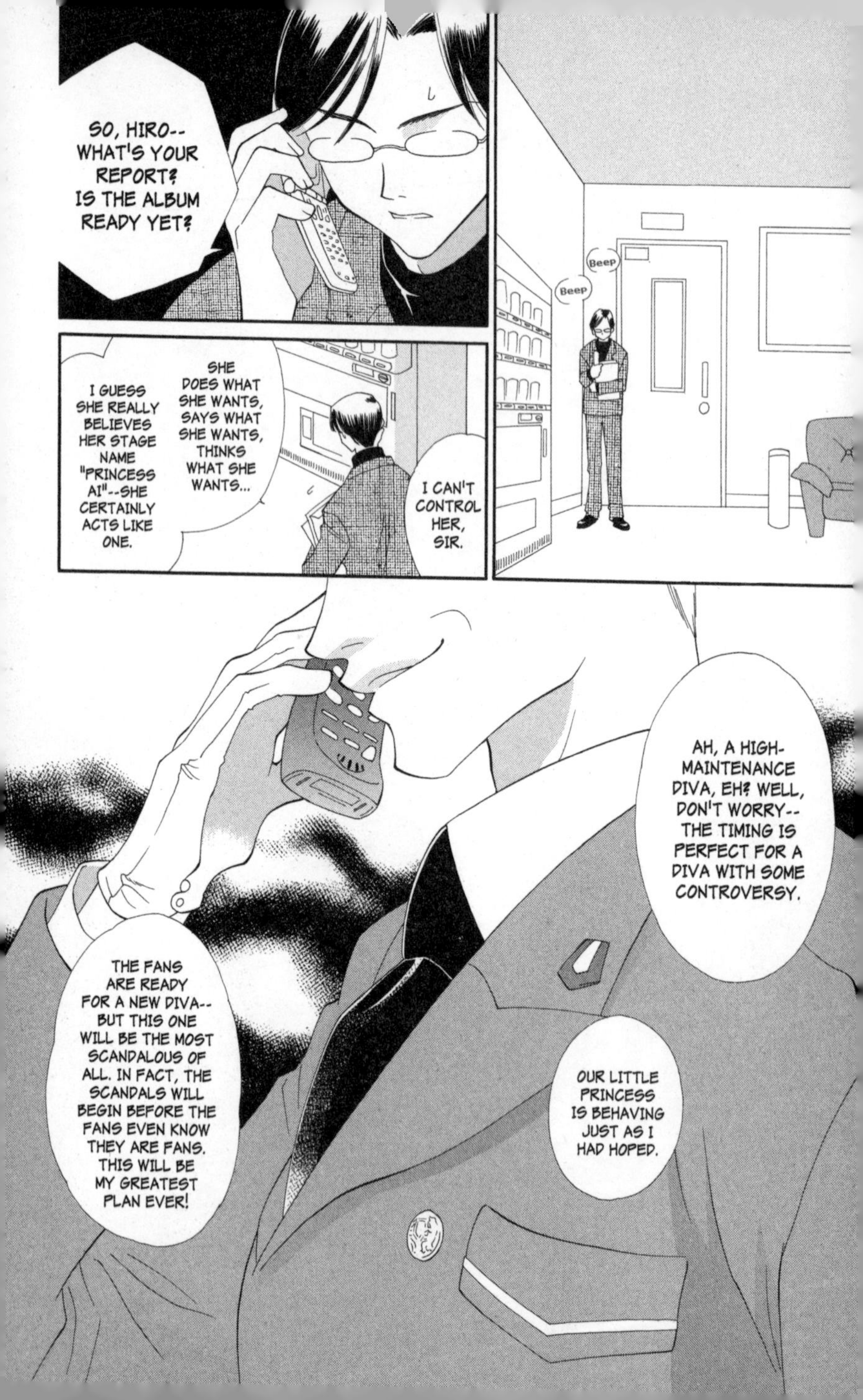
Beep
Beep
SO, HIRO-- WHAT'S YOUR REPORT? IS THE ALBUM READY YET?
I CAN'T CONTROL HER, SIR.
SHE DOES WHAT SHE WANTS, SAYS WHAT SHE WANTS, THINKS WHAT SHE WANTS...
I GUESS SHE REALLY BELIEVES HER STAGE NAME "PRINCESS AI"--SHE CERTAINLY ACTS LIKE ONE.
AH, A HIGH-MAINTENANCE DIVA, EH? WELL, DON'T WORRY-- THE TIMING IS PERFECT FOR A DIVA WITH SOME CONTROVERSY.
OUR LITTLE PRINCESS IS BEHAVING JUST AS I HAD HOPED.
THE FANS ARE READY FOR A NEW DIVA-- BUT THIS ONE WILL BE THE MOST SCANDALOUS OF ALL. IN FACT, THE SCANDALS WILL BEGIN BEFORE THE FANS EVEN KNOW THEY ARE FANS. THIS WILL BE MY GREATEST PLAN EVER!

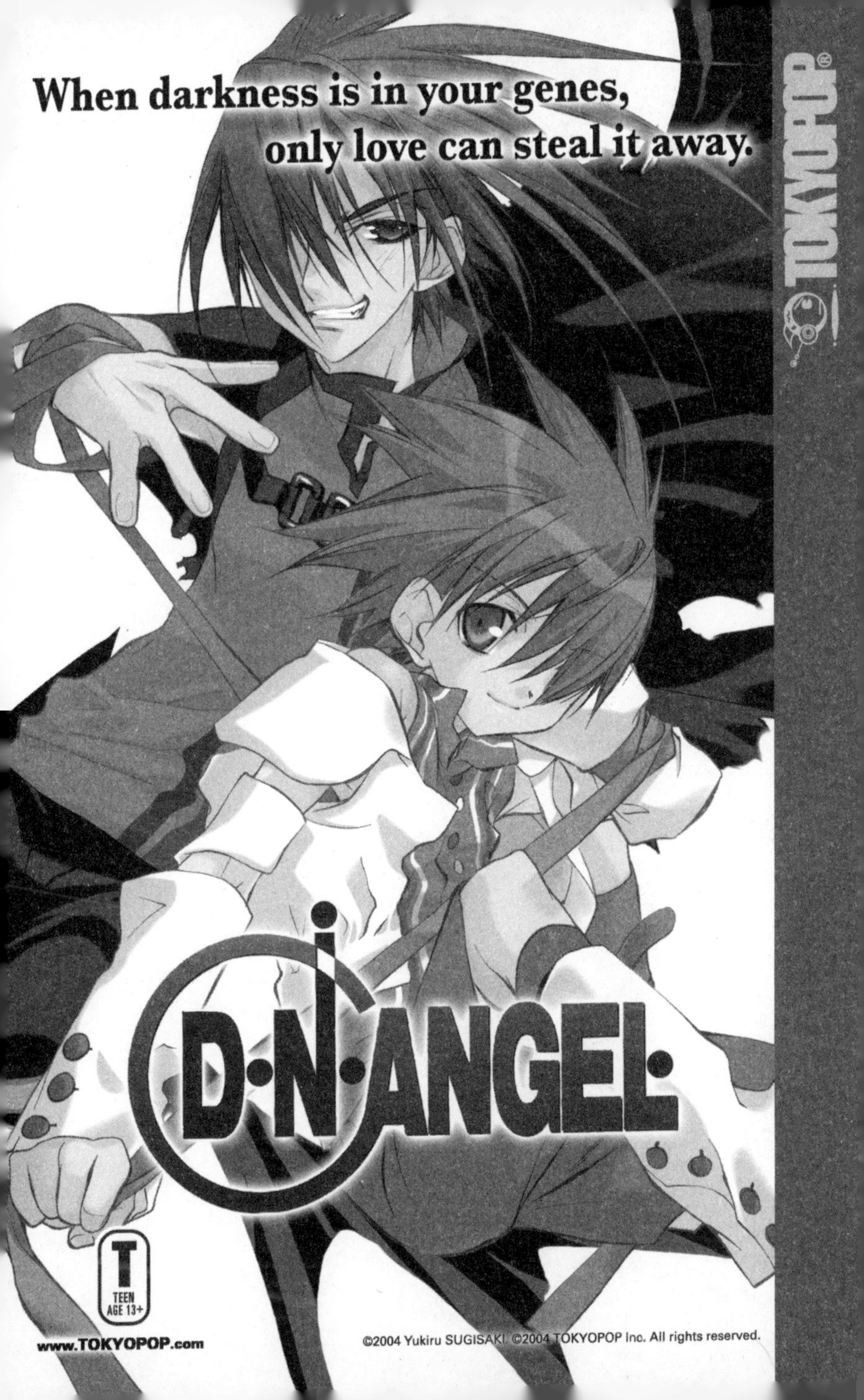

When darkness is in your genes,
only love can steal it away.
TOKYOPOP
D•N•ANGEL
T
TEEN
AGE 13+
www.TOKYOPOP.com
©2004 Yukiru SUGISAKI. ©2004 TOKYOPOP Inc. All rights reserved.

The Story:

In the mystical land of ancient China, where magical beings intermingle with everyday life, Qwan is a strange boy who devours demons and absorbs their powers. However, he's looking for more than a quick bite. Qwan's quest is to find the sutra known as the Essential Arts of Peace—an ancient scroll that will reveal the ultimate purpose of his existence!

The Creator:

Aki Shimizu

Behind the Manga:

• From the artist of Suikoden III: The Successor of Fate.
• Fantastic art and quirky characters all wrapped up in high adventure!
• Demons...they're not just for breakfast anymore.

Genre:

Fantasy

SRP:

£ 6.99

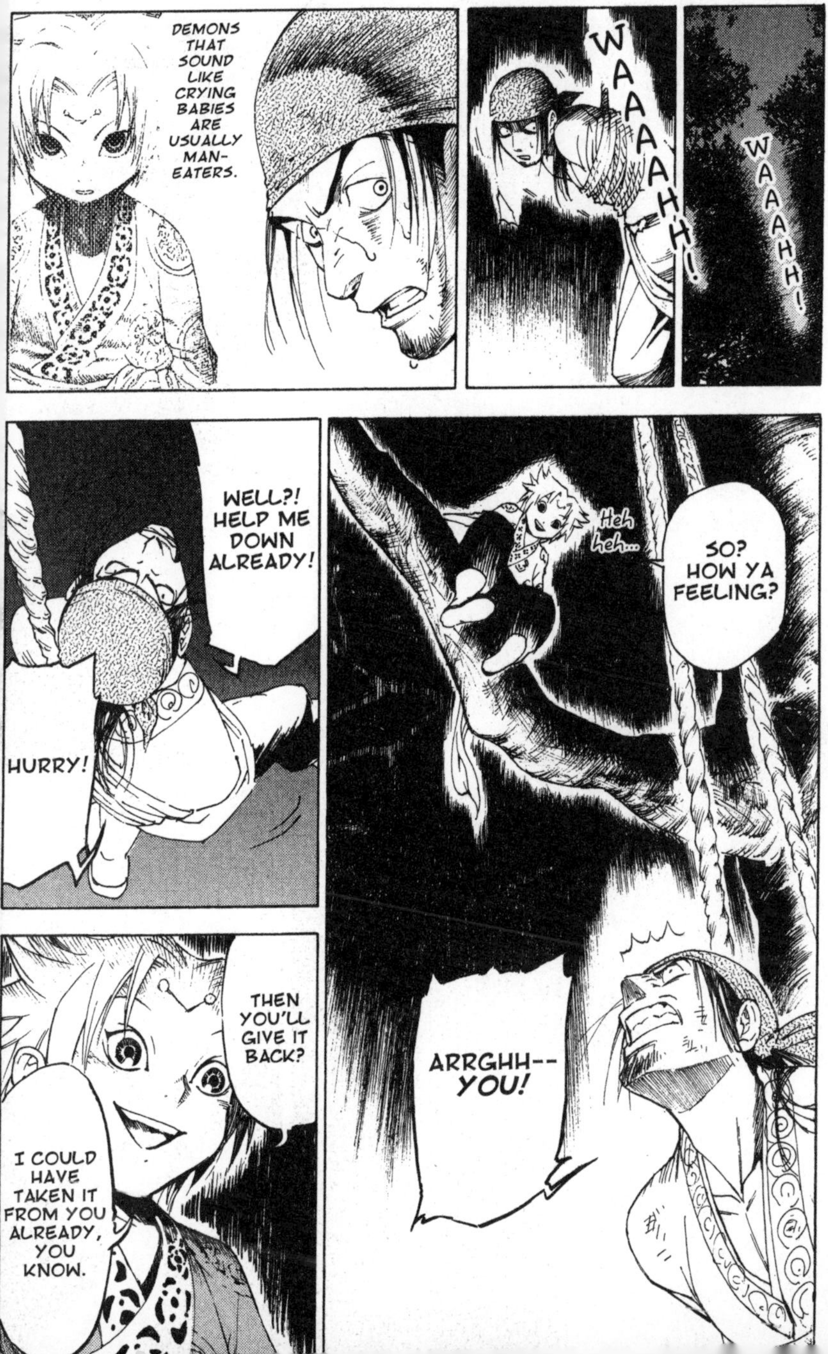
WAAAAHH!
WAAAAAHH!
DEMONS THAT SOUND LIKE CRYING BABIES ARE USUALLY MAN-EATERS.
Heh heh...
SO? HOW YA FEELING?
ARRGHH-- YOU!
WELL?! HELP ME DOWN ALREADY!
HURRY!
THEN YOU'LL GIVE IT BACK?
I COULD HAVE TAKEN IT FROM YOU ALREADY, YOU KNOW.

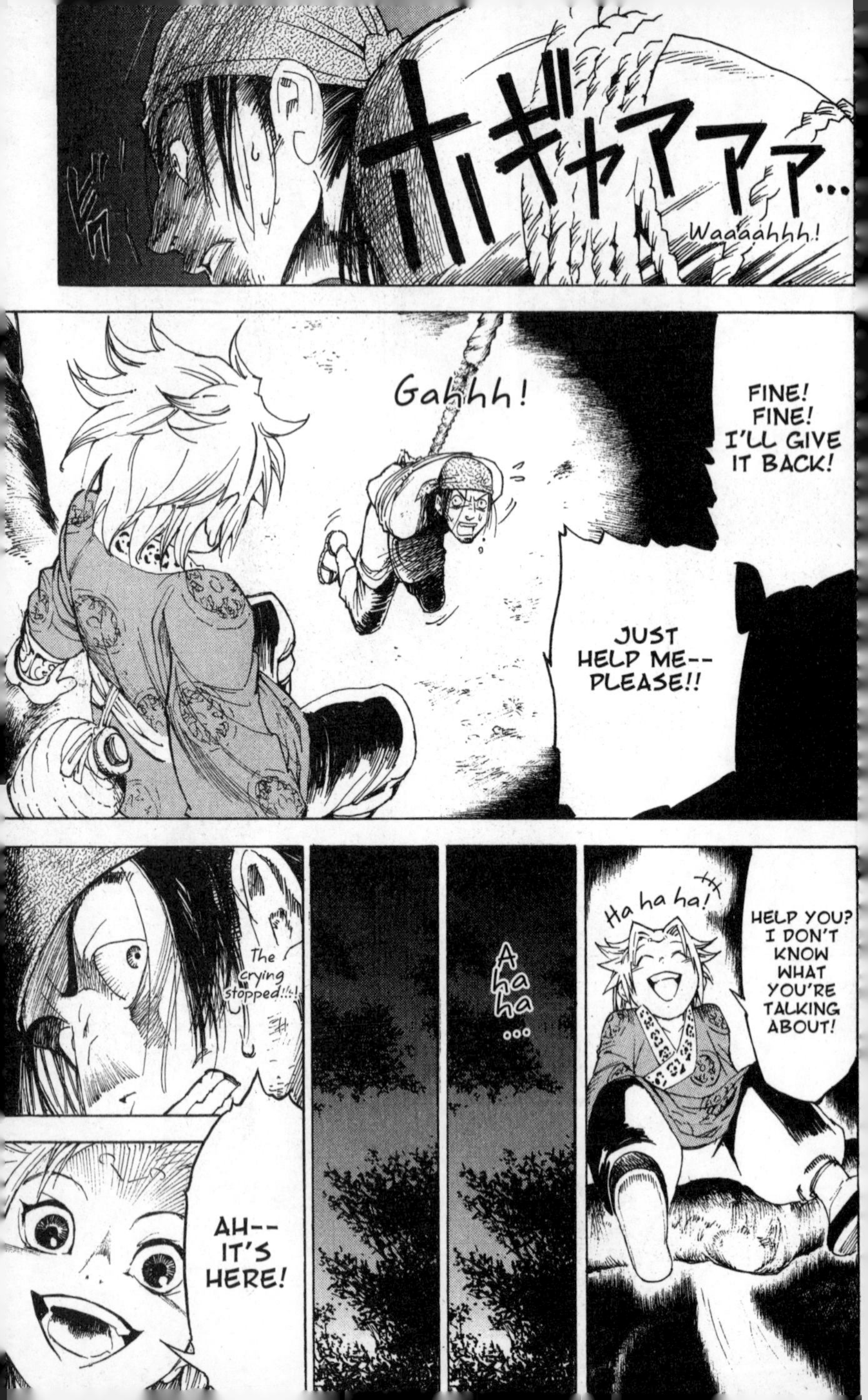
ホギャアァァ…
Waaaahhh!
FINE! FINE! I'LL GIVE IT BACK!
JUST HELP ME-- PLEASE!!
Gahhh!
Ha ha ha!
HELP YOU? I DON'T KNOW WHAT YOU'RE TALKING ABOUT!
Ahaha...
The crying stopped!!!
AH-- IT'S HERE!

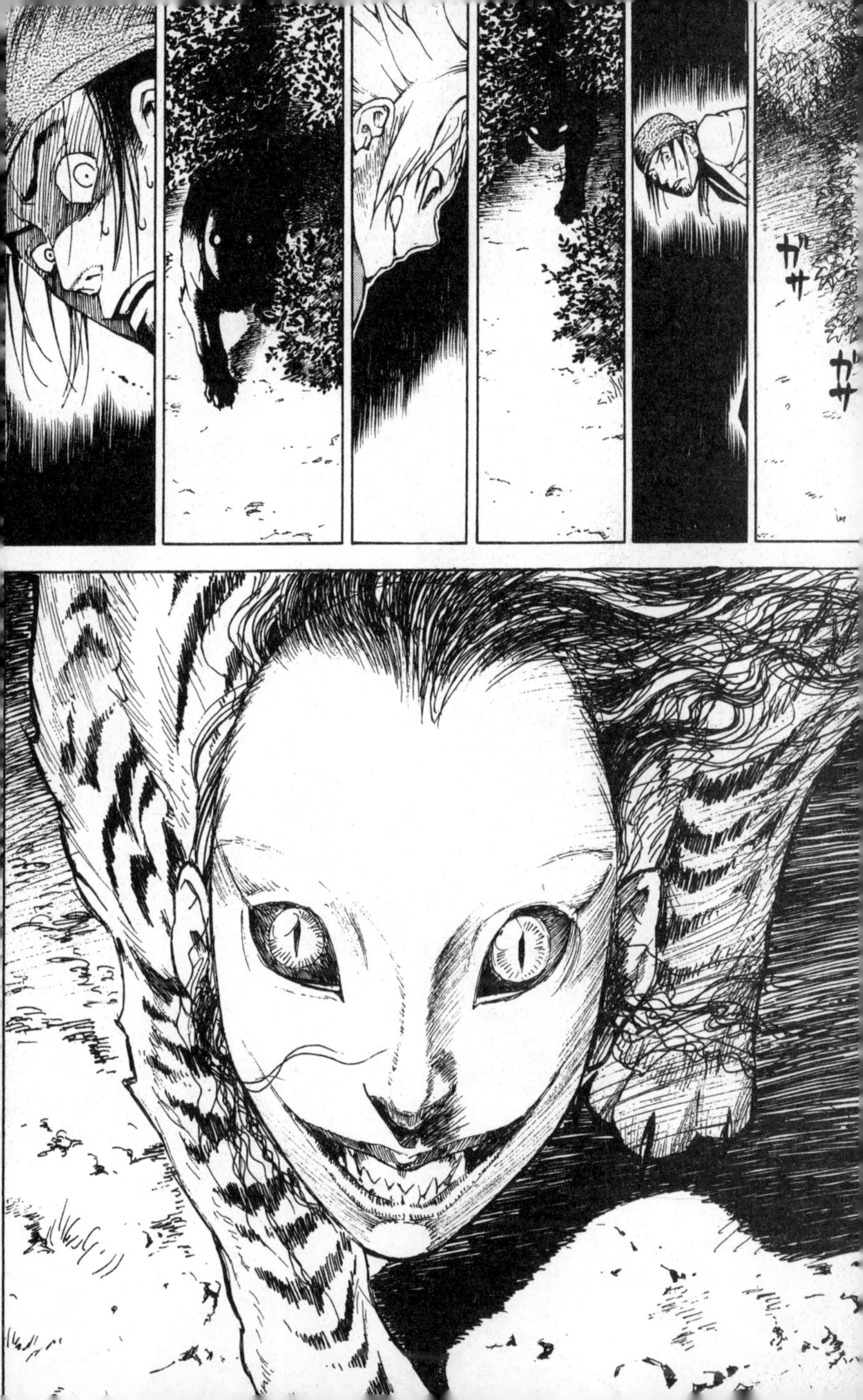
ガサ
ガサ

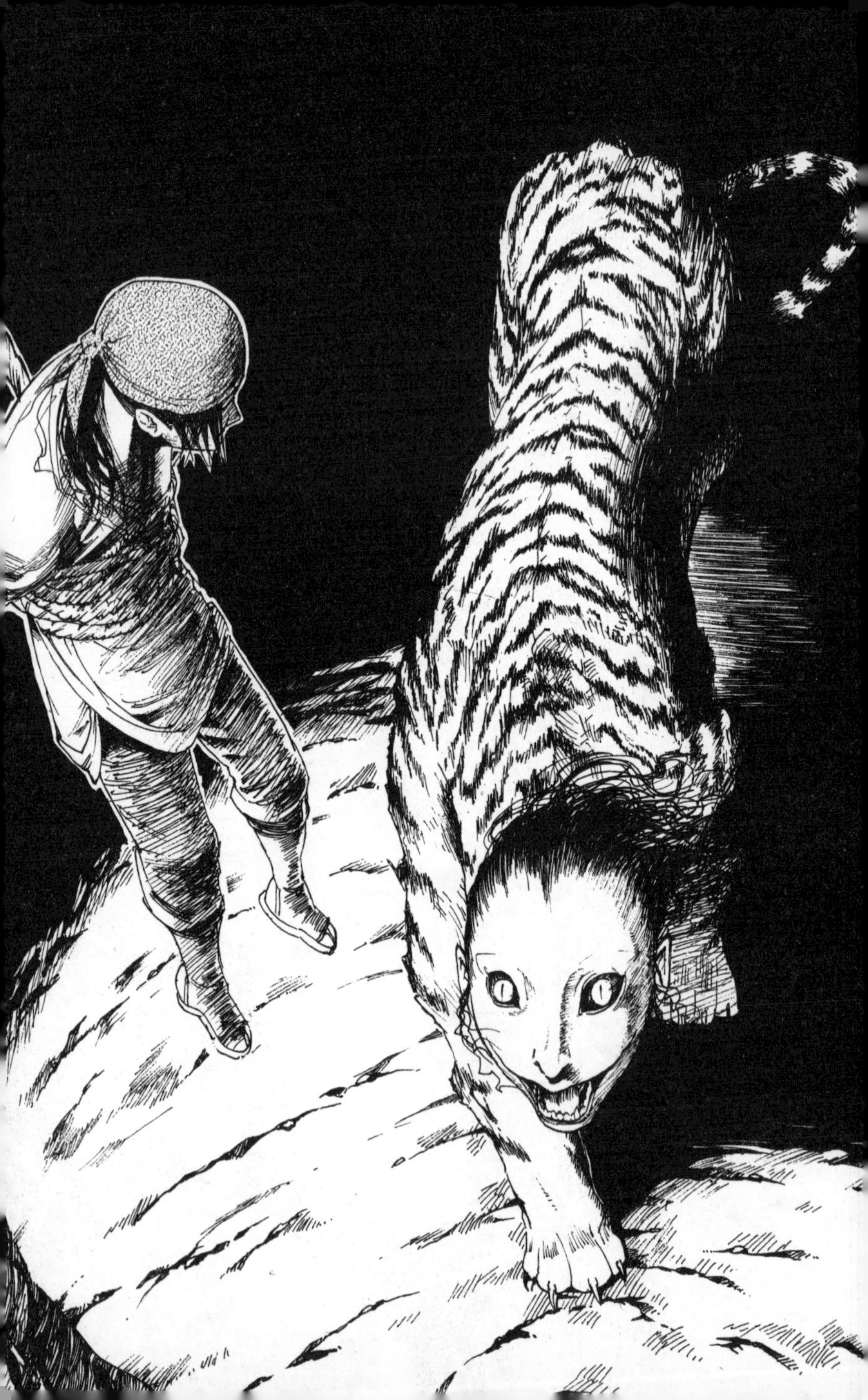

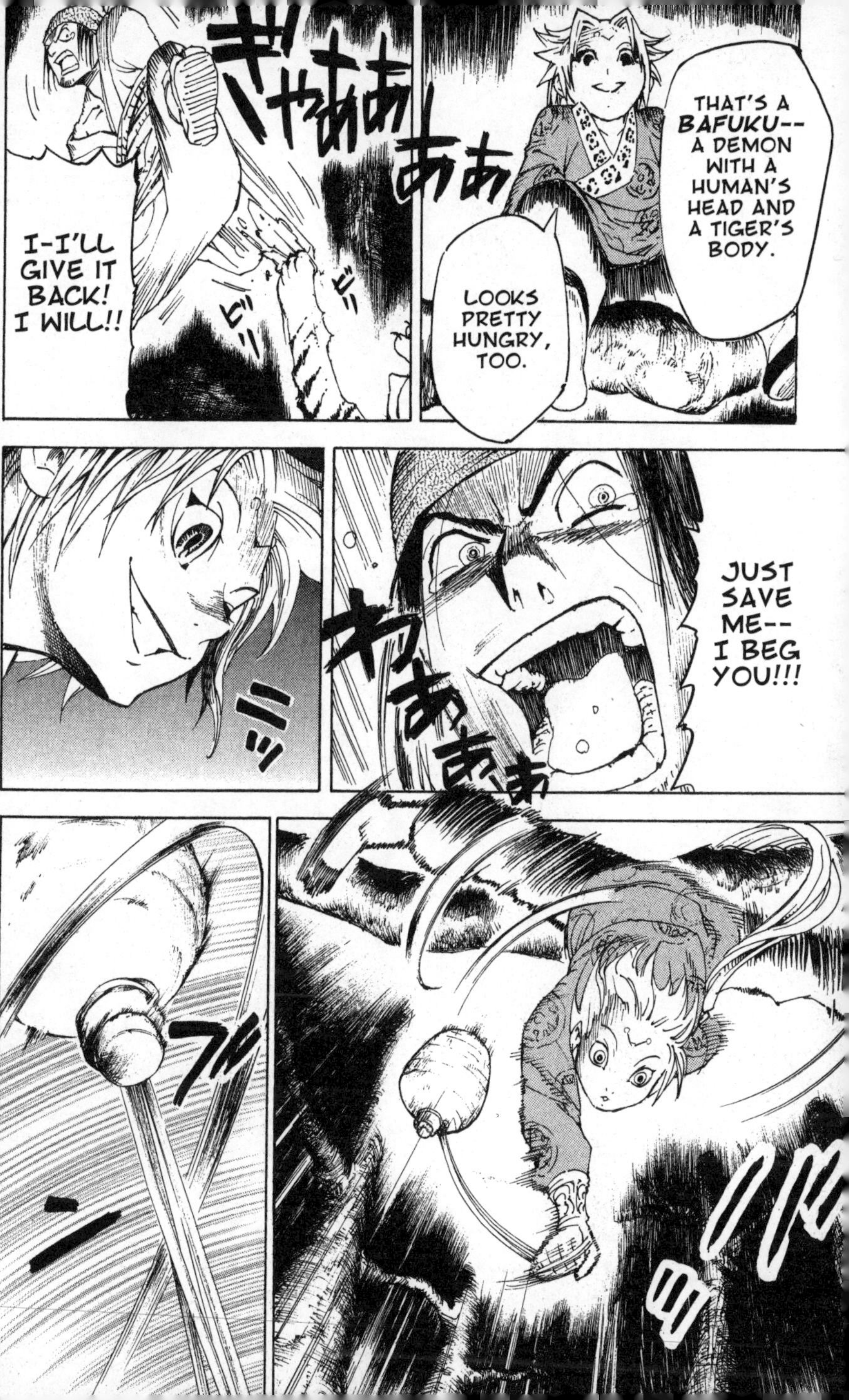
THAT'S A BAFUKU-- A DEMON WITH A HUMAN'S HEAD AND A TIGER'S BODY.
LOOKS PRETTY HUNGRY, TOO.
ぎゃあああああ
I-I'LL GIVE IT BACK! I WILL!!
ビリ
ビリ
JUST SAVE ME-- I BEG YOU!!!
ギャあああ
ニッ
フ

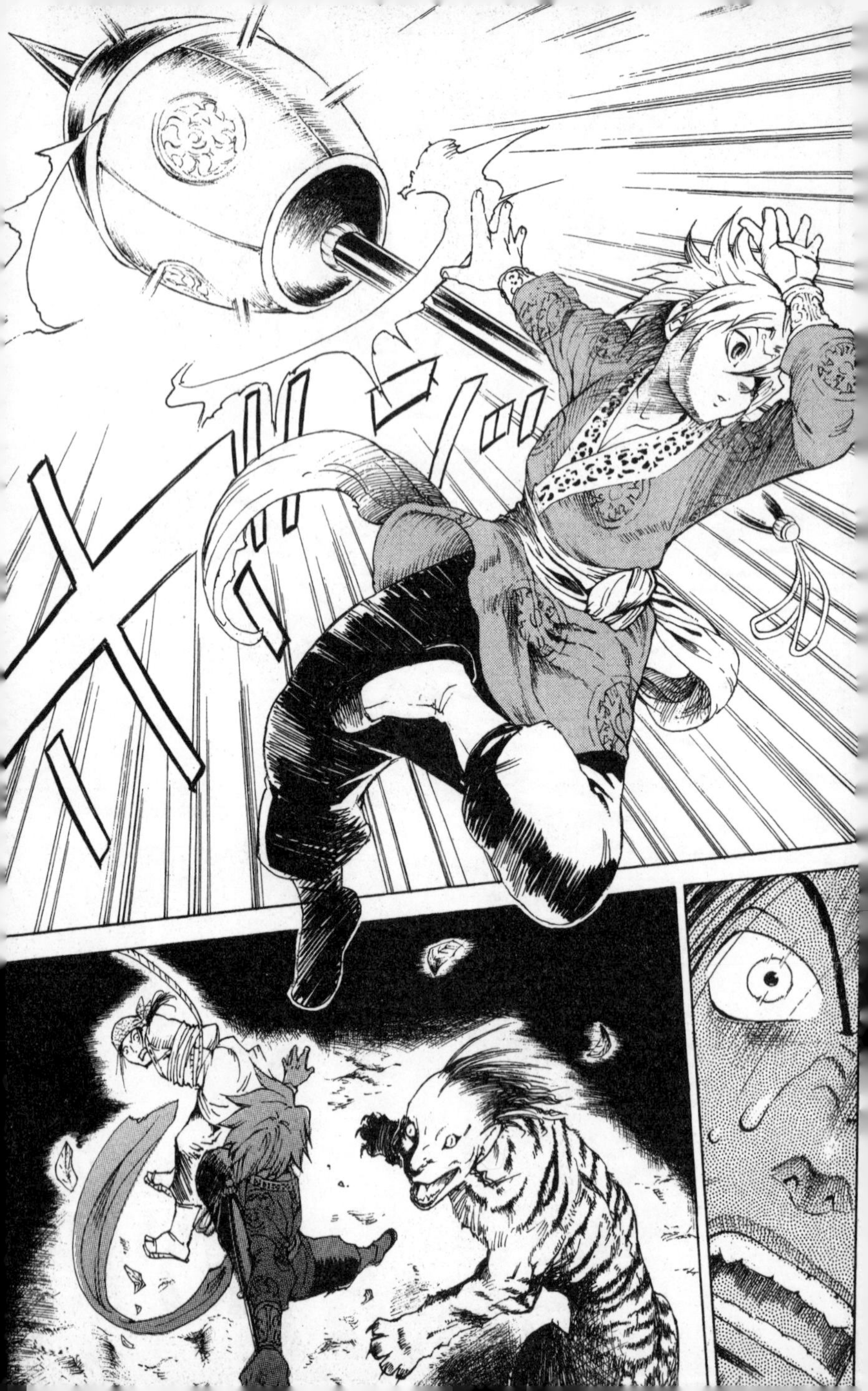

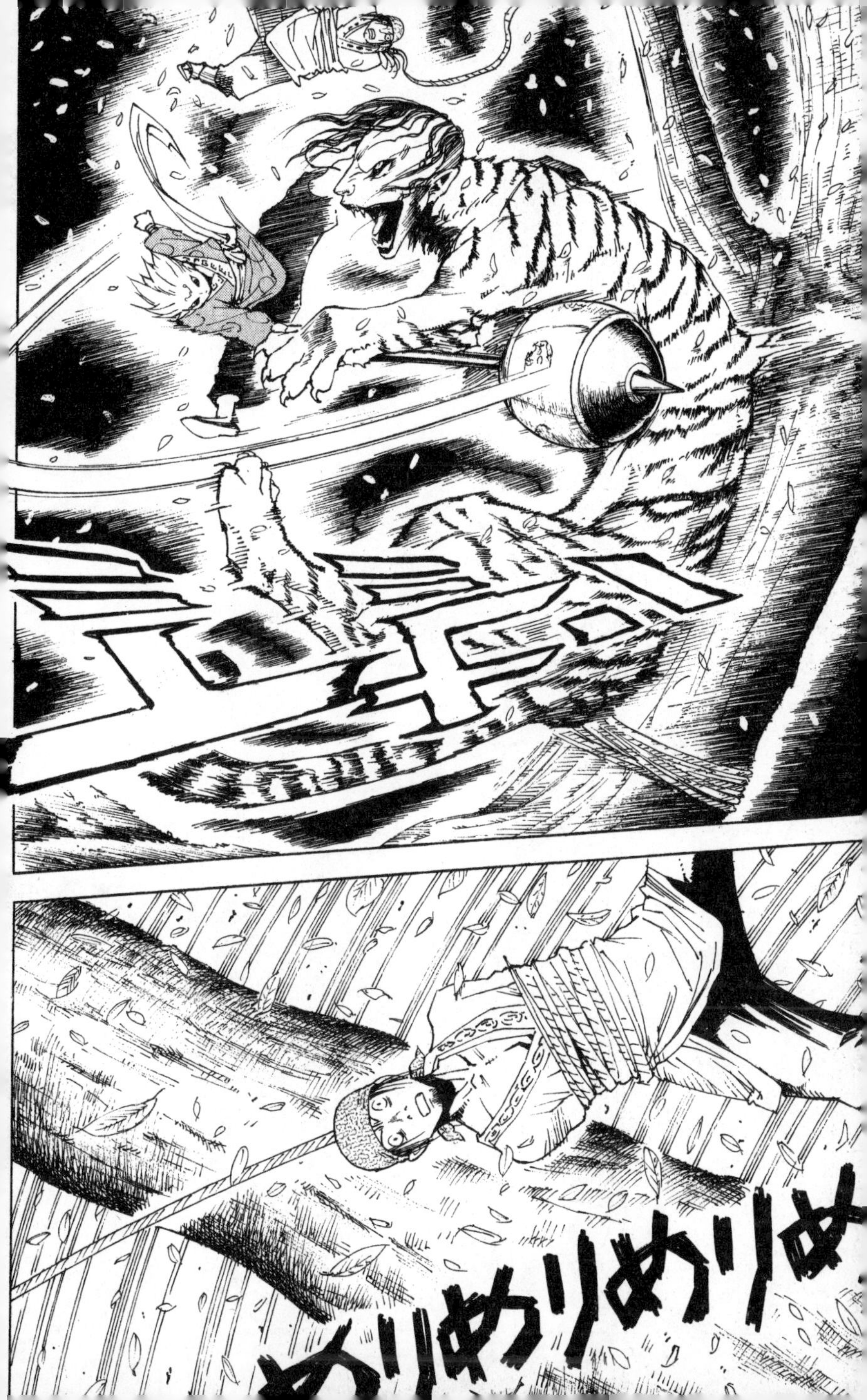
めりめりめりめ

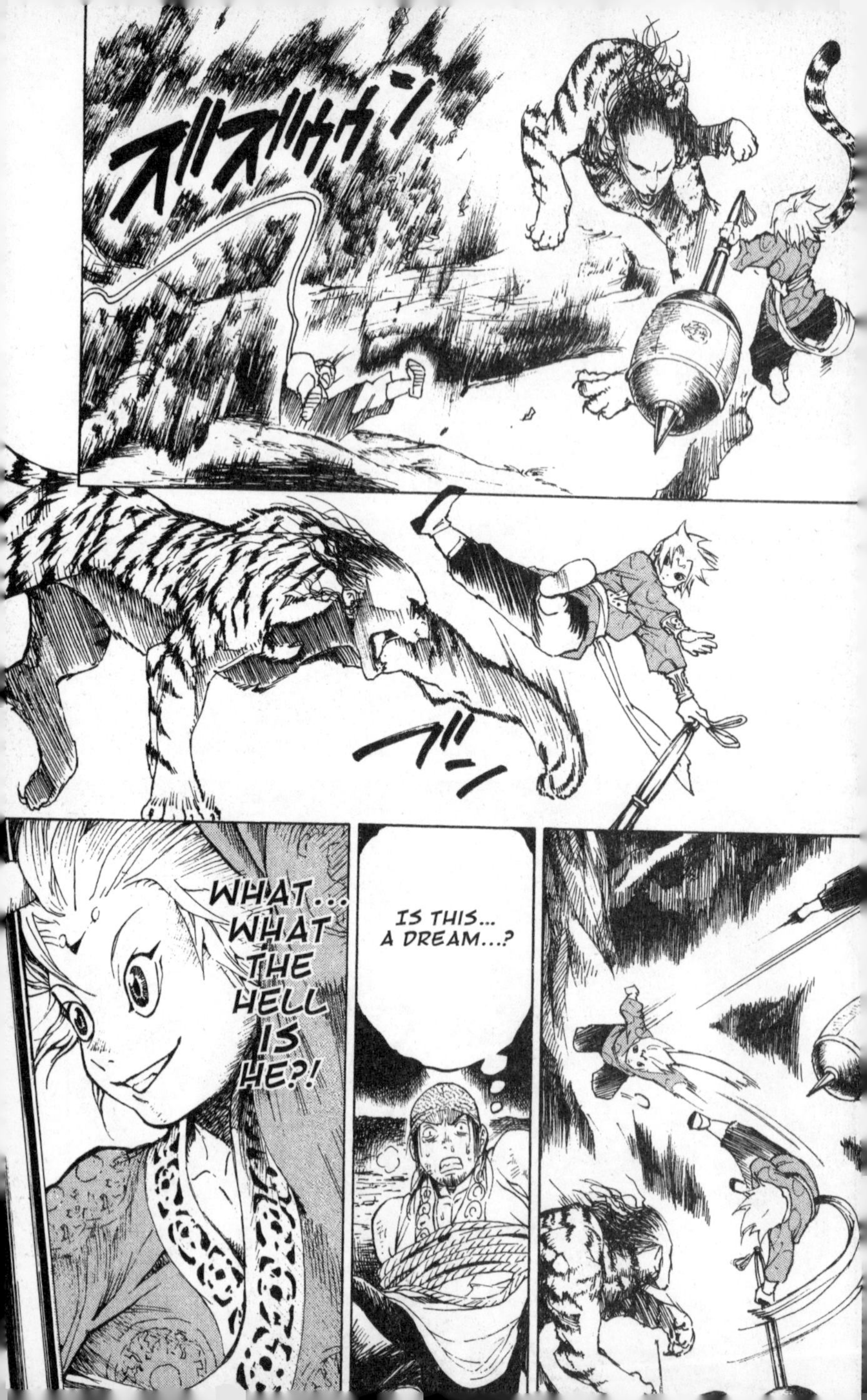
IS THIS... A DREAM...?
WHAT... WHAT THE HELL IS HE?!

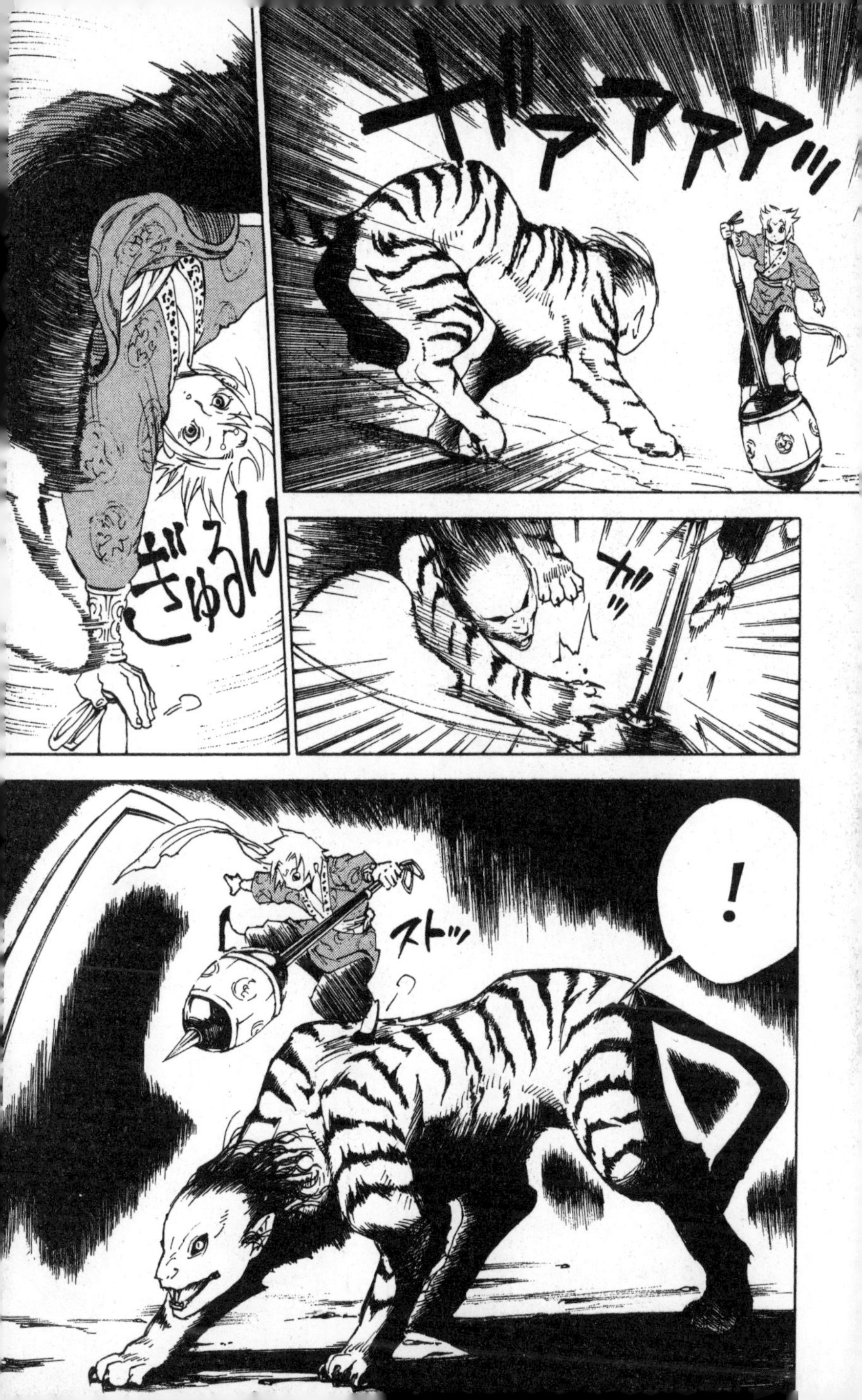
ガアアアアッ
ガッ
ぎゅるん
ストッ
!

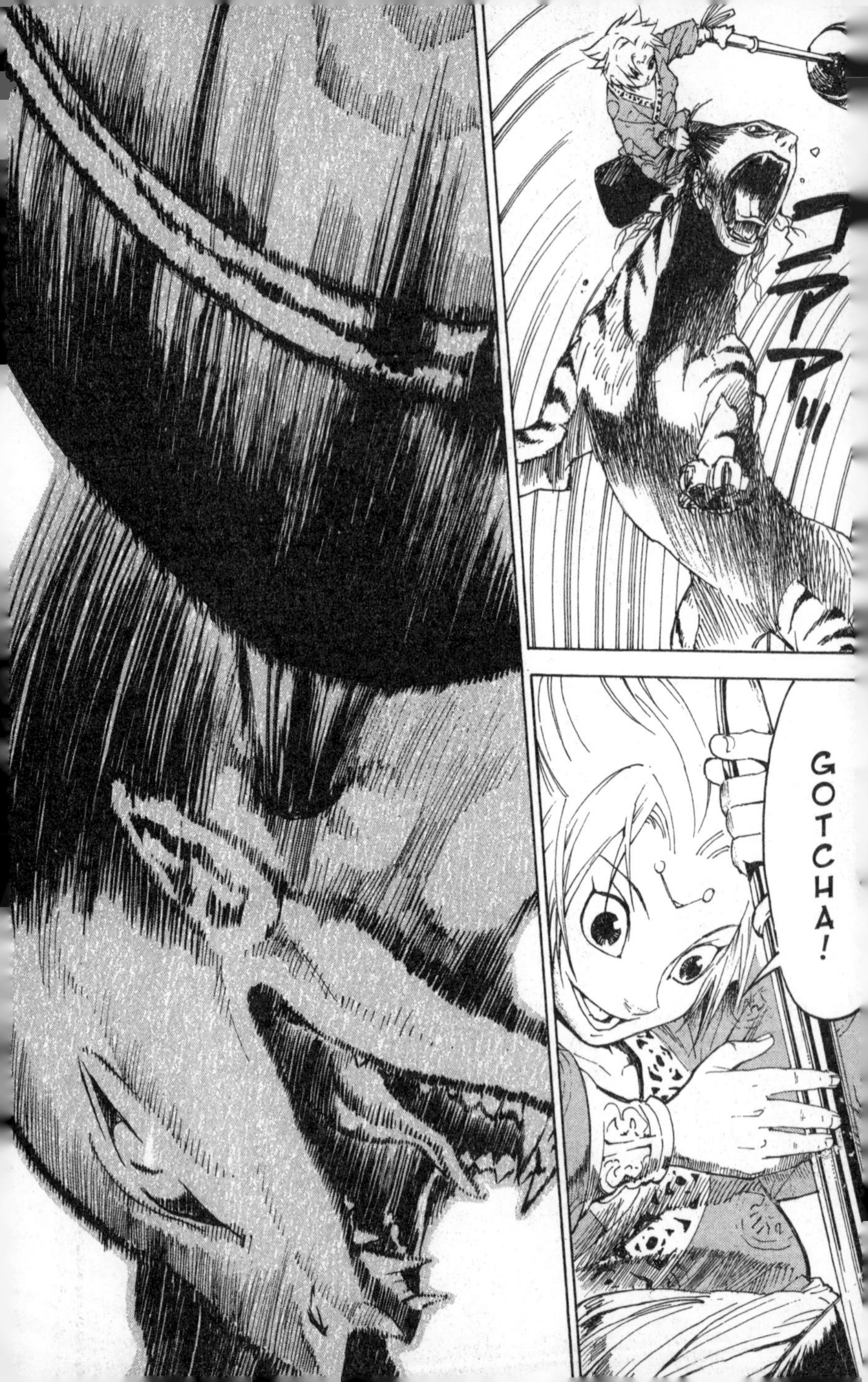
コアアッ
GOTCHA!

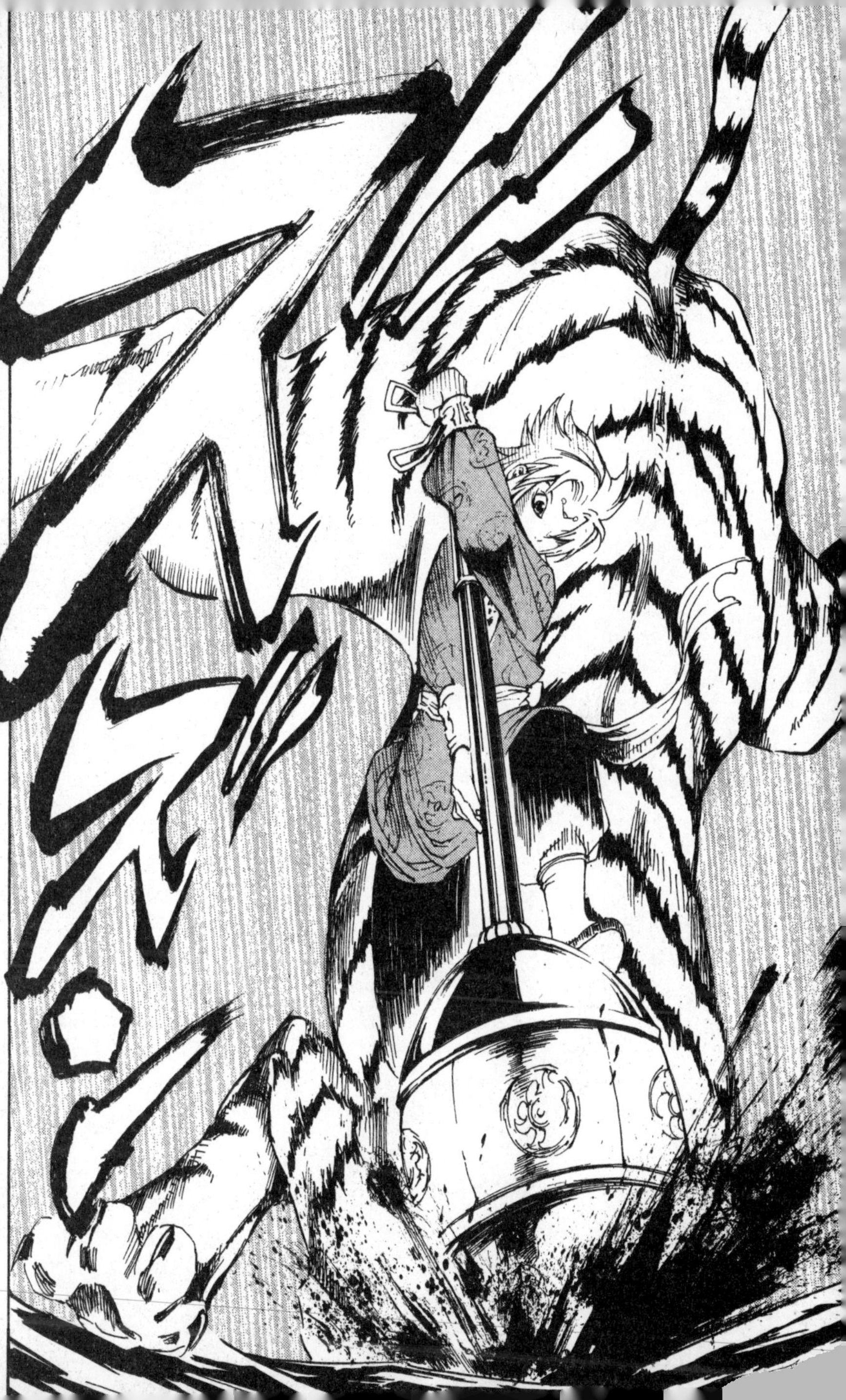

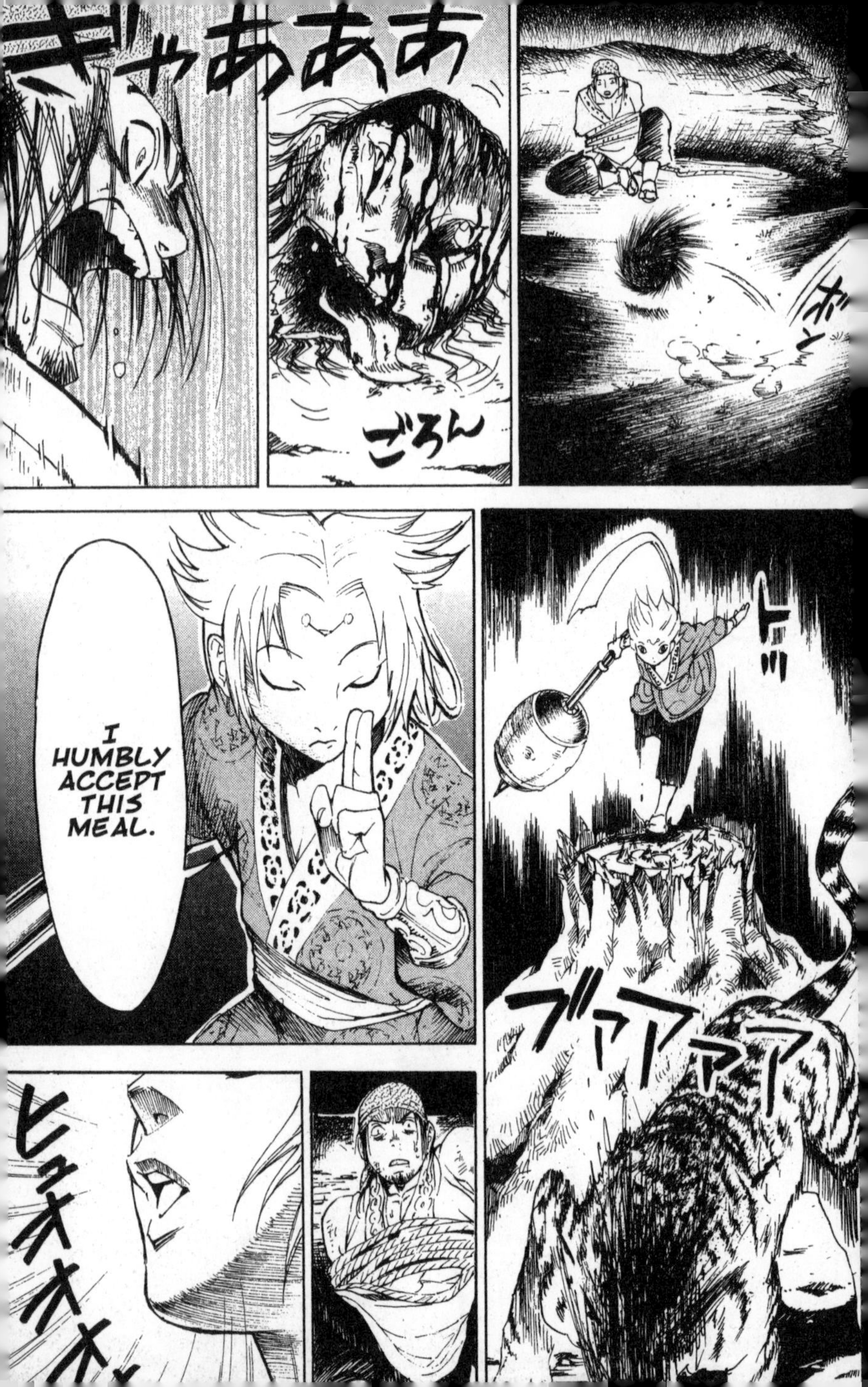

ボン
ごろん
ぎゃあああ
ドッ
ブァアアア
I HUMBLY ACCEPT THIS MEAL.
ヒュオオオ

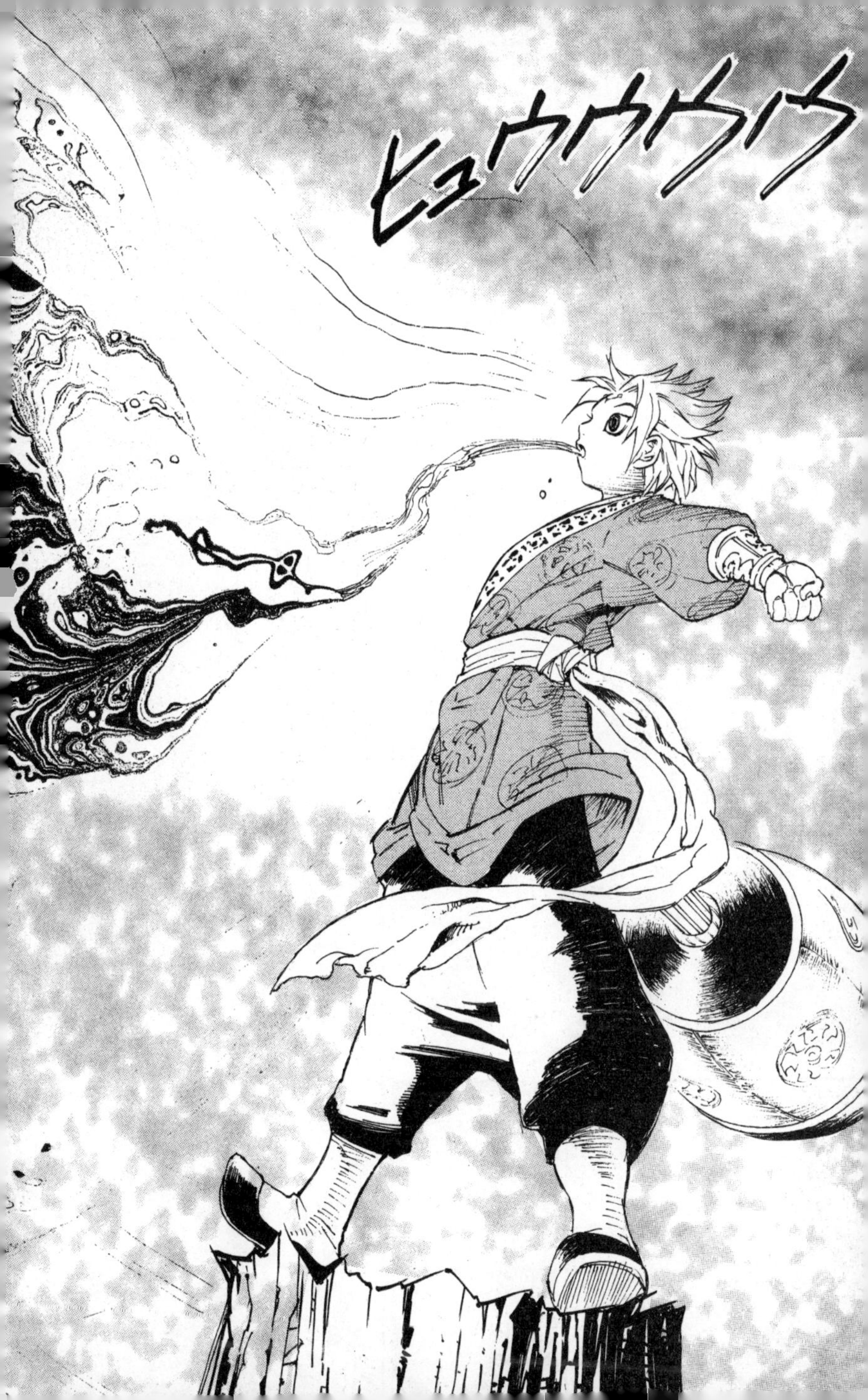
ヒュウウウウ

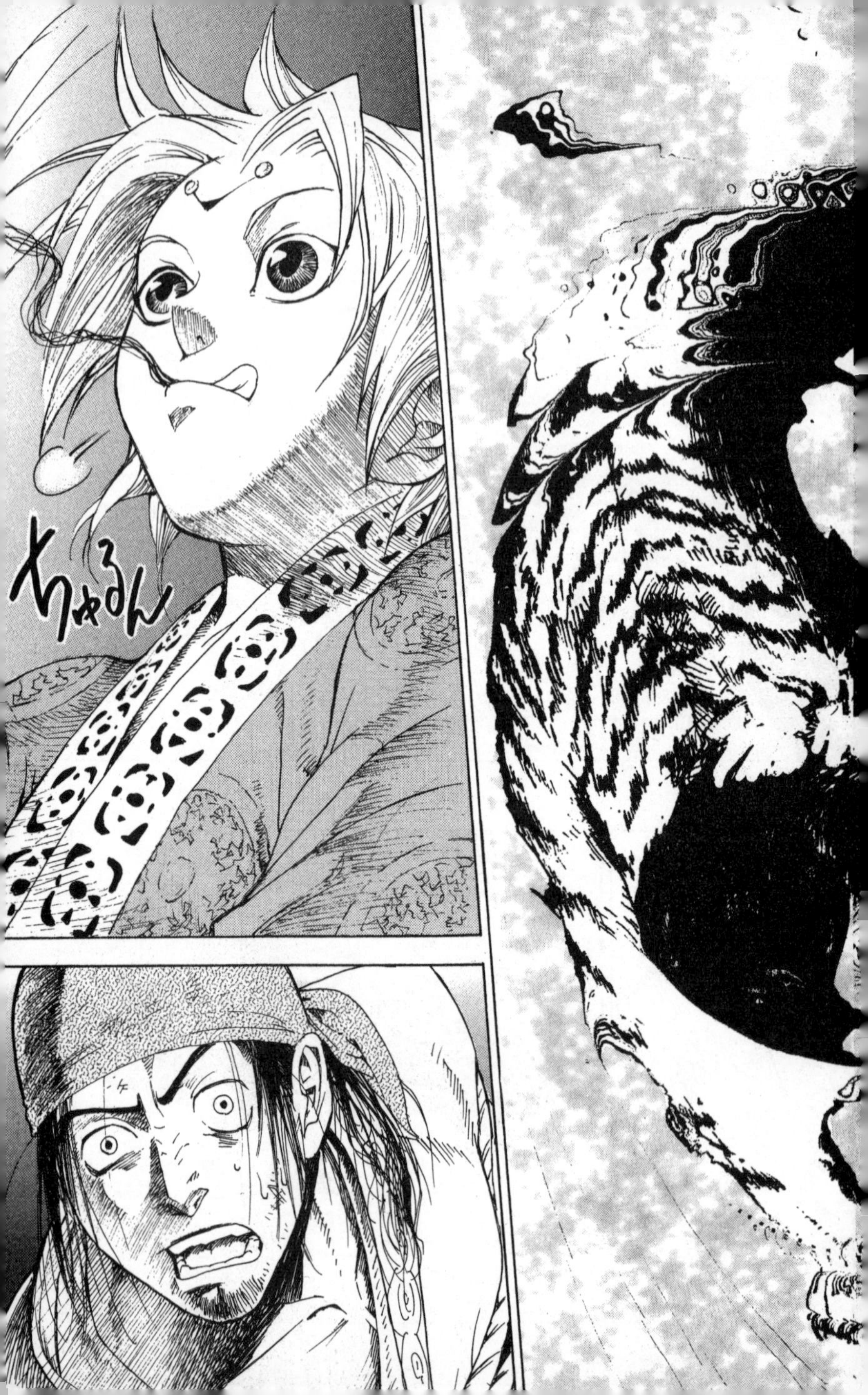
ちゃるん

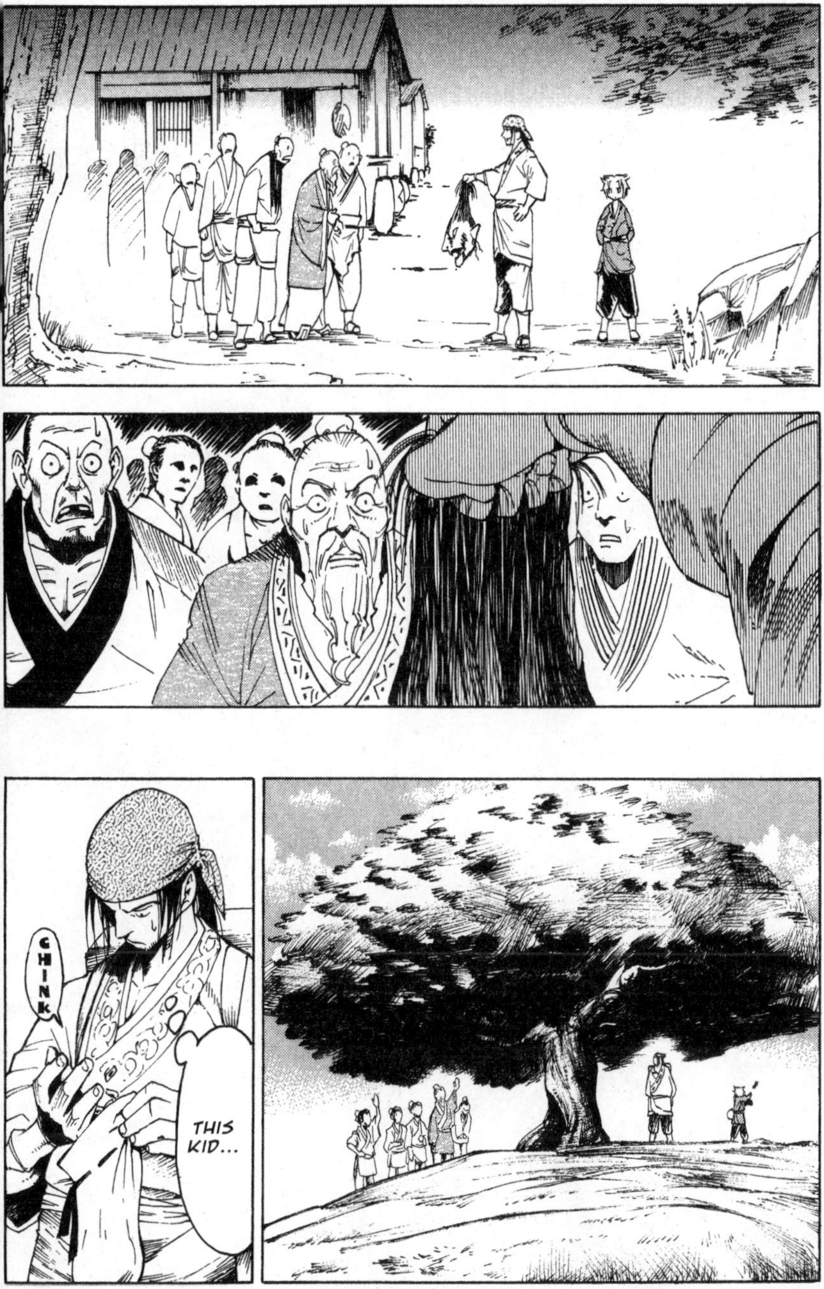
CHINK
THIS KID...

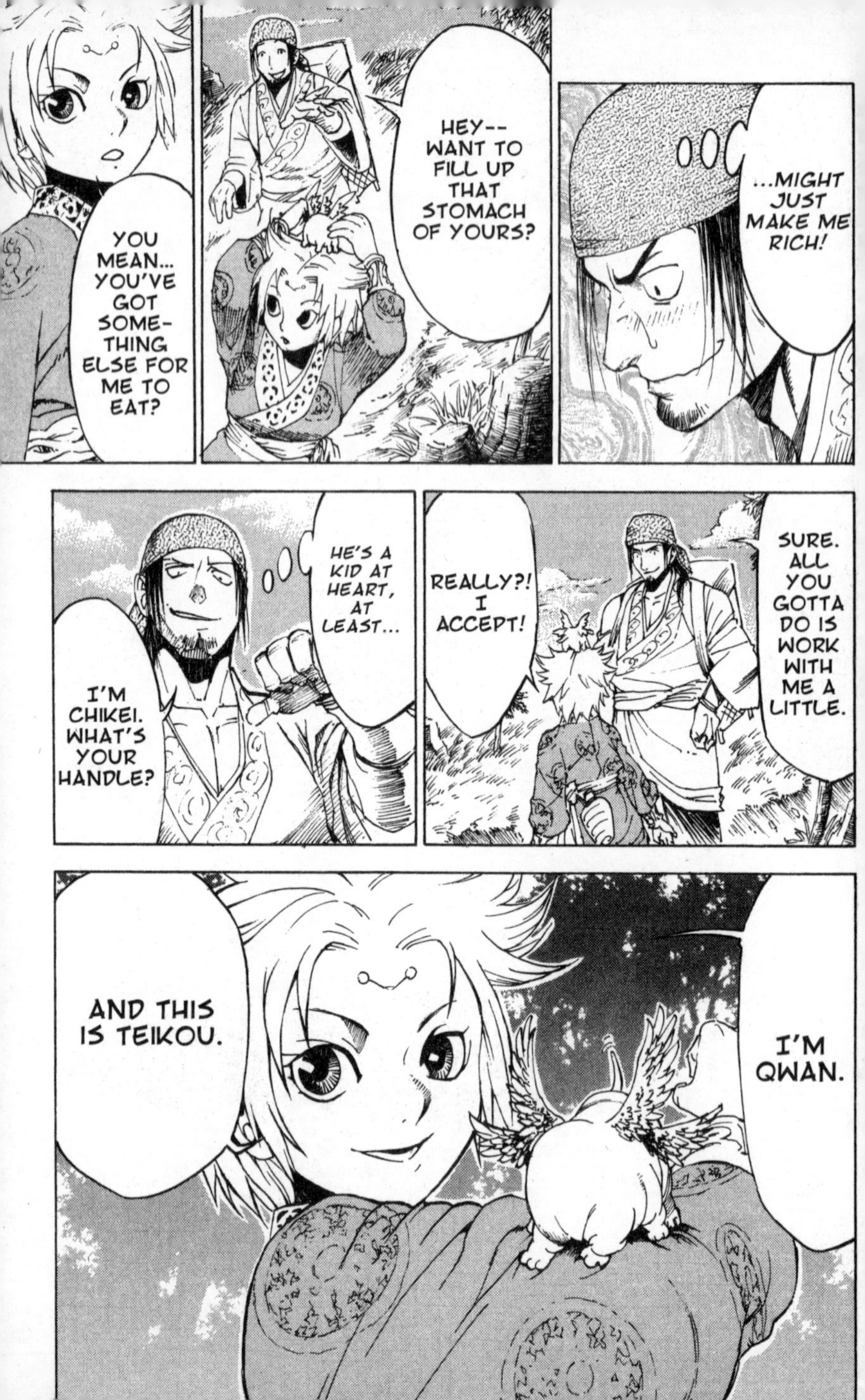

...MIGHT JUST MAKE ME RICH!
HEY-- WANT TO FILL UP THAT STOMACH OF YOURS?
YOU MEAN... YOU'VE GOT SOME-THING ELSE FOR ME TO EAT?
SURE. ALL YOU GOTTA DO IS WORK WITH ME A LITTLE.
REALLY?! I ACCEPT!
HE'S A KID AT HEART, AT LEAST...
I'M CHIKEI. WHAT'S YOUR HANDLE?
I'M QWAN.
AND THIS IS TEIKOU.

SORCERER HUNTERS

The Story:

In the land of Spoolner there live the Sorcerers who possess magical abilities and the Parsoners who do not. For ages, the Parsoners have been the subjects of abject cruelty at the hands of rogue sorcerers. Enter the Sorcerer Hunters: champions of justice who protect the world from wizards gone wrong!

The Creators:

Ray Omishi and Satoru Akahori

Behind the Manga:

• With its romantic misadventures and disturbing monsters, Sorcerer Hunters is on the cutting edge in Japanese comics for mature readers.
• A successful series of Sorcerer Hunters videos has been released nationally.
• Fan-service, fantasy and comedy all in one!

Genre:

Action / Comedy / Fantasy

SRP:

£ 6.99

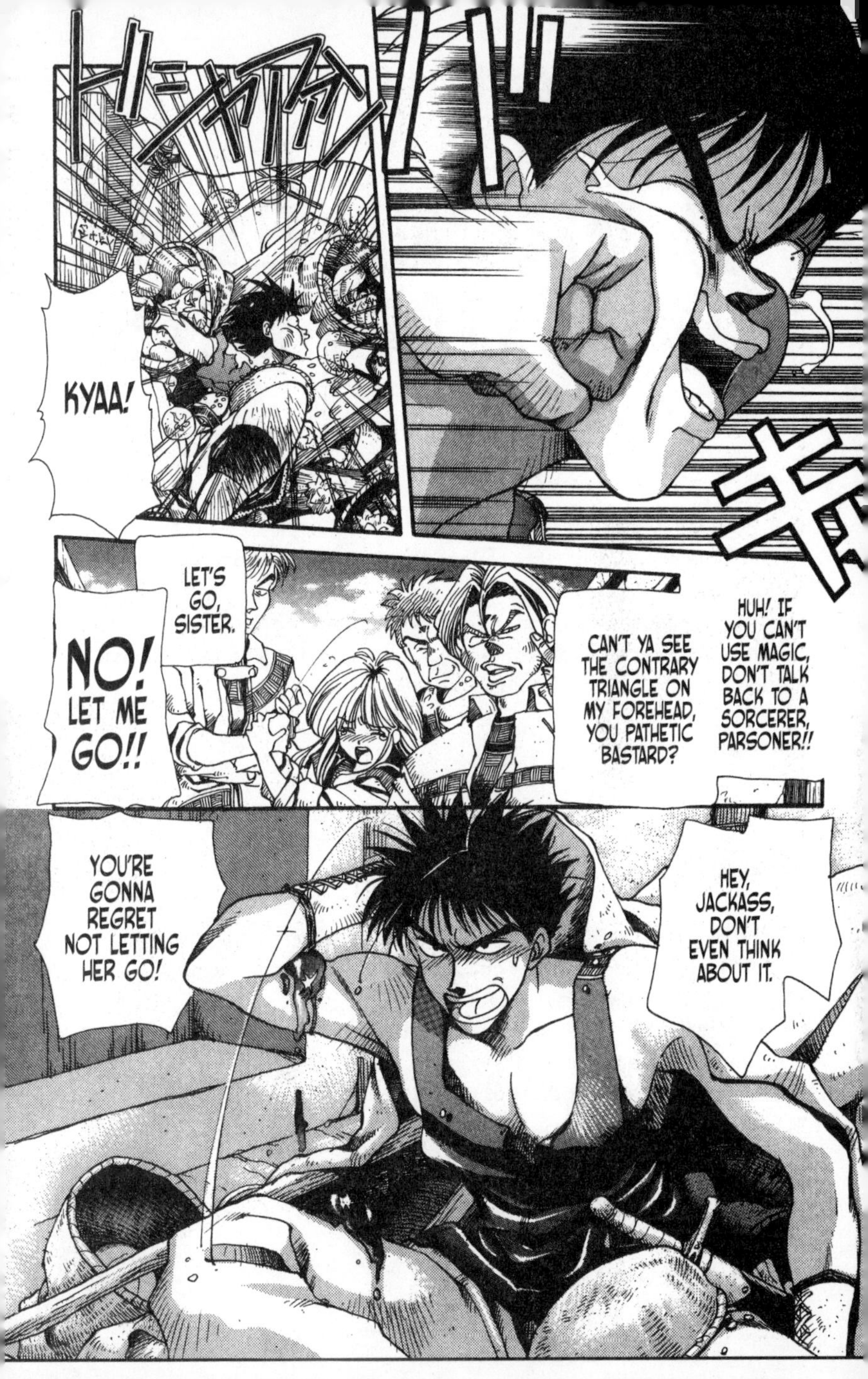
KYAA!
HUH! IF YOU CAN'T USE MAGIC, DON'T TALK BACK TO A SORCERER, PARSONER!!
CAN'T YA SEE THE CONTRARY TRIANGLE ON MY FOREHEAD, YOU PATHETIC BASTARD?
LET'S GO, SISTER.
NO! LET ME GO!!
HEY, JACKASS, DON'T EVEN THINK ABOUT IT.
YOU'RE GONNA REGRET NOT LETTING HER GO!

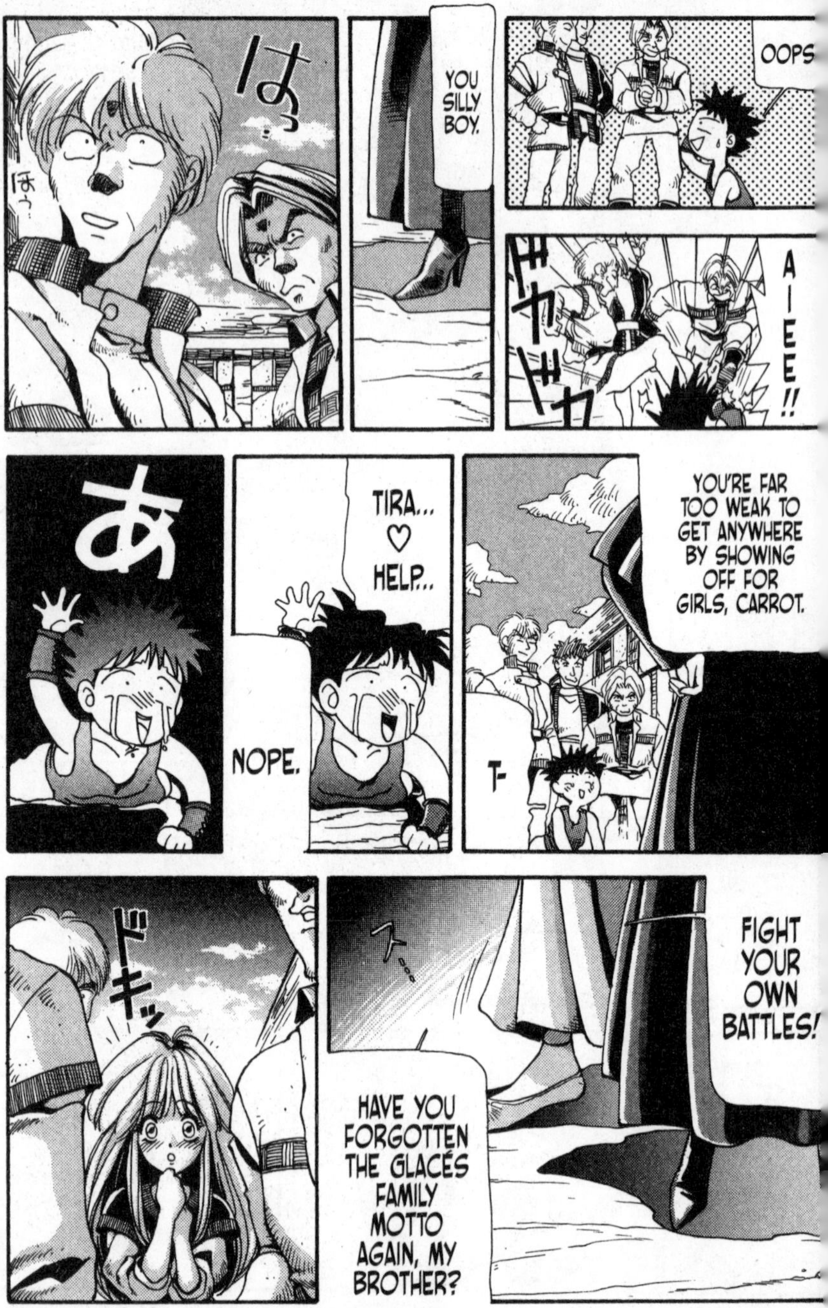
OOPS
AIEEE!!
YOU SILLY BOY.
はっ
YOU'RE FAR TOO WEAK TO GET ANYWHERE BY SHOWING OFF FOR GIRLS, CARROT.
T-
TIRA... ♡ HELP...
NOPE.
あ
FIGHT YOUR OWN BATTLES!
HAVE YOU FORGOTTEN THE GLACÉS FAMILY MOTTO AGAIN, MY BROTHER?
ドキッ

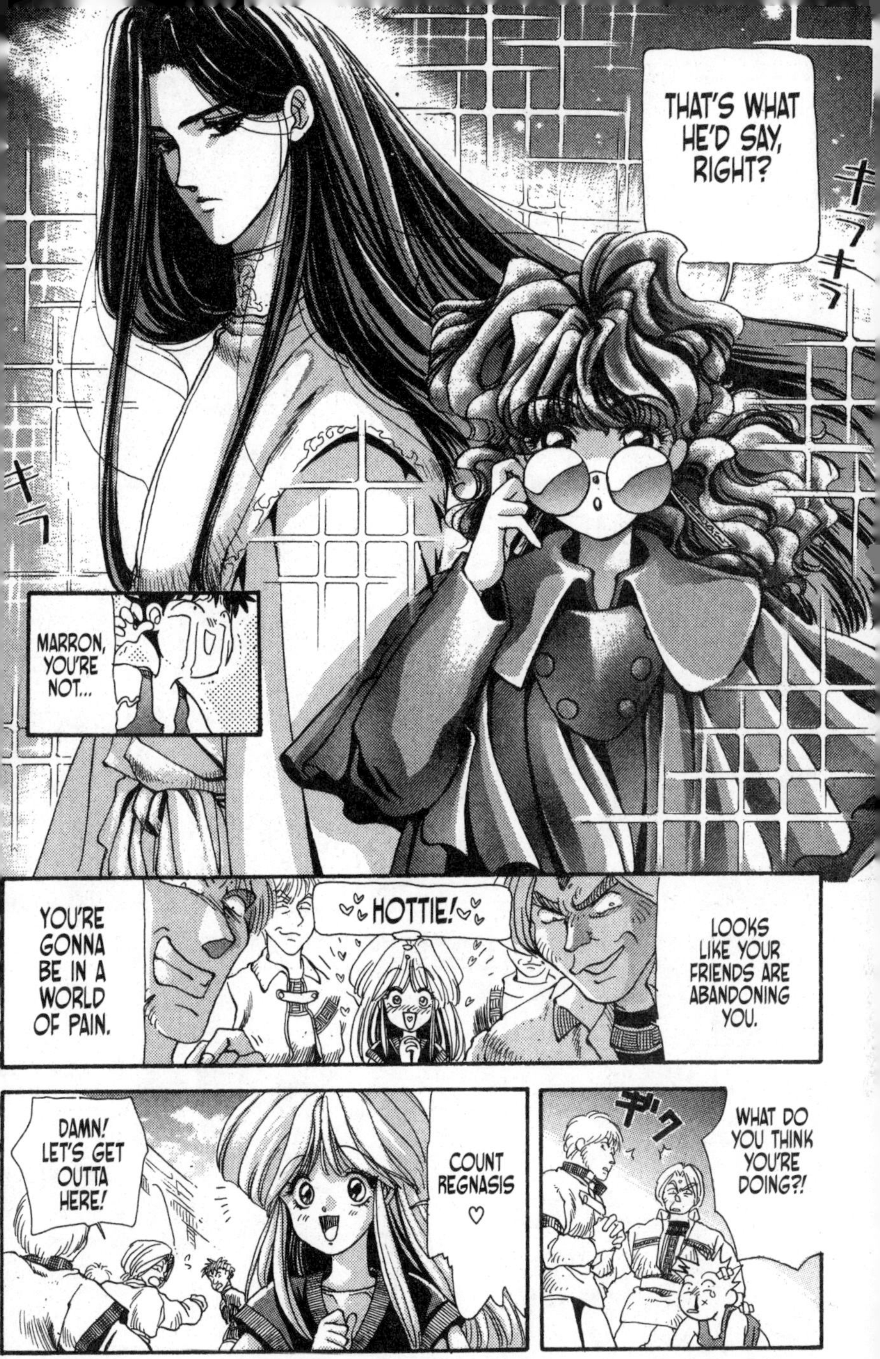
THAT'S WHAT HE'D SAY, RIGHT?
キラキラ
キラ
MARRON, YOU'RE NOT...
LOOKS LIKE YOUR FRIENDS ARE ABANDONING YOU.
HOTTIE!
YOU'RE GONNA BE IN A WORLD OF PAIN.
ギク
WHAT DO YOU THINK YOU'RE DOING?!
COUNT REGNASIS ♡
DAMN! LET'S GET OUTTA HERE!

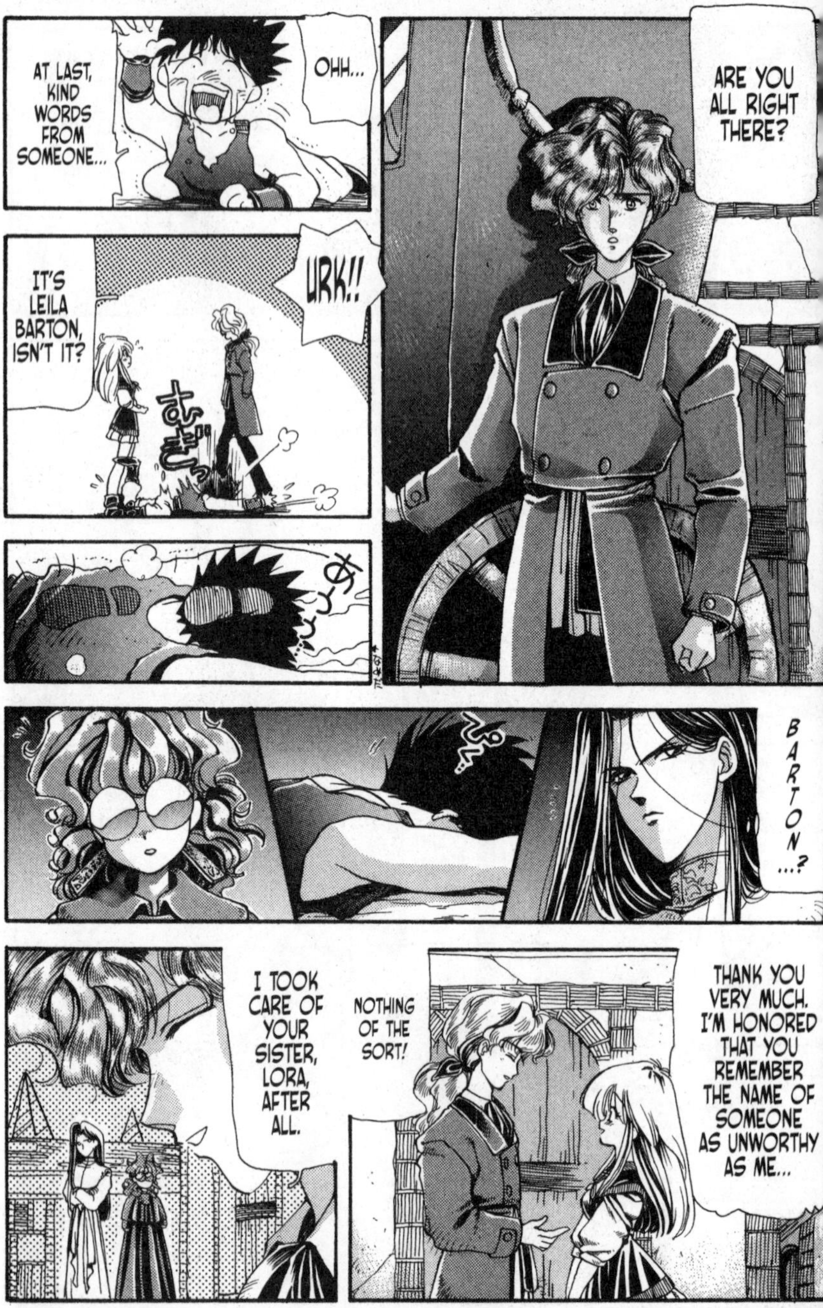
ARE YOU ALL RIGHT THERE?
OHH...
AT LAST, KIND WORDS FROM SOMEONE...
URK!!
IT'S LEILA BARTON, ISN'T IT?
BARTON...?
THANK YOU VERY MUCH. I'M HONORED THAT YOU REMEMBER THE NAME OF SOMEONE AS UNWORTHY AS ME...
NOTHING OF THE SORT!
I TOOK CARE OF YOUR SISTER, LORA, AFTER ALL.

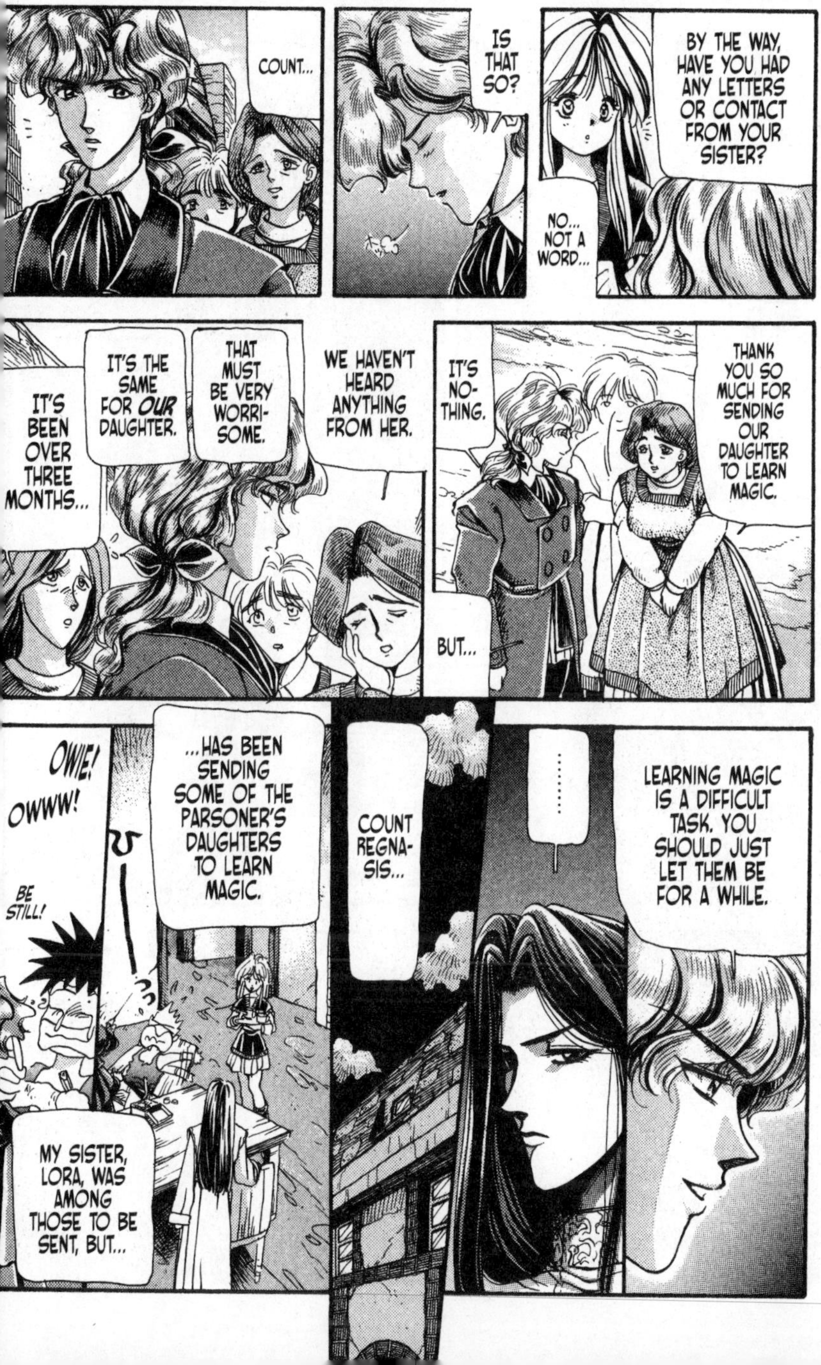
BY THE WAY, HAVE YOU HAD ANY LETTERS OR CONTACT FROM YOUR SISTER?
NO... NOT A WORD...
IS THAT SO?
COUNT...
THANK YOU SO MUCH FOR SENDING OUR DAUGHTER TO LEARN MAGIC.
IT'S NO-THING.
BUT...
WE HAVEN'T HEARD ANYTHING FROM HER.
THAT MUST BE VERY WORRI-SOME.
IT'S THE SAME FOR *OUR* DAUGHTER.
IT'S BEEN OVER THREE MONTHS...
LEARNING MAGIC IS A DIFFICULT TASK. YOU SHOULD JUST LET THEM BE FOR A WHILE.
......
COUNT REGNA-SIS...
...HAS BEEN SENDING SOME OF THE PARSONER'S DAUGHTERS TO LEARN MAGIC.
OWIE!
OWWW!
BE STILL!
MY SISTER, LORA, WAS AMONG THOSE TO BE SENT, BUT...

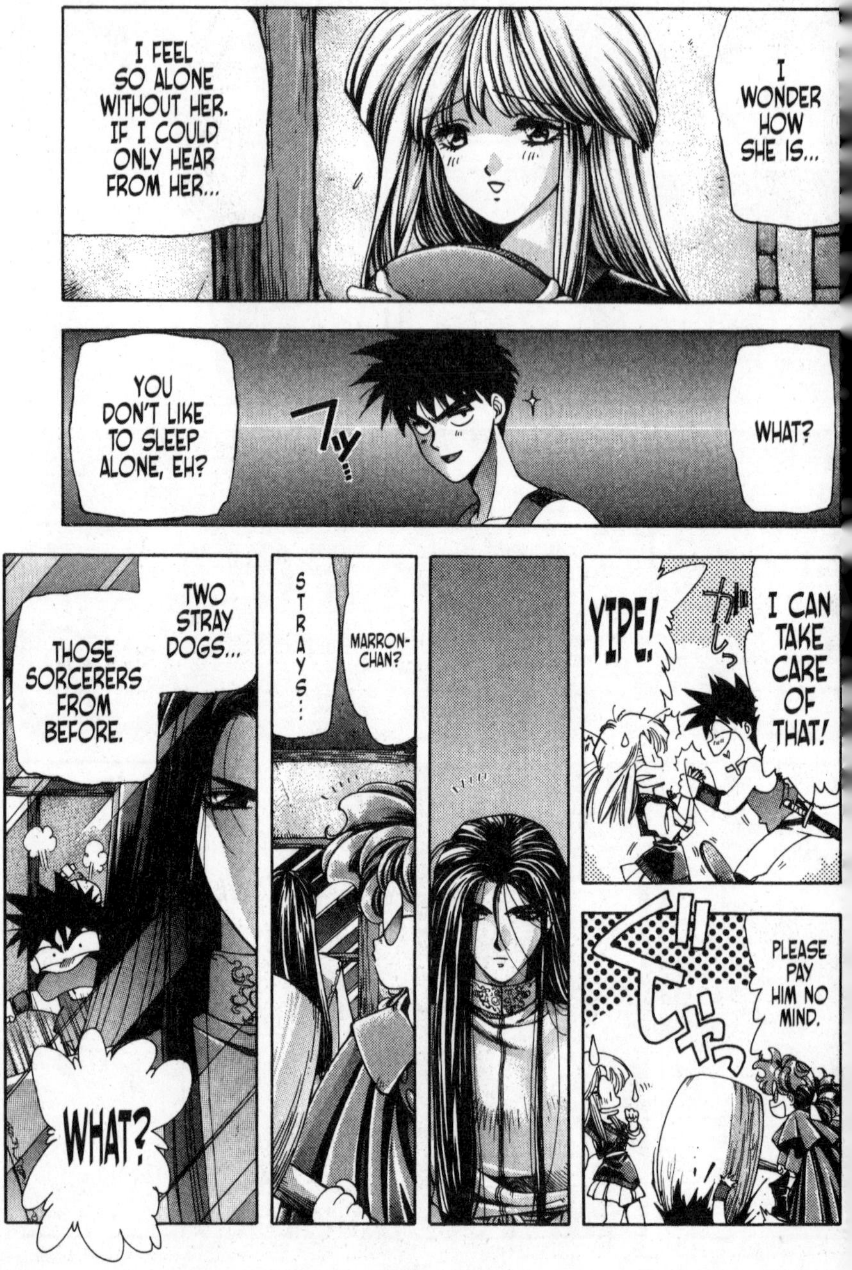
I WONDER HOW SHE IS...
I FEEL SO ALONE WITHOUT HER. IF I COULD ONLY HEAR FROM HER...
WHAT?
YOU DON'T LIKE TO SLEEP ALONE, EH?
I CAN TAKE CARE OF THAT!
YIPE!
PLEASE PAY HIM NO MIND.
MARRON-CHAN?
STRAYS...
TWO STRAY DOGS...
THOSE SORCERERS FROM BEFORE.
WHAT?

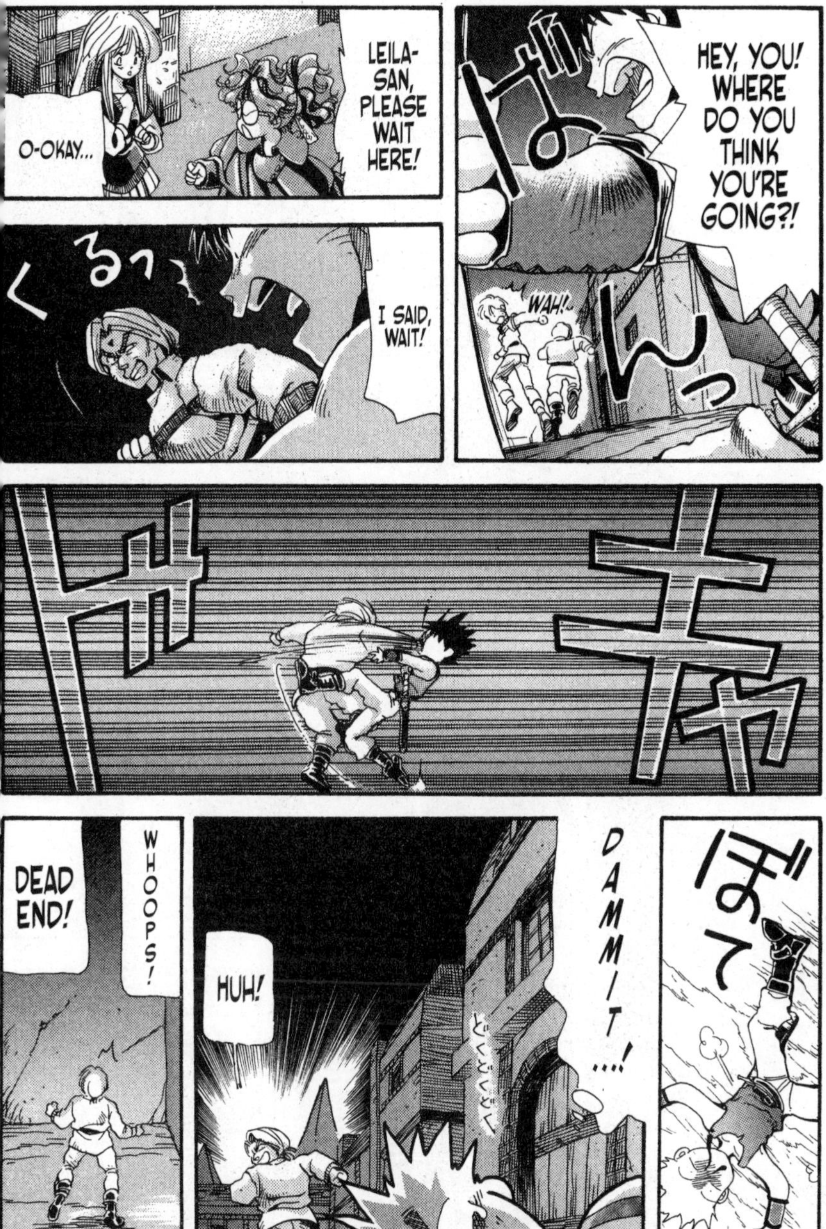
HEY, YOU! WHERE DO YOU THINK YOU'RE GOING?!
WAH!
LEILA-SAN, PLEASE WAIT HERE!
O-OKAY...
I SAID, WAIT!
DAMMIT...!
HUH!
WHOOPS!
DEAD END!

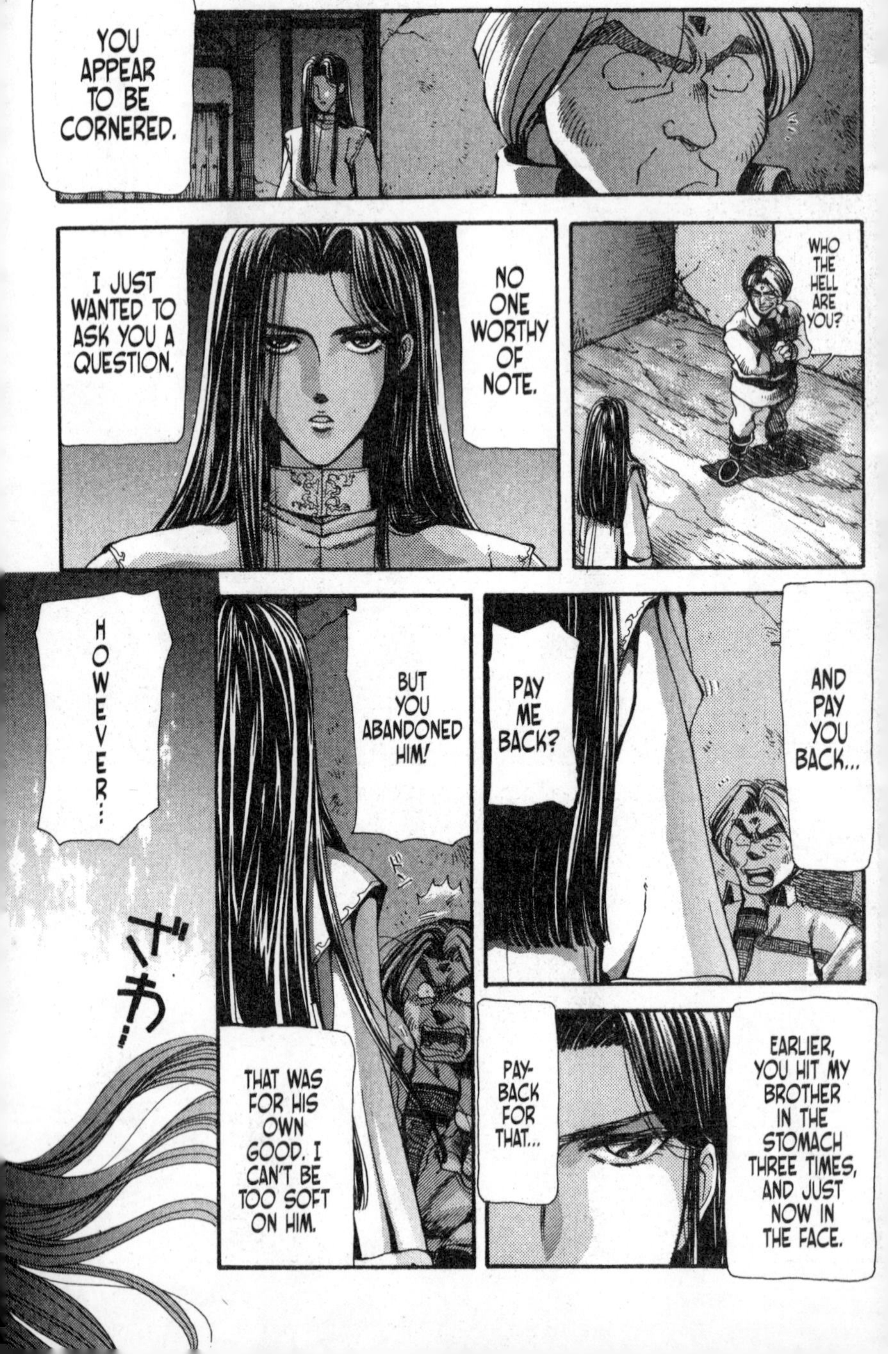

YOU APPEAR TO BE CORNERED.
WHO THE HELL ARE YOU?
NO ONE WORTHY OF NOTE.
I JUST WANTED TO ASK YOU A QUESTION.
AND PAY YOU BACK...
PAY ME BACK?
EARLIER, YOU HIT MY BROTHER IN THE STOMACH THREE TIMES, AND JUST NOW IN THE FACE.
PAY-BACK FOR THAT...
BUT YOU ABANDONED HIM!
THAT WAS FOR HIS OWN GOOD. I CAN'T BE TOO SOFT ON HIM.
HOWEVER...
ザッ

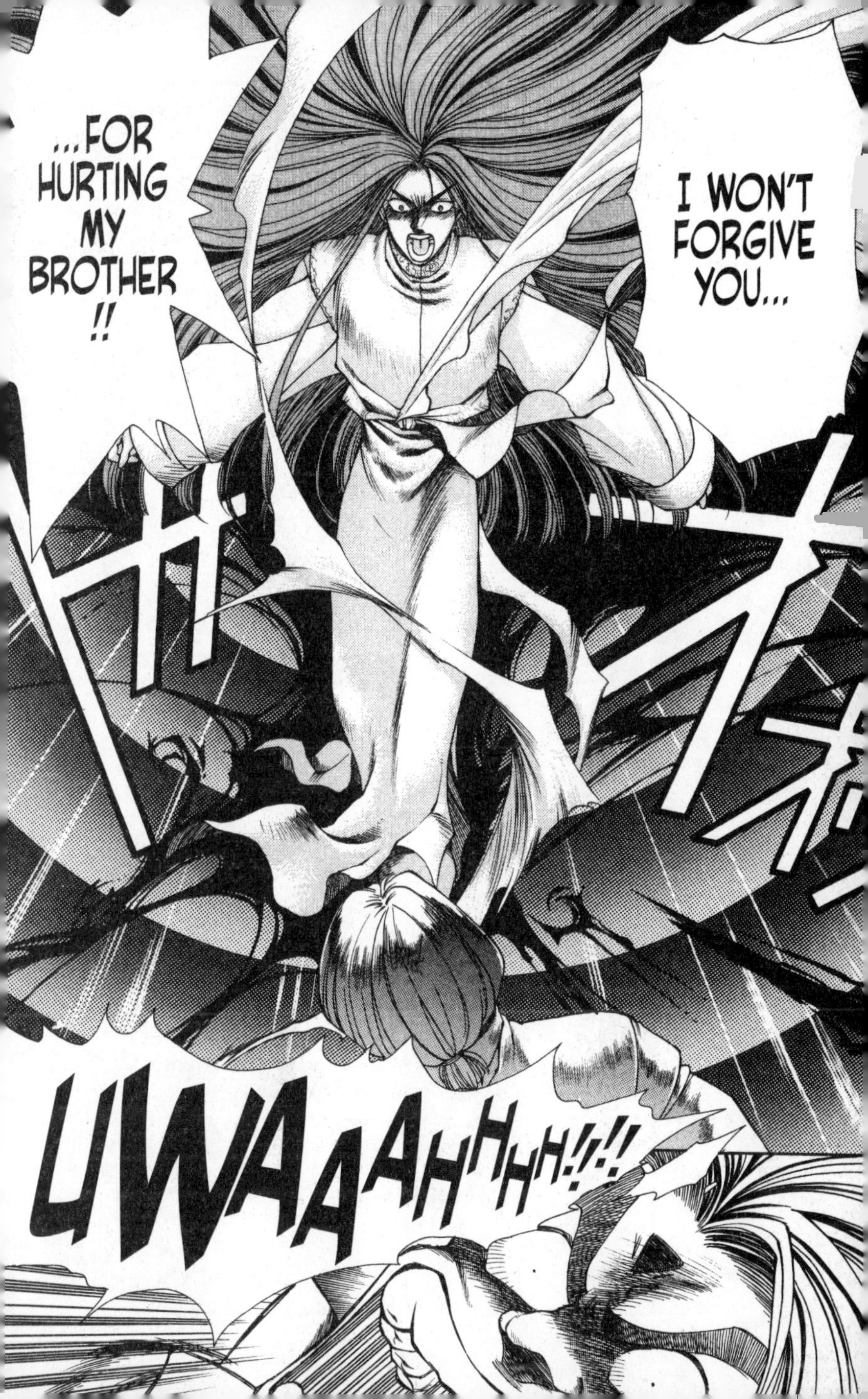

I WON'T FORGIVE YOU...
...FOR HURTING MY BROTHER !!
UWAAAHHHH!!!!

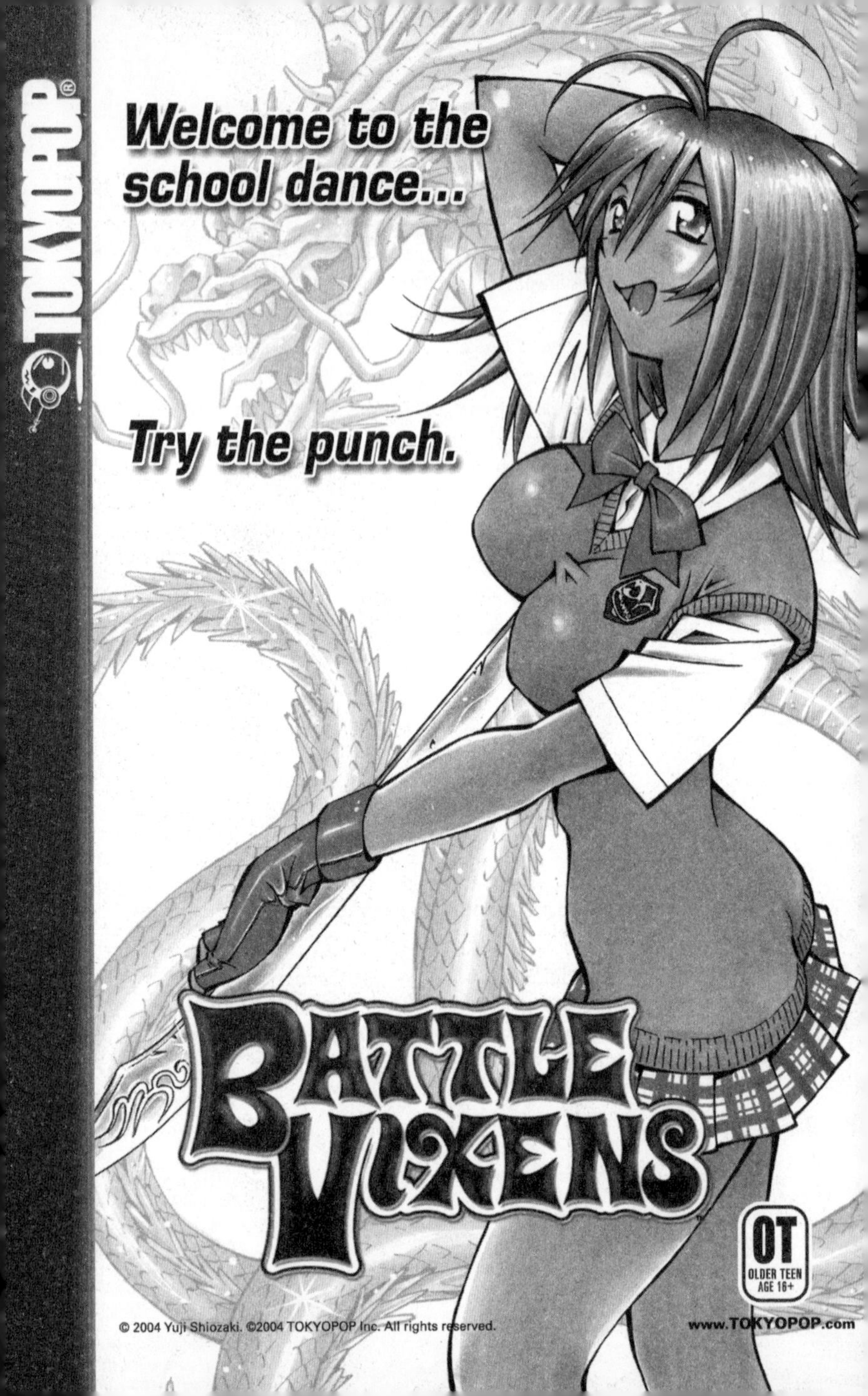
TOKYOPOP
Welcome to the school dance...
Try the punch.
BATTLE VIXENS
OT
OLDER TEEN AGE 16+
© 2004 Yuji Shiozaki. ©2004 TOKYOPOP Inc. All rights reserved.
www.TOKYOPOP.com

TOKYO TRIBES

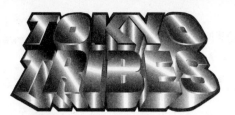

The Story:

Originating in the pages of Japan's hip skateboarder fashion magazine known as *Boon* (rather than in a weekly manga anthology magazine), *Tokyo Tribes* already sets itself apart from the din of manga publishing. But manga-ka Santa Inoue's hard-hitting tale of Tokyo street gangs battling it out in the concrete sprawl of Japan's capital raises the bar for manga storytelling, transcending genres, conventions and even hemispheres.

Ornate with hip-hop trappings and packed with gangland grit, *Tokyo Tribes* paints a vivid, somewhat surreal vision of urban youth. Rival gangs from various Tokyo barrios press each other for turf, leaving many a foot soldier dead in the violent clashes. But when the heat between two of the clans gets personal, a bitter rivalry explodes into all-out warfare.

The Creator:

Santa Inoue

Behind the Manga:

- *Tokyo Tribes* was featured in Japan's hip skateboarder fashion magazine *Boon*.
- *Kill Bill* meets *Menace 2 Society*.
- Created by Santa Inoue, famous for his hyper-real urban action dramas such as *Tamashii Rettsusha, Born to Die, Neighborhood 13* and the original gangland epic *Tokyo Tribe*.

Genre:

Action / Drama

SRP:

£ 6.99

OT
OLDER TEEN
AGE 16+

YOU REMIND ME SUMTHIN, SUMTHIN

THE TOKYO TRIBES

VOL. 5

REMINISCE, REMINISCE......

remi-nice〔reminis〕vi.
思い出にふける〔を語る〕
追憶にふける

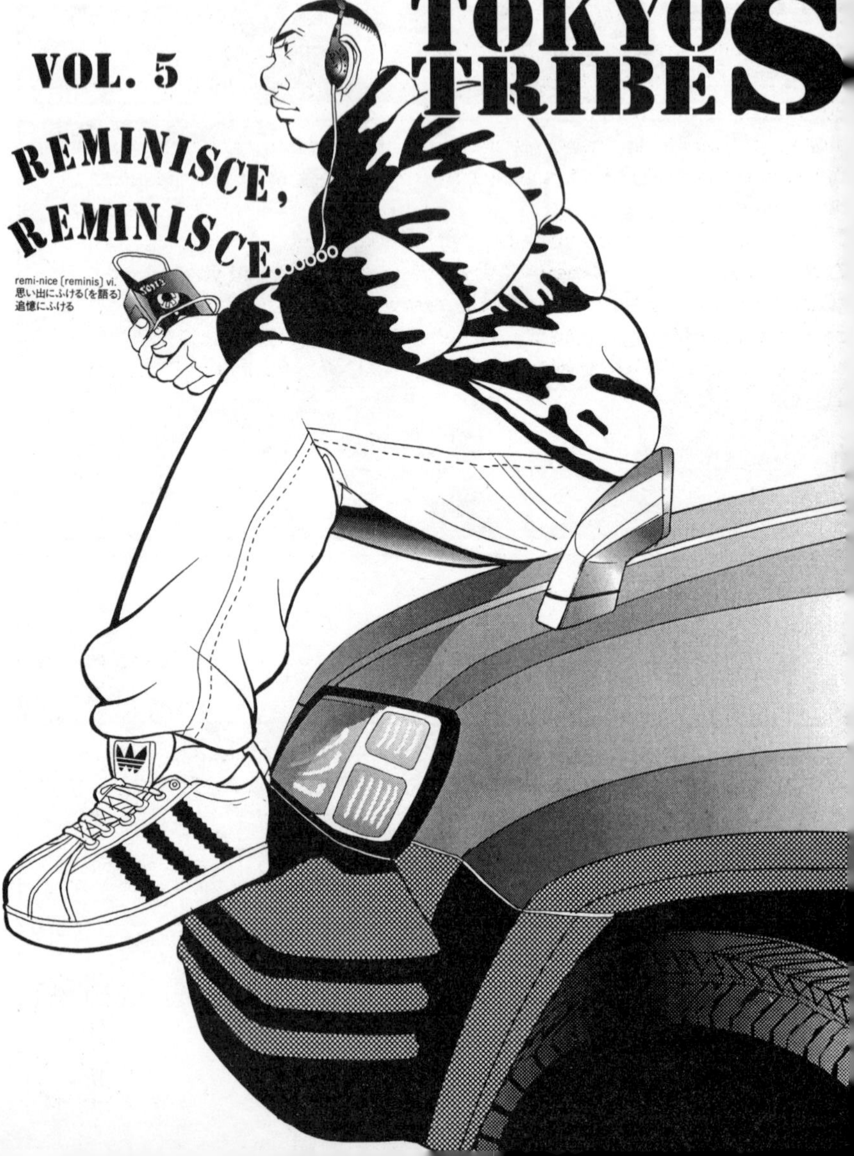

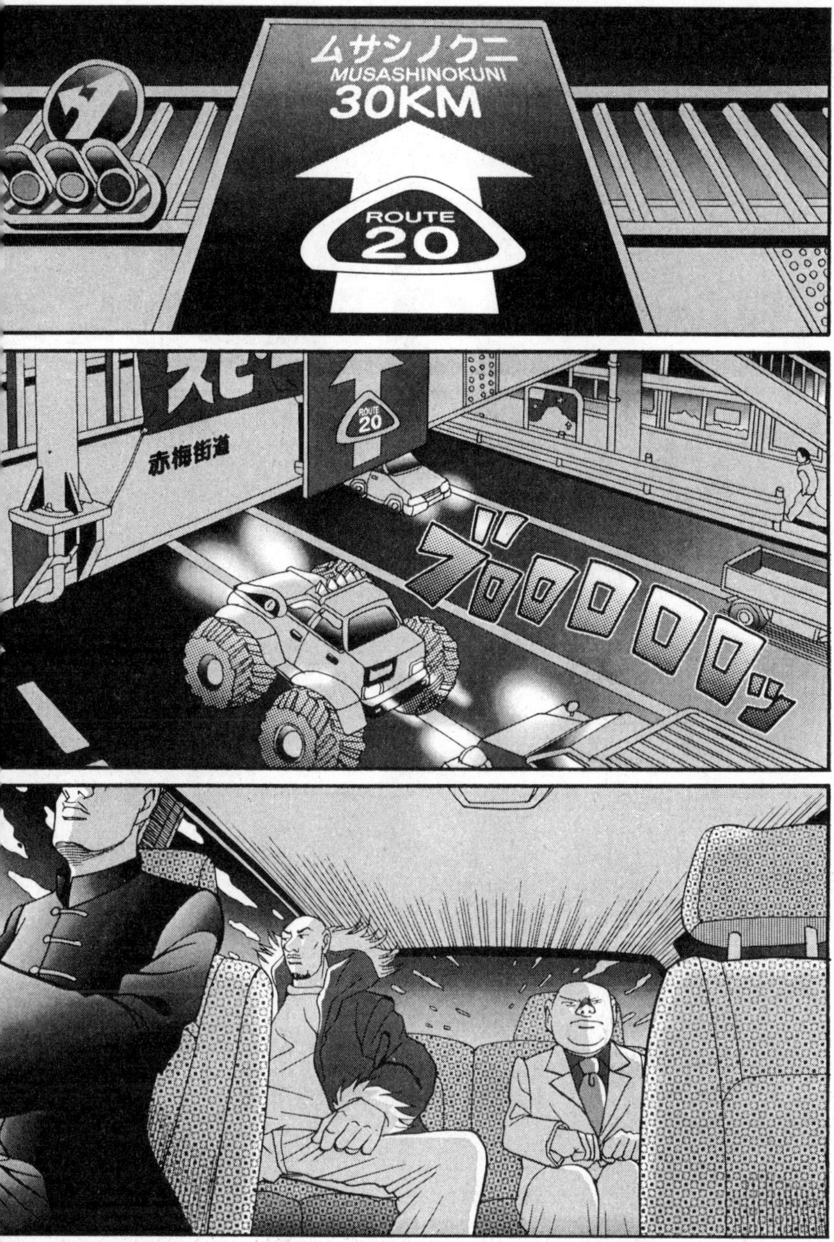
ムサシノクニ
MUSASHINOKUNI
30KM
ROUTE
20
ROUTE
20
赤梅街道
ブロロロロロッ

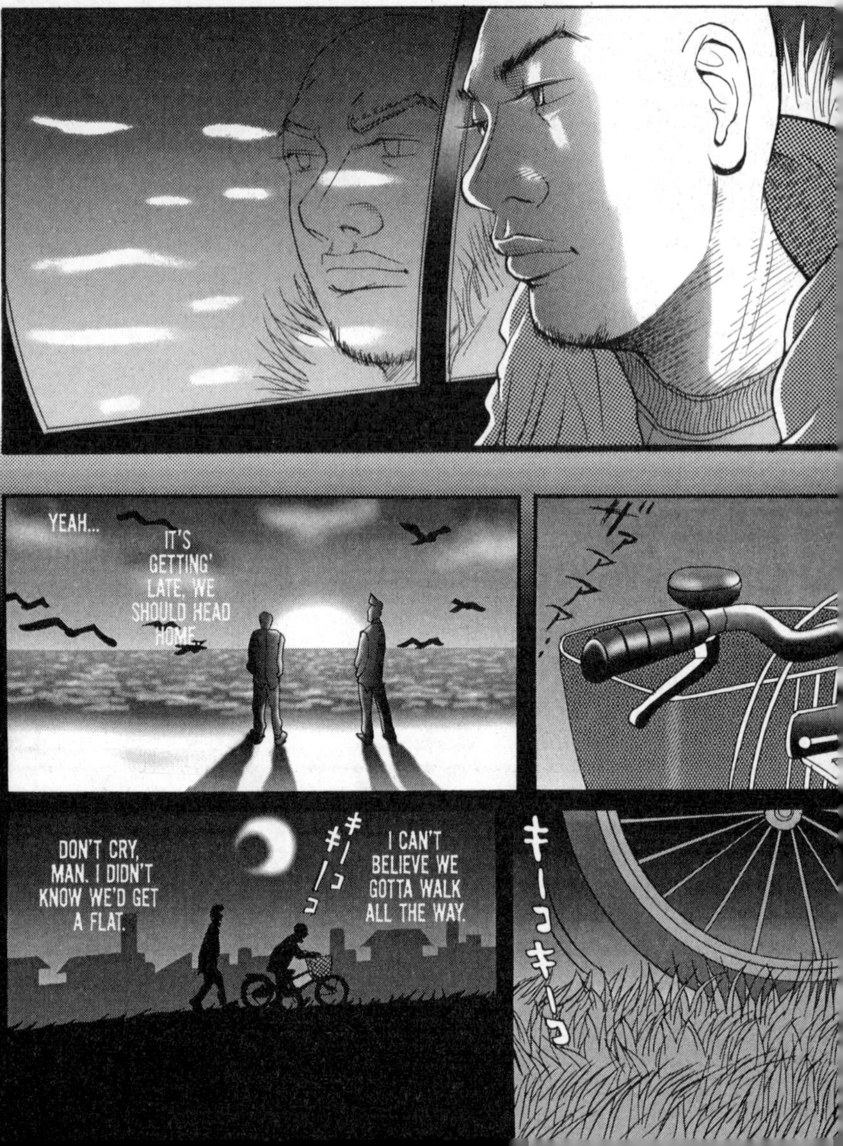
ザァアアア…
YEAH...
IT'S GETTING' LATE, WE SHOULD HEAD HOME.
キーコキーコ
キーコ
キーコ
I CAN'T BELIEVE WE GOTTA WALK ALL THE WAY.
DON'T CRY, MAN. I DIDN'T KNOW WE'D GET A FLAT.

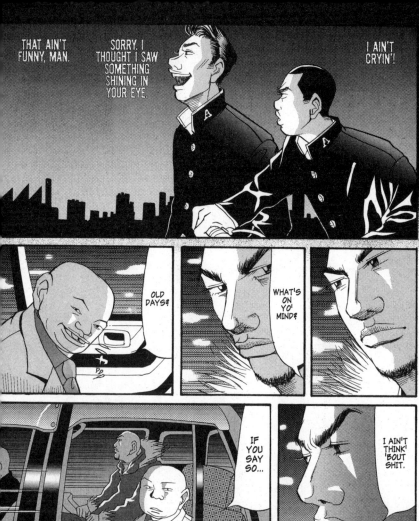

I AIN'T CRYIN'!
SORRY. I THOUGHT I SAW SOMETHING SHINING IN YOUR EYE.
THAT AIN'T FUNNY, MAN.
WHAT'S ON YO' MIND?
OLD DAYS?
I AIN'T THINK' 'BOUT SHIT.
IF YOU SAY SO...

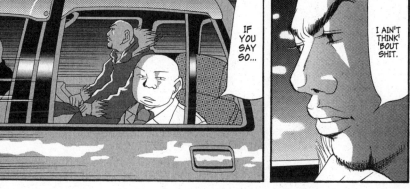

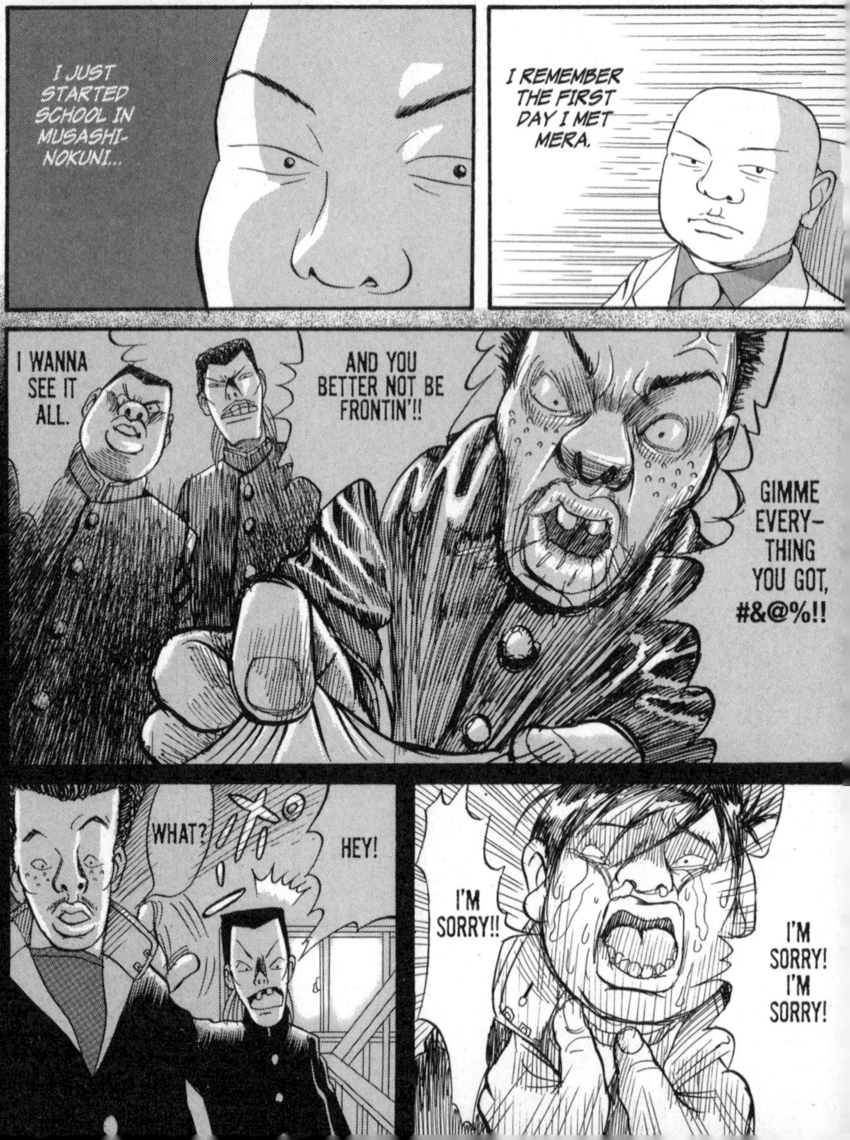
I REMEMBER THE FIRST DAY I MET MERA.
I JUST STARTED SCHOOL IN MUSASHI-NOKUNI...
GIMME EVERY-THING YOU GOT, #&@%!!
AND YOU BETTER NOT BE FRONTIN'!!
I WANNA SEE IT ALL.
I'M SORRY! I'M SORRY!
I'M SORRY!!
HEY!
WHAT?

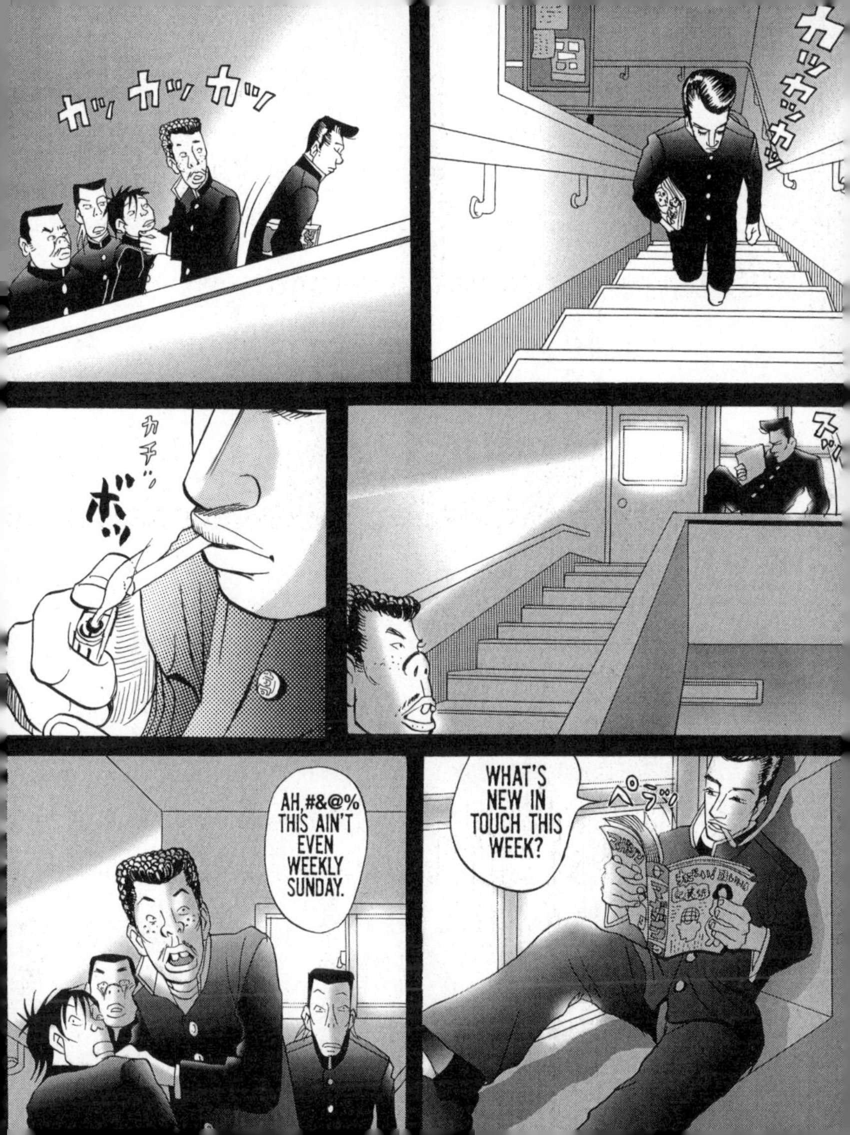

カッカッカッ
カッカッカッ
スッ
カチッ
ボッ
WHAT'S NEW IN TOUCH THIS WEEK?
ペラッ
AH, #&@% THIS AIN'T EVEN WEEKLY SUNDAY.

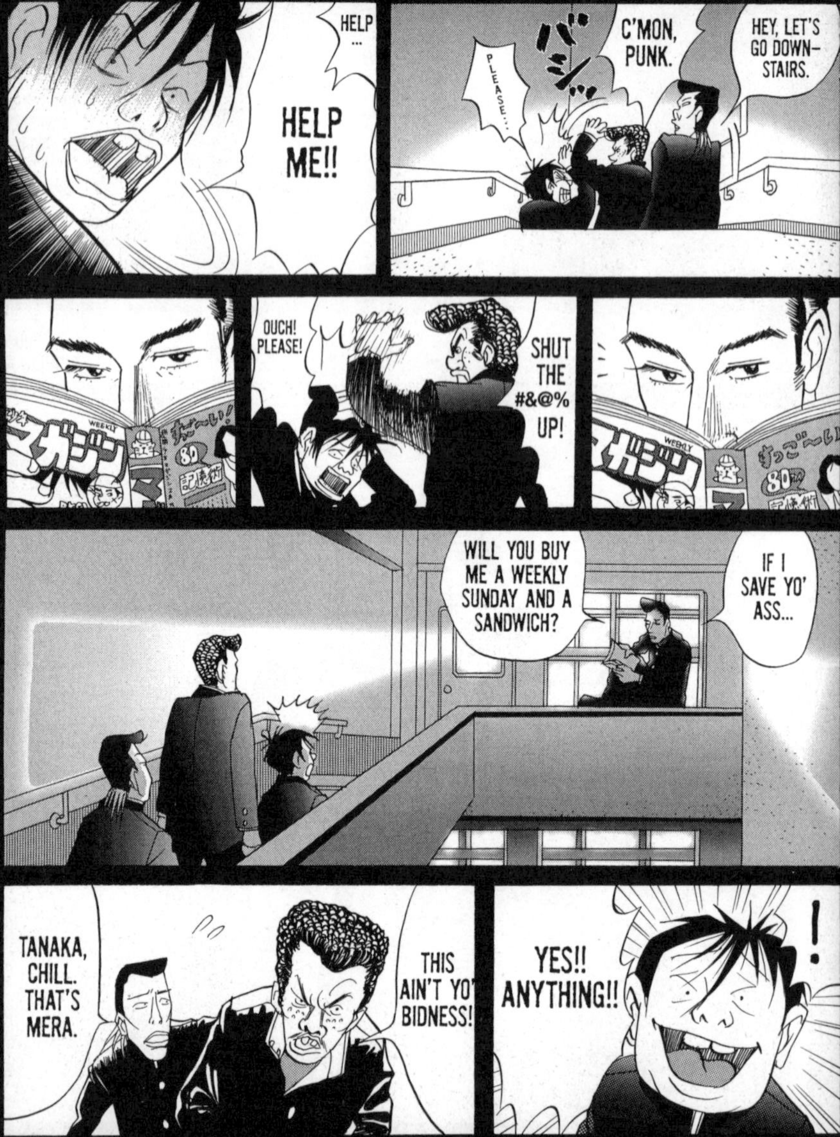
HEY, LET'S GO DOWN-STAIRS.
C'MON, PUNK.
PLEASE...
HELP ...
HELP ME!!
SHUT THE #&@% UP!
OUCH! PLEASE!
WEEKLY
WEEKLY
IF I SAVE YO' ASS...
WILL YOU BUY ME A WEEKLY SUNDAY AND A SANDWICH?
!
YES!! ANYTHING!!
THIS AIN'T YO' BIDNESS!
TANAKA, CHILL. THAT'S MERA.

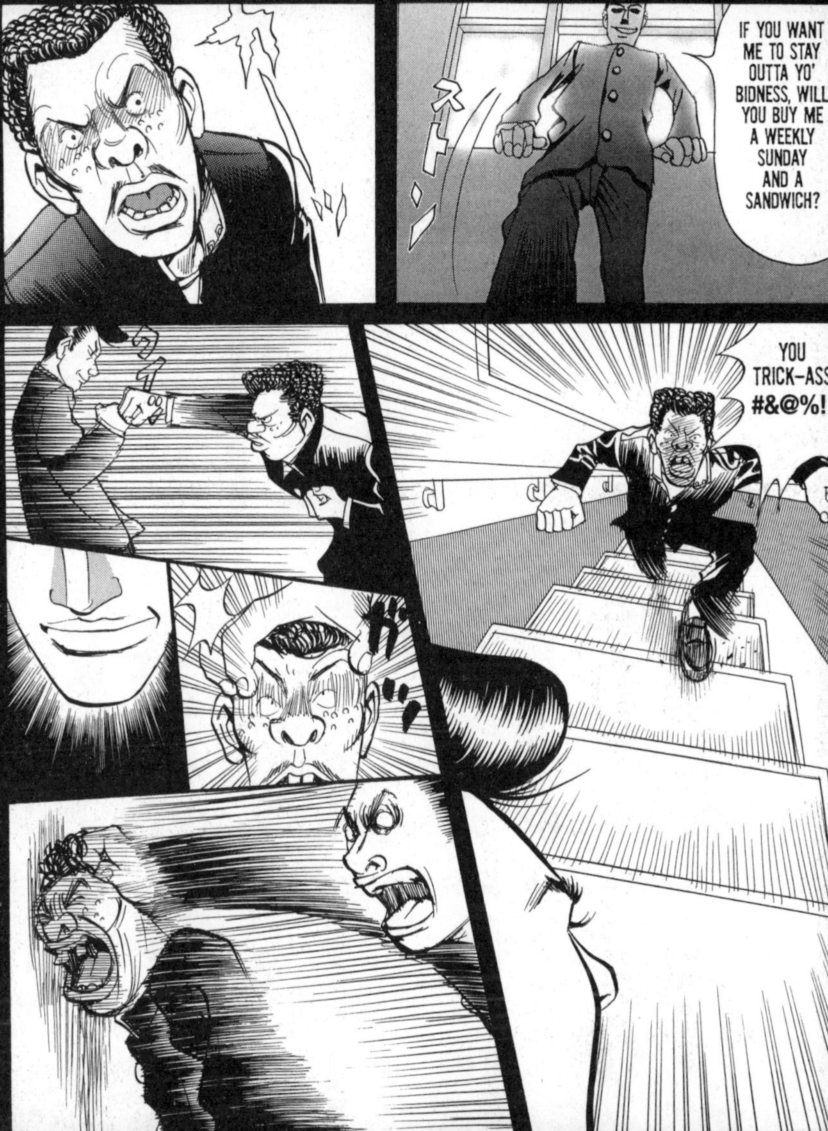
IF YOU WANT ME TO STAY OUTTA YO' BIDNESS, WILL YOU BUY ME A WEEKLY SUNDAY AND A SANDWICH?
YOU TRICK-ASS #&@%!!

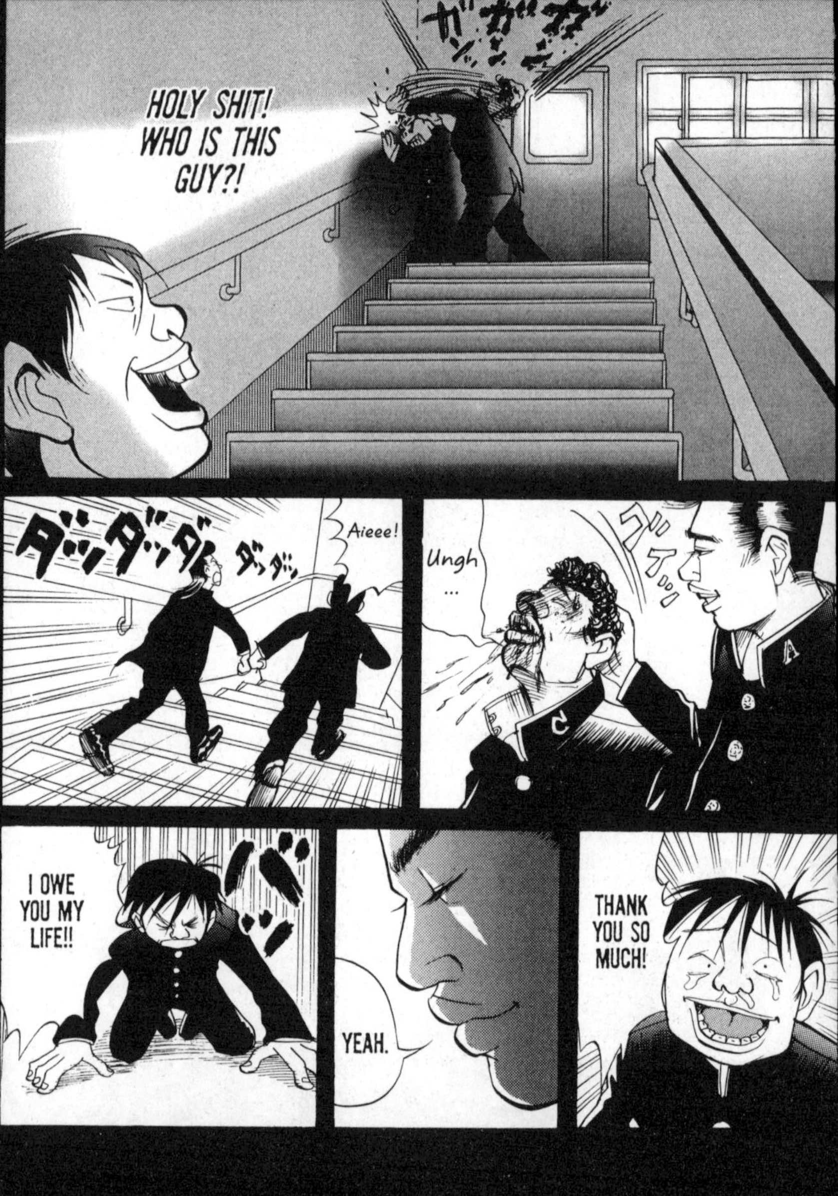
HOLY SHIT! WHO IS THIS GUY?!
Ungh ...
Aieee!
THANK YOU SO MUCH!
YEAH.
I OWE YOU MY LIFE!!

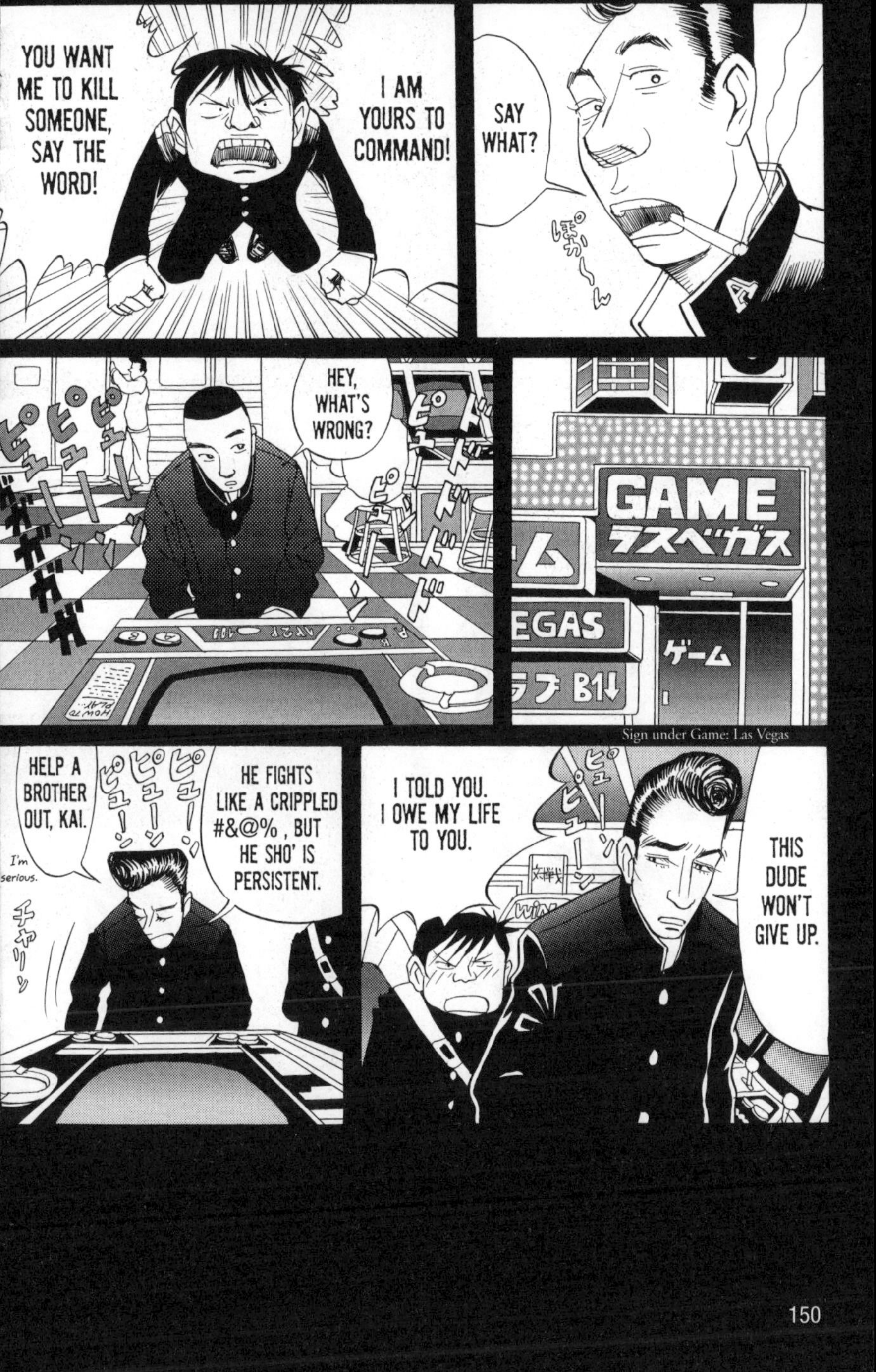
SAY WHAT?
ぽか〜ん
I AM YOURS TO COMMAND!
YOU WANT ME TO KILL SOMEONE, SAY THE WORD!
GAME
ラスベガス
EGAS
ゲーム
B1↓
Sign under Game: Las Vegas
HEY, WHAT'S WRONG?
THIS DUDE WON'T GIVE UP.
I TOLD YOU. I OWE MY LIFE TO YOU.
HE FIGHTS LIKE A CRIPPLED #&@% , BUT HE SHO' IS PERSISTENT.
HELP A BROTHER OUT, KAI.
I'm serious.
チャリーン

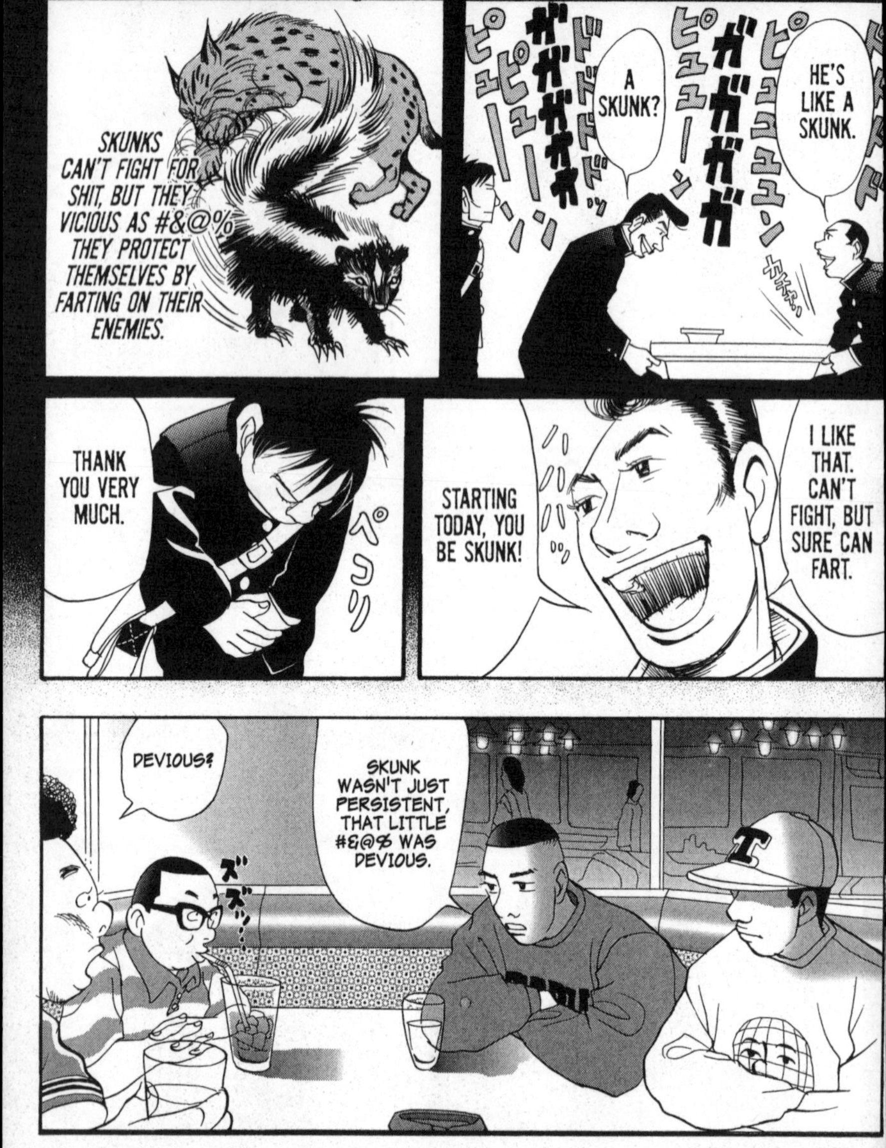
HE'S LIKE A SKUNK.
A SKUNK?
SKUNKS CAN'T FIGHT FOR SHIT, BUT THEY VICIOUS AS #&@% THEY PROTECT THEMSELVES BY FARTING ON THEIR ENEMIES.
I LIKE THAT. CAN'T FIGHT, BUT SURE CAN FART.
STARTING TODAY, YOU BE SKUNK!
THANK YOU VERY MUCH.
ペコリ
SKUNK WASN'T JUST PERSISTENT, THAT LITTLE #&@% WAS DEVIOUS.
DEVIOUS?
ズズッ

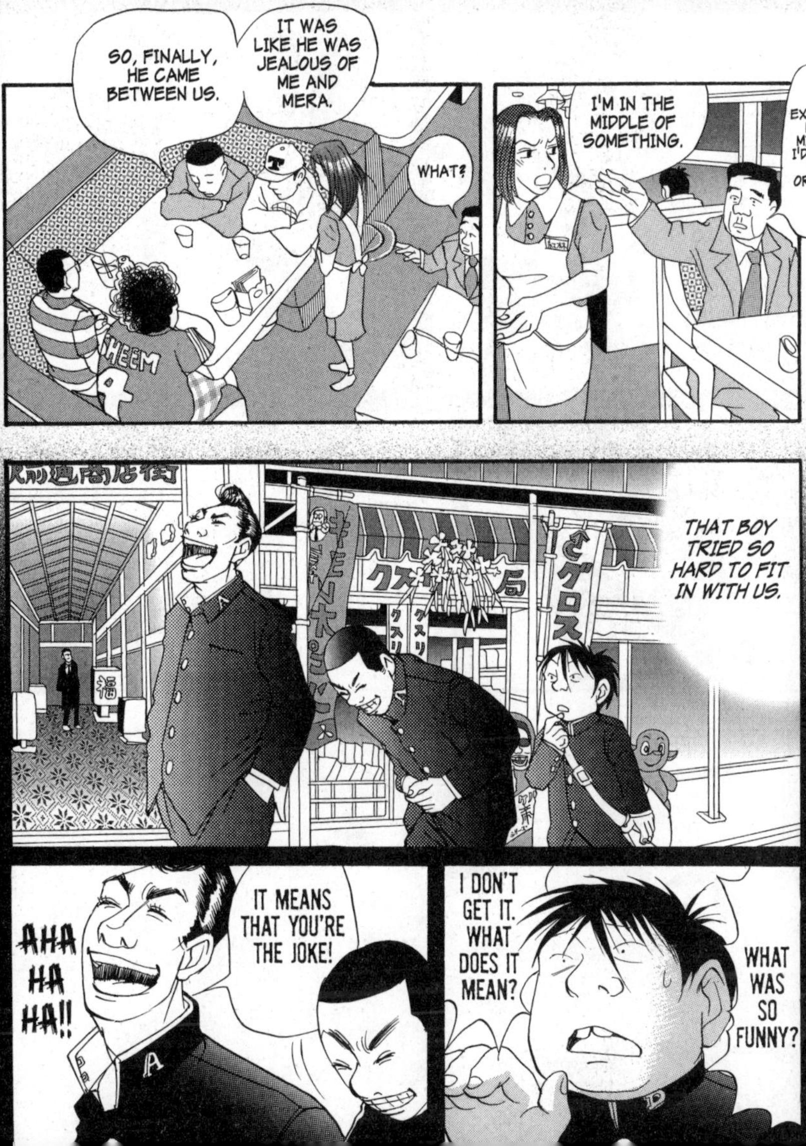
EXCUSE ME, MISS? I'D LIKE TO ORDER.
I'M IN THE MIDDLE OF SOMETHING.
IT WAS LIKE HE WAS JEALOUS OF ME AND MERA.
SO, FINALLY, HE CAME BETWEEN US.
WHAT?
THAT BOY TRIED SO HARD TO FIT IN WITH US.
WHAT WAS SO FUNNY?
I DON'T GET IT. WHAT DOES IT MEAN?
IT MEANS THAT YOU'RE THE JOKE!
AHA HA HA!!

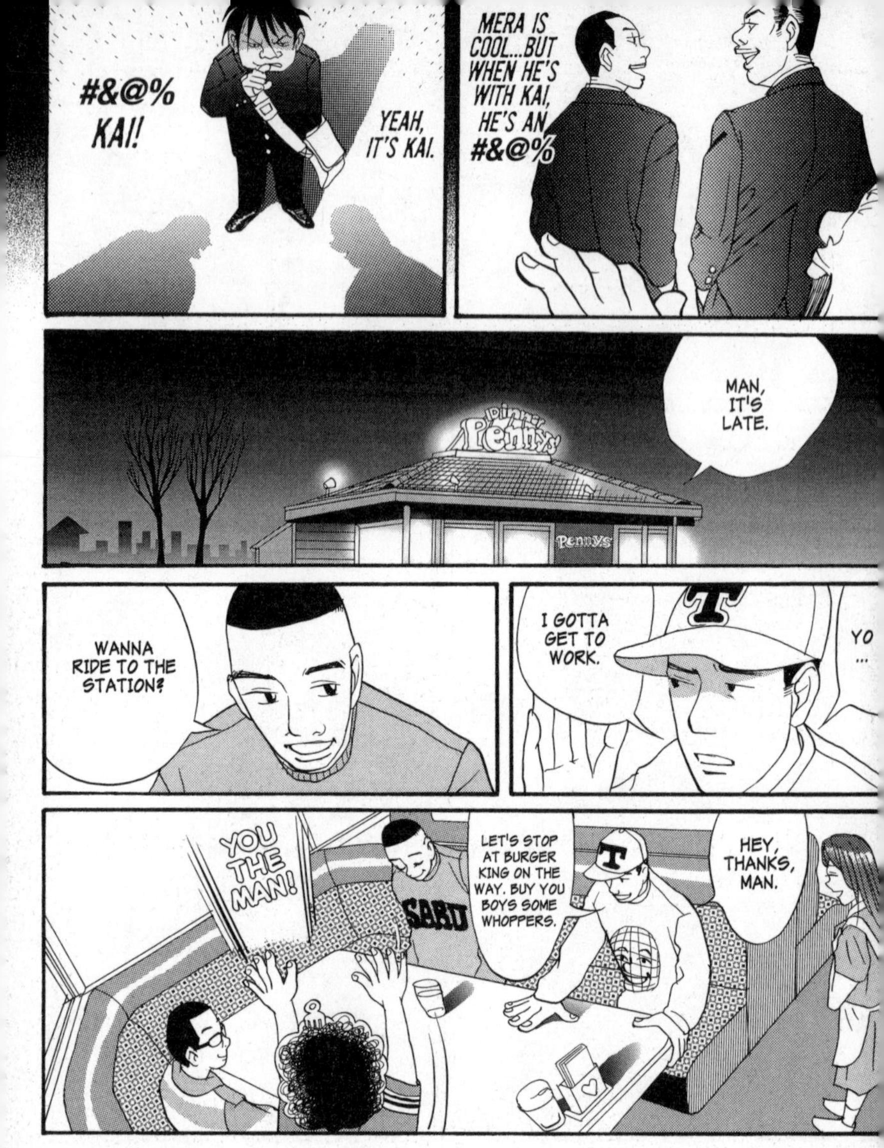
MERA IS COOL...BUT WHEN HE'S WITH KAI, HE'S AN #&@%
YEAH, IT'S KAI.
#&@% KAI!
Dinner Penny's
MAN, IT'S LATE.
Penny's
YO ...
I GOTTA GET TO WORK.
WANNA RIDE TO THE STATION?
HEY, THANKS, MAN.
LET'S STOP AT BURGER KING ON THE WAY. BUY YOU BOYS SOME WHOPPERS.
YOU THE MAN!
SABU

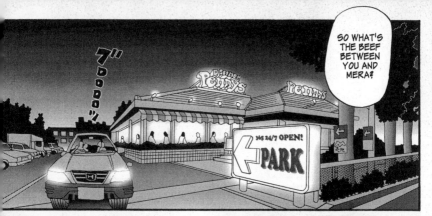

DOOOOO
SO WHAT'S THE BEEF BETWEEN YOU AND MERA?
PARK
WHY DOES THIS DUDE HATE MUSASHI-NOKUNI NOW?
IT'S ME.
IT AIN'T THE CITY HE HATES.
WHAT? YOU?

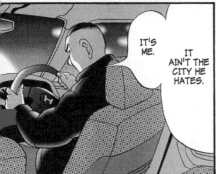

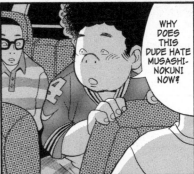

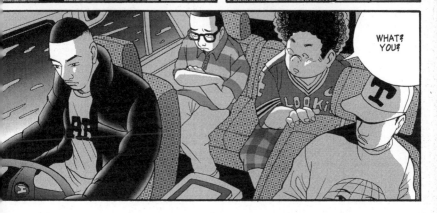

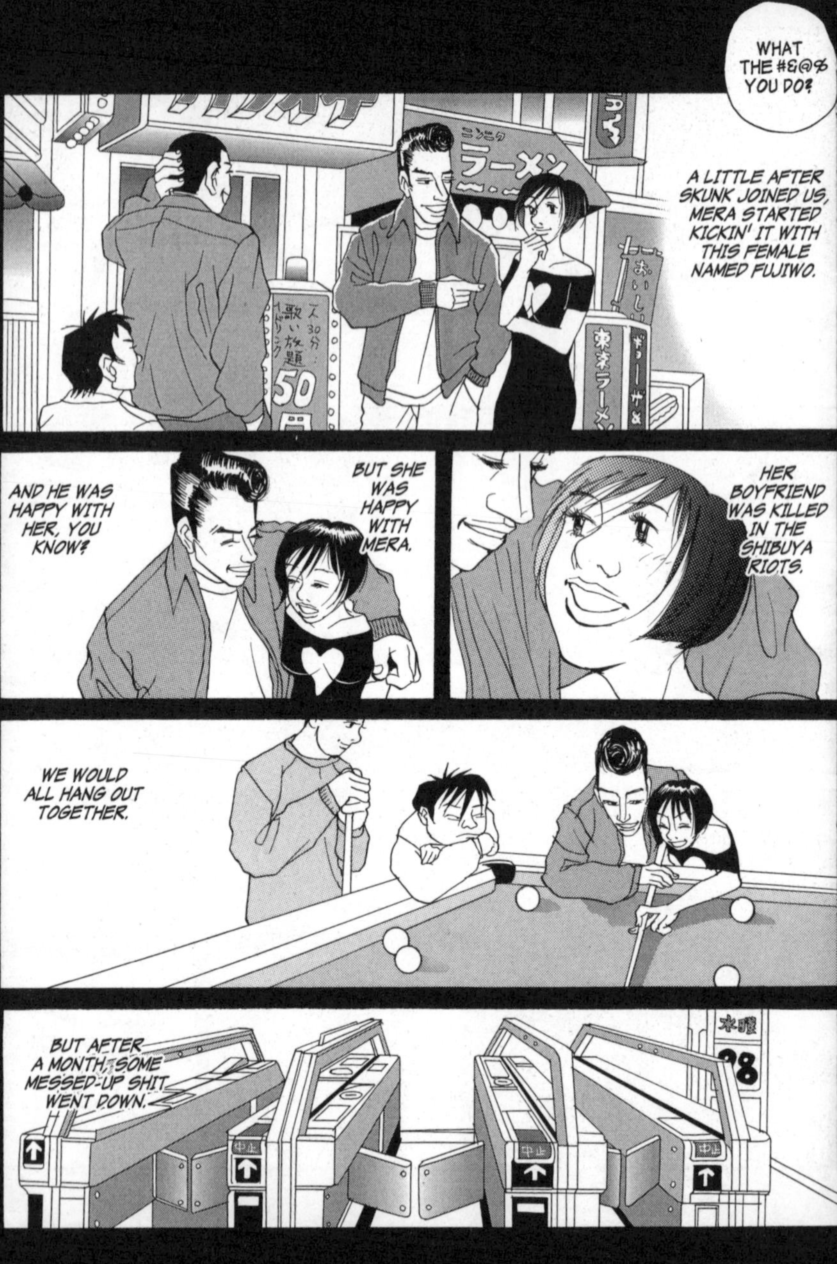
WHAT THE #&@% YOU DO?
A LITTLE AFTER SKUNK JOINED US, MERA STARTED KICKIN' IT WITH THIS FEMALE NAMED FUJIWO.
ラーメン
HER BOYFRIEND WAS KILLED IN THE SHIBUYA RIOTS.
BUT SHE WAS HAPPY WITH MERA.
AND HE WAS HAPPY WITH HER, YOU KNOW?
WE WOULD ALL HANG OUT TOGETHER.
BUT AFTER A MONTH, SOME MESSED-UP SHIT WENT DOWN.

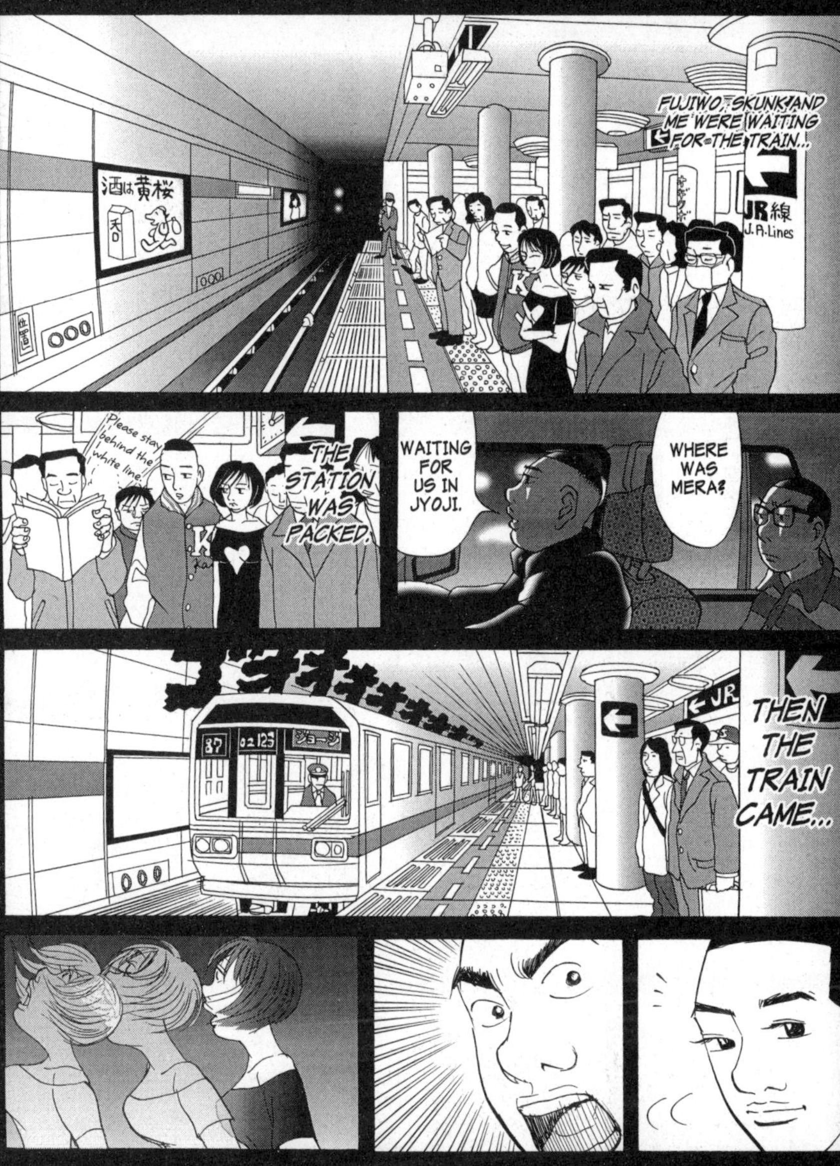
FUJIWO, SKUNK AND ME WERE WAITING FOR THE TRAIN...
酒は黄桜
JR線
J.A. Lines
WHERE WAS MERA?
WAITING FOR US IN JYOJI.
THE STATION WAS PACKED.
Please stay behind the white line.
THEN THE TRAIN CAME...
JR
ジョージ

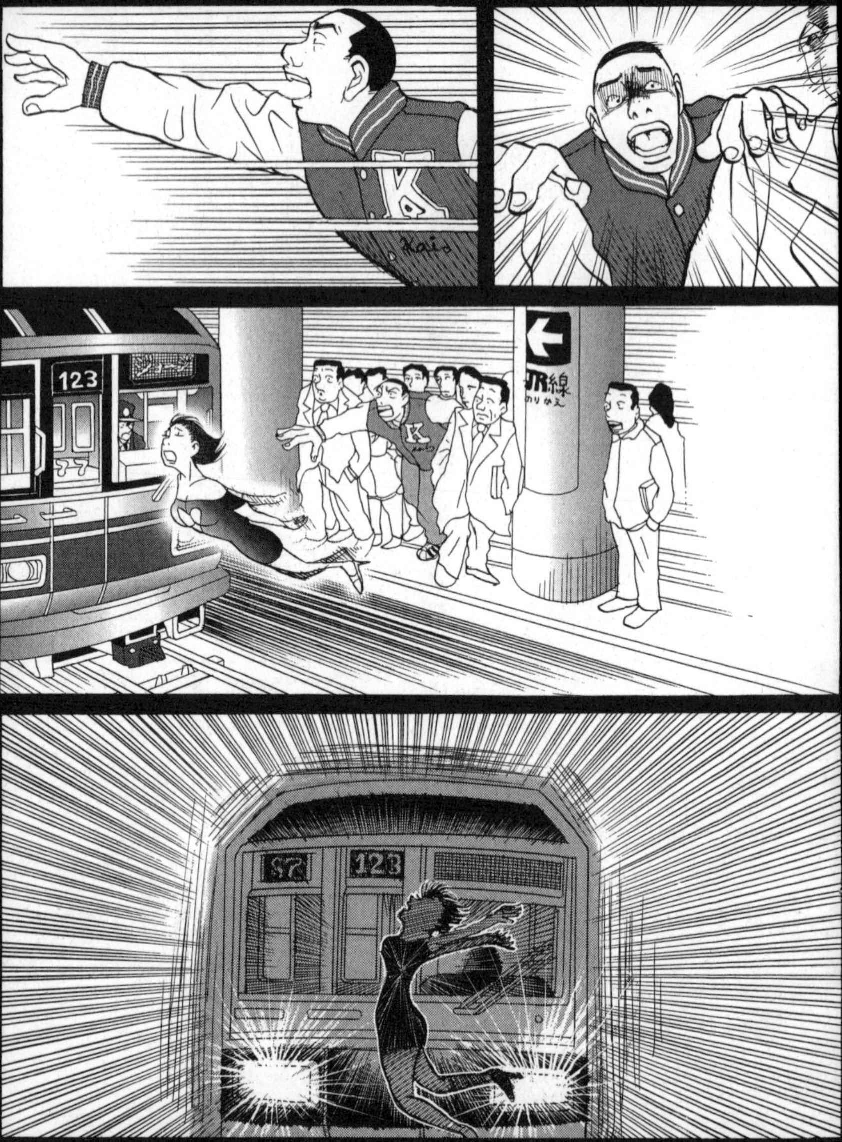
Kaio
JR線
のりかえ
123

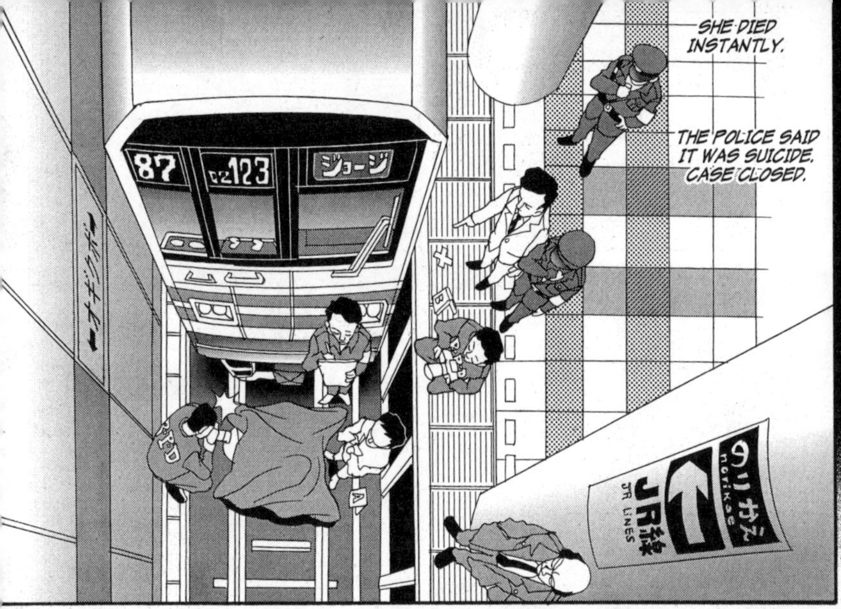
SHE DIED INSTANTLY.
THE POLICE SAID IT WAS SUICIDE. CASE CLOSED.
87
02 123
ジョージ
のりかえ
norikae
JR線
JR LINES

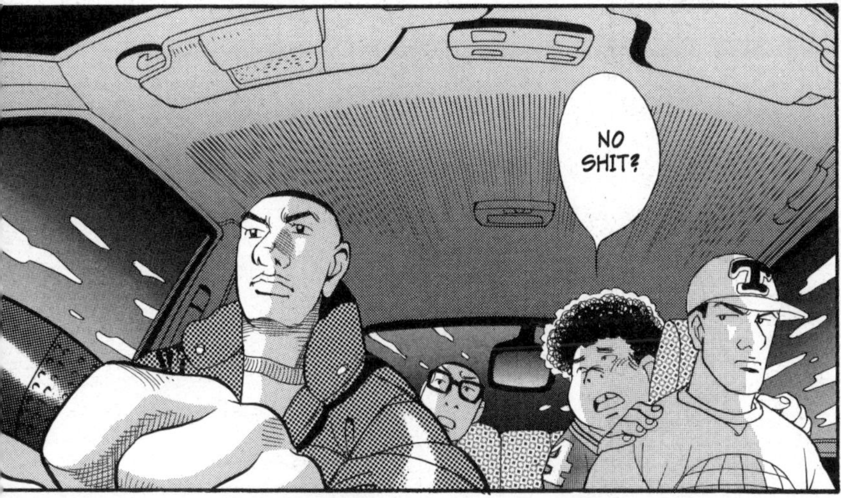
NO SHIT?

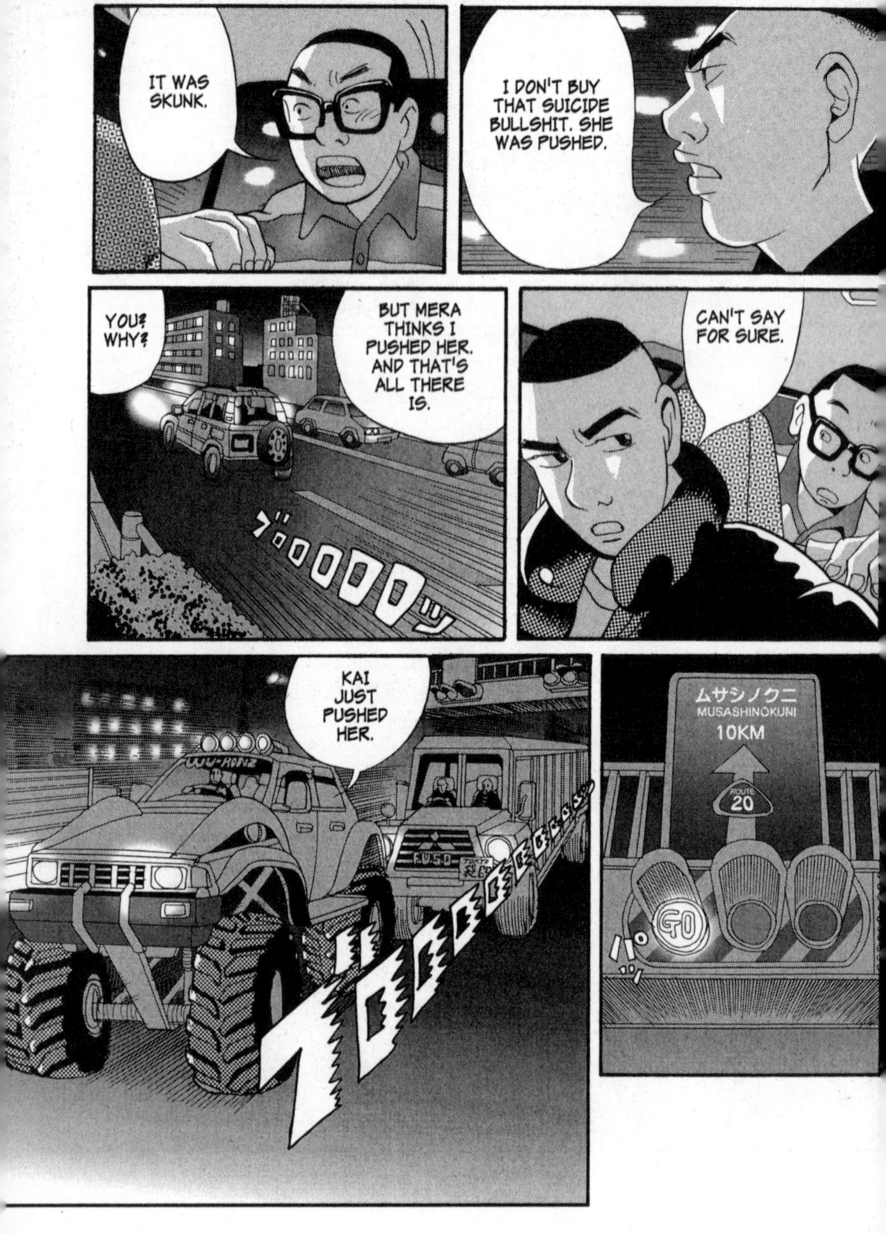
I DON'T BUY THAT SUICIDE BULLSHIT. SHE WAS PUSHED.
IT WAS SKUNK.
CAN'T SAY FOR SURE.
BUT MERA THINKS I PUSHED HER. AND THAT'S ALL THERE IS.
YOU? WHY?
ムサシノクニ
MUSASHINOKUNI
10KM
ROUTE 20
GO
KAI JUST PUSHED HER.

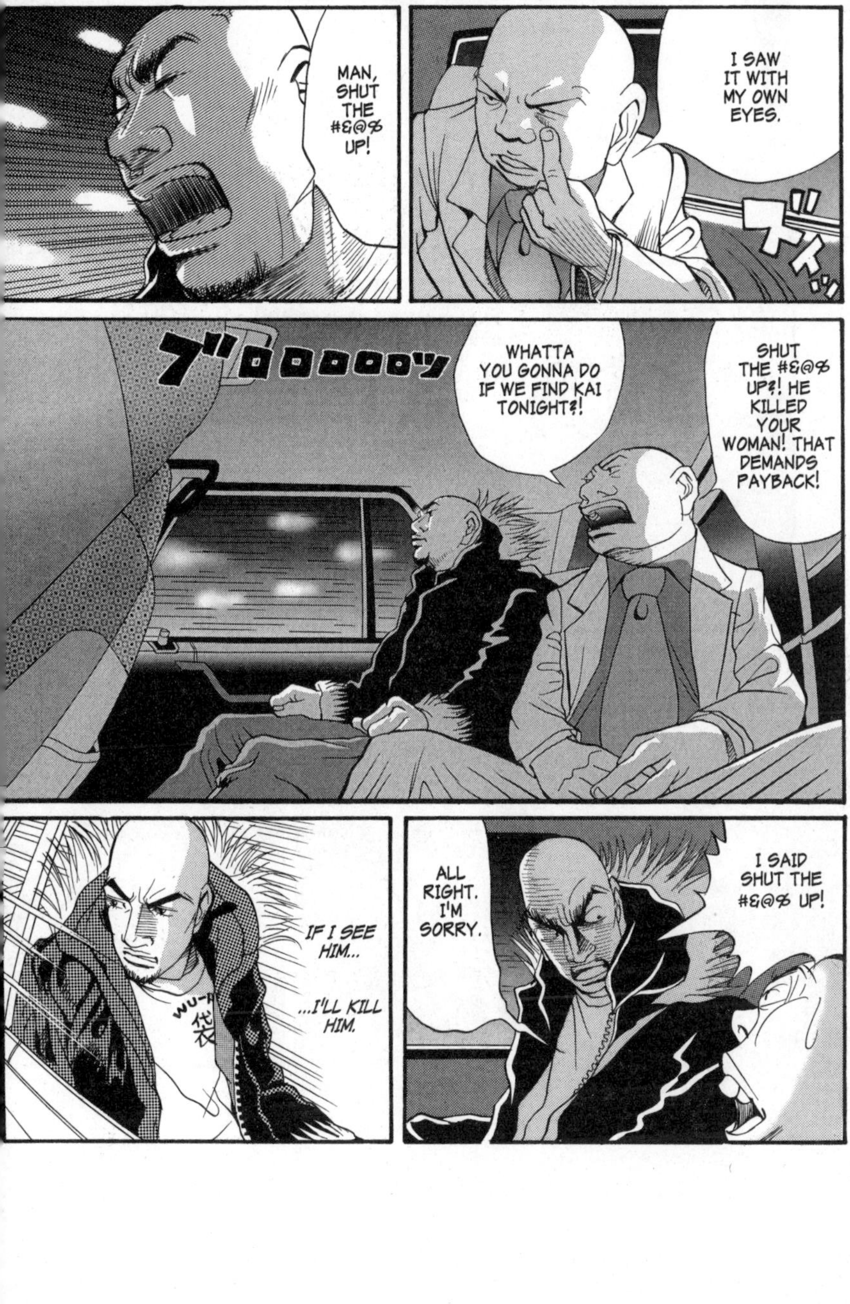
I SAW IT WITH MY OWN EYES.
MAN, SHUT THE #&@% UP!
SHUT THE #&@% UP?! HE KILLED YOUR WOMAN! THAT DEMANDS PAYBACK!
WHATTA YOU GONNA DO IF WE FIND KAI TONIGHT?!
I SAID SHUT THE #&@% UP!
ALL RIGHT. I'M SORRY.
IF I SEE HIM...
...I'LL KILL HIM.